BROADCAST JOURNALISM

Other titles in the series

ESSENTIAL FEATURE WRITING   Brendan Hennessy
HANDLING NEWSPAPER TEXT   Harold Evans
THE LAW AND THE MEDIA   Tom Crone
MAGAZINE JOURNALISM TODAY   Anthony Davis
MODERN NEWSPAPER EDITING AND PRODUCTION   F.W. Hodgson
MODERN NEWSPAPER PRACTICE   F.W. Hodgson
NEWSMAN'S ENGLISH   Harold Evans
NEWSPAPER DESIGN   Harold Evans
PICTURES ON A PAGE   Harold Evans

BROADCAST JOURNALISM

Techniques of Radio and TV News

ANDREW BOYD

Heinemann Professional Publishing

To Michael and Laura and all my students
– the voices of tomorrow

Heinemann Professional Publishing Ltd
Halley Court, Jordan Hill, Oxford OX2 8EJ

OXFORD LONDON MELBOURNE AUCKLAND

First published 1988

British Library Cataloguing in Publication Data
Boyd, Andrew
Broadcast journalism: techniques of radio
and t.v. news.
1. Broadcast journalism – Great Britain
I. Title
070.1'9'0941 PN4888.B74

ISBN 0 434 90175 X

Printed in Great Britain by
Butler and Tanner Ltd, Frome

CONTENTS

Acknowledgements x

Foreword xi

How to use this book xiii

List of illustrations xiv

Part One

BROADCAST JOURNALISM

NEWS GATHERING

1 What is news? 3
Proximity 3
Relevance 4
Immediacy 4
Interest 4
Drama 5
Entertainment 5
Different types of news 5
  Emergencies 6
  Crime 6
  Local and national government 7
  Planning and developments 7
  Conflict and controversy 7
  Pressure groups 7
  Industry 8
  Health 8
  Human interest 8
  Personalities 8
  Sport 8
  Seasonal news 8
  Special local interest 8
  Weather 8
  Traffic 9
  Animals 10
Checklist 10
Fieldwork 10

2 News sources 12
Reporters 13
Contacts 13
Newsroom diary 13
Files 14
Check calls 15
Emergency services radio 16
  The ten code 16
Politicians 17
Pressure groups 17
Staged events 17
  The protest 17
  The announcement 18
  The set piece 18
News releases 18
Syndicated tapes 20
Freelances 20
  Advantages and disadvantages of using stringers 21
Tip-offs 21
Hoaxes 22
Wire services and news agencies 23
The network 24
Other news media 26
  'Get the father . . .' 26
Shared material 27
Fieldwork 27

3 Getting the story 29
Newsroom conference 29
Copytasting 30
Balance of news 30
Visuals and actuality 31
The brief 31
The angle 32
Chasing the contact 33
Staged news conferences 35
Beating the clock 36
  Work to sequence 36
  Don't panic 36
Fieldwork 37

WRITING FOR BROADCAST

4 Conversational writing 38
Telling the story 39
Writing for a mass audience 40
No second chance 41
Confusing clauses 42
Inverted sentences 43
Plain English 43
Familiar words 44
Easy listening 44
Accurate English 44
Keep it concrete 45
Make it interesting 46
Contractions 47
Rhythm 47
Fieldwork 48

5 Newswriting 50
The news angle 50
Multi-angled stories 51
Hard news formula 52
The intro 52
Placing key words 53
Feature openers 55
Developing the story 56
The WHAT formula 57
Signposting 57
Last line 57
Last words 58
Accuracy 58
Fieldwork 61

6 Broadcast style book 62
Clichés 62
Journalese 64
Hyperbole 65

Adjectives 65
Quotations 66
Attribution 66
Contentious statements 67
Immediacy 68
Active 69
Positive 69
Redundancies 70
Repetition 70
Homonyms 70
Singular or plural? 71
Pronouns 71
Punctuation 71
Spelling 71
Abbreviations 72
Figures 72
Proof reading 72
Ambiguity 73
Fieldwork 74

INTERVIEWING

7 The interview 75
The interviewer's skill 76
Different types of interview 76
A disaster story? 76
Hard news 78
Informational 79
Investigative 79
Adversarial 80
Interpretative 81
Personal 81
Emotional 82
Entertainment 82
Actuality only 82
Telephone or remote 83
Vox pop and multiple 83
Grabbed 84
The disaster story continues . . . 85
Fieldwork 86

8 Setting up the interview 87
Background 88
A plan of campaign – the questions 88
Get your facts right 88
Fit the brief 89
Check arrangements 89
Approach 89
Pre-chat 90
Body language 91
Discussing the questions 91
The questions 92
Using notes 92
Ask questions that will get answers 93
Yes/no questions 94
Avoid questions that call for monologues 94
Short, single idea questions 95
Progress from point to point 95
Building bridges 95
Avoid double questions 96
Keep the questions relevant 96
Avoid leading questions 96
Mixing statements with questions 97
Beware of questions that would be out of date 98
Avoid sounding ignorant 98
Winding up the interview 98
Finish strongly 98
Being interviewed yourself: the Q & A 99
Introducing actuality 100
Fieldwork 100

THE NEWS PROGRAMME

9 From 2 minute headlines to 24 hour news 102
The bulletin 103
News programmes 103
Documentary 103
Vérite 103
24 hour news 105
Who does what? 106
Network TV news 106
Local radio news 107
Fieldwork 107

10 Item selection and order
'A fair picture . . .' 108
Second thoughts 108
Item order 110
1 The significance of the story 110
2 The material impact of the story 111
3 Audience reaction 111
4 The topicality of the story 111
5 The immediacy factor 111
6 Sport/specialisms 111
7 Linking items 112
8 Actuality/pictures 112
9 'And finally . . .' 112
Local considerations 112
Foreign coverage 112
Producing a running order 113
Fieldwork 116

11 Putting the show together
Establishing programme identity 117
Winning an audience – the openers 117
Keeping an audience – headlines and promotions 118
Actuality 119
Pictures 120
Graphics 121
Programme balance – being all things to all people 121
Groupings and variety 122
Rhythm and pace 125
Fieldwork 126

12 Making the programme fit 127
Cutting 127
Filling 128
Backtiming 130
Fieldwork 130

PRESENTING THE NEWS

13 News anchors and presenters 131
The talent 131
Anchors versus newsreaders 132
Qualities of a newscaster 133
Women newscasters 133
More than just a newsreader . . . 134
Professionalism 135
Voice 136
Fieldwork 137

14 'On-air!' 138
Performance 138
Presence 139
Getting through to the audience: rapport 140
Know your material 141
Ad-libs 141
The gate 142
Making a swift recovery 142
Corpsing 145
Relaxation 145
Fieldwork 146

15 Newsreading mechanics 147
Speed 147
Breathing 147
Projection 148
Emphasis 149
Pitch 150
Microphone technique 150
Using the prompter 151
Noise, noise, noise 153
Bringing the story to life 154
Fieldwork 155

DUTIES AND DILEMMAS

16 Power, freedom and responsibility 157
Power 157
Regulation 158
'Independence' 158
Censorship in developing nations 159
The myth of objectivity 160
Opinion and comment 161
Campaigning journalism 162
Impartiality under fire 162
Responsible reporting 163
Reporting disorder 163
Camera bias 164
Distortion 165
Sensationalism 166
Good taste 166
Privacy 167
Internal pressures on reporting 169
Resources 169
Selection 169
Pressures of ratings 169
Pressures of advertising 170
The law 170
Libel 170
National Union of Journalists' code of professional conduct 171
Fieldwork 172

Part Two

RADIO

INSIDE THE BBC WORLD SERVICE

17 The best of British 175
The service 177
The system 177
Independence 179
The newsroom conference 180
The stories 180
Accuracy 182
Radio newsreel 182
Foreign correspondents 185
Sponsored stringers 187
Newsreaders 187
The way ahead? 187
Fieldwork 188

RADIO NEWS COVERAGE

18 Story treatment 190
Newsflash 191
Headline 192
Copy story 193
Voicer or voice report 193
Teaser or taster 194
Voice report from the scene 195
Interview 197
Newsclip 199
Package 199
Mini-wrap 202
Fieldwork 204

THE EQUIPMENT

19 Principles of recording 205
Tape 206
Reclaiming tape 207
Care of tapes 208
Cartridges 208
Pros and cons of carts
Digital carts 209
Principles of recording 209
Sound 210
How recordings are made 210
Tape heads 210
Tracks 210
Video recording 210
Digital recording 211
Bias 211
Equalization 211
Noise reduction 212
Types of microphone 212
Fieldwork 212
213

20 Using portable recorders 214
Reel-to-reel versus cassette: advantages and disadvantages 214
Reel-to-reel: The Uher 216
Cassette: The Marantz 218
Before the interview 220
Mike handling 220

Lining up the victim 221
Setting up the room 221
Dealing with distractions 221
The level check 221
Are you sitting comfortably? 222
Logging the tape 222
Maintain eye contact 222
Adjusting levels 222
Fieldwork 223

21 Editing 224
Studio tape decks 225
Marking and cutting 226
The editing block 228
Leader tape 228
Dub editing 228
'You can't see the join . . .' 229
Editing a thirty second bulletin clip 229
Unethical editing 230
Mixing 230
Setting levels 231
Types of fade 232
Fieldwork 234

22 The studio today and radio tomorrow 235
On-air studio 235
Talks studio 236
The contributions studio 236
Remote studios 237
Radio car 237
Outside broadcast vehicle 238
Cellular telephone 238
Telephone reports 238
Phone levels 240
Obscenity button 240
The touchscreen studio 241
Tomorrow? 242
Fieldwork 244

Part Three

TELEVISION

INSIDE ITN

23 Independent Television News 247
Getting the news 248
The editors 250
The producers 251
Getting the programme on air 254
Fieldwork 255

24 A story is born 254
Panning for gold 256
The interview 257
Compiling the report 259
'Going live . . .' 266
Fieldwork 267

HOW TELEVISION WORKS

25 The story of TV 268
Early days 268
The camera 271
How television pictures are transmitted 271
The TV set 272
Satellite TV 273
Fieldwork 274

TV NEWS COVERAGE

26 Gathering the news 275
Film versus videotape 275
The camera crew 275
Cameraperson 277
Recordist 279
Lighting technician 280
The outside broadcast 283
Getting the story back 285
Master control room 286
Fieldwork 286

27 Camera shots 287
The shots 287
Camera positions 289
Sequence of shots 289
Shot length 290
Grab action shots first 291
Shoot for impact 291
Context 291
Pictures should complement the narrative 292
Sound 292
Cutaways 293
Telescoping the action 294
Reverses 294
The line 295
Continuity 296
Pieces to camera 296
Planning – the full treatment 298
Fieldwork 299

TV SCRIPTWRITING

28 Writing the script 300
The cue (lead, or link) 301
Writing to sound 301
Keep detail to a minimum 303
Script layout 303
Balancing words with pictures 306
Using the library 307
Fieldwork 308

COMPILING THE REPORT

29 Editing videotape and film 310
Editing videotape 311
The tape 311
The tape editor 311
The editing suite 311
The timer 311
The edit controller 312
Video mixing 312
Recording the commentary 312
Audio mixing 312
Playing the tape on air 313
The video cartridge 313

VTR playback 313
Editing film 314
The film 314
Different types of film 314
Editing sound on film 315
The double system 315
The film editor's equipment 316
The enemy within 316
The editing bench 317
The sound reader 317
Marking the edits 318
Splicing 318
Leadering and cues 318
Assembling the print 319
Playing the film on air 320
Telecine 320
The roll through 320
Fieldwork 320

30 Visuals 321
Stills 321
Screening stills 322
Film library 323
Electronic graphics 323
Graphic stills and animations 324
Painting with light 324
Titles and captions 325
Overlays 327
Chromakey 327
Back projection 328
Inlay 328
Fieldwork 329

THE NEWS STUDIO

31 'Standby for transmission . . .' 330
The set 330
Lighting 331
Cameras 332
Sound 332
The floor manager 333
Prompting 333
Control room 334
The director 335
Other personnel 336
Running order 337
Fieldwork 338

PUSHING BACK THE FRONTIERS

32 Tomorrow 339
The computerized newsroom 339
Teletext 341
Next steps 343
And then? 343
Digital TV 343
Developments in space 344
Fieldwork 346

APPENDICES 347

1 A career in TV and radio 347
Jobs in radio 348
Television 348
Freelancing 349
Union membership 349
Getting started 349
Approaching news editors 350
The interview 351
Training courses 353
Degree or not degree . . .? 353
Personal qualities 353

2 Addresses of vocational and pre-vocational courses in broadcasting 355

Glossary 360
Further reading 367
Index 368

ACKNOWLEDGEMENTS

Sincere and grateful thanks to all the following who have borne with me, opened their doors to me, put themselves out for me, supplied pictures, information and advice, and managed to keep smiling throughout my barrage of foolish questions. Without your help and support this book would not have been possible.

ITN David Nicholas, Editor in Chief; Norman Rees, Chief Assistant Editor; Michael Morris, Managing Editor; Geraldine Sharpe Newton, Head of Public Relations; Jill Dennis, Press Officer; Malcolm Johnson, Director; Phil Moger, Producer; Peter Hall, Manager, ORACLE; Trevor McDonald, Presenter *Channel 4 News*; Mark Webster, Industrial Correspondent; Michael Sheridan, Reporter; Kim Sabido, Reporter.

BBC External Services Terry Heron, former Editor; David Spaull, Deputy Editor; James Edwards, Assistant Editor; Peter Brooks, Intake Editor; Tony Dunn, Senior Duty Editor; Chris Tye, Duty Editor, Radio Newsreel; John Rhettie, Sri Lanka Correspondent; Hans Bremer; Newsreaders Lawrence Reeve-Jones and John Touhey. Thanks also to all in the Press Office.

Technical Advisors Peter Heaps, ITN Chief Engineer; Alison Sargent, BBC Radio Cambridgeshire; Jim Gregory, Senior Maintenance Engineer, Radio Services (Technical), Central Office of Information; Brian Hoey and Ian Johnston, Lecturers, London College of Printing. Many thanks for casting a watchful eye over my material and for all your welcome suggestions.

Thanks also to Paul Cleveland, ABC; Judith Melby, Canadian Broadcasting Corporation; Harry Radcliffe, CBS; Freda Morris, NBC; Malcolm Downing and Ian Henderson, Australian Broadcasting Corporation; John Rodman and Annette Bosworth, WEEI, Boston; Broadcast News, Canada; Federation of Australian Broadcasters; Canadian Bureau for International Education; Broadcasting Corporation of New Zealand; Simon Ellis, BBC Essex; Katrina Balmforth, Chiltern Radio; Penny Young, BBC Northampton; Gerry Radcliffe and Tony Delahunty, Pennine Radio; Henry Yelf, BBC Radio Solent; Jim Greensmith, Radio Hallam; Chris Rider, Ocean Sound; Richard Bestic, IRN; Rob McKenzie and the Press Office, Capital Radio; Peter Everett, BBC; LBC/IRN; BBC General News Service; Reuters News Agency; Visnews; WTN; Tyne Tees TV; HTV; Grampian TV; County Sound; Uher; Marantz Audio UK; EDS Portaprompt; Nagra Kudelski SA; E.W.O. Bauch Ltd; Sony Broadcast Ltd; UK Press Gazette; British Rail Press Office, Southern Region; Miles Kington, Writer; Posy Simmonds, Cartoonist; Martin Romanwicz, illustrator, also Dr Philip Jupp and John Wigley for photographic services.

Special thanks to Gerard Mansell, former Managing Director, BBC External Services; colleagues Ian Hyams, John Turner and Adam Hopkins and to the London College of Printing for its support. Also to my editor Freddie Hodgson for his invaluable guidance and encouragement. And last but not least, unstinting thanks to my long-suffering wife, Anne Marie.

During the writing of this book some of the above titles will almost certainly have changed as friends and colleagues moved on to better things.

Whilst every effort has been made to contact copyright holders, the publisher would like to hear from anyone whose copyright has unwittingly been infringed.

FOREWORD

It is barely fifty years since broadcast news began to take over from the press as the prime source of up-to-date information about current events in the world at large. The turning point was almost certainly the European crisis which culminated in the Munich agreement of September 1938. Then war seemed inevitable and radio, for the first time, showed that it could deliver news to an anxious audience faster and with more immediacy than the best run newspapers. The Second World War confirmed the trend, not just in Britain itself, where the nation gathered each night round its wireless sets to listen to the *Nine O'Clock News* for an authoritative account of the swaying fortunes of war, but more widely through the BBC's European and Overseas Services, which established then standards of reliability and professionalism which have been maintained to this day.

Yet the BBC, then a monopoly, had been slow in appreciating the importance of broadcast news. Reith, its founder, and his senior colleagues were deeply suspicious of journalists, and it was not until 1937 that the BBC appointed its first professional, R. T. Clark, to be its News Editor. The previous year, a proposal by a young, newly-recruited Topical Talks Assistant, Richard Dimbleby, for the creation of a team of BBC reporters and the introduction of voiced reports in bulletins had fallen on deaf ears. So had a proposal for the setting up of a corps of BBC correspondents put forward by Commander Stephen King-Hall, a noted broadcaster of the period.

Andrew Boyd's book vividly reflects the distance travelled since those early days and graphically portrays the vast new industry which the growth of the broadcast news media has brought into being. It is not just that news has become the staple ingredient *par excellence* of both radio and television. Nor is it just that nowadays far more people get their daily ration of news from hearing it or seeing it, than from reading it. It is also that the number of sources of broadcast news has greatly increased with the proliferation of radio and television channels, and that technological advances have brought the gathering, processing and presentation of news to a remarkably high pitch of speed and sophistication.

Andrew Boyd rightly focuses on the skills required in a profession which long ago ceased to be the province of talented amateurs. Young people who read his book will find in it not only a profusion of first-hand information about what it is like to work 'at the coal face' in this demanding trade and on how news is gathered, processed, edited and packaged in the various sectors of the television and radio industries, but also a great deal of practical instruction on the craft of television and radio news broadcasting, from the first indications of a breaking story to the full treatment in a news programme. But behind the hard-nosed, down-to-earth approach of the experienced news editor there is the frequently reaffirmed awareness of the special responsibilities of broadcasting journalists and of the fundamental values – independence, integrity, dedication to the truth – without which there can be no good journalism, however well developed the skills.

Gerard Mansell
Former Managing Director, BBC External Services

HOW TO USE THIS BOOK

Broadcast Journalism: Techniques of Radio and TV News is a practical manual for reporters and would-be journalists eager to make a career in the hectic world of broadcasting. It offers a clear insight into the arena of electronic news and, with extensive illustrations, provides step-by-step practical instruction in all the essential skills of broadcast reporting.

The three main parts – Broadcast Journalism, Radio, and Television – systematically lay the foundations required by the aspiring broadcast journalist.

Part One deals with the business of newswriting, newsgathering, interviewing, programme making and presentation, focusing on the common ground between radio and television.

Parts Two and Three place those skills firmly in the context of the radio and TV newsroom. Each begins by taking the reader behind the scenes, first to experience the atmosphere in the internationally respected newsroom of the BBC External Services in London and then to the stimulating world of Independent Television News.

Today's broadcast industry has been shaped by rapid advances in technology. How the equipment works and how the reporter should use it is clearly explained in the sections on television and radio which offer instruction in the basics of camerawork, recording for radio, editing pictures and audio, and TV scriptwriting.

A section on the career outlines the jobs available and offers a plan of campaign for those determined to break into broadcasting, from the first approach to preparing for the interview. The question of training is covered and a preliminary list of courses is given.

For readers using the book as a reference, the detailed contents at the start and extensive cross-referencing signpost your route and encourage you to dip in and out as you please.

Each chapter ends with a set of practical suggestions for developing the skills outlined. These form the basis of a training course which you can use to teach yourself or others.

The aim has been to produce a comprehensive manual – a tool – to be grasped and used by students, teachers and practitioners of broadcast journalism alike.

Andrew Boyd

LIST OF ILLUSTRATIONS

Figure 1 IRN newsroom 2
Figure 2 Weather graphics 9
Figure 3 Capital Radio Flying Eye 9
Figure 4 BBC Monitoring Unit 12
Figure 5 News sources – contacts board 14
Figure 6 BBC External Services news diary 14
Figure 7 Embargoed news release 19
Figure 8 Sample of agency copy (Reuters) 23
Figure 9 BBC GNS rip and read news summary 25
Figure 10 TV editorial conference 29
Figure 11 Recording an interview with a Uher portable tape recorder 34
Figure 12 Dictating news copy onto computer 39
Figure 13 News cue sheet 54
Figure 14 Maintaining eye contact during a location interview for TV 75
Figure 15 Setting the interviewee at ease 81
Figure 16 Setting up the interview on the phone 87
Figure 17 TV interview with Mrs Indira Ghandi 93
Figure 18 Chairing a radio discussion in the talks studio 99
Figure 19 Reading the news on BBC local radio 102
Figure 20 Programme running order for radio 114
Figure 21 Visuals running order for TV 115
Figure 22 Double-headed radio news presentation 125
Figure 23 'Voice is music' 131
Figure 24 BBC job advert for a reporter 136
Figure 25 Live presentation from a BBC control desk 138
Figure 26 BBC World Service newsreader 151
Figure 27 TV studio Portaprompt 152
Figure 28 Idiot guide to appropriate newsreading 154
Figure 29 Posy cartoon: 'We bring you – live from the scene of the tragedy . . .' 156
Figure 30 War reporting. When do freedom fighters become terrorists? 163
Figure 31 Camera crew under fire. Wherever they stand someone will accuse them of bias 164
Figure 32 Unfair film editing – accusation 165
Figure 33 Should cameras intrude on grief? 168
Figure 34 Newsroom of BBC External Services 174
Figure 35 Agency copy pours into the BBC 176
Figure 36 Bulletin running order for BBC External Services 178
Figure 37 Marking up system for BBC World Service copy 181
Figure 38 Behind the scenes of *Radio Newsreel* 183
Figure 39 BBC World Service foreign correspondents 186
Figure 40 Reporting for radio on location 190
Figure 41 The radio car 195
Figure 42 BBC war correspondent using 'portable' disc recorder 205
Figure 43 Bulk eraser 207
Figure 44 Cutaway of a tape cartridge 208
Figure 45 Tape tracks 211

Figure 46 Microphone directivity patterns 212
Figure 47 Uher portable tape recorder 215
Figure 48 Tape laced up on portable tape recorder 216
Figure 49 Marantz portable cassette recorder 218
Figure 50 Nagra miniature tape recorder 219
Figure 51 Microphone handling 220
Figure 52 Editing a radio report in a mixing studio 224
Figure 53 Studio tape decks, analogue and digital 226
Figure 54 Editing reel to reel tape (sequence) 227
Figure 55 Setting tape levels on PPM meters 231
Figure 56 Different types of fade 233
Figure 57 Radio studios – BBC and Independent 235
Figure 58 Communications between talks studio and control desk 236
Figure 59 Self-operation in the newsbooth 237
Figure 60 Sending a taped report back to base on the telephone 239
Figure 61 The Touchscreen studio 241
Figure 62 Behind the scenes in a TV news studio 246
Figure 63 Senior presenters at the newsdesk 247
Figure 64 TV news prospects 250
Figure 65 Countdown to a programme – role of the TV news producer 252
Figure 66 The TV interview – camera and lighting 258
Figure 67 Camera shots bring home the reality 260
Figure 68 Matching TV script to pictures 261
Figure 69 TV commentary booth 264
Figure 70 Computer printout of TV script 265
Figure 71 Autocue script 266
Figure 72 Model of John Logie Baird's first mechanical TV camera 269
Figure 73 First electronic television camera 269
Figure 74 From TV camera to TV screen – how sound and pictures are transmitted 270
Figure 75 Intelsat V 273
Figure 76 TV location interview using sound reflector 276
Figure 77 On location with an ENG camera 278
Figure 78 Lighting for shots in poor daylight 281
Figure 79 Hand-held Sun Gun to boost the light 282
Figure 80 Outside broadcast units in action 283
Figure 81 Interior of OB scanner 284
Figure 82 Portable satellite ground station 285
Figure 83 Sequence of different camera shots 288
Figure 84 Crossing the line 295
Figure 85 Reporter doing piece to camera (stand-upper) on location 296
Figure 86 Prompting on location 297
Figure 87 TV editing suite 310
Figure 88 Countdown clock 313
Figure 89 Clapperboard (clapstick) 316
Figure 90 Steenbeck film editing machine 317
Figure 91 Film synchronizer 317
Figure 92 Film editing marks 318
Figure 93 Using a film joiner 319
Figure 94 Studio camera focusing on a picture stand 322
Figure 95 Composite shot 323
Figure 96 Graphics help explain figures and numerical relationships 324
Figure 97 Graphics operator at work 325
Figure 98 Chromakey window and full-screen backdrop 327
Figure 99 Floor manager's instructions 333

Figure 100 Camera operator's cribcards and automatic prompter 334
Figure 101 Corrections to Autocue script 334
Figure 102 *News at 5.45* control room 335
Figure 103 The computerized newsroom 339
Figure 104 Teletext journalists at work 341
Figure 105 Satellite earth station 345
Figure 106 A student journalist presents a programme 352

Part One

BROADCAST JOURNALISM

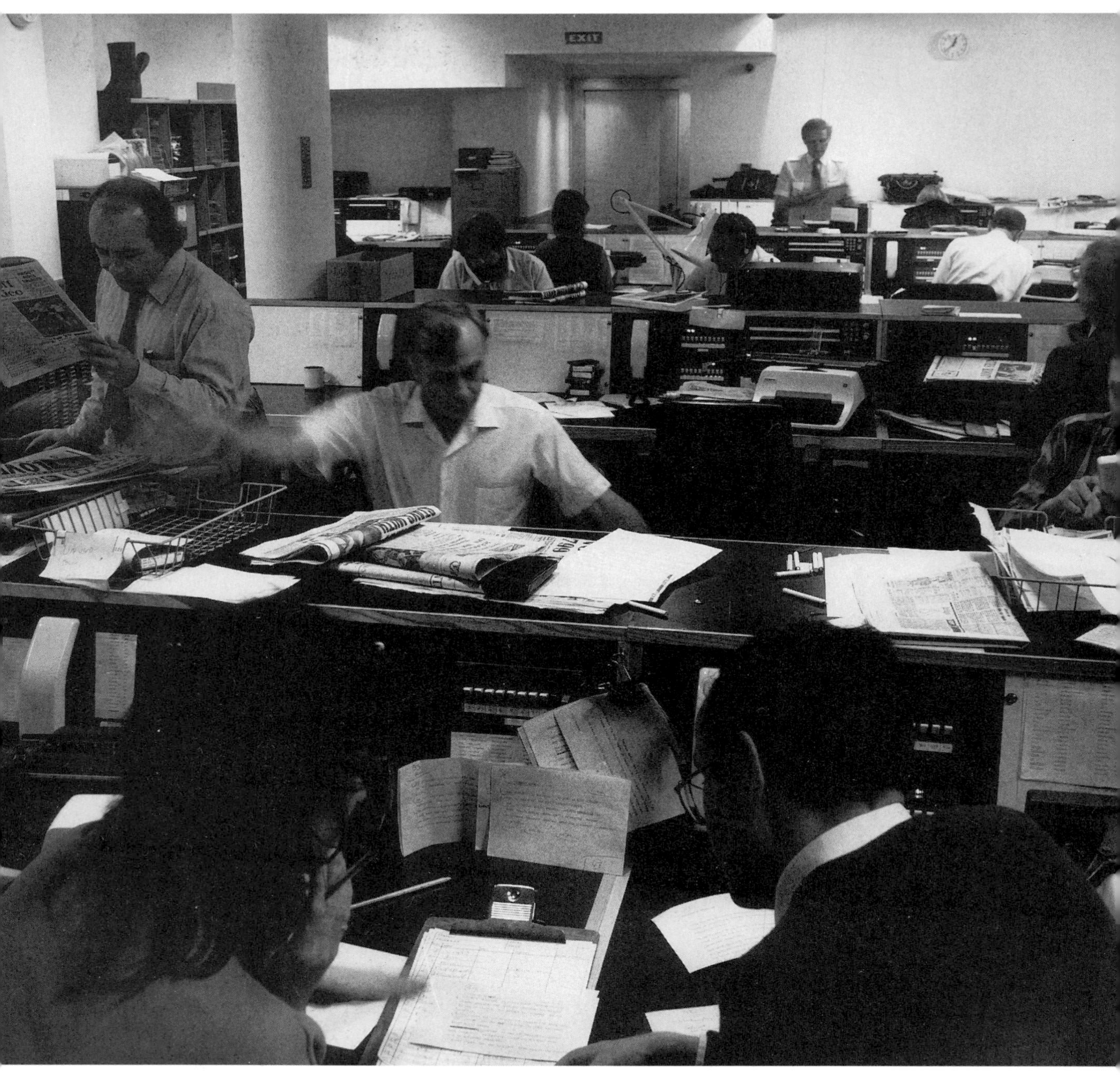

Figure 1 'On the hour, every hour . . .' The pace, the hustle, the pressure of the IRN (Independent Radio News) 24 hour newsroom (courtesy IRN)

NEWS GATHERING

1 What is news?

'Tidings, new or interesting information, fresh events reported.'
– *CONCISE OXFORD DICTIONARY*

'News is the first rough draft of history.' – BEN BRADLEE

'News is anything that makes a reader say, "Gee Whiz!"'
– ARTHUR McEWEN

'News is the immediate, the important, the things that have impact on our lives.'
– FREDA MORRIS, NBC

'When a dog bites a man, that is not news, but when a man bites a dog, that is news.' – CHARLES DANA

'Women, wampum and wrongdoing are always news.' – STANLEY WALKER

PROXIMITY

In a contest to come up with the dullest headline imaginable, a *Times* sub-editor managed to slip the following into the paper:

SMALL EARTHQUAKE IN CHILE – NOT MANY DEAD

The headline has all the resounding impact of a damp squib. It turns the story into everything news is not – by making an earth-shattering event sound small in scale and undramatic, remote and unimportant. It may have produced a smile at *The Times* – thousands of miles from the earthquake – but the irony would have been lost on anyone living in Chile.

Yet this spoof has something to say about the nature of news. For a story to have impact, it has to be *relevant*. For news to be relevant, it has to have *proximity* to an audience.

Somebody once described news as an acronym for North, East, West and South. But news is narrower than that – the tremors in South America would be unlikely to trouble the Eskimos of the northern Arctic wastes – the problem is simply too far away.

RELEVANCE

Even when the proximity gap is narrowed, a news item may fail to interest different groups within the *same* country. A surge in the price of coffee might shake up the businessmen of Nairobi, but fail to stir the fishermen and woodcarvers of Mombasa. But if the price of coffee crashed, the item would come home to everyone in Kenya – the economy would slump and they would *all* be affected.

But even when a story has both proximity and relevance, the reaction it provokes in *you* will depend on your upbringing, environment, education, background, beliefs, and morality. In other words, news values are subjective, and for most news editors, the selection of news is more of an art than a science. Stories are weighed up by an instinctive process they would put down to *news sense*.

Despite that, every editor would agree that the greater the effect of a story on listeners' lives, their incomes and emotions, the more important that item will be. And every editor knows that if a news service is to win and hold an audience, the bulk of its stories must have impact on most of the people most of the time.

IMMEDIACY

> *'Yesterday's newspaper is used to wrap fish and yesterday's broadcast does not exist at all.'* – MARTIN MAYER
>
> *'The strength of radio is its immediacy. Exploit that by constantly up-dating stories and keeping them fresh. We're telling people what's happening* now.*'* – MALCOLM SHAW, NEWS EDITOR, RADIO MERCURY
>
> *'Radio news is what happened five minutes ago and its impact on what is going to happen in the next five minutes.'*
> – RICHARD BESTIC, IRN PARLIAMENTARY CORRESPONDENT

News is about what is happening now, or the first inkling of something that happened earlier but was hushed up. And nowhere is news more immediate than in broadcasting. '*You catch it live!*' used to be the catchphrase of one radio station's sports service. It is a boast the printed word can never match.

To the broadcast journalist, what happened yesterday is dead and buried. There has to be something new to say, some fresh angle. And with hourly deadlines, even what went on air at eleven will have to be updated for noon.

To put it another way: *news is only news while it is new.*

INTEREST

'*Worthy, but dull*' is one of the most damning indictments you could make about a news report. News should make you suck in your breath and exclaim, sit up, take notice and listen.

Broadcast news is often criticized for pandering to the popular taste, but by its very nature, *broad*casting caters for the mass interest, rather than that of a minority. Stories must have a wide appeal or most of the audience will change channels.

The skill of the newswriter comes in drawing out the relevance of a story and presenting it clearly and factually while making the most of every scrap of interest. This way the newswriter can give the audience what it *needs* to know – as well as what it *wants* to know.

The most interesting element in news is often people – showbusiness personalities, celebrities, big-name politicians, royalty – elite people, who we know only from a distance and who interest us out of curiosity, envy, admiration, malice or affection; people through whom we live our lives vicariously, or whose actions and decisions influence and shape our existence.

DRAMA

Dramatic events of the stranger-than-fiction variety make striking headlines. Shotgun sieges, violent crime, car chases, cliff-top rescues – the greater the drama, the greater its prominence in a bulletin. Excitement, danger, adventure, conflict, have as great an appeal to the newswriter as the novelist or movie-maker.

The art of newswriting is closely related to storytelling – news items are referred to as stories – but if the writer is to maintain integrity and credibility, the temptation to dress up the facts to make them more like fiction has to be avoided.

ENTERTAINMENT

In some journalistic circles entertainment is still a dirty word, but news and showbusiness often go hand in glove. There is an element of performance in the presentation of news and sometimes pure entertainment in its writing. The *kicker* or *tailpiece* is a prime example. This is the light or humorous story at the end of a bulletin, immortalized in the UK by Independent Television News (ITN), whose policy to 'leave 'em smiling' is pure showbiz.

Information and entertainment are often held in tension. Where news ends and entertainment begins is more than a matter of house style. It is one of the more important questions facing the news media today. Where that line is drawn will depend on the target audience for a programme and the priority that is placed on high ratings. The surest way to boost those ratings is to increase the amount of entertainment that goes into the mix.

For more on item selection see Chapter 10, page 108.

DIFFERENT TYPES OF NEWS

Many first-time visitors to a newsroom ask the same question: 'where do you *get* all your news?' The answer is, it may not grow on trees, but there is usually plenty to be found if you know where to look, as the rest of this chapter explains.

'Steven McBride is 20 years old.'

So what? It might be information, but it is not news.

'Half his short life has been spent in prisons, borstals and other institutions.'

Well, that is sad and may be of some interest to somebody because it is unusual, but it is still not *news.*

'Steven McBride is coming out today... a free man.'

It is information, it has some interest and it is new because he is coming out *today*, but it is still not *news.*

'Three months ago, McBride was sentenced to ***life*** *for the murder of his parents.'*

His *parents.* Now this is important. How can a man who has been charged with murdering his parents be let out of prison after only three months?

'New evidence has come to light to show conclusively that McBride did not commit the murders and that the killer is still on the loose and has ***already*** *struck again.'*

The information is new, interesting, and important, but for it to be newsworthy, it would have to be relevant to *you*, the audience. If the murders were committed in *your* home town – that is news – and local radio and TV there would almost certainly run it as their lead.

The starting place for most broadcast journalists is in the local or regional radio newsroom. Here, the *local angle* is all-important. Where the audience lives, the people they know, the matters and events that directly affect them give the story its point of relevance.

Once reporters have cut their teeth on the bread and butter stories many will think about moving into network news or television. Many items of national news begin in the local newsroom. The writing style is similar, the mechanics of the piece unchanged, but the scale of the event gives the story a wider significance.

Whether a news story is local, national or international, it will usually fall into one or more of the following categories:

Emergencies

The emergency services deal with the high points of human drama – fires, sea or mountain rescues – whenever human life is at risk there is a story.

Accidents are a steady but unpredictable source of news, but the larger the area covered by the news service, the more serious these will have to be to warrant coverage, otherwise the bulletins would be full of little else, so reporting of accidents is usually confined to death or serious injury.

Crime

Rising crime rates offer a steady source of news. The larger the area, the more crime there will be, so only more serious offences are likely to be reported.

> *'Crime is still a big one. People love crime stories, they really do, no matter where in the world you are people want to know about what is happening on the streets; the murder, the rapes, the robberies – that occupies a fairly large chunk of time.'*
>
> – ANNETTE BOSWORTH, ASSISTANT TO THE VICE PRESIDENT, NEWS AND PROGRAMMING, WEEI, BOSTON*

Crime stories have many phases, from the actual incident, to the police raid, arrest, and eventual appearance in court.

Local and national government

Every action of government – locally or nationally – has a bearing on a potential audience, and whatever affects an audience is news. To prevent bulletins becoming swamped with items from city hall, news policy is usually to report only the stories that have the greatest effect on the largest number of people.

Planning and developments

Local building developments would include new projects, leisure complexes, shopping centres, housing schemes and any big development that will impact on an area. Nationally, the difference is one of scale. Newsworthy developments would include major road building schemes, new townships, dams and other large projects.

But the concept of developments as news expands beyond public works to mean any form of major change that is happening or is about to happen that will affect a given audience.

Conflict and controversy

> *'Almost inevitably, anything that threatens people's peace, prosperity or well-being is news and likely to make headlines.'*
>
> – ALASTAIR HETHERINGTON†

News is about change – events that shape our society and alter the way we live. Conflict is the essence of drama, and the dramatic makes news.

This can be physical clashes in the streets or a conflict of ideals – a row at the local council or in Parliament. Where actions or ideas mean upheavals in society, then that conflict is news.

Every issue in the public eye has those who are for it and those who are against it. Broadcast journalism can cover what is happening, stimulate debate, and bring important issues into sharper focus.

Pressure groups

Pressure groups are people who have organized themselves to stir up controversy. They either want change or are opposed to it, so their demands are usually news. Reaction to government policy, events or developments can be an effective follow-up to a story. The reporter seeks

*From WEEI, video by Ian Hyams.

† From *News, Newspapers and Television*, Macmillan 1985.

out the players in the underlying conflict, exposes the controversy and so uncovers the news.

Industry Employment is a major factor in most people's lives, so developments in industry make big news, whether they concern layoffs or increased job recruitment which will affect the workforce and prosperity of an area.

Health From outbreaks of AIDS, illness and disease, to a shortage of blood donors.

Human interest A human interest story may be defined as an extraordinary thing that has happened to an ordinary person. Soft news is lightweight material which people like to hear, such as who has won the pools or discovered a Ming vase in their shed. It is the unusual, ironic, or offbeat; the sort of story that people enjoy talking about in pubs and bars.

Personalities Visiting personalities, royalty or politicians are usually good for a local news item, especially if their visit is linked to a local event or occasion. Nationally, the bigger the name, the more likely it is to make news. The more entertainment a station mixes with its news, the more prominently personalities – especially from showbusiness – are likely to feature.

Sport Many in the audience tolerate the news only because they know if they stay tuned they will get the latest football, cricket or rugby results. Local teams and clubs often feature strongly in the local news, especially if they are doing well or badly in their leagues, and this is reflected at a national level, where news usually focuses on the promotion battles and relegation struggles that mark the changing fortunes of the top and bottom teams.

Seasonal news Seasonal news includes Christmas shopping, January sales, the first cuckoo, the tourist season, seasonal unemployment.

Special local interest No two news areas are the same. Each will throw up stories peculiar to its own geography and make-up. An area with a car factory will create news about recruitment, layoffs, new models and the fortunes of the company. A seaport with a naval base will produce stories of warships stationed there and naval exercises involving local ships and men. A mountainous region will generate items about missing climbers and mountain rescues.

Special features give an area its identify. Audience loyalty is built when a station is seen to be providing a truly local news service.

Weather (Figure 2) Regular weather updates are one of the main features in the local news.

TV companies spend a great deal of money providing a high quality weather service. On the national news satellite pictures are often combined with detailed graphics and elaborate weather maps.

Weather normally follows the news, but at times of extreme conditions, the weather itself will make headlines. Radio comes into its own when there are flash floods, droughts or serious snowfalls. CBC in Wales picked up huge audiences by running snowdesks one particularly severe winter. Residents and travellers regarded it as a life-line as people were being literally snowed under or cut off for days at a time. CBC put out a constant stream of information and answered people's inquiries by telephone. Nothing can touch radio for its immediacy in times of crisis.

Traffic

Next to the weather, the first thing many people want to know in the morning is whether the roads will be clear for getting to work. Radio is the only medium motorists can safely take in while driving. In car-orientated societies where large numbers commute to work, traffic and travel news can pick up big audiences. These periods are known as *drive-time*. Radio stations can give up-to-the-minute information on which roads are blocked and where there are traffic jams.

Some car radios can automatically scan channels and seek out the latest traffic reports. In Britain, the Automobile Association (AA) has its own reporters who go live into local radio drive-time programmes from AA offices around the country.

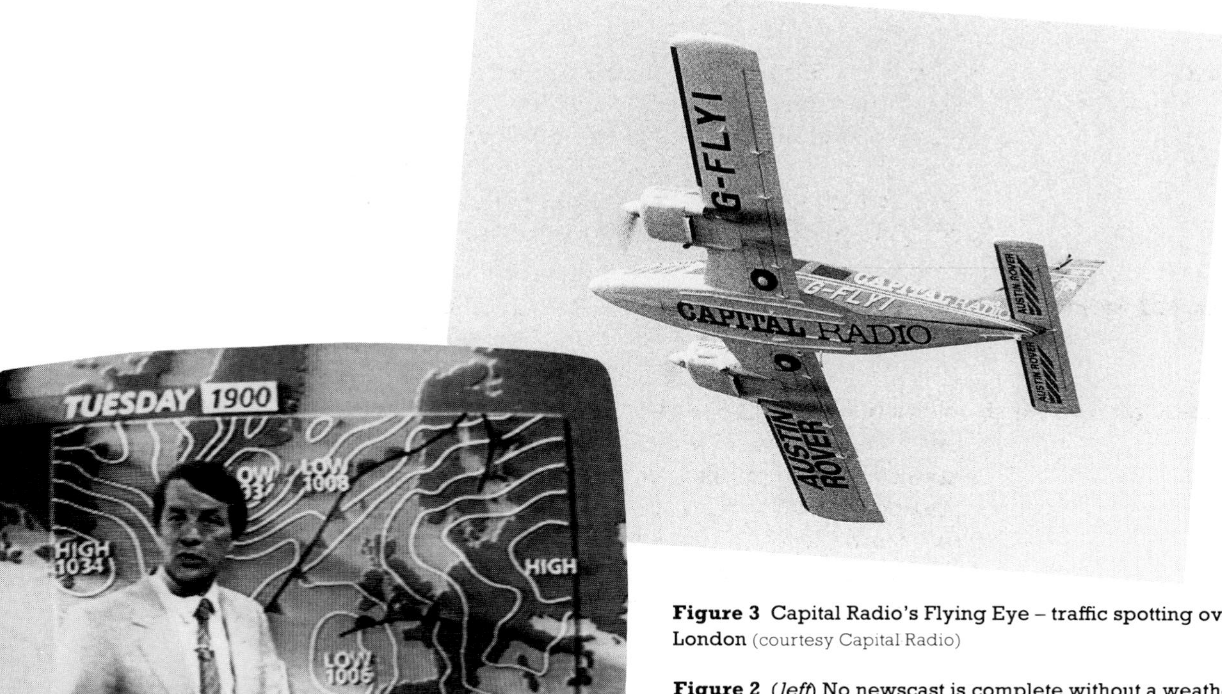

Figure 3 Capital Radio's Flying Eye – traffic spotting over London (courtesy Capital Radio)

Figure 2 (*left*) No newscast is complete without a weather report and, increasingly elaborate ways are being found to display the forecasts. Unseen to the audience, the weatherman in this picture holds a switch which changes the electronic backdrop at the press of a button (courtesy BBC)

Some larger stations, such as Capital Radio in London and Radio Clyde in Glasgow, have their own aircraft scanning the roads for traffic snarl-ups, with a reporter on board who can send back live updates over a radio link (Figure 3).

Citizens' band radio is also frequently used to get a first-hand picture of the build up of traffic from the motorists who are trapped in it. Many stations extend their service to cover all types of commuting by providing drive-time reports about buses, trains, ferries and flights.

Animals

Few items prompt greater reaction from the legions of pet lovers than shaggy dog stories. Men, women and babies may die in fires but fail to provoke a murmur, but if anyone tries to poison a poodle, the switchboards are likely to be jammed with calls.

CHECKLIST

For any item which does not fall into the above categories, the test of whether or not it is news to a given audience is:

Is it:

- Relevant
- Important
- Tragic
- Unusual
- The last
- The most expensive
- Immediate or imminent
- Interesting
- Controversial
- The first
- The biggest
- Funny, or Ironic

But the first question an editor will ask is: *Does it affect* ***our*** *audience*? And for the local newsroom that means: *Is it local?*

FIELDWORK

1 Video record a local TV news programme and list the stories that appear. See if each of the items will fit into one or more of the categories in the summary above. If you cannot place any of the items, work out suitable new categories into which they will fit.

2 Record national and local radio bulletins of comparable lengths on the same day and list the stories in each.

Go through each story to see how it rates in your view in terms of *relevance*, *importance*, *immediacy*, *interest* and *entertainment*. Award each story points out of three under each category, where three is the maximum score (*Very important*, etc.) and zero is the lowest. Add up the totals and see which bulletin scores the highest overall. Is that the one you preferred? If not, why do you think it rated so highly?

3 Which stories did you find the most *relevant* and why? In what way is the relevance of those stories determined by their geographical *proximity* to you?

Which stories did you find the most *important* and what made some stories more *interesting* than others? Why?

Decide which you think is the most controversial story in each bulletin and why.

4 Focusing on the idea that News = Change, work out what are the biggest changes happening in your local area at the moment that might find their way into a news bulletin.

5 News has just come in of a big fire in a chemical warehouse in the centre of town. Some of the chemicals are highly explosive. Police say the whole warehouse is like a giant bomb and are evacuating the area. Given unlimited resources, how would you cover the story for TV? (Split into teams of four if you are in a class and discuss.)

2 News sources

There are some days when news just seems to fall into your lap. Everywhere you turn another story is breaking. Days like these are a journalist's dream.

The nightmare begins with the holiday season when nothing seems to happen. Local check calls to the police elicit jokey offers from bored constables to *'go out and bite a dog for you.'*

And so the media resorts to clutching at flying saucers and running items about nude bathing on the beaches. This is known as the *silly season*.

Figure 4 Part of the BBC's massive news monitoring service at Caversham which listens in to broadcast stations and agency reports throughout the world and feeds information to BBC newsrooms, Parliament and the press (courtesy BBC External Services)

Most times the newsperson's lot is somewhere between these extremes. What stories there are have to be dug for. Graft is required to turn a tip-off into hard facts.

REPORTERS

The biggest source of news for any radio or TV station should be its reporting staff. Many local stations rightly insist that their journalists live in the community to which they are broadcasting. Through everyday contact with people in the area, from their observations as they do their shopping or drive to work, will come ideas for stories.

From the car window the reporter notices that the construction of a new factory seems to be behind time. There has been little progress for almost a month; so the reporter pulls in at the roadside and asks the foreman why. Closer to the station, rows of publically-owned houses on an inner city site seem to be rotting away; what can the authorities do to make them habitable? Squatters are moving in; are the neighbours concerned? Would the squatters resist attempts to evict them? Reporters should keep their eyes and ears open.

Wealthier stations are able to employ *specialists* – reporters who are experts in certain areas, with experience behind them and a key set of contacts. Chief fields are local government, industry, or crime.

The job of the *investigative journalist* is to find something wrong and expose it. He or she is a positive force for change, a professional with the ability to penetrate the closed ranks of vested interests and free imprisoned information from behind enemy lines. Investigative reporters may also work in teams on projects such as documentaries.

Not every station can spare the time or has the scope to permit an ordinary reporter to develop into an investigative journalist, but all reporters have to be investigators at heart.

CONTACTS
(Figure 5)

When the big story breaks, the first thing reporters reach for is their contacts book. This is their most valuable resource. It contains the names and phone numbers of everyone in their area who regularly makes, or comments on, the news, plus national figures whose sphere of influence may include their own 'beat'.

The relationship between reporters and their contacts is doubled-edged. The newswriter needs a story, the newsmaker needs publicity.

Clearly, a line has to be drawn, and the place to draw it is well before the point where editorial freedom and integrity begin to be compromised.

After a while, reporters may find some of their regular contacts become their friends. That may be fine if there is good news involving that contact, but if the news is bad, it still has to be reported. In the end, reporters must maintain their independence. They can never afford to owe anyone favours.

NEWSROOM DIARY
(Figure 6)

Newsrooms keep a diary, which is made up each day by the news editor. It gives details of stories the newsroom will cover, the times of events and the reporters alloted to them.

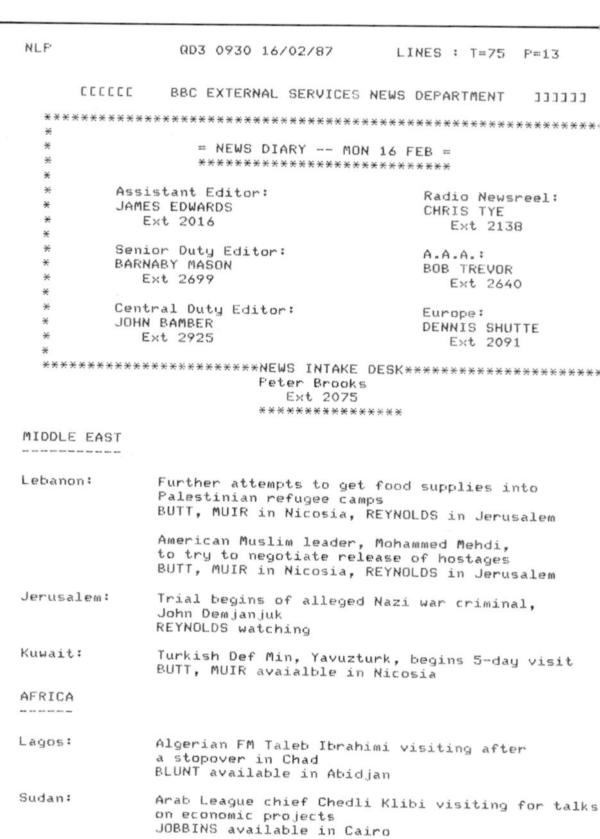

NLP QD3 0930 16/02/87 LINES : T=75 P=13

[[[[[[BBC EXTERNAL SERVICES NEWS DEPARTMENT]]]]]]

= NEWS DIARY -- MON 16 FEB =

Assistant Editor:
JAMES EDWARDS
Ext 2016

Radio Newsreel:
CHRIS TYE
Ext 2138

Senior Duty Editor:
BARNABY MASON
Ext 2699

A.A.A.:
BOB TREVOR
Ext 2640

Central Duty Editor:
JOHN BAMBER
Ext 2925

Europe:
DENNIS SHUTTE
Ext 2091

NEWS INTAKE DESK
Peter Brooks
Ext 2075

MIDDLE EAST

Lebanon:	Further attempts to get food supplies into Palestinian refugee camps BUTT, MUIR in Nicosia, REYNOLDS in Jerusalem
	American Muslim leader, Mohammed Mehdi, to try to negotiate release of hostages BUTT, MUIR in Nicosia, REYNOLDS in Jerusalem
Jerusalem:	Trial begins of alleged Nazi war criminal, John Demjanjuk REYNOLDS watching
Kuwait:	Turkish Def Min, Yavuzturk, begins 5-day visit BUTT, MUIR avaialble in Nicosia

AFRICA

Lagos:	Algerian FM Taleb Ibrahimi visiting after a stopover in Chad BLUNT available in Abidjan
Sudan:	Arab League chief Chedli Klibi visiting for talks on economic projects JOBBINS available in Cairo

Figure 5 News sources – almost a full contacts book chalked up on the board at BBC Radio Solent (Andrew Boyd)

Figure 6 Most newsrooms produce a diary each day to show what stories they plan to cover and which reporter has been assigned to them. The BBC External Services diary extends to four pages and covers Asia, America, Europe and Britain (courtesy BBC External Services)

The diary, or a list of prospects drawn from that diary, is the first thing reporters look at when they arrive on shift. It is the day's plan of action; the newsroom route map.

The editor makes up the diary from information in the post, tips from reporters and stories which are known to be breaking. Files are usually kept on major stories containing up-to-date cuttings and background information. Bigger stations have libraries and news information services to help with more extensive research.

FILES

In its simplest form the *futures file* can be a single drawer in a filing cabinet with drop-files numbered 1 to 31, one for each day of the month.

Selected news releases about events at some future date are noted in the diary and put on file. Court appearances for newsworthy cases are filed ahead, with copy relating to earlier hearings.

An *archive* may be developed by transferring the month's files to an identical filing drawer with all the copy used and possibly tapes of the output. Bulletins and news programmes may also be recorded and stored in the archive.

All incoming copy of interest, but which has failed to make the bulletins, is impaled on a spike or kept in a basket.

The trouble with storing information on paper is that it takes too much space to allow files to go back a long way, and increasingly stations are keeping their files on computer databases.

Stories can be instantly recalled, even if the operator has forgotten the date or author of the copy. One or two key words are typed into the computer and, providing those words featured in the story, the copy will quickly come up on the screen. (See also the computerized newsroom, page 339).

The WPB is often the biggest file of all. Newsrooms get flooded with useless information and propaganda, most of which ends up, with scarcely a glance, where it belongs, in the waste paper bin.

CHECK CALLS

A story which is happening right *now*, such as an armed robbery, fire, or air crash, is known in Britain as a breaking news item, and in America as a *spot story*.

Prime sources of breaking news are emergency services – fire, police, ambulance, coastguard, etc. – which are contacted regularly. These inquiries are known as *check calls*.

There are problems with such calls. In an area which is rich in news media, overworked police officers may be tempted to shake off callers by saying nothing is happening even when it is.

Shift changes may mean a call is made before the new duty officer has managed to catch up on the paperwork, so he or she is unaware of the events of the previous few hours and gives the reporter a false impression.

A common mistake is for the reporter to try to get information from the wrong person. In provincial British police stations constables are rarely authorized to talk to the media, who should instead refer inquiries to duty inspectors or station sergeants instead. If a serious crime has been committed, a station sergeant may know little about it, so the best contact would be the detective from CID (Criminal Investigation Department) or equivalent, who is handling the case.

Constabularies may be organized on a county basis, each with its own press officer, whose task it is to collate important news from police stations and release it to the media. This can overlook the bread and butter items and be too slow off the mark with breaking stories.

Press officers are distant from the scene of the crime, so information can take some time to get to them. To make matters worse, local police, who do know what is happening, are often instructed in major crimes to redirect all inquiries to the press officer.

There are times when the police need the media as much as the media needs the police, for making appeals for witnesses and help in tracing missing persons. Reporters are not obliged to co-operate, but goodwill is often the best way of ensuring a steady flow of information.

EMERGENCY SERVICES RADIO

The surest way to keep in touch with major breaking news is to tune in to emergency services radio.

By monitoring the transmissions of police and fire services you can hear the news as it is actually happening, instead of waiting for the official version to be collated and sanitized by a spokesperson.

In Britain it is illegal to listen to police radio and take action as a result of that information. The law is intended to deter criminals from listening to police activity. To make it harder, messages from base are given on one frequency and mobile units reply on another, so only half the conversation can be heard at one time.

In America it is common for reporters to turn up at an incident before the police, but British law means that writing a story from a police broadcast, or sending a reporter to the scene could result in a prosecution. In practice it would be impossible to prove the reporter had been listening to police radio.

A more likely outcome would be the straining of relationships between the newsroom and the police, which could result in a loss of goodwill and stem the flow of official information.

In places where listening in is legal, newsrooms commonly use radio *scanners*. These monitor the emergency airwaves for a transmission and home in on the conversation.

The 10 code

In many countries the police talk to one another in a code designed to help them communicate clearly and rapidly over the air, while at the same time mystifying unauthorized eavesdroppers.

Frequently the code used is a variation of the 10 code. Instead of saying '*Fight in progress*', for example, an officer might say '*10–10*', followed by the location. Each force may haves its own version of the code where the numbers mean something different.

Some of the key messages in one variation of the 10 code are:

10–31	Crime in progress
10–32	Man with a gun
10–33	Emergency
10–34	Riot
10–35	Major crime alert
10–50	Accident
10–57	Hit and run
10–79	Notify coroner

Whatever is heard over police radio *must* be checked before use. Frequently police get called to 'emergencies' only to discover a storm in a teacup. A 'riot' can turn out to be a gang of kids establishing who's boss in the park; reports of a murder attempt in an apartment or block of flats might be a husband and wife settling their differences with a crockery-throwing contest.

POLITICIANS

> ***'Too much of what I see is press release broadcasting. You automatically go and get a ministry, then somebody from the opposition. All these people do is give you party political statements. I find that boring and can't believe the public learns anything. You already know what the political parties are going to say, and I can't see where any of that does a damn thing to improve the quality of our understanding.'*** – HARRY RADLIFFE, BUREAU CHIEF, CBS NEWS

Local politicians are a prime source of news for a local newsroom. Usually they are happy to oblige as this raises their profile and may win votes. A reporter should be wise to that and make sure legitimate news, rather than vote-catching rhetoric, gets on air.

Every journalist should know the names of the area's representatives in both local and national government, and should have contact numbers for them at work and at home.

When politicians are not making news themselves, they are usually good for a comment or reaction to stories that affect their constituencies or wards. Political comment is cheap and readily available and this type of reaction can be overdone, lead to accusations of political bias, and leave a bulletin sounding as dull as a party political broadcast. Use sparingly.

PRESSURE GROUPS

A similar warning applies to using pressure groups for reaction and comment: beware of vested interests. Big pressure groups include trades unions and employers' organizations. Smaller groups abound such as the Lord's Day Observance Society which wants to keep Sundays free from commercialism, and the Animal Liberation Front, which sometimes takes criminal action against vivisection laboratories. Many charities also act as pressure groups.

Beware of unrepresentative groups with only a handful of members. Bona fide pressure groups have an important contribution to make to public debate.

STAGED EVENTS

Staging a news event is the pressure group's ultimate way of winning attention. These usually fall into one of three categories: the *protest*; *announcement* and *set-piece*.

The protest

This is the pressure group trying to give its voice as wide a public hearing as possible. A three-lane highway is to be constructed across green fields to run alongside a housing estate. Residents, environmentalists, and opposition politicians form an action group to stage a march on the town hall. To make sure the cameras are there they make the event as visual as possible, with people dressed in fancy costumes and carrying banners. To ensure radio coverage they chant and sing specially written protest songs.

The announcement

This is more formal, and often takes the shape of a news conference. When the town planners announce their three-lane highway they do so with a lavish presentation. All the media is invited to a conference in the chandeliered opulence of the town hall banqueting room. Drinks are laid on and a buffet provided.

When reporters have been wined and dined and their journalistic sensibilities submerged beneath a stupor of alcohol, the mayor and other senior officials are ceremoniously invited to make their presentation.

The road scheme is flourished with neat and convincing rhetoric about better traffic flow, reduced accident figures and the positive effect on trade in the town. For the cameras, there are stylish mock-ups of the road and artists' impressions. For the media, press packs are provided with slickly written articles which the organizers hope will be published unaltered. Key speakers are available immediately after the presentation for photocalls and interviews. (See also news conferences, page 35.)

The set-piece

This is usually staged simply for publicity. The new highway has been built, and a TV personality hired to open it by leading a cavalcade of vintage cars along its length – very visual and almost assured of TV coverage. At its best the set-piece provides a bright and appealing story for the bulletin, at its worst it can be news manipulation of the first order.

A prime example was the funeral of an IRA hunger striker which received widespread coverage on British television. This was largely thanks to the specially constructed grandstand provided by the terrorist organization for the cameras.

At the other extreme was the 'Great Auk Story'. Reporters from British newspapers and a TV journalist were lured to the remote Orkney Islands where a team of five eccentrics was believed to be embarking on an expedition to find the Great Auk, a seabird thought to have been extinct for 150 years. Hopes were fuelled by reported sightings by islanders. When the bird eventually did make an appearance it was not only extinct, it was stuffed. It turned out to be a stunt for a whisky company. It was not wholly successful. At least one reporter, peeved at being taken on a wild Auk chase, refused to name the distillery which had organized the stunt.

Where news events are a lavish attempt at news management by publicity seekers, journalists should be aware of this and not let it influence their news judgement. Money talks, but it is up to you whether you listen.

NEWS RELEASES

> ***'Is there anything more useless than a PR agency, I ask myself? Every morning I have to devote half an hour of my precious time to opening mail: 99 per cent of it describes a graceful arc into the waste paper basket.'*** – LETTER IN THE *UK PRESS GAZETTE*

Each morning, editors in broadcast newsrooms have a pile of mail dumped before them on their desks. Yet most of the items posted to the media will end up in the waste paper bin after scarcely a second glance. That is because so much is irrelevant and of little interest to the audience. Middle Eastern countries have been known to send regular bulletins on their economic progress and internal politics to small-town radio stations in England.

To sift the wheat from the chaff, the mail is *copytasted*, but to scrutinize each item carefully could take hours, so each envelope is ripped open and its contents hastily scanned. Unless a news angle presents itself almost immediately the copy is filed in the bin.

Most of the mailbag comprises public relations handouts – usually dressed-up advertising the writers hope will pass as news. They are usually disappointed.

If the handout is one of the small percentage that does contain a possible story, it will be checked and written up into copy (Figure 7).

Some news releases carry *embargoes*, which means they are not to be used before a certain release date. Public relations people use the embargo to try to control the flow of news, and prevent stories being run in what they would regard as a haphazard fashion. On the plus side, the embargo gives the newsroom time to prepare its report by giving advanced warning of the event.

Figure 7 Embargoed news releases give advance information on the understanding that it will not be published until the release date, giving the newsroom time to prepare the story

OVERSEAS
DEVELOPMENT

NEWS RELEASE ~ Press Office 01·213 4909

Overseas Development Administration, Eland House, Stag Place, London SW1E 5DH

EMBARGO: NOT FOR PUBLICATION BEFORE 1700 HOURS, 26 JANUARY

26 January

MINISTER PLEDGES ECO-CONCERN IN AID PROGRAMME

Mr Chris Patten MP, Minister for Overseas Development today said that eco-concern and not eco-hysteria was the right response to environmental problems in developing countries.

The Queen's New Year's Honours List is a good example of embargoed material. The list is sent by teleprinter well before the official announcement. Local stations can then produce stories about people in their area ready to run the moment the embargo is lifted.

> *'In America there would be no arrangements with the Government to hold a story for release. In the States there would be an effort to prevent us knowing, because if we know, we go with the story. There just isn't that kind of cooperation, except in matters of extremely high security.'*
>
> 'You mean there are no gentlemen's agreements?'
>
> *'There are no gentlemen!'* – FREDA MORRIS, LONDON BUREAU CHIEF, NBC NEWS

SYNDICATED TAPES

Among the daily plethora of unsolicited material which arrives in the newsroom may be a number of recorded interviews sent by public relations companies. These are often available free of charge and usually have some advertising tie-up.

This more sophisticated variation of the news release appeals to producers who are slothful or overstretched and who may be grateful to receive something for nothing. But as the saying goes, there is no such thing as a free lunch. The PR company hopes stations will find a slot for the tape and play it on air unedited. Used in this way, syndicated tapes are simply free, unadulterated, publicity.

They may be interviews with airline bosses talking about new or cheaper flights; company directors explaining plans for a superstore in the area, or, even agricultural hints and tips from a government agency.

At best, syndicated tapes are harmless, even useful, fillers. At worst they can be scarcely disguised adverts or propaganda. No unsolicited tapes should be used without checking for violations of the advertising code, and that journalistically and technically the tape is up to standard and is relevant to the audience. Handle with care.

There is also the syndicated programme. Like the syndicated column in a newspaper, this is produced for regular subscribers or distribution on a wider scale. Again, advertising can play a major part, as many of these programmes will be sponsored. They are often available at no cost to the station, provided references to the sponsor's name are not edited out. Syndicated programmes include, in the US, Monitor Radio, from the Christian Science Monitor newspaper, and, in the UK, a sponsored chart show which is broadcast by stations in the independent radio network.

FREELANCES

Most newsrooms supplement their own material by buying news tip-offs and stories from freelances. Non-staff members who contribute regularly are known as stringers or correspondents; working journalists who add considerably to the eyes and ears of a station. Freelances may also be employed to fill for absent staff members. (See also career, page 347.)

Stringers are often local newspaper reporters boosting their incomes by selling copy to other media in the area – with or without the blessing of their editors. Some will make their living this way.

The most organized may band together to form a local news agency. These often specialize in fields such as court, council, or sports reporting – assignments which would often take too much time to make it worth an editor's while to cover. Instead, a stringer will be commissioned to cover the event, and will usually file for a number of stations.

Stringers will either be specially commissioned to report a story, or will offer their copy 'on spec.', in the hope that the station will buy it.

Advantages and disadvantages of using stringers

Advantages

- Stringers are cost-effective because they are often paid only for work that gets used on air;
- They enhance a station's 'ground cover', by using local or specialist knowledge to get stories that might not be available to staff reporters.
- They can be commissioned to cover stories that would be too time-consuming to warrant staff coverage;
- Experienced broadcast freelances can fill for staff members who are sick or on holiday.

Disadvantages

- Stringer copy is seldom exclusive as their living depends on supplying news to as many outlets as possible;
- Copy is seldom in broadcast style, as many stringers are newspaper journalists more familiar with writing for print;
- Stringers have to sell their copy to make a living, so stories may be dressed up to make them more marketable;
- Stringers are less accountable than staffers who can be more readily disciplined for their mistakes.

TIP-OFFS

Another source of news is the *tip-off*, from known contacts or members of the audience, who may phone in with what they consider to be news items. In the US, where union regulations permit, some stations appoint a number of authorised tipsters from the audience who call in when they spot a possible story. WGST in Atlanta, Georgia, has even gone to the length of issuing tipsters with car stickers and giving a cash bonus for the tip of the week.*

Items from tipsters cannot be given the same weight as tip-offs from bona fide stringers or correspondents: the information is not from a trained journalist, the source may be unreliable, the facts confused or even libellous. Also, every station has its time wasters and hangers-on who phone in or call round out of sheer self-importance. Worst of all, the tipster may be malicious, and the information a hoax.

* Phillip O. Kierstead, *All-News Radio*, TAB Books, 1980, p. 198.

HOAXES

MISSING ARISTOCRAT LORD LUCAN SPOTTED IN SOUTH AFRICA
GADAFFI ORDERS DEATH OF EXPELLED DIPLOMATS
PRINCE CHARLES ATTACKS ARCHITECT
ROBERT DE NIRO TO STAR IN YORKSHIRE RIPPER MOVIE
DIRTY DEN (BRITISH SOAP STAR) TO QUIT

These *hoaxes* are the work of one man: mass-hoaxer Rocky Ryan who has been waging a one-man campaign to pull the wool over the eyes of the British media ever since a *Sun* newspaper reporter had him arrested at gunpoint.

'Ryan is a pain in the rear but knowing there are hoaxers like him about ought to make all of us more careful about thorough checking of the facts. In a way he actually might be good for us.'
—NEWSDESK EXECUTIVE QUOTED IN *UK PRESS GAZETTE*

Broadcast news, with its quick-fire deadlines and lack of time for checks and balances, sometimes falls prey to the most elaborate of hoaxes. People ring up claiming to be contacts who are known by the station, such as police inspectors, and offer phoney information.

In 1982, someone who claimed to be a well-known sports commentator telephoned the BBC's national radio newsroom claiming racing driver John Watson had been killed. The information was broadcast. It was a hoax.

BBC TV news has been hoaxed about an air crash, and a tip-off on April fool's day caused the independent station, Essex Radio, to put out news of an armed man holding a hostage. This tip, on the newsroom's ex-directory hot-line, came three minutes before the bulletin. When the police heard the news they panicked and sent their cars racing to the scene only to discover that they and the radio station had been duped.

If in doubt, check it out. The only sure protection against the hoaxer is a set of sharp wits and the common sense to check the information.

If someone rings up claiming to be a regular contact and does not ring true for some reason, get his number and check it against the known contact's number. Even if it matches, ring him back to make sure he had not simply looked up the number in the phone book. If the caller is genuine, he should not object to the care with which his information is being checked.

Occasionally, a tip-off will yield some useful information, but for safety's sake *all* tip-offs, whether they appear genuine or not, must be checked before running – even if it does mean missing the deadline. In the end, accuracy counts for more than speed – ***if it doesn't check out, chuck it out***.

WIRE SERVICES AND NEWS AGENCIES

Major outside sources of news are the wire services and big news agencies. Among the biggest are Reuters, United Press International (UPI) and Associated Press (AP) which cover global news.

Among the domestic agencies are the Press Association (PA) which reports on all aspects of British national news, and the Australian Associated Press (AAP). The oldest agency in Africa is the South African Press Association, and the largest in India is the Press Trust of India.

The biggest television news agency in the world is Visnews, which is controlled by Reuters. Visnews is also the largest daily user of satellites for TV, supplying news to more than 400 stations in close to 90 countries, including the BBC. Rival WTN (Worldwide Television News) is jointly owned by ITN, the American ABC network and Channel 9 of Australia.

Agencies employ correspondents who send their reports back to base. From there they are relayed to subscribers as hard copy on teleprinters or are fed directly into newsroom computers. Audio and video reports are beamed to newsrooms by satellite or piped in by landline, where they are re-recorded for later use.

Agency correspondents can effectively boost even the smallest station's coverage to incorporate national or international news, multiplying by many times the number of reporters at that station's disposal.

Figure 8 News agencies pump out reams of copy on teleprinters each day swelling the reporting strength of the newsroom. Before agency copy can be used on air, stories have to be rewritten to suit station style. This extract is part of a 750 word report by Reuters which might have to be boiled down to 90 words or less and reworked to make it possible to read out loud (courtesy Reuters)

KAMPALA REJOICES AS GUERRILLAS TAKE OVER:

By Michael Rank

KAMPALA, Jan 27, Reuter - The people of Uganda's capital, Kampala, today celebrated the capture of the city by well-disciplined guerrillas who spared them the looting and mayhem that has accompanied past upheavals.

National Resistance Army (NRA) guerrillas, who took over government yesterday, were greeted with applause and gifts of fruit and drinks as they toured the capital in open trucks.

"They treat us really well. They never steal from us or give us any trouble. They are good people," said one Kampala resident, expressing the views of many who believe the NRA offers real hope of ending the bloodshed of the last 20 years.

Thousands of people returned to their homes in Kampala's suburbs early today after more than a week of fighting.

A few corpses littering streets in the city centre were quickly removed and by afternoon Kampala's sprawling markets were busy with vendors selling tropical fruit and vegetables.

NRA chairman Yoweri Museveni, the country's new de facto head of state, pledged at an open-air news conference to form a broad-based government which would include all factions, but exclude officials responsible for atrocities. These would be put on trial, he added.

Usually, once a wire is installed and the subscription charges paid, a station can use any amount of material. This copy is known as *rip and read*, because in theory it can ripped off the printers and read straight on air. Extensive use of rip and read means that many stations in remote areas are able to employ small newsrooms, and in some cases make do without any journalists at all.

There are disadvantages. The news may be national or international but it is seldom local. Rip and read copy is also often long winded and in a literary style which would need rewriting (Figure 8).

As well as news, some agencies offer specialized wires, covering fields of interest such as weather, sport, or business news.

THE NETWORK

A logical step from relying on the resources of agencies or freelances is for broadcast organizations to pool their news stories and programmes.

This produces economies of scale. If five stations take the same programme, then the costs are spread five ways. When stations work together more cash can be found to produce higher quality programmes. Material which would have been beyond the reach of a small station, may now be made available under a pooling scheme. This is the principle behind networking.

Networking can take place in a loose federation, as with independent radio in Britain, where each station is an autonomous company, or in a formalized system where all the stations are owned and regulated by a single body such as the BBC.

In America, the first national network came into operation in 1928, with fifty-six stations under the control of the National Broadcasting Company (NBC). This was to later spawn the ABC network (American Broadcasting Company) with four separate news and music services. Others include CBS (the Columbia Broadcasting System), MBS (Mutual Broadcasting System), and NPR (National Public Radio). When it comes to television, the USA has the biggest concentration of TV companies and TV sets in the world.

In Canada, CBC (the Canadian Broadcasting Corporation) operates twin radio networks and a TV network. A large number of homes also take cable TV. Australia has public and private radio and TV networks, while the publically-owned Broadcasting Corporation of New Zealand controls two TV networks, more than thirty community radio stations and two-non commerical radio networks. In Africa also, the state retains control over TV and radio. All India Radio is regulated by government and broadcasts in more than 90 different dialects. India has also developed a satellite TV network, beaming mainly educational programmes to ground stations for distribution across the country.

Many networks feed their string of local stations with national news from a centralized newsroom, and those stations in turn send back reports of major stories to the network.

IRN (Independent Radio News), in London, is a wholly-owned subsidiary of LBC, the London Broadcasting Company. It provides

RIP'N READ NEWS SUMMARY FOR 1300

VIA GNS

LEYLAND VEHICLES HAVE ANNOUNCED WHAT THEY CALL ' SUBSTANTIAL REDUNDANCIES' AT THEIR PLANTS IN GLASGOW, WATFORD AND AT LEYLAND IN LANCASHIRE+ THE COMPANY SAYS WORKERS AT THE THREE PLANTS ARE BEING TOLD OF THE DECISION OVER THE NEXT TWO DAYS+ UNION LEADERS ARE BEING GIVEN DETAILS OF THE REDUNDANCIES AT A MEETING IN LONDON TODAY+

Figure 9 The BBC's General News Service sends out rip and read summaries of national news which network stations can pull from the printers and read on air. Illustrated is the lead story for the major one o'clock bulletin (courtesy BBC GNS)

independent stations with news bulletins on the hour and a teleprinter and audio service, so they can take the national news live, or assemble and read their own version of the IRN bulletin.

Some stations in remote regions such as Scotland prefer to compile their own national bulletins which can be angled to suit their Scottish audiences, rather than settle for news with a London emphasis.

Network stations pay for the IRN service with a fixed percentage of their revenue. This means prosperous stations pay more and subsidize the smaller ones.

The BBC's network service operates differently. GNS (the General News Service) provides copy and audio, but does not offer a live bulletin which stations can pipe-in on the hour (Figure 9).

In the US, regional networks range from groups of stations who exchange tapes on a regular basis, to scaled down national networks with a centrally produced bulletin piped-in on the hour.

When a station switches over to take the network news, this is called *opting-in* to the network. The process of switching back is called *opting-out*.

Where opt-outs are used, bulletins will end with a readily indentifiable *outcue* such as a timecheck, which is the presenter's cue for switching back to local programming.

Many radio stations follow the national news with a local bulletin, others precede it with local news, and some prefer to combine the two in a single bulletin, which is known as a *news-mix*. Many television stations produce their own regional news but take a networked national news service.

Local TV and radio stations will also be expected to contribute to the pool of news stories available to the network. Material is supplied to and from the network along a *contribution circuit*. Stations with similar interests may install their own contribution circuits and supply one another with material, operating like a network within a network.

OTHER NEWS MEDIA

Journalists take a professional pride in beating their fellows to a story. Most news editors monitor the rival media to make sure they are ahead with the news, and to see if there is anything they have missed.

One of the news editor's first tasks each day is usually to go through the national and local papers to see if there are any stories referring to the area which need to be followed-up.

Following-up a news item means checking and developing it to find a new angle. This is different from taking a story from a newspaper and rewriting it for broadcast. That would be plagiarism – stealing somebody's work. Facts may also be wrong and errors repeated.

There is no copyright on ideas, however, and journalists often feed on one another for their leads and inspiration, as in this actual example:

'Get the father . . .'

Two rival TV news programmes go on air close to one another in the evening: *Coast to Coast*, the independent programme, between 6 and 6.30; *South Today*, the BBC service, from 6.35 to 7.

Coast to Coast picked up a breaking news story. A local businessman had been held in Libya because his boss's company there had run into debt and he was being held responsible. The news broke that he was finally to be allowed to return to Britain, and was flying home that night. *Coast to Coast* had just got the information and carried it as a copy story.

South Today was monitoring the programme and immediately got a reporter to phone Gatwick airport to try to interview the father, who was waiting for his son's flight.

Meanwhile, *Coast to Coast* has just finished and the opening sequences of *South Today* are going out on air. The presenters are told to stand by for late breaking news.

Minutes later copy comes in saying the businessman is due to arrive within the hour, and a presenter breaks from the script to read the story unrehearsed.

At the airport, public relations staff are busily trying to find the father.

Twenty minutes into the programme and all that remains is the weather and the headlines. The father has not been found and time is running out. The producer takes over the story. He gets through to the father even as the closing headlines are being read.

The director quickly tells one of the presenters through his earpiece that the father is on the phone waiting to be interviewed. The presenter has 45 seconds to ad-lib the interview before the programme ends and transmission returns to the network. It is not possible to overrun by even a second.

The businessman's father says he is delighted his son is returning home. The Foreign Office confirmed the news yesterday. Alcohol is forbidden in Libya, so they will celebrate with some bottles of his son's favourite beer.

The director counts down the closing seconds while the presenter thanks the father for talking to him and wishes the viewers a calm good evening. The programme ends bang on time and as coolly as if it had all been planned from the start. Independent television had led the way, but the BBC got the better story.

SHARED MATERIAL A number of BBC TV and radio newsrooms share the same building, so there is a crossover of ideas. Joint newsrooms, such as BBC Radio Bristol and BBC Television South and West take this one step further. Story ideas are swapped and stringer and agency copy pooled.

On occasions, radio will use the soundtrack of TV interviews in a bulletin, and TV stations may make use of radio reporters to supply phone reports on breaking stories.

In Britain, independent radio frequently uses material recorded off-air from independent television, although the two have no corporate tie-up. The arrangement usually requires the radio station to credit the TV company for using its audio.

In Coventry, a cable television company uses reporters from Mercia Sound, the local independent station, to produce and present its news output.

At an international level, news services frequently buy and exchange reports with one another to enhance their worldwide coverage. A number of broadcasting unions have been set up to act as clearing houses. These include the Inter-American Association of Broadcasters (AIR), the European Broadcasting Union (EBU), the Union of National Radio and Television Organisations of Africa (URTNA), and the Caribbean Broadcasting Union (CBU). (See also Inside ITN, page 247.)

FIELDWORK

1 It is a quiet day on the radio station. No news is breaking; there is nothing to follow up. You are sent out by your news editor to find a story. If you are able to, go out into your neighbourhood and see what you can come up with. (Go in pairs if you are in a class.) If you can't get out, discuss what stories you might cover.

2 You are setting up TV news coverage in a brand new area. Think of ten important contacts you would make in the community. Then find out the name, job title and phone number of the major contacts you would expect to call each day in your area to make the check calls to the emergency services.

3 If it is legal, listen in to the emergency services band on the radio and see if you can work out what they are covering. If they use a variation of the 10 Code, jot down the codes used and find out what they mean.

4 From your own TV viewing and radio listening, which do you think are the most active pressure groups in your area and how do they get their message across to the media? Do they come across favourably or badly? Why?

5 A caller on the line to your newsroom says large quantities of lethal waste have leaked from a nearby industrial plant. The toxic chemical is spilling into a reservoir which directly feeds the local water supply. He says he is the manager at the plant and is urging you to put out a message immediately warning people to stop drinking the water as it could poison them. What do you do?

3 Getting the story

News editors are to broadcast journalism what generals are to warfare. They set the objectives, weigh the resources and draw up the plan of campaign. Under their command are the officers and troops on the ground.

Some news editors prefer to be in the thick of battle, directing the action from the front line, while others favour a loftier perspective, set back from the heat of the action. These will oversee strategy, but delegate a number two to be responsible for tactics. In larger newsrooms, this may be the deputy news editor, senior producer, or bulletin producer. Working to the news editor's plan of campaign he/she will keep in touch with the news as it develops and arrange coverage.

NEWSROOM CONFERENCE (Figure 10)

In larger newsrooms the plan of campaign is drawn up at the morning conference. Producers and senior staff put their heads together with the news editor to map out the day's coverage.

Figure 10 Morning news conference for the programme *Northern Life.* Journalists gather in the newsroom to discuss the day's coverage. The news editor decides which stories to pursue and allocates reporters to cover them (courtesy Tyne Tees Television)

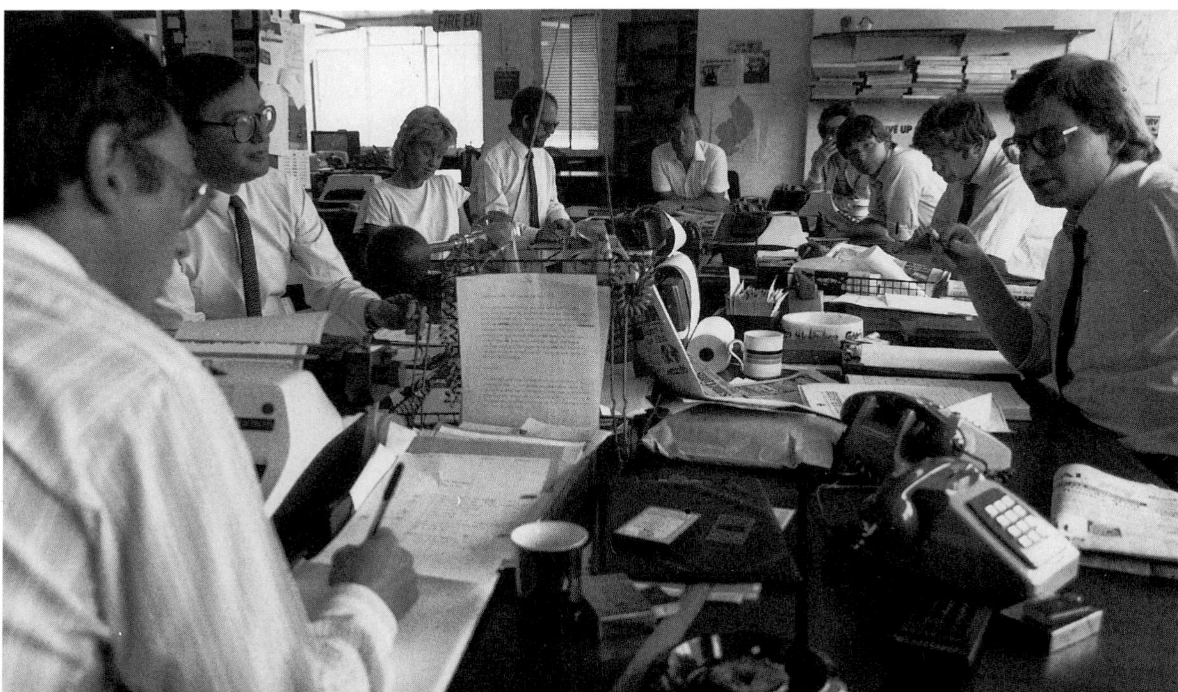

Many stories will already be in the diary or on the files; some of yesterday's items will still be current and will need to be followed-up to find new angles. The news wires may produce items which can be used or pursued. Producers and reporters will be expected to come forward with their own ideas, and other leads may come in the post or from rival media.

Stories are then ranked in order of importance and in line with station policy and resources are allocated accordingly. (See also item selection, page 108.)

If more stories present themselves than staff reporters can cover, the news editor will bring in freelance support or put some stories 'on ice,' to be followed only if others fall down.

On a thin day, the news editor may have to rely on back-up material to fill the programme. Most stations have a small collection of timeless features which have been kept for such emergencies, called *fillers* or *padding*. Where there is little hard news to cover, reporters and crews may be sent out to get more filler material to top up the reserves.

If the station is running news on the hour, the news editor will attempt to spread coverage throughout the day to provide an even balance, with the emphasis on peak-time listening. For longer news programmes, producers arrange coverage to ensure reports are back in time to make those deadlines.

COPYTASTING

Each newsroom will have someone in charge of the newsdesk at all times, keeping a close eye on agency tapes and breaking stories. As news comes in, a senior journalist will copytaste each item to see if it is worth running or pursuing or offers new information on an existing story.

When a good story breaks unexpectedly, the news editor, like the general, must be prepared to switch forces rapidly from one front to another to meet the new challenge.

Reporters may be asked to drop what they are doing and cover the new story instead; old running orders will be scrapped and new ones devised. This demand for sharp reflexes, total flexibility and all-stops-out performance puts the buzz into news reporting.

BALANCE OF NEWS

Chasing breaking news is only half the story. The news editor or producer also has the overall balance of the programme to consider.

In a 30-minute TV programme time will be set aside for regular slots or segments, such as sport, headlines and the weather, and material will have to be found to fill them.

In any audience will be some who would prefer to unwind to light items at the end of a working day, rather than endure heavyweight stories; others will prefer national news to local, and commerical stations may be expected to inject enough entertainment into the show to shore-up audience ratings. All these conflicting demands will be brought to bear in shaping the news priorities and arranging coverage at the start of the day. (See also the news programme, page 102.)

VISUALS AND ACTUALITY

Getting the story in radio and TV means more than simply gathering the facts. How those facts are illustrated is also important. Like newspapers with their photographs, radio has its sounds, recorded at the scene. These are called *actuality*.

Radio brings a report to life by painting a picture in the imagination of the listener, while TV takes its audience to the scene through the use of film and video footage. And TV can add to its armoury sound effects, graphics and still photographs. The cost of all this artistry is to make TV sometimes slower and less flexible than radio, but attractive visuals and interesting actuality breathe life into the coverage of news. Good illustrations can boost the position of a report in the programme, and poor actuality or footage may make a producer think twice about running it at all.

THE BRIEF

The ideal brief would be a typewritten note giving details of the story, saying who the interviewee was, the time and place of the interview, with the relevant press clippings, background and a selection of suitable questions. But reality usually falls short of the ideal. News editors are busy people who say the reason they have two ears is so they can perch a telephone under each. Most reporters will be all too familiar with the phrase that greets them when they arrive for work: '*Don't take your coat off . . .*'.

Sometimes 'brief' is the operative word . . . It may go something like this: '*The strike at the car plant – the MD's in his office, he'll see you in ten minutes. Give me holding for 11, a clip for noon and I'll take 2 and a half for the 1 o'clock.*'

No typewritten note; no background list of questions. Not even a '*please.*'

The reporter is already expected to know that the strike has been called, which car plant it concerns, where it is, how to get there, who the managing director is, all the necessary background to produce three separate items, and to have the know-how to come up with a line of questioning which perfectly matches the unspoken ideas in the news editor's head. So what is unreasonable about that?

However frantic the news editor may be, the reporter will have to prise out the answers to three questions before setting out on the assignment:

- What do you want?
- When do you want it for?
- How long do you want it to run?

With the car workers' strike, the plant's managing director will be asked: '*What's your reaction to the stoppage? How damaging could it be for the company? Will jobs or orders be lost? How long can the company survive the action?*'. The union point of view will also be required.

Knowing the time of transmission and the length of the item is vital. There would be no point in returning to the newsroom at 3 o'clock with enough material to make a half-hour documentary when what was wanted was a 35-second interview for the lunchtime news. No one will see this masterpiece if it arrives too late or runs too long to go in the programme.

News reporters usually work to the next bulletin deadline. On some stations deadlines crop up every fifteen minutes, so when reporters go out on a story, that story must not vanish with them. Hence the instruction to write *holding copy*. This is a short news item that can be run in the next bulletin or headlines to tide the newsroom over until reporters return with the interview.

If they are likely to be out for some time, say, at a conference, they may be expected to phone in regular reports from the venue to keep the bulletins topped up with the latest news. Recorded interviews can also be fed back down the phone as a last resort. (See telephone reports, page 238.)

The next directive is to provide a clip for noon: that would be the best 35 seconds or so from the interview to illustrate the story.

Lastly, the reporter here has been asked to produce an interview of 2 minutes 30 seconds for the 1 o'clock news programme. The questions above on page 31 would satisfy that, with any leads picked up from the managing director which give a new slant on the story.

Many news editors would argue that an elaborate brief should not be necessary, as reporters are expected to have a good working knowledge of their area and keep abreast of breaking news. But things are not always so hectic. When reporters arrive on duty, they may be given time to catch up by reading through the output of the previous shift. *Reading-in* helps reporters familiarize themselves with what has already gone on air.

Where more background is required, reporters on small stations would be expected to research it themselves, while those on larger stations may be able to call upon a researcher or the station's news information service or library.

> ***'What you need is a wide background knowledge, rather than narrow specialization, and you need to keep it up to date.'***
> *— BBC EXTERNAL SERVICES NEWSROOM GUIDE*

THE ANGLE

Think of a news story as a diamond. A diamond has many facets, and whichever way you hold it, it is impossible to look at them all at once. Some will always be hidden from view. Likewise, it may be impossible to cover every aspect of a news story at once – there is seldom the time or space. The reporter will be forced to concentrate on a few of the story's facets. Each facet represents a different angle. The angle is the part of the story which the reporter chooses to hold up to the light at any one time. Most stories will have a number of different angles and news editors and producers usually spell out which particular one they want reporters to focus on.

Take a story about a big new contract at a steelworks: the fact of the contract is the story, but that may not be reason enough for running it. Information only becomes news when it affects a given audience. If the contract is big enough, it might make national news, but the editor in a local newsroom would run the story only if the steelworks is in his/her area. The story would then have a *local angle*. With national news, the main angle is often the importance or significance of the story to the nation. At a local level, the importance to the community comes first.

Once the news editor is satisfied the story is relevant to the audience, he/she may want to cover it a number of different ways. The angle will change according to viewpoint, and with the steelworks, the obvious viewpoints to go for would be those of the management and workforce.

An interview will be arranged with the company about the size of the contract, the effect on the company's prospects and the likelihood of more jobs.

If the reporter discovers 500 new jobs will be offered over the coming three years, the follow-up angle would shift to the union viewpoint. The major union would be asked to comment.

So far, both interviews have been with spokespeople; one to establish the facts of the story and the other to react to them, and there is a constant danger in journalism of always talking to experts, or *talking heads*, and overlooking ordinary people with grassroots opinions.

Another viewpoint, closer to the audience, would be that of the workers at the steelworks. The reporter would ask some for their reactions to the news and might follow that by talking to several unemployed people who now have their first chance for some time of finding a job.

Workers and unemployed alike are the people whose lives will be affected by the contract, and they and their dependents will probably make a significant part of the station's audience. In the end, it is their reactions that matter the most.

Using extracts from all the interviews, a comprehensive and well-rounded report could be built up, with background material filled in by the reporter. This is known as a *package*.

TV reporters will want to illustrate their item with good footage of the steelworks in action. Dramatic images of red hot molten steel and flying sparks would feature with shots of blue-collar workers with their protective facemasks, contrasting perhaps with images of a be-suited director in a plush office.

Radio will certainly go for the noise of the steelworks, the clashing of metal and the voices of people at work.

CHASING THE CONTACT
(Figure 11)

Once the reporter has been briefed and found out exactly *what* is wanted and *when*, the process of getting the story begins with the contacts file.

Much precious time on a sixty-minute deadline can be saved by going for the right person from the start. Go straight to the top. Don't waste time with minor officials who will only refer you upwards. If you are dealing with a company, go for the managing director. Only settle for the

Figure 11 Getting the story with what the BBC describes as the radio reporter's notebook – the portable reel-to-reel tape recorder (Andrew Boyd)

press office if the MD or his/her secretary insists. A press officer is at best one step away from the person you want to interview and may have reasons for putting you off.

Some organizations will insist you use their press officers – that is what they pay them for – and it is possible to build up a good working relationship with the best of them, but remember that behind every plausible statement and off-the-record remark there lurks a vested interest.

> *'I don't want any of my journalists talking to press officers. Press officers are paid to conceal the truth, not to tell it.'* – STEWART STEPHEN, EDITOR

Setting up the interview can be the dullest, most time-consuming chore in journalism. Sometimes the ringing round can seem interminable and more time can be spent waiting for people to phone you back than in reporting.

To save time, the best tip is never to rely on anyone to call you back. If a secretary tells you your contact is speaking on another line and will return your call, politely insist on holding on while he/she finishes the conversation. If you hang up, your name will be added to the list of callbacks, and that list could be a long one. Also, if the story might mean adverse publicity, you could find yourself waiting by the phone for ever.

If your contact is out, leave a message stressing the urgency of your business, and ask if there is someone else who could handle your inquiry.

If they try to put you off, be polite but persistent, and if that fails, go above their heads to someone more senior. If no one can talk to you, find out where your contact is and try to call him/her there. Don't be fobbed off. Remember, every minute wasted brings you closer to your deadline. The approach should be assertive rather than aggressive and tenacious but always polite.

If, after that, your interviewee is still playing hard to get, then put that angle 'on hold' and approach the story from another direction.

With the steelworks item, if management is being elusive, go instead for the union line. With a more controversial story, such as plans to build a prison in the area, if those behind the scheme will not talk, go directly to the opposition or to the grassroots and interview residents who may be frightened about the prospect of prisoners escaping near their homes.

All too often, despite your best endeavours, you will find yourself staring at the telephone, willing for it to ring, while messages and repeated messages lie neglected in a heap on your contact's desk.

At this stage, you are wasting time and should go back to your news editor. Say what steps you have taken, and seek further direction. Should you continue to wait by the phone, firing off still more messages, or should you cut your losses and try a different angle or abandon this and get on with another item?

STAGED NEWS CONFERENCES

News conferences can be a time-consuming way of getting a story. Having sat through a forty-minute presentation, when questions are invited from the floor, the tendency is for reporters to talk over each other and fire their questions at once, often in pursuit of different angles. This kind of anarchy, induced by approaching deadlines, can make for a garbled recording.

Set presentations can be difficult to record if the speakers are some distance from the microphone, and much of the material may be irrelevant to the report and can swallow up yards of tape which makes for troublesome editing. The reporter should always take extra tape and note when the interesting points were made.

Press conferences generally live up to their name. The format was devised for print journalism and is largely unsuited to the electronic era. The opportunity to record interviews usually comes *after* the conference. Some newsrooms refuse to give coverage unless the main speakers make themselves available for private interviews well in advance and provide copies of speeches so questions can be prepared.

The alternatives are to hang around for interviews until the conference is finished, or record them on location before the conference gets under way, but there may well be a queue of other reporters with the same idea.

Radio has an advantage. When TV moves in to do an interview, the crews usually take a little time to set up their lights and cameras, so radio reporters are advised to be assertive and to get in first, pleading that the interview will take only a few minutes. Cooling your heels while TV completes the cumbrous operation of lights, colour check, pre-chat, interview and cutaways, will only push you closer to your deadline.

BEATING THE CLOCK

The fastest way to get a report on air is via the telephone, and live pieces may sometimes be taken into news programmes or bulletins. But telephone items (*phonos*) are mushy in quality and lack that essential visual element for TV.

Stations which have few reporters will often rely on interviewees to come to them. This practice frees the journalist to remain in the newsroom and chase more stories, but is better suited to radio than TV where the choice of location is often determined by the need for interesting visuals.

If time is short, and the reporter is having to travel to the interview, precious minutes can be clawed back by planning the route. Rush hour delays should be taken into consideration. Detailed street maps are essential, and travelling by cab can put a taxi driver's expert knowledge at your disposal.

If the station has a radio car or outside broadcast vehicle, live reports can be sent back which save time and add considerably to the sense of occasion and urgency.

Work to sequence

Another way to claw back precious minutes is to arrange to do your interviews in the order in which they will appear on air. This keeps the tapes or film in a logical sequence and helps with the preparation of questions.

Make sure all the key phrases and quotes you intend to keep are noted either during the interview or after it, and log the points where those quotes occur. This can be done from a stop-watch, or by using the counter on the tape recorder. Jotting down single trigger words such as 'angry' or 'delighted' can help you plan your editing.

Many radio reporters listen to their interviews in the car on the way back to the station and the editing process is well advanced in their minds even before they return.

Don't panic

In the editing room, many inexperienced journalists, sweating against the clock, let circumstances panic them. There is always the hope that you *will* be able to turn round that three minute package in the last moments before the programme, and an experienced hand will have little trouble in doing just that. But the old adage about more haste, less speed, is especially true in broadcasting.

Be realistic. If you doubt your ability to get the piece on air by the deadline, then warn the producer or news editor that it may not be coming. Give them time to prepare a standby. Whatever you do, do not leave them without that safety net. If they are banking on your item and it fails to turn up, at best you will try the patience of your colleagues, and at worst you will leave a hole in the programme which could prove impossible to fill, throw

the presentation team into confusion and lead to a disaster on air.

Similarly, by rushing your piece you could easily make a mistake and the first time you realize your blunder may be when you see or hear it going on air. When a deadline is rapidly approaching, the temptation to run the piece without checking it through can be almost irresistible.

If mistakes do appear, the station's credibility takes a nosedive, and the authority of that bulletin is knocked. The audience and your colleagues will judge you, not by the amount of well-intentioned effort that went into your work, but by the results as they appear on air. In the end, that is all that really matters.

> *'The most important thing about news is the listener – most radio journalists think getting the last-minute story into the bulletin is more important than presentation, and getting the facts absolutely right – they are mistaken.'* – SIMON ELLIS, NEWS EDITOR, BBC ESSEX

FIELDWORK

1 Find out the names of the news editors at your nearest radio and TV stations and ask if you can visit their newsrooms for a day (longer if possible) to observe what goes on. Talk to the journalists about their jobs without getting in their way and ask if you can go with any of the reporters on a story. Watch how the news develops from an idea to a full-blown report.

2 Listen to the main local news programme on the radio and see if you can work out which, if any, of the stories are being used as padding or fillers. Listen especially to any actuality in the bulletin and discuss whether it added anything to the story, or if the story would have been clearer without it. Was there too much or too little actuality in the bulletin?

3 Read through a local newspaper and make a list of stories that could be followed-up. Think about the angles you could take to develop the story further. Then plan your coverage for each of them. Work out contacts and questions and draw up briefs for your reporters.

4 For TV, work out what footage you would want to take to illustrate those different stories. Go for a good a mix of coverage with plenty of variety. Be creative.

5 If you have access to radio or TV recording equipment, find a contact involved in one of the stories who is willing to be interviewed. Compare your finished report with those in the next radio and TV bulletins and discuss how your own work could be improved.

4 Conversational writing

'Writing, when properly managed . . . is but another name for conversation.' — LAURENCE STERNE

'For years, editors told reporters: "Don't tell me about it, write it." Turn that around, and you have a good rule for the broadcast journalist: "Don't just write it, TELL ME ABOUT IT."'
— BROADCAST NEWS OF CANADA, *STYLE BOOK*

Anyone with ambition towards writing will probably appreciate a lively piece of prose. We all have our journalistic giants and literary heroes. But what may be clear and sparkling to the eye, may be confused and baffling to the ear. It may also prove impossible to read out loud. The following is from Hemingway's *For Whom the Bell Tolls.* A Spanish gypsy, Rafael, is describing a machine gun attack on a Facist train. Read it out loud and see how you get on:

> *'The train was coming steadily. We saw it far away. And I had an excitement so great that I cannot tell it. We saw steam from it and then later came the noise of the whistle. Then it came chu-chu-chu-chu-chu-chu steadily larger and larger and then, at the moment of the explosion, the front wheels of the engine rose up and all of the earth seemed to rise in a great cloud of blackness and a roar and the engine rose high in the cloud of dirt and of the wooden ties rising in the air as in a dream and then it fell on to its side like a great wounded animal and there was an explosion of white steam before the clods of the other explosion had ceased to fall on us and the* maquina *commenced to speak ta-tat-tat-ta!' went the gypsy, shaking his two clenched fists up and down in front of him, thumbs up, on an imaginary machine gun.'**

Breathless? Punctuation is minimal to drive the speech forward and convey a sense of excitement, but although it makes compelling reading on paper, it is almost impossible to read aloud without suffering from oxygen starvation. Even conventional prose can cause problems, because the writing obeys the rules of the written, rather than the spoken word.

Writing for broadcast can mean tossing away literary conventions, including the rules of grammar, if the words are to make sense to the ear,

* Penguin, 1969, page 31.

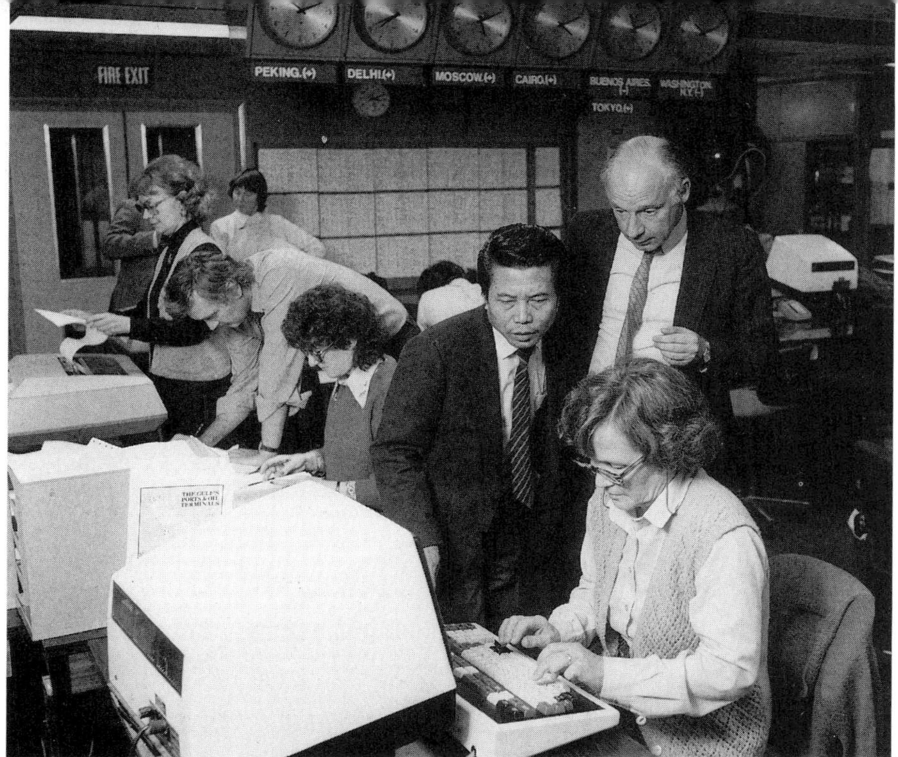

Figure 12 Newswriting for the computer age – writers for the BBC's External Services dictate their copy directly to a computer operator. On-screen it can be rapidly edited and updated and different versions produced (courtesy BBC External Services)

rather than the eye. In print, shades of meaning are conveyed with choice adjectives and skilful prose, but the spoken word makes use of a medium which is altogether more subtle and powerful – the human voice.

An accomplished reader can breathe life into the flat black marks on a page, investing them with shades of light and dark, irony, pleasure or distaste with nothing more than a minor variation in the pitch or tone of his voice.

TELLING THE STORY

> *'If you find it difficult to put your thoughts down on paper clearly and simply, use the trick of telling someone out loud what you want to say. Your brain will throw out most of the padding automatically. People talk more clearly than they write; so make your writing more like your talking and your viewers will understand you better.'* – HARRIS WATTS*

For print journalists making the crossover into broadcasting and graduates embarking on a career in radio or TV, the hardest adjustment can be to break out of the literary mould imposed on us since our schooldays. All the emphasis then was on the written word, but everything in broadcasting is written to be spoken.

* *On Camera*, BBC, 1984.

The technique of the broadcast newswriter has been described as '*talking into the typewriter*'*, and for many years some BBC reporters have dictated copy directly to secretaries without first drafting it on paper, to make sure the story is in a conversational style. A piece of broadcast copy should sound natural to the ear and be easy to read out loud, without causing the reader to stumble over words and gasp for breath.

Newswriting, which may look fine in print, can often *sound* stilted and peculiar:

> *'Judge Theodore T. Townshend (43), of 17 Withy Grove, Edmonton, Alberta, has been found guilty of being in charge of a motor vehicle whilst under the influence of alcohol.'*

Picture yourself leaning on a bar telling the same story to a friend. Chances are you would say something like, '*Hey, have you heard – an Alberta Judge has been found guilty of drunken driving*!'

Without realizing it, you would have translated the written word into the spoken word, and the broadcaster would do the same, leaving out, of course, the '*Hey, have you heard*...?' The broadcasting equivalent of that is the urgent jingle (sounder, US) into the news bulletin.

The conversational approach would continue for the rest of the item: *Judge Theodore Townshend, who's 43 and lives at Withy Grove, Edmonton*... etc.' The middle initial and road number only clutter up the story and so have been dropped. Any facts that are not vital should be scrapped.

Similarly, broadcast news has no need of a mass of adjectives. For television, the saying '*a picture is worth a thousand words*' holds true and the images presented by the camera will tell the story more effectively than any description. Where there are no accompanying illustrations, the nuances of inflection in the newsreader's voice will paint a picture as colourful as the most purple of prose.

WRITING FOR A MASS AUDIENCE

> *'At all times remember you are communicating with ONE person. ONE-TO-ONE means YOU and just ONE listener.'*
>
> – COUNTY SOUND RADIO STYLEBOOK

For the professional broadcaster there must be no such thing as '*the masses out there*'. Images of a sea of upturned faces somewhere beyond the studio lead only to megaphone newsreading and a style of writing which turns every story into a proclamation.

The secret of communicating with an audience, however large, is to write and speak as though you were talking to only one person, and it helps if that person is someone you know and like, rather than your worst enemy or boss.

Visualizing a single well-disposed listener warms up the approach,

*Carolyn Diana Lewis, in *Reporting for Television*, Columbia University Press, 1984.

makes it more personal, and avoids the trap of sounding patronizing. Aim to talk *to* the audience and not *at* them.

The most important technique in communication is to meet people where they are – at their level. Nothing enrages an audience more than being talked down to, and few things bore them faster than hearing talk which is above their heads. Broadcasting means just that: reaching out to a broad cross-section of the community, and the skill lies in pitching it so what you say satisfies roadsweepers and university dons alike – no mean task.

When reporters learn to *tell* the story rather than write it they are half-way there. The next stage is to realize that the broadcast audience has different needs to the newspaper reader, and that those needs differ again between radio and television.

NO SECOND CHANCE

Newspaper readers have one big advantage: they can read and re-read the same item until they can make sense of it. But broadcasters have only one chance to score with their audience. The information is fleeting. As soon as it has passed, it has vanished into the ether and is lost until the broadcast is repeated the following hour – if it is repeated at all.

The onus on making sense of the news lies always with the newswriter and newsreader, never with the audience. This means the broadcast story has to be crystal clear the first time of hearing. Clutter has to go and convoluted writing has to be ironed out; clauses and sub-clauses dismantled and reconstructed as new sentences if necessary.

The writer has to wield a ruthless logic in the way he/she explains the story, moving the information unswervingly forward from point to point. Mark Twain described the way a good writer constructed a sentence:

> *'He will make sure there are no folds in it, no vaguenesses, no parenthetical interruptions of its view as a whole; when he has done with it, it won't be a sea-serpent, with half of its arches under the water; it will be a torch-light procession.'*

What do you think Mark Twain would have made of the following?

> *'The docks' dispute, which is now in its 17th day, as 300 members of the Transport Union, Britain's largest union, take strike action, because of an overtime ban which has been in operation since February 9, as well as unsocial hours, shows no sign of letting up, despite warnings by the TGWU that lorry drivers could be asked to black the port.'*

Chances are you would have to read that through twice to be clear about it, which means the story would have failed on radio or TV. Yet all it needs is a little unravelling:

> *'There's still no sign of a let-up in the docks' dispute, now in its 17th day. This is despite warnings by the Transport Union, Britain's biggest, that lorry drivers might be called on to black the port. 300 members of the TGWU have walked out in protest at unsocial hours and a ban on overtime. The ban was imposed on February the 9th.'*

In this rewritten version, the one sentence of the original has become four. The tangle of subsidiary clauses has been unravelled and chopped into three short sentences. The story progresses logically and the only kink which remains is the tiny subsidiary clause, '*Britain's biggest,*' which is too small to restrict the flow of the sentence.

Notice too, that '*February 9*' which is standard newspaper style, has been changed to the slightly longer, but more conversational, '*February the 9th*'.

Sentences for broadcast need to be clear and declarative, containing a minimum of different ideas. Simplicity and conciseness are the watchwords, yet that does not mean that writing for the voice should be devoid of style, energy or colour. Poetry, which is intended for reading aloud, is often vivid and bursting with life.

Canada's Broadcast News organization recommends a sentence length of 20 to 25 words with one thought per sentence, but recognizes the danger that, '*strings of short sentences can be just as deadly as overlong sentences, because they produce a staccato effect.*'

Newspaper readers have the food in their own hands, they can feed themselves and decide how long they want to spend chewing over an item. But radio and TV audiences have to be fed the news. Many stations assume an average attention span of about three minutes; some rate it even shorter – around 90 seconds – but for even three minutes of spoken information to be digested it has to be chopped up into small chunks which are easy to swallow.

> ***'A high school teacher of mine once said short declarative sentences are the best kind of writing. Writing should be as concise and clear as possible.'*** – PAUL CLEVELAND, ABC ASSIGNMENT MANAGER, ABC NEWS (US) LONDON

CONFUSING CLAUSES

An item which makes sense on paper where the punctuation is visible can have an altogether different meaning when read aloud:

> *'South Africa said the Zambian leader has been found negligent in the area of human rights.'*

Just *who* has been found negligent and by *whom* comes down to a little matter of punctuation, or lack of it, which can completely alter the sense of the story:

> *'South Africa,'* said the Zambian leader, *'has been found negligent in the area of human rights.'*

For broadcast, the copy style has to be unambiguous. Assuming the second version of this hypothetical story is the correct one, it should be re-written as follows:

> *'The Zambian leader says South Africa has been found negligent in the area of human rights.'*

INVERTED SENTENCES

Because listeners have to hold in their memory what has been said, inverted sentences such as the one you are reading are to be avoided.

An inversion often demands that listeners retain information that is without meaning until it is put into context. By the time that context comes listeners may have forgotten what they were supposed to remember or be terminally confused. This is how *not* to do it:

> *'Because of the fall in the mortgage rate, which has stimulated home buying, house prices are going up again.'*
>
> **Rather:** *'House prices are going up again. The fall in the mortgage rate has led to an increase in home buying.'*

State the point to begin with and then explain it, not the other way round, and avoid beginning a sentence with 'Because' or 'According to'. Listeners can never refer back.

PLAIN ENGLISH

Plain English should not be confused with dull language; the English tongue is too rich and varied for it ever to need to be boring. Plain English does away with woolliness, wordiness, officialese and circumlocution and replaces it with words and descriptions that are concrete and direct.

Plain English is about rat-catchers and road sweepers, never rodent operators or highway sanitation operatives. It is about straightforward writing using commonly understood words, rather than those of a Greek or Latin origin. As journalist Harold Evans put it, it is about calling a spade a spade and not a factor of production.

General Montgomery said if you intend to fight a battle you should first *know your enemy*. The enemy of good writing is the official, the bureaucrat and the so-called expert who uses words as a barrier to understanding instead of as a means of communication. Their aim is to mystify rather than enlighten. A good deal of the journalist's time is spent translating their gobbledygook into plain English so ordinary people can make sense of it.

The danger is that some reporters, out of deadline pressure or laziness, may put something down on paper which they do not really understand in the hope that those who hear it will. They will not.

Never run anything on air that does not make complete sense to you. You will lose your audience and be playing into the hands of the exponents of gobbledygook, who will chalk up another victory.

> ***'. . . politicians, spokesmen, communiqué drafters, academics and all too many others, have their reasons for using their own jargons. We have no reason to follow theirs or to create ours. Our job is to de-jargonize, to declichefy, to make everything clear, simple and concise.'***
>
> *— BBC BUSH HOUSE NEWSROOM GUIDE*

FAMILIAR WORDS

Speaking the layperson's language also means using familiar words. Prefer:

• Cut out	to	Excise
• Destroy	to	Obliterate
• Against	to	Antagonistic to
• Talkative	to	Loquacious
• Truthful	to	Veracious
• Cancel	to	Abrogate
• Poverty	to	Penury
• Highest point	to	Zenith

If you use a word your listeners may not immediately understand, while they are puzzling over its meaning, the information that follows will vanish into the ether. By the time they reach for a dictionary or, more likely, shrug and give up, they will have missed the rest of the news.

EASY LISTENING

American broadcaster Irving E. Fang has researched into what makes broadcast copy easy or difficult to understand. He devised the Easy Listening Formula, which is based on the length of words in a sentence. The idea is to add up all the syllables in a sentence, then subtract from that the number of words. If the final score is higher than 20, the sentence contains too many long and abstract words that would make it hard to understand, and it should be subbed down.* For example:

'Kenya's Health Minister, Mr Peter Nyakiamo, has announced that there is absolutely no scientific evidence for the recent "hysterical and alarmist" media reports that Mombasa and Melindi in Kenya are a source of the killer disease Aids.' (Score 32)

Rewrite: *'Kenya's Health Minister is denying reports that Mombasa and Melindi are a source of the killer disease Aids.'* (Score 12) *'Mr Peter Nyakiamo says there is no scientific proof for what he calls the "hysterical and alarmist" media reports.'* (Score 15)

ACCURATE ENGLISH

Taking shades of grey and turning them into black and white for the sake of simplifying an issue is often the mark of an inexperienced journalist. Some precision might have to be sacrificed for the sake of simplicity, but the final story should still give the facts accurately.

How would you translate the following ghastly, but typical, example of officialese?

'The Chairman observed that the Government loan of one million dollars may serve to obviate the immediate necessity for the termination of the contracts in question among non-full time ancillary staff, but that this contingency could not be discounted at a later period in the financial year in the event that funds became exhausted.'

* *Television News*, Hasting House, 1972, p. 176.

The following version, distilled from the facts above, may look plausible, but would be completely misleading:

> *'The Chairman said the jobs of support staff had been spared for the time being thanks to a million dollar handout by the Government, but when the cash runs out later in the year, their jobs will have to go.'*

The above 'translation' makes the following fatal errors:

- First, the staff are part-time and on contract, which makes the stakes arguably less high than if they had been full-time employees, as the rewritten version implies by omission.
- Second, there is nothing definite about these contracts being spared; '*may* serve to obviate', were the Chairman's words.
- Third, the 'Government handout' is not a handout at all, but a loan, and loans, unlike handouts, need repaying.
- Fourth, it is not certain the cash will run out later in the year, and,
- Fifth, even if it does, it is by no means definite that those contracts will be cut.

Below is a more accurate translation:

> *'The Chairman said the jobs of part-time ancillary staff, whose contracts have been under threat, may be safe for the time being, thanks to a million dollar loan from the Government. But he added that job cuts could not be ruled out later if the money ran out.'*

If you really want to bewilder your listeners, try sprinkling in the odd word that means something other than most people imagine:

> 'When asked about the road building, Councillor Joe McFlagherty said he viewed the scheme with complete disinterest.'

To translate that as, '*Councillor Joe McFlagherty said he could not care less about the scheme*' would be to get the wrong end of the stick. Disinterested should not be confused with uninterested which suggests a lack of concern. 'Disinterested' means he had no personal or vested interest in the project.

'*His alibi was that he had no reason to kill his own mother*' does not make sense. *Alibi* means a plea that someone was somewhere else at the time. Alibi is not synonymous with *excuse*.

KEEP IT CONCRETE

The fleeting nature of broadcasting means that information tends to be impressionistic, and radio in particular finds it difficult to convey technical details or abstract ideas. Precise instructions, complex abstractions or statistics – anything, in fact, which is hard to picture in the mind, does not come across well. Television has the powerful advantage of being able to use graphics, captions and illustrations to bring home a point, but even then, it is easy to overload the medium with too much information. As somebody once said: '*Half of what you say is forgotten; the rest gets twisted.*'

The way to use the medium successfully is to keep statements simple, direct, concrete and to the point, and to express them in a way that everyone will readily understand.

Colloquialisms are acceptable for bringing home the meaning of a story, but in-words and slang that have grown stale through overuse will irritate listeners and should be avoided.

Metaphors and examples also help in putting over an idea. Radio paints a picture in someone's mind, but you cannot paint a picture of an idea, a concept or an abstraction. You have to relate that to things people are already familiar with, and that means using illustrations. For example:

Not: *'The Chancellor is increasing taxation on spirits by imposing a 5 per cent increase in prices from midnight tonight.'*
But: *'A bottle of whisky will cost around 40 pence more from midnight tonight. The Chancellor's putting 5 per cent on all spirits, which will push up the price of a short by about 4 pence.'*

Not: *'The Government's given the go-ahead for a massive new tower block in the centre of Wellington. Crane Towers is to be nine hundred and eighty seven feet high.'*
But: *'... Crane Towers is to be almost a thousand feet high ... that's taller than the Eiffel Tower and almost three times the height of St Paul's Cathedral.'*

The more abstract the words, the harder it gets to visualize what is meant by them and the more likely we are to end up with a different picture to the one the writer had in mind.

S. I. Hayakawa explains this with his ladder of abstraction idea, which uses Bessie the cow as an example*. To the cowhand, Bessie is a loveable old friend who gazes at him with her big brown eyes while she chews the cud. To a visitor she is merely an old brown cow. To the farm manager every cow on the farm is an item of livestock. To the bookkeeper, livestock comes under the heading of farm assets. To the accountant, assets are synonymous with wealth. Each step up the abstraction ladder takes us one step further from faithful old Bessie.

Ask someone to imagine a cow and they might picture a beast very different from Bessie; tell them 'livestock' and they could imagine a pig or a sheep; 'farm assets' could be tractors or ploughs; 'assets' could be anything saleable and 'wealth' may simply conjure up a picture of a wad of notes. Poor old Bessie!

MAKE IT INTERESTING

The journalist has something the audience wants – information. They want it because it is new, important, and relevant to them. But however much they may need it, they will receive it only if it is presented in a way that is interesting and entertaining.

At times, broadcasters will be required to tell their audience not simply what they want to hear, but what they need to know. In newsroom par-

**Language in Thought and Action*', Harcourt Brace and World, 1964, pp. 176–9, quoted in *Television News*, p. 176.

lance, not every story is 'sexy' with instant listener appeal. Some have to be worked at to draw out the point of interest.

The goings-on in the Common Market, debates in the Commonwealth or Congress and the workings of local government are important areas which traditionally turn off a mass audience. The challenge to the broadcaster is to demystify those issues by pointing up their relevance in concrete terms that people can readily grasp and relate to. To get that far, you have to begin by capturing audience interest.

Turn people off, and they will simply turn *you* off. Hold their interest, and you will help bring issues home to the people they affect, and, by raising public awareness, increase the accountability of those who make the decisions.

CONTRACTIONS

One of the most obvious differences between written and spoken English is the use of contractions. Words like, *can't*, *couldn't*, *wouldn't*, *shouldn't*, *we'll*, *she'll*, *they'll*, *wasn't*, *didn't*; and even, *shouldn't've* and *can't've*, might look peculiar on paper, but are the substance of spoken English. In your next conversation, try to avoid contractions and see how difficult you find it and how stilted it sounds. Broadcasting is about conversation, so contractions are a must.

> *'The Fire Chief said they had tried everything but had not succeeded in rescuing the mother and her child from the upper window. "We are giving it all that we have got, but we cannot do miracles. There has been no sign of them now for some time, and we are afraid that it is probably already too late."'*

This might pass in print, but read out loud it becomes obvious the story would not work on radio or TV. All it takes is a few deletions and a smattering of apostrophes:

> *'The Fire Chief said they'd tried everything but hadn't succeeded in rescuing the mother and her child from the upper window. "We're giving it all we've got, but we can't do miracles. There's been no sign of them now for some time, and we're afraid it's probably already too late."'*

A little contraction can be a dangerous thing. The shortened form can confuse the ear and be misleading to the listener. 'He *couldn't* agree to the proposal', sounds very much like, 'He *could* agree to the proposal,' and 'She *didn't* know who committed the murder', could, to someone listening with half an ear, sound like, 'She *did* know who committed the murder.'

There are times when NOT is too important a word to risk skipping over it with a contraction. Put it in CAPITALS.

RHYTHM

Spoken English has a rhythm of its own that differs from the written word. The simple reason is that, with the exception of Hemingway's gypsy quoted above, people have to come up for breath every now and again.

Sometimes sentences which look fine in print, sound unfinished when read aloud, because they stray from the conventional rhythms of speech. Usually where English is spoken, sentences will rise and fall and end with the voice turned down; unless that sentence is a question, when the voice will rise at the end. (See also pitch, page 150.)

While print journalists concentrate on cutting words out, broadcasters will sometimes extend sentences to make them sound more natural:

'The trial resumes at one,' may sound unfinished, while 'the trial is due to resume at one o'clock' is longer but more rhythmic with a more definite shape and conclusion.

The only rule, which supersedes most rules of grammar, is, if it *sounds* right, it probably *is* right. In the end the copy has to communicate, and if that means driving a coach and horses through the flower beds of the Queen's English, then so be it.

Another problem which can often show up only when the copy is read out loud is that of the unintentional rhyme:

> *'Defence Counsel Simon Crayle said the Jury could not fail to set these men free on their not guilty plea, but the judge gave them three months in jail.*
>
> *'One defendant, a stocky Croatian, yelled no justice was done in this nation. For disturbance in court, the Judge said he ought to serve six further months on probation.'*

Jarring clashes of sound and potential tongue-twisters should also be avoided:

> *'At election offices throughout Throstlebury today, each party is preparing to grind into gear for the great haul towards the imminent general election.'*

A little alliteration may occasionally be acceptable, but sometimes several similar sounds spoken aloud sound stupid, while a superfluity of hissing *s* and *c* sounds sound sibilant. Say this sentence yourself and see.

FIELDWORK

1 Take two daily newspapers, one popular, the other serious, and read some of the stories out loud. Which newspaper style sounds more like conversational English – the popular style or the serious style? What makes the difference?

Take the hardest story to read aloud and go through it using Fang's Easy Listening Formula (page 44) and give a score for each sentence. Then rewrite the story using shorter sentences and words with fewer syllables until it satisfies the Easy Listening Formula. Now read it out loud and see how it sounds. Is it any better? Can it still be improved?

2 Find a better way to write this story and to bring the point home:

> *'The rate of inflation has continued to rise over the past 12 month period, according to today's figures, which show that the retail price of staple foodstuffs has increased by 10 per cent – 5 per cent higher than the average inflation rate.'*

3 Discuss the differences between:

Assassinate and Execute
Billion and Million
Injured and Wounded
Claim and Say
Imply and Infer
Fewer and Less
Black and Coloured

4 A new agricultural strategy for the country has been launched which requires increased productivity by farmers. How would you cover the story to make it sound interesting to a typical audience?

5 Translate the following gobbledygook into plain English:

'The Managing Director unequivocally reiterated his observation to the Board that there was an immediate necessity for the augmentation of differentials within the company to offer an extended programme of pecuniary incrementation for senior executives, for the prevention of the continuing and increasing recruitment of not inconsiderable numbers of personnel in higher management by overseas companies currently offering enhanced salaries and more attractive inducements.'

5 Newswriting

> *'When you've got a thing to say,*
> *Say it! Don't take half a day...*
> *Life is short – a fleeting vapour –*
> *Don't you fill the whole blamed paper*
> *With a tale, which at a pinch,*
> *Could be covered in an inch!*
> *Boil her down until she simmers,*
> *Polish her until she glimmers.'*
> —JOEL CHANDLER HARRIS

Hard news is new and important information about events of significance. Soft news and human interest items are stories run for their entertainment value first and their information second.

In the hard news story for broadcast there is no room for padding. The information must have the impact of an uppercut and connect with the audience in the first sentence.

THE NEWS ANGLE

Before so much as rattling the keyboard, the journalist has to be clear about which angle to take on the story. This will depend on where the story occurred, what has been reported already, and what new facts have emerged.

Take the example of an air crash. All 329 people on board were killed when an Air India jumbo jet crashed off the west coast of Ireland. The disaster made headlines throughout the world, but had special significance in India and Canada. The Indian national airline was involved and the plane had taken off from Toronto, bound for Bombay.

Apart from the international importance of the event, news media of both nations had major *local* stories on their hands. The local angle resurfaced time and again in India, Canada and around the world in the villages, towns and cities where the passengers and crew had lived.

A number of different angles would have to be pursued. The first is the fact of the crash, and the questions, '*When, where, why and how many dead*?'

That same day two people die when a bomb explodes in a suitcase unloaded from another Canadian flight, from Vancouver. The events are too similar to be a coincidence. So the next angle is who planted the bomb? Two militant groups claim responsibility; the Kashmir Liberation Army, and the Sikh Dashmesh Regiment.

A reporter is assigned to produce a background item about terrorism in the sub-continent, looking at the history of these groups and their possible motives.

As the names of local people on the passenger list filter back to newsrooms stories would be prepared about the deceased, to be followed perhaps by interviews with relatives.

Meanwhile, a new angle comes into play when search teams set out to recover the wreckage. Eighteen days after the crash, the digital flight recorder is found, putting the story back in the headlines. Three months to the day after the plane went down, it makes big news again when the inquest takes place at Cork, in Ireland.

Developing stories, which constantly throw up new angles and call for different versions, are known as *running stories*. When a major running story breaks, it is often more than a single reporter can do to keep up with it, so a team is usually assigned to cover every possible angle.

MULTI-ANGLED STORIES

Broadcast news can handle more complex stories by breaking the information down point by point and giving it out in a logical sequence. But another problem can arise when the story has two angles of near equal importance which both deserve a place in the introduction. This is known as the *multi-angled* or *umbrella* story.

The way to tackle this is with a double intro – which is not to say the intro should be double the length:

> *'Today's record crime figures reveal violence and sex attacks at an all-time high . . . Police chiefs say the streets are turning into no-go areas because of the shortage of trained officers.'*

Here we have two stories, the first the escalating crime figures and the second the equally dramatic police reaction to them – both would be developed in the rest of the report.

Multi-angled stories may arise from one good story leading to an equally good follow-up which beg to be combined. These can be refreshed and kept running by updating and emphasizing different angles in subsequent bulletins. Sometimes two stories arise separately which need to be run together under an umbrella:

> *'Sport . . . and it's been a tremendous day for New Zealand's athletes, with success in the hundred metres at home and a swimming triumph in Europe.'*

> **Or:** *'More bad news for industry . . . A smelting plant in Tema is to close with the loss of more than 130 jobs, and 50 workers are to be made redundant at a nearby steelworks.'*

Both examples begin with an umbrella statement which covers the two stories in each and signposts what is to follow.

HARD NEWS FORMULA

There is a tried and tested hard news formula which is used in newspapers, radio and TV. It constructs the story by asking *who*, *what*, *when*, *where*, *why* and *how* questions. Answers to these should give most of the information required.

- ***What*** has happened?
- ***Where*** did it happen?
- ***When*** did it happen?
- ***Who*** was involved?
- ***How*** did it happen?
- ***Why*** did it happen?
- ***What*** does it mean?

Plus *extra information*, if there is time.

The news story begins with the most important facts, and backs those up with detail, background and interpretation, constructed to get the story across in a logical way that is clear and commands attention. Newswriters for the BBC's World Service are advised to tell listeners all they need to know to understand the story and to stop there. No question should be raised that cannot be answered.

THE INTRO

> *'The first sentence in a radio news story is all-important. It must have, partly, the character of a headline. It must instantly establish the subject in the listener's mind, show him why the story is worth hearing and signpost the direction it is going to take, But it should not try to say too much.'* – BBC BUSH HOUSE NEWSROOM GUIDE
>
> *'The story should* **'sell'** *itself in the first line which should be simple and punchy. My philosophy is that news should be lively rather than worthy. Even if it's serious it doesn't have to be boring. The key is . . . if you enjoy the story, so will the audience.'*
> – KATRINA BALMFORTH, NEWS EDITOR, CHILTERN RADIO

Once the angle is established, the writer has to work out his/her introduction (also known as *intro* or *lead* – UK, or *headline sentence* – US) This is the first sentence or paragraph of the story and also the most important. It's function is to:

- State the most significant point.
- Grab attention.
- Whet the appetite.
- Signpost the way into the rest of the story.

The first twenty or thirty words are like the ornate fly which an angler uses to lure the fish. The story opening has to be bright, attractive, skilfully constructed and worthy of further investigation. Once listeners are interested and take the bait you can reel them in with the rest of the story.

The intro contains the most important point. If there has been an art auction at which a masterpiece by Rubens has fetched a record price, the main point will be the record sums paid for the painting.

To make it easier to select the main point, it can help to choose a key word or short phrase which sums up whatever is most important about the story.

The key word in the art auction story is 'record.' If the story concerned a car crash which had killed sixteen, the most important point would be the sixteen deaths, not the crash. Car crashes happen all the time, but they seldom claim so many lives, so '*16 dead*' becomes the key phrase.

To build up the story, it may help to imagine a newspaper headline which could be worked up into an introduction. So, '*Record price for masterpiece*' would be the starting place for the art auction story, and '*Car crash kills 16*' would do for the other.

Both stories would probably make national news, and would lead a local news bulletin if they happened in an area covered by a radio or TV station. The locality would become central to the story and the line would change to, '*Record price for masterpiece at New York art auction*', and '*Car crash in Lagos kills 16*.'

Some stations also require the *today* angle to be pointed up in the intro to heighten the immediacy of the story.

Lastly, as it would not do for broadcasters to speak in headlines, these stories need reworking to turn them into conversational speech, which is easily done.

'The highest price ever paid for a masterpiece has been reached at an art auction in New York.'

'A multiple car crash in downtown Lagos has this morning claimed the lives of 16 people.'

The ideal hard news intro or headline sentence should be short – no longer than twenty to thirty words; uncluttered and with no unnecessary detail; simple; direct and capable of grabbing and holding interest.

PLACING KEY WORDS

Looking more closely at the second example above, it might seem more direct to say, '*16 people were killed this morning in a multiple car crash in downtown Lagos*.' This would get over the important information and communicate well enough in print, but for broadcast news, putting the main point right at the beginning of the story could create a problem.

The reader of a newspaper is led around the printed page by its layout. Each story is clearly separated from the one before it and the reader can choose which items to look at and which to ignore from the headlines which also prepare for the information to come. Television approaches this with its graphics and strong visual element, but in radio the layout is invisible and sometimes inaudible. Stories are separated by pauses and there is only the reader's voice and the writer's ability to help the listener tell where one story ends and the next begins.

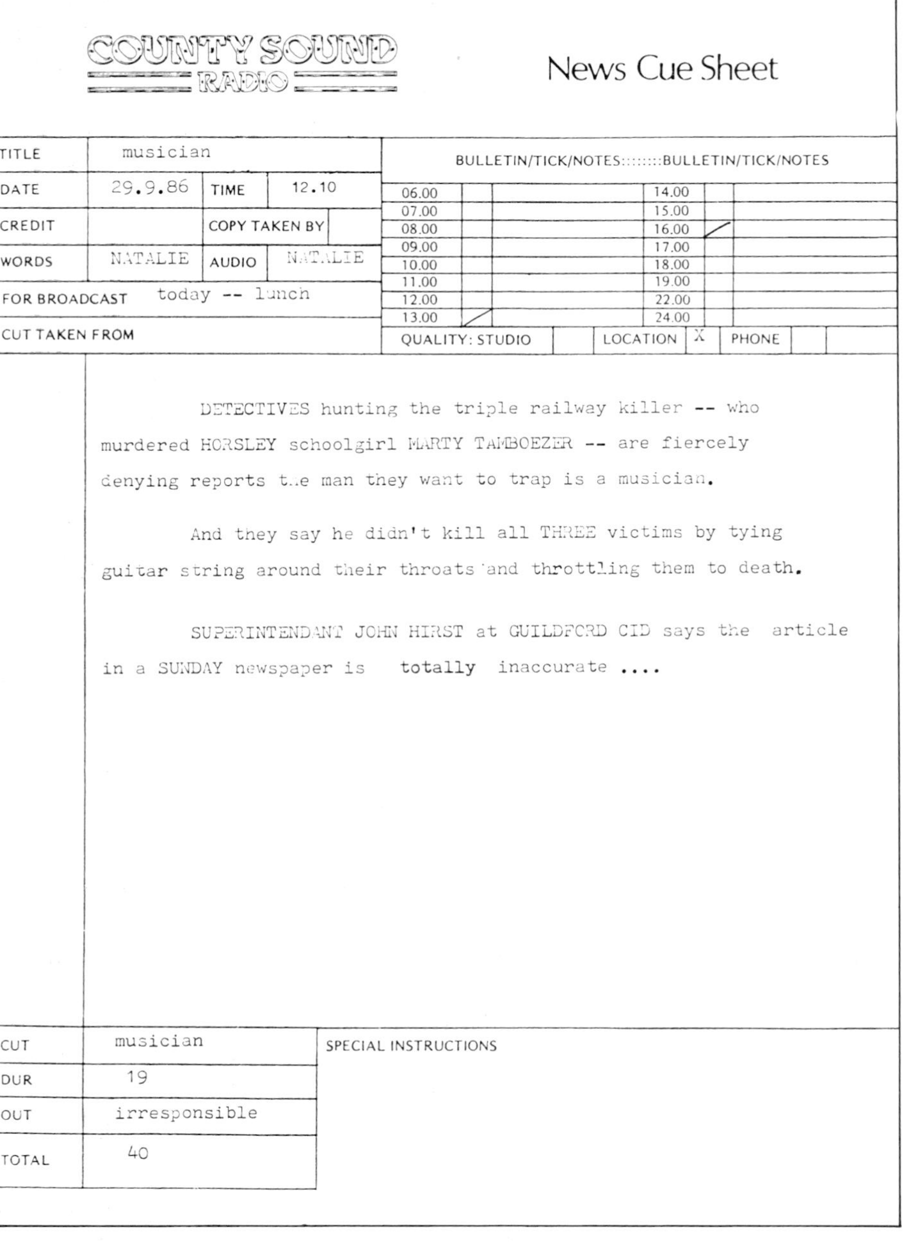

COUNTY SOUND RADIO

News Cue Sheet

TITLE	musician		
DATE	29.9.86	TIME	12.10
CREDIT		COPY TAKEN BY	
WORDS	NATALIE	AUDIO	NATALIE
FOR BROADCAST	today -- lunch		
CUT TAKEN FROM			

BULLETIN/TICK/NOTES::::::::BULLETIN/TICK/NOTES

06.00			14.00	
07.00			15.00	
08.00			16.00	✓
09.00			17.00	
10.00			18.00	
11.00			19.00	
12.00			22.00	
13.00	✓		24.00	

QUALITY: STUDIO | LOCATION X | PHONE

DETECTIVES hunting the triple railway killer -- who murdered HORSLEY schoolgirl MARTY TAMBOEZER -- are fiercely denying reports the man they want to trap is a musician.

And they say he didn't kill all THREE victims by tying guitar string around their throats and throttling them to death.

SUPERINTENDANT JOHN HIRST at GUILDFORD CID says the article in a SUNDAY newspaper is totally inaccurate ....

CUT	musician
DUR	19
OUT	irresponsible
TOTAL	40

SPECIAL INSTRUCTIONS

Figure 13 Some news editors insist that copy is prepared on special cue sheets. This example gives detailed information about when the story was written, when it was intended for use and when it was actually broadcast. It also shows the recording was made on location rather than in the studio or over the phone. This helps the producer avoid putting too many similar sounding items in the bulletin.

The box at the bottom left of the sheet gives the title of the tape accompanying the cue, its duration and last word, and the combined duration of the cue and tape.

The cue itself points up the local angle in the introduction and stress words are marked by putting them in capitals (courtesy County Sound)

With radio the problem is compounded because people tend to listen with half an ear while they tinker with the car, splash paint over the ceiling or shout at the children. Absolute attention is usually reserved for times of national crisis when the family huddles in silent anticipation around the receiver. Under normal circumstances, the first few words of a story may easily slip by unnoticed. If the main point does escape the audience, then by the time their attention is drawn back to the story, the whole meaning of the piece may be lost. The broadcaster should avoid putting the key words right at the beginning (Figure 13).

FEATURE OPENERS

Not all opening sentences follow the hard news formula. The feature, human interest or soft news story is primarily for entertainment, so the order in which the information is given becomes less important. What matters most is that the story brings a moment of light relief to the audience, and this calls for a different writing technique:

> *'If you've got a thing about creepy crawlies and the thought of stepping on a snake makes you sick, then spare a thought for Jeb Winston from Canberra.*
>
> *'Jeb's going to be surrounded by snakes.. many of them poisonous... for up to a fortnight. He's planning to sit cross legged in an eight by six tank with more than forty serpents to keep him company in a bid to break the world record for snake-sitting.'*

The hard news formula calls for the meat of the story in the first line, but the introductory paragraph here teases the audience into wanting to get to the bottom of the story by beginning with a tantalizing appeal to the emotions.

The style is conversational, even anecdotal, and contrasts with the brisk formality of hard news. The story is relaxed, and so is the style of its writing and delivery. This easy-going and informal approach is often used for cheerful end-of-bulletin items.

Most bulletin stories will be written in the straight-backed, concise, hard news style. But the same story can undergo a revolution in style when written in greater detail for a longer programme. Where the presenter is given room to be a 'personality', the writing will often loosen up to take on a chattier, more relaxed and discursive approach:

> **Bulletin intro:** *'Three counties in New Mexico have been declared disaster areas after a winter storm claimed the lives of five people.'*
>
> **Programme intro:** *'The weather continues to make big news. Some places have more snow than they can handle and others, it seems, can not get enough of it. While St Paul in Minnesota is having to import 600 tons of snow before it can stage its Winter Carnival, elsewhere snowdrifts of up to seven feet are paralysing whole areas and claiming lives. In New Mexico, three counties have been declared disaster areas, after being hit by savage winter storms which killed five people.'*

The feature style, which leads the audience into the story rather than presenting them with the facts in the first line, is used more freely wherever greater emphasis is placed on entertainment and a lighter touch than on straightforward and sometimes impersonal, hard news.

DEVELOPING THE STORY

> *'A story has to be built up logically. Start with an attention-grabbing development – something new. Then give the story a beginning, a middle and an end. You have to tell a tale.'* – MALCOLM DOWNING, CHIEF CORRESPONDENT, AUSTRALIAN BROADCASTING CORPORATION, LONDON

Finding the intro is the hardest task in newswriting. Once that is settled the rest of the item will usually fall into place.

The next step is to list the points in their logical order, constructing a story that progresses from point to point without turning back on itself or leaving the listener dangling for an explanation.

Explanation usually follows the introduction, and after that comes more detail (beware of clutter), and the tying up of loose ends. This has been described as the *what formula*:

The WHAT formula

W What has happened? The introduction tells the story in brief.
H How did it happen? Explain the immediate background or context.
A Amplify the introduction. Flesh out the main points in order of importance.
T Tie up loose ends. Give additional background material.

The final story should answer the questions, *who*, *what*, *when*, *where*, *why* and *how*, though not necessarily in that order.

The trickiest part is deciding which facts to include and which to leave out. A 20-second copy story is only sixty words long, which leaves no room for superfluous detail. Frequently, important points have to give way if vital points are to remain.

The test of non-essential information is, does the audience need it to make sense of the story, or will the story stand up without it?

In the case of our snake sitter above, his name and where he comes from are important, but his middle names, the name of his road and the number of his house are irrelevant. The details of how he and the snakes will be fed over the fortnight may be interesting, but could be dropped if space is short, while his chances of surviving unbitten and what would happen if a snake did sink its fangs into him would be well worth a mention.

Simply stated, the skill is to write up the information in order of importance until space runs out and then leave the rest.

SIGNPOSTING

> *'Tell 'em you're gonna tell 'em; tell 'em you're tellin' 'em. and tell 'em you've told 'em.'* ANON.

Broadcasting has one major limitation – the spoken word has an infuriating habit of going in one ear and out the other. Research has shown that people can only recall about two items in eight from the previous night's TV news.*

To beat these odds, the journalist has to write to create an impression rather than trying to forcefeed an audience with facts which are no sooner heard than forgotten. The art is to decide on the one lasting impression you want to leave your audience, which will usually be the main point of the story, and then to subtly push that point home throughout. This is called signposting, and it works like this:

'A homeland of their own . . . the dream for Canada's Eskimos for many years . . . could soon become reality.

'The Canadian Government is planning to divide the vast expanse of the Northwest Territories to given Indians and Eskimos a greater say in their own affairs.

'More than a million square miles would be split into Eastern and Western Territories, giving the Eskimos wider control of the East which has only 4000 white settlers.

'Their dream – which has been talked about for decades – is to be put to the Canadian people in a referendum. If they agree, the Eskimos will call their new territory Nunevut, which means "Our Land".'

The scene is set at the beginning with a simple declaration of what the story is about: the dream of a homeland for the Eskimos. How this would happen, where this would be and the history of the idea is amplified over the next three paragraphs, before returning at the end to the central theme of the homeland.

Most listeners will forget the details, but if they can recall ten minutes later that Canada's Eskimos could soon have a homeland of their own, the signposting will have worked and the story will have succeeded. The aim is to make the message of the story inescapably clear, but the skill lies in reiterating the main points without making them *sound* like repetition.

Signposting picks out the thread of an argument without requiring the audience to backtrack, which is impossible over the air. It also acts as the broadcasting equivalent of the cross-heads in a newspaper which highlight and bring home the important points.

LAST LINE

The last line should round off the story and point ahead to any next developments. This is the *'tell 'em you've told em'* part of the signposting. A story about trouble on the roads could end:

'. . . and difficult driving conditions are expected to continue until much later this evening.'

*Laurie Taylor and Bob Mullen, *Uninvited Guests*, Chatto and Windus, 1986.

A story about an unofficial bus strike, could finish:

'Bus drivers will be meeting their union leaders this afternoon to try to persuade them to make the strike official.'

Both closings refer back to the events in question (conditions on the roads; the bus strike) and show the way ahead (difficult conditions continuing into the evening; the meeting with union leaders).

Another way to round off a story is for the presenter to pick up on the end of audio or film footage with a final comment. This is known as a *back announcement* (or *back anno, BA*). It is a useful device for giving out phone numbers or updating an item recorded earlier with new information:

BA: *'And we've just heard that the road is now clear and traffic is starting to move. Tailbacks are still expected for the next half hour.'*

Back announcements are commonly used in radio to remind an audience who or what they have been listening to and as a bridge between items where some natural link can be found:

BA: *'Mary Fernandez reporting on the growing numbers of teenagers who run away from home... Well, one of the biggest dangers to those children must come from the drug pushers, and there's worrying news of yet another kind of drug that is now being sold on the streets... etc.'*

LAST WORDS

The lasting impression of any programme or item is usually made by the first and last words, and as much care should be taken on ending the story as in writing the intro. As well as beginning strongly, the story should end on a positive note, and not be allowed to tail off weakly or to fizzle out.

News stories should end with a bang rather than a whimper. Strong, definite and emphatic last words are preferable to limp endings:

Prefer: *'she said the investigation would be launched at once.'*
To: *'... the investigation would be launched at once, she said.'*

Weak: *'... the gunmen are threatening to shoot the hostages at midnight unless the Government gives in to them.'*
Stronger: *'... the gunmen are threatening to shoot the hostages at midnight, unless the Government gives in to their demands.*

The last words are the ones the audience will remember – so make them memorable.

ACCURACY

> *'In the case of news we should always wait for the sacrament of confirmation.'* – VOLTAIRE

'*A journalist is someone who finds a story and then lures the facts towards it*', and '*Never let the facts get in the way of a good story*', are jokes which, unfortunately, sometimes contain more than a grain of truth.

But nothing devalues a reporter's credibility faster than getting the facts wrong.

Mispronouncing place names irritates listeners and getting wrong someone's name or job title can sour a valued contact. More seriously, an inaccurate court report could lead to a libel suit or an action for contempt. The best maxim for the journalist is: '*If in doubt . . . check it out*'.

The main points of the story should always be verified, so no contentious or uncertain points are left to chance. *If they can't be checked out, they should be chucked out.*

The example below illustrates how difficult it can be to get the facts right, especially on a breaking story. This snap arrived on the telex from a news agency:

86626 MYNEWS G

M AND Y NEWSAGENCY, PORTSMOUTH

OIL RIG

A 400 TON SUPPLY SHIP HAS COLLIDED WITH ONE OF THE LEGS OF THE PENROD THREE OIL RIG, 20 MILES SOUTH OF THE ISLE OF WIGHT AND IS TRAPPED IN THE OIL RIG AND SINKING, WITH EIGHT PEOPLE ON BOARD.

IT'S POSSIBLE THAT THE DAMAGE TO THE OIL RIG WILL CAUSE IT TO COLLAPSE.

THE SAR HELICOPTER FROM LEE ON SOLENT HAS BEEN SCRAMBLED.

MORE FOLLOWS LATER.

86626 MYNEWS G

A battery of quick fire calls was made to the coastguard and the search and rescue (SAR) service among others. These threw up the following conflicting information:

Name of oil rig	*Name of ship*	*Size of ship*
Penrod 3	Spearfish	150 tons
Penrod No. 3	Spearship	400 tons
Penrod 83		500 tons
Penrod 85		
Penrose 85		
Number of crew	*Damage to rig*	*State of ship*
6	Slight	Sunk
7	In danger of collapse	Not sunk
8		Partially sunk
		Being towed ashore
		Scuttled
Method of scuttling	*Number of helicopters at scene*	*Location*
Blown up	1	10 miles south of island
Shot out of the water	2	15 miles south of island
		20 miles south of island

Fast moving events, inaccessible location and lack of official comment from experts too tied up in the operation to talk made the facts difficult to establish.

In the end, the story was that the 143 ton trawler *Spearfish* had become entangled in one of the legs of the *Penrod* 85 oil rig when it was trying to land supplies. The *six* man crew was winched to safety by *one* helicopter before the ship was towed clear by a frigate and sunk by *anti-aircraft fire*.

The best angle did not emerge until later, when an inspection of the helicopter rotors revealed they had flown so close to the rig that the blades had clipped the superstructure. One inch closer and the helicopter would have crashed.

With news flashes and breaking news some reshuffling of the facts is expected as the story becomes clearer. But there are times when getting the facts wrong can have disastrous consequences.

Reports of accidents, air crashes and loss of life must be handled with utmost care. If a crowded passenger train has been derailed and passengers killed, there can be no excuse for confusing the time of the train with that of another. Much anxiety can be averted by giving specific and accurate details, and with an air crash, by broadcasting the flight number.

When names of the dead are released, those names have to be got right, and if the name is a common one, like Smith, Brown or Patel, details of the address should be given to prevent needless worry.

A slip of the eye or stumble on the keyboard can render numbers wildly out, which can have a dramatic effect on a story, as happened with this example from the BBC's General News Service:

THE HEALTH MINISTRY IN WEST GERMANY IS SENDING, TO EVERY HOUSEHOLD IN THE COUNTRY, A COPY OF A PAMPHLET ABOUT THE DANGERS OF THE DISEASE, AIDS – THAT'S ACQUIRED IMMUNE DEFICIENCY SYNDROME. THE TWENTY-SEVEN-MILLION BOOKLETS WILL COST MORE THAN A MILLION AND A QUARTER POUNDS TO PRINT.

WEST GERMANY HAS HAD THREE AND A QUARTER MILLION CASES OF AIDS REPORTED SO FAR.

CORRECTION TO RIP 'N READ

IN LAST LINE PLEASE READ ...... WEST GERMANY HAS HAD THREE HUNDRED AND FORTY CASES OF AIDS REPORTED SO FAR.

****

****

051285/1250 DB

Wire services alert the network to a correction in a story by ringing a bell on the teleprinter. Usually, a couple of rings is enough. The above example was serious enough to warrant 100 bells – represented by the rows of stars on the copy.

FIELDWORK

1 Put the hard news formula to the test. Go through a couple of meaty newspaper stories marking out where the story answers the questions, *who*, *what*, *when*, *where*, *why* and *how*. Then list the order in which those answers appeared.

2 Sum up the main point of each story in a key phrase of five words or less. Then compare your key phrases to the newspaper headlines. How similar are they? Do the headlines home in on different points? Why?

Next develop your key phrases into an intro for each story. Keep each intro down to thirty words maximum. Then compare your intros with the ones used by the newspaper. What are the differences?

3 Construct a hard news story from the following collection of facts:

The Bantry Bay Company employs a workforce of 3000.
There are no plans to cut shopfloor workers.
The company makes widgits.
10 per cent of the clerical workers are to lose their jobs.
The company lost £2m in the first half of last year.
The cuts are to try to improve efficiency and reduce costs.
There are 1000 white collar (clerical) workers.
The company says that early retirement and voluntary redundancies should account for most of the job cuts.
The last redundancies at the Bantry Bay Company took place five years ago.

4 Now put together a soft news feature from the following facts. Remember, the style needs to be less terse and more entertaining. You will need to think of livelier ways to present the facts than they are given here and should try to avoid repeating the word 'alligator' too often.

The trapper's name was John Tanner.
The alligator weighed 150 pounds.
Mr Tanner took with him only a rope lassoo and miner's lamp.
The alligator tried to bite through the noose. With moments to spare, Mr Tanner managed to bind its jaws with electrical tape.
The alligator was caught in the sewers beneath Orlando, in Florida.
Alligator meat is a local delicacy. He could have sold it for its meat and its hide.
He wrestled with the alligator and managed to slip the noose around its neck.
He did not get any money for his efforts. 'It wasn't hurting anybody,' he said.
He got the alligator to come to him by imitating the mating call of the female alligator.
The authorities sent for Mr Tanner after state trappers had failed to catch the reptile, which had tried to bite four drainage inspectors.
He took it to a remote part of the country and let it go.

5 Now turn that feature item into a hard news story of fewer than 100 words. Then go back over your stories and check they are well signposted, end strongly and are easy to read out loud. Finally, if you are in a class, swap your work with someone else, and sub-edit their versions, making any alterations you think are necessary.

6 Broadcast style book

Good style
'If I had a donkey as wouldn't go,
do you think I'd wallop him? Oh no.
I'd give him some corn and cry out 'Whoa,
Gee up, Neddy.'

Bad style
'If I had an ass that refused to proceed,
Do you suppose that I should castigate him?
No indeed.
I should present him with some cereals and
observe proceed,
Continue, Edward.' – HAROLD EVANS*

Most broadcast organizations have a view about good style, and though they differ in detail, most would agree that good style is usually whatever makes good sense.

George Orwell wrote *Politics and the English Language* in 1946, but his advice still holds true today;

- Never use a metaphor, simile or other figure of speech which you are used to seeing in print.
- Never use a long word where a short one will do.
- If it is possible to cut out a word, always cut it out.
- Never use the passive where you can use the active.
- Never use a foreign phrase, scientific word or a jargon word if you can think of an everyday English equivalent.
- Break any of these rules sooner than say anything outright barbarous.[†]

CLICHÉS

Eric Partridge, in his *Dictionary of Clichés*, defines the cliché as 'a phrase so hackneyed as to be knock-kneed and spavined.'[‡]

**Newsman's English*, Heinemann, 1972.
[†] George Orwell, *Politics and the English Language*.
[‡] Routledge, 1940

They not only fail to enliven dull copy, clichés make even the most significant item sound trite. If we accuse ratepayers of taking up cudgels against city hall whenever they write a letter of complaint, what are we to say the day owner-occupiers really *do* drive nails through wooden clubs and set about their elected representatives?

What will be left to say when war *is* declared?

Hyperbole and clichés are for hacks. This, then, is a dictionary for hacks:

absolute farce
acid test
all-out-effort
anybody's guess
around the table
as sick as a parrot
at this point in time

balanced on a knife edge
beat a hasty retreat
bid (for attempt)
bitter end
bolt from the blue
bombshell
boost
boss
brutal reminder

calm before the storm
calm but tense
cash boost
chequered career
chief
clampdown
crackdown

daylight robbery
deciding factor
desperate attempt/bid
doctors fought
drama
dramatic decision/new move
dug in their heels

effortless victory

fell on deaf ears

gave as good as he got
gay (for homosexual)
get under way
given the green light
going walkabout
got the message

headache
heart of gold
heated debate
high-ranking
horror
how does it feel?

in a nutshell
in due course
in full swing
iron out the problem

jobless youngsters
just like the Blitz

lashed out at
last but not least
last ditch effort
last minute decision
leading the hunt
leaps and bounds
leave no stone unturned
limped into port
loud and clear
lucky few
luxury liner

major new development/project
marked contrast
mercy dash
miracle cure
mindless vandals
mine of information

news leaked out
nipped in the bud
none the worse for wear
not to be outdone

one in the eye
over and above
over the moon

paid the penalty
painted a grim picture
part and parcel
picking up the pieces
point in time
pool of blood
pride and joy
probe
pull out the stops
put into perspective

quiz (for question)

rushed to the scene

selling like hot cakes
shock
short and sweet
shot in the arm
show of force
sitting on a goldmine
sitting on the fence
$64,000 question
square peg in a round hole
still anybody's guess
stuck to his/her guns
sweeping changes

up in arms
up in the air

vanished into thin air
vast amount
virtual standstill
voiced his approval

weighty matter
what of the future?
whole new ball game
wreak havoc
writing on the wall

No doubt you will have your own favourites to add to the list. With technology making strides, it may soon be possible to program an elaborate lexicon of clichés into a computer, enter the type of the story, say, *murder*; key in details such as the name of the victim, and within a matter of seconds, we could be reading printouts of sparkling news copy, such as the following:

> *'Police are hunting a vicious killer following the brutal murder of* (FILL IN NAME) *in his opulent country house in the secluded backwater of* (FILL IN NAME) *this morning.*
>
> '(FILL IN NAME) *'s mutilated body was found lying in a pool of blood in the bedroom. A sawn off shotgun lay nearby. Police discovered the corpse after a dawn raid on the mansion in the early hours of the morning, following a tip from an underworld supergrass.*
>
> *'Detective Inspector* (FILL IN NAME) *who's leading the hunt, said the killer had vanished into thin air. Police with tracker dogs were now combing nearby woods, and pledged to leave no stone unturned until the butcher of* (FILL IN NAME) *had been brought to justice.*
>
> '(FILL IN NAME) *was described by stunned and grief-stricken neighbours as "a pillar of society".'*
>
> '(FILL IN NAME) *'s widow, shapely blonde* (FILL IN NAME) *told us how she felt...'*

JOURNALESE

A kissing cousin of the cliché is journalese, described by writer John Leo as the native tongue of newsgatherers and pundits. It is the language of the label and instant metaphor, drawing its inspiration from newspaper headlines to make pronouncements of stunning clarity over matters which to everybody else appear decidedly muddied.

> *'Every cub reporter... knows that fires rage out of control, minor mischief is perpetrated by Vandals (never Visigoths, Franks or a single Vandal working alone) and key labour accords are hammered out by weary negotiators in marathon, round-the-clock bargaining sessions, thus narrowly averting threatened walkouts.'* – JOHN LEO*

More disturbingly, an evening's sport of name-calling, stone throwing and petty crimes against property by rival gangs of schoolboys in Northern Ireland (which is divided along sectarian, religious, tribal and political lines, and suffers the worst unemployment in the UK) becomes a '*fresh outbreak of violence between loyalists and republican supporters...*'

Clichés and journalese are devils disguised as angels. They lie in wait for the moment Inspiration turns her back, before overpowering her, stealing her clothes and sneaking up on the reporter as a deadline approaches.

*'Journalese for the Lay Reader,' *Time*, 18 March, 1985.

Hapless hacks are usually so intent on beating the clock that they fail to see through the disguise and welcome these saboteurs as saviours. So resigned are reporters to their infiltration and so dependent on their support, that, even when their disguise wears thin through over-use, the two are often left to wreak their havoc unchecked. The alternative is to waste precious minutes attempting to revive Inspiration, who has an infuriating habit of succumbing whenever deadlines draw near.

Even books are written to deadlines, and it is not inconceivable that you may unmask the odd cliché within these pages. Feel free to strike the offender through with a biro and, if you find Inspiration at her post, make some suitable correction.

HYPERBOLE

Definition of hype

'Exaggerated statement not meant to be taken literally.'
– CONCISE OXFORD DICTIONARY

'Headlines twice the size of the events.' – JOHN GALSWORTHY

Another blood relation of journalese is hype, seen in the Northern Ireland example above. Hype can be found scattered throughout the media, and in especially large concentrations wherever advertising copywriters gather.

Many journalists readily call on hype's assistance to lend support to a flaccid story on a quiet news day.

'Children's lives could be at risk if they swallow quantities of a lethal drug which has gone missing in Harare.'

Translated: Somebody dropped their sleeping tablets on their way home from the shops.

'A man has been arrested in Perth after an appalling and unprovoked sex attack on a defenceless three year old girl.'

But: All sex attacks are *appalling:*
NO three year old girl is likely to *provoke* such an attack
ALL small girls are *defenceless.*

Hype of this order is unpleasant, distasteful and unnecessary. If the story can't stand up without it, it should not be run.

If the news is to remain a reliable source of factual information, hype should be kept within the confines of the commerical break.

ADJECTIVES

'I will rarely use an adjective and only because I think it's important, and then I will ask for it to be taken out in the next bulletin.'
– PENNY YOUNG, NEWS EDITOR BBC RADIO NORTHAMPTON

How many adjectives you use will depend on your house style and whether the station's image is 'quality' or 'popular'. Contrast the versions below:

'Firemen with oxy-acetylene cutters took three hours to free the body from the wreckage. They said it was one of the worst crashes they'd seen.'	*'Firemen with oxy-acetylene cutters struggled for three hours to free the mangled body from the shattered cab. They said the horrific crash was one of the worst they'd seen.'*

Most stations would think twice about the tasteless 'mangled'. Adjectives add colour but too many make the piece sound like an extract from a lurid novel. Remove them all and the item can sound dull or bland. Handle with care.

QUOTATIONS

A choice quotation can add considerably to the flavour of a report, but there are hazards in using quotes in broadcasting.

In print a quote is immediately obvious because of the quotation marks, but broadcast audiences can not *hear* when a quote begins and ends, so they should be kept short and clearly attributed:

> *'The Prime Minister rounded on the protestors, accusing them of "behaving like a bunch of anarchists".'*

The newsreader can help with the signposting, by pausing for a fraction of a second before reading the quote.

ATTRIBUTION

Information should be attributed clearly to leave the audience in no doubt about who is speaking – remember, listeners can never refer back. This said, attribution can be overdone and badly clutter a piece of copy:

> *'The honourable Peter Threeple, Junior Minister in the Department of Health, said today that an injection of 20 million pounds would be made available to improve wages in the National Health Service.'*

Not exactly an attention grabber, so the sentence should be turned around to put the facts before the attribution, and the attribution shortened to be still accurate, but much more manageable:

> *'A cash injection of 20 million pounds is to be made available to improve wages in the Health Service.*
>
> *'Health Minister Peter Threeple told the Commons today that the money . . . etc.'*

The message is often more important than the messenger. In this case the news of the funding is more important than the name of the minister, so the information should be run before the attribution.

Stories should begin with a person's name only when that name is widely known. If the audience cannot immediately identify the person, this becomes a point of confusion at the start of a story.

To avoid cluttering an introduction it is sometimes necessary to choose between giving a person's name or title in the first line. If their name is better known than their job or organization, then the name should be given before the title, and vice-versa.

> *'The Director General of the CBI, John Banham, has called on the Government to provide tax concessions to make Britain's businesses more profitable.'*

This may work satisfactorily in print, but spoken out loud the first line becomes cluttered and the title CBI may not be universally understood. The attribution should be spread over two sentences and some clear signposting provided:

> *'The leader of Britain's employers is calling for tax concessions to make businesses more profitable.*
>
> *'John Banham, Director General of the Confederation of British Industry, wants the Government to . . . etc.'*

The art is to attribute a statement clearly without letting the attribution get in the way. Television has a major advantage over radio – interviewees can appear without an introduction because their names and titles can be displayed on the screen over their pictures.

CONTENTIOUS STATEMENTS

When statements are controversial or contentious the attribution has to be made clearly and cannot be held back until the second sentence:

> *'America's unemployed are a shiftless, lazy bunch of spongers, who should be forced to sweep the streets until they find a decent job.' So said Governor Richman at a news conference today . . .'*

This first sentence has turned a highly debatable assertion into a statement of fact, and the danger is that the audience may miss the attribution which follows and identify the opinion with the newsreader. The station could lose a large section of its audience – the unemployed. The broadcaster must maintain impartiality by distancing him/herself from such statements.

This problem is avoided by giving the attribution in the same sentence and signposting that we are dealing with opinions and not facts:

> *'Governor Richman launched a scathing attack on America's unemployed today . . . calling them a shiftless, lazy bunch of spongers. And, speaking at a news conference, he said they should be forced to sweep the streets until they could get themselves decent jobs.'*

This gets the broadcaster off the hook and leaves Governor Richman dangling firmly *on* it.

Careful attribution is crucial where facts are being asserted which have yet to be proven true. It is not uncommon with war reporting to find both sides claiming substantial victories over each other at the same time. Unless the facts can be confirmed from independent sources, such statements should never be given without qualification:

> *'Cornish and Devonian forces are both claiming significant victories today. The Cornish airforce **say** they shot down 14 Devonian bombers with no losses of their own and the Devonian airforce is **claiming** to have destroyed every Cornish airfield. Both sides now **say** they have total air superiority and in official statements today each side **alleges** the other is lying.'*

Say, *claim* and *allege* are useful qualifications for suspect information and distance the newsreader enough to avoid sounding like a propaganda mouthpiece. *Claim* and *allege* should be avoided where no doubt is meant to be implied, and repetition of the word '*said*' can be avoided by using phrases like '*he added*' or '*pointed out*'.

IMMEDIACY

One of the great strengths of broadcast news is its immediacy. It wipes the floor with newspapers when it comes to reacting quickly to changing events. The Cuban missile crisis in 1962 when the world stood on the brink of nuclear war, has been accredited as the catalyst which caused the switch from papers to TV as the prime source of news.*

While newspapers have no option but to examine old news, broadcasters are able to follow events as they unfold. Broadcasters understandably play to their strengths, and most newsrooms heighten the sense of immediacy in their copy by using the present or perfect tenses. While tomorrow's newspaper will tell us:

> *'In Delhi, a leading Hindu activist escaped unharmed yesterday in an assassination attempt. . . .' (past tense)*

Today's bulletin will say,

> *'In Delhi today, a leading Hindu activist has escaped unharmed, following an assassination attempt.' (perfect tense)*

The present tense is even more immediate:

> *'The Nigerian Government is requesting the extradition of four leading politicians who fled to London after a military coup.'*

Tomorrow's newspaper, which will be inherently backward-looking, would alter that tense, to 'has requested', or 'requested', each of which retreats from the immediacy of the action.

The word 'yesterday' is taboo in broadcasting. Nothing sounds more incongruous than a station with hourly bulletins giving a time reference which harks back 24 hours. If 'yesterday' or 'last night' have to be used, they should be kept out of the opening sentences and buried further down in the story.

Similarly, phrases such as '*this morning*,' '*this afternoon*', or '*this evening*' can date copy. So, for inclusion in the 6 o'clock news, the following story would have to be rewritten:

*Anthony Davis, *Television: Here is the news*, Independent Books Ltd, 1976, p. 23.

> *'In Kampala, military authorities this morning arrested a number of trigger-happy soldiers who were using army vehicles for private errands and shooting unnecessarily at criminals.'*

The phrase '*this morning*', which would stand out like a sore thumb by the evening, would be replaced with the words '*have*', or '*have today.*' Some news editors object to prolific use of the word '*today*' arguing that all broadcasting is about what happened today, so the word is redundant and can be omitted.

Similarly, exact times, such as, '*at seven minutes past twelve*' should be rounded off to, '*just after midday*', and specific times should be used only if they are essential to the story or heighten the immediacy of the coverage:

> *'News just in.... Within the past five minutes Congress has voted to defeat the President's plans to increase financial aid to right wing guerrillas in Central America...'*

For those listening in the small hours of the morning, references to events '*last night*' can be confusing, and should be replaced with '*overnight*' or '*during the night*'.

Time references have to be handled even more carefully when a station is broadcasting over several time zones. Canada, for example, spans seven such zones. To avoid confusion over their copy, news agencies which file stories over a wide area usually include the day of the week in brackets.

ACTIVE

News is about movement, change and action. Yet too often newswriting is reduced to the passive voice – instead of actions that produce change, we hear of changes that have occured as a result of actions. '*The car smashed into the brick wall*', becomes the limp and soft-centred, '*the brick wall was smashed into by the car*'.

Hickory Dickory Dock	Hickory Dickory Dock
The clock was run up by the mouse	The mouse ran up the clock
One o'clock was struck	The clock struck one
Down the mouse ran	The mouse ran down
Hickory Dickory Dock.	Hickory Dickory Dock.

The passive version on the left could be said to be lacking something of the snap of the original. The active voice is tighter, crisper and more concrete.

POSITIVE

> *'Good style is when you can see pictures in your writing, but just as important is a good grasp of the English language – and that's getting rarer and rarer to find.'*
>
> —JUDITH MELBY, NETWORK PRODUCER, CANADIAN BROADCASTING CORPORATION

News is about what is happening, so even what is *not* happening should be expressed in an active, positive way. '*He did not succeed*', becomes '*he failed*'; '*He was asked to move, but didn't*', becomes '*he refused to move*'; '*Plans for the hospital would not go ahead for the time being*', becomes, '*Plans for the hospital have been shelved*'.

Double negatives should be unravelled; '*Doctors say it is improbable that the illness will not prove terminal,*' becomes, '*Doctors admit the patient will probably die*'.

REDUNDANCIES

Redundancies are words that serve only to clutter up the copy. They should be ruthlessly elminated:

Check *out*
End result
Eye witness
Period of a week, etc.

One of the worst offenders is the little word, '*that*', which can straddle the middle of a sentence like a roadblock:

> *'New Zealand's Prime Minister said* ***that*** *the country's anti-nuclear policy was here to stay.'*

The can also be a pain. To be extreme about about them both:

> *'When asked about* ***the*** *possible strike action,* ***the*** *Dockers' leaders said* ***that*** they hoped ***that*** *that would not be necessary.*

Now read those sentences again and leave out the words in bold.

Every word should earn its place in the copy. Newswriting is too streamlined to carry any passengers. Modifiers such as '*very*', '*quite*', and '*almost*' are excess baggage and should be dumped.

REPETITION

> *'The obvious is better than the obvious avoidance of it'*
> —FOWLER'S MODERN ENGLISH USAGE

Unnecessary repetition of words can jar the ear and should be avoided, but if no alternative can be found, and if it *sounds* right, then do not be afraid to repeat. No one has yet come up with a way of avoiding saying 'fire' in a story about a . . . well, a conflagration, without sounding absurd. Common practice is to alternate the words 'fire' and 'blaze'.

Where a *proposal* is involved, alternatives such as *scheme*, *plan*, *project* or *programme* may be used.

HOMONYMS

These are words which sound like others with different meanings:

Bare	and	Bear
Blight	and	Plight
Might	and	Might
Ate	and	Eight
Billion	and	Million
Fatal	and	Facial

Confusing fatal and facial injuries in an accident report could give somebody's mother a heart attack! Usually the context will make the meaning of the word clear, but beware of baffling the listener.

SINGULAR OR PLURAL?

Should it be the Government *says* or the Government *say*? Opinions differ and many newsrooms settle the issue by writing whatever sounds right to the ear. The trouble starts when inconsistencies creep into the copy:

> *'The Labour party say their policies will put Britain back to work. Labour wants a massive increase in public spending.'*

'*The Labour party say*,' and '*Labour wants*' may both sound right individually, but they do not sound right together. Journalists must make up their own mind.

PRONOUNS

Using pronouns in broadcasting requires a special discipline to get round the problem of muddling the listener who can not go back over what has been said:

> *'Film star Clark Cooper was involved in an ugly scene with fellow actor Gary Gable outside a Hollywood restaurant today. Cooper called Gable a has-been, and Gable responded by casting doubt on Cooper's parentage. He said he would sue.'*

Is Gable suing Cooper or is Cooper suing Gable? The way around this is to swap the pronoun for a name:

> *'Cooper said he would sue.'*

PUNCTUATION

Writing for broadcast is writing to be read aloud. Sentences should be broken into groups of meaning and these should be separated by a visible pause. Semi-colons and colons do not work well, because they are visually too similar to the full stop (period) or comma.

Pauses that are intended to be longer than a comma can be indicated by the dash -- hyphen - ellipsis ... or slash /. The ellipsis or dash (double hyphen) are perhaps the most effective indicators of pauses because they create more physical space between words than other forms of punctuation. Each new idea should be separated by a longer pause, and the best way to indicate this is to begin a new paragraph.

Capital letters can be used for names or to create emphasis, but if the story is written entirely in capitals, as is often the case (sic), the emphasis and visual signal at the start of the sentence is lost.

SPELLING

> *'The names of people represent an enormous threat, particularly if they're foreign names that you suddenly see for the first time.'*
> —ANNA FORD, UK NEWSREADER AND PRESENTER
>
> *'If you get a difficult name to pronounce and you're fairly uncertain in your own mind about it, there's one golden rule – look the viewer straight in the eye through the camera lens, and say the first thing that comes into your head.'* —ANDREW GARDNER, BRITISH NEWSREADER*

**It'll Be Alright on the Night*, London Weekend Television

Some people say spelling does not matter in broadcasting, but that is not strictly true. The listener may not know if the wurds are speld gud, but a misspelled word can act like a banana skin beneath an unwary newsreader and cause him or her to stumble or trip.

Foreign and unfamiliar names can also be a problem. The solution is to spell them *fon-et-ik-lee* (phonetically) – as they sound. It is also a good idea to warn newsreaders of a pronunciation trap by marking the top of the page. They can then rehearse the troublesome word.

ABBREVIATIONS

Abbreviations generally make sense to the eye, but not to the ear. All but the most common, such as Mr and Mrs and USA, should be avoided.

Names of organizations should be spelled out unless they are commonly known by their initials, such as the BBC. Never use abbreviations that the newsreader would have to translate, such as C-in-C for Commander in Chief. The newsreader may be thrown for a second or get them wrong.

Some stations require abbreviations to be hyphenated, for example P-T-A, A-N-C, unless they form recognizable words (acronyms), when they should be left intact, for example SWAPO or NATO.

FIGURES

Nothing clutters copy quicker or confuses the ear more than a collection of figures. Even a short figure on a piece of paper can take a surprisingly long time to read aloud.

A single story should contain as few figures as possible, and within the bounds of accuracy numbers should always be rounded up or down to make them easier to take in: for 246,326, write 'almost 250,000', or, even better, 'nearly a quarter of a million'.

Broadcast stations vary in their approach to figures, but whatever the house style, clarity is the aim, for the sake of the newsreader as well as the listener. Resist the temptation to use '*a million*' instead of '*one million*', as listeners could easily confuse it for eight million. '*Billion*' should also be avoided as this means different things in different countries. Refer to so many thousands of millions instead.

PROOF READING

Copy should always be read out loud, to check for the sense and make sure no traps lie in wait for the unwary newsreader. Never leave it to the reader to check the copy through. A sudden rush before the bulletin could leave no time to prepare. The acid test of good copy is whether someone else could read it out loud, having never before clapped eyes on it, and get through without tripping over his tongue.

Below are some examples of hastily written copy which were actually submitted to be read on air:

*****

HEALTH OFFICERS THROUGHOUT THE COUNTRY ARE BEING PUT ON THE ALERT FOR TYPYOID CASES . . . AFTER SIX PEOPLE RETURNING FROM A GREEK HOLIDAY WERE FOUND TO HAVE THE DISEASE TAKES TWENTY ONE DAYS TO INCUBATE AND IT'S THOUGHT MORE CASES COULD DEVELOP IN THE NEXT FEW DAYS.

*****

*****
ALBOUR LEFT WINGER . . . MICHAEL MEACHER . . . HAS DEFENDED HIS PROPOSAL THAT A FUTURE LABOUR GOVERNMENT SHOULD HOLD A REFERENDUM ON WHETHER BRITIAN SHOULD HAVE NUCLEAR WEAPOSN.
HE SAYS IT'S A LIFE AND DEATH ISSUE . . . AND ONE THOUSAND THAT OVERRIDES ALL OTHER MATTERS.
*****

*****
ENGLAND BEAT THE REPUBLIC OF IRELAND TWO NIL LAST NIGHT AT WEMBLEY. IT WAS AN EASY WIN, AND ENGLAND WERE ON TOP UNTIL THE CLOSING MINUTES WHEN BRADY SCORED FOR IRELAND.
*****

Apart from the spelling mistakes, these stories may look feasible at first glance. Only when they are read through do the problems become obvious.

Even the most innocent words and phrases can sometimes conspire to trap you. Find another way of saying it *before* you go on air:

> *'Avon's ambulamencement . . . Avon's ambulaments . . . Avon's ambulen . . . Avon's ambewlamence . . .* (Pause. Deep breath) *The ambulancemen of Avon . . .'* – British TV.

AMBIGUITY

Ambiguity offers the audience a rich source of humour at the newsreader's expense. Howlers can range from the simple snigger:

> *'Orchestra musicians at the Royal Opera House are threatening to strike next week, if the management turn down a 10 per cent no-strings pay rise.'*

to the cringingly embarrassing:

> *'. . . the batsman's Holding . . . the bowler's Willey . . .'*

Here are some other examples which might have been caught in time if the writer had troubled to read them through:

> *'Teams of traditional dancers from various parts of Kenya exposed themselves to world scouts delegates in a grand performance.'*

> *'About 50 students broke into the college, smashing glass and chanting, "No cuts, no cuts", A porter had his hand injured . . .'*

> *'During evidence, PC John Wilkinson said that John Depledge had given him a violent blow to the testicles. They both fell to the ground . . .'*

FIELDWORK

1 Compare two radio bulletins on different stations that vary in style. Which do you prefer and why? Jot down the clichés and journalese that appear in each. See if you can come up with less hackneyed ways of saying the same thing.

2 Scan the pages of a popular newspaper for examples of journalese. How many of these phrases do you occasionally hear in radio or TV news broadcasts? Again, see if you can come up with alternatives.

3 The following story needs rewriting to clarify it, tidy up the attribution, simplify the figures and generally knock it into shape. Have a go.

> Flagham Council leader and Housing Chairman, Councillor Fred Bunter MA, has dismissed opposition plans to cut council rents as 'absurd'. Rent cuts of up to 19 per cent had been suggested to help out the 6883 tenants who had fallen badly into arears. Councillor Bunter said the rent cuts would penalise the council's other 63,722 tenants who had managed to keep up with their rent. The cut price rents scheme was proposed by opposition spokesman on Housing, Councillor Bob Taylor, who said, 'Many of these tenants have no way of paying their rent. They are in severe difficulties, often through no fault of their own, and must be helped.'

4 Rewrite the following headlines into a more immediate, direct and active broadcast style:

> In connection with the Security Holdings armed robbery in Parkerville last month, four men appeared briefly in court today. An adjournment was granted for a week.
>
> The search for twelve fishermen from a Danish trawler in the North Sea ended when they were found safe and well drifting on the sea in a small boat.
>
> Three schoolchildren died after their school bus was hit by a car on the M1. Other vehicles were not involved.

5 The following story is a complete mess. Whoever wrote it should fear for his/her job. The angle needs pointing up, it has unnecessary repetition, redundancies, convolution, singular/plural problems, hopeless punctuation and too many adjectives. Hammer it into shape and rewrite it to broadcast style.

> The Police Department is urgently calling for eye-witnesses following a tragic and fatal fire at hospital in Brunton. The fire broke out in the third floor laundry room at the modern 300-bed General Hospital in Brunton and quickly spread to the casualty ward. Frightened patients in the casualty ward hastily raised the alarm and worried doctors and nurses had to evacuate them from the ward along with all the other patients in the rest of the hospital who later heard the distressing news that an ancilliary worker in the laundry room where the fire began was overcome by the fumes and sadly died in the horrific fire which is still burning fiercely as firemen continue bravely to fight the flames which are still lighting up the night sky. The police say that they think that the fire may have been started on purpose. The flames have badly damaged about half of the hospital. No other patient or member of staff was injured in the fire.

7 The interview

> *'It's marvellous! I have the opportunity to be impertinent to people I'd never normally meet and I can say what would be considered rude things and they have to answer. It's a position of great responsibility and I'm privileged to do it.'* – RICHARD BESTIC, IRN PARLIAMENTARY CORRESPONDENT

Every scrap of information that reaches the airwaves stems from an interview of some sort – a chat at a bar to get some background, an informal phone call to clear up some details, or a recording for transmission.

Broadcasting's great appeal is that the audience can hear the facts straight from the horse's mouth. The speaker's own words lend greater authority to a report than any number of quotes in next day's newspaper. Listeners can follow events as they happen – live.

Figure 14 All eyes on the interviewee during location filming for the news programme *Wales at Six*. Eye contact between reporter and interviewee keeps the information flowing (courtesy HTV)

THE INTERVIEWER'S SKILL

Interviewers are brokers of information. Their skill lies in matching the goods on offer with the needs of their customers. Their art is to tease out the story in the teller's own words, while making sure every word will be clearly understood by their audience.

Listeners can then make up their own minds about whether or not to believe what is being said. The function of exposing viewpoints to public debate and criticism is one of the major planks in the argument that a free news media is essential to democracy.

To the best of their ability, reporters must lay aside their own interests, points of view and prejudices. The reporter's job is not to produce propaganda, however noble the cause: that is the task of the politician and public relations officer. Reporters are watchdogs for their audience, and it is with them that their loyalties must lie.

Reporters' skills, their knowledge of the subject, and their access to the interviewee give them the means and the responsibility to ask the sort of 'Yes, but...' questions their audience would love to ask in their place. The reporter is the bridge between the layperson and the expert, the person in the street and the official, and a good interview will often test the validity of an argument by exploring its points of tension or controversy.

DIFFERENT TYPES OF INTERVIEW

The BBC tells its trainees that there are three basic types of interview:

1 The *hard exposure* interview which investigates a subject.
2 The *informational* interview which puts the audience in the picture.
3 The *emotional* interview which aims to reveal an interviewee's state of mind.

These three paint a broad picture of the art of the interview, which we can develop further into twelve different types, all with special functions:

- Hard news
- Information
- Investigation
- Adversarial
- Interpretative
- Vox pop and multiple
- Personal
- Emotional
- Entertainment
- Actuality only
- Telephone or remote
- Grabbed

A DISASTER STORY?

The following extraordinary interview was heard on IRN (Independent Radio News), the British commerical network news service. It was with a militant union leader during a long lasting and bitter strike. The man facing the microphone was miner's leader Arthur Scargill, a Yorkshireman not known for his gentle touch with interviewers, or for giving any ground in an argument. But this reporter thought he could take him on and beat him at his own game – live on peak-time radio. Decide for yourself whether he succeeded and whether the result made good or bad radio.

The first major stumbling block came near the beginning when the interviewer asked the militant miners' leader to admit defeat:

> *'Five weeks into the dispute the membership... is still divided over whether to follow your call. Would you concede that the strike is a bitter one and that like never before miner is pitched against miner?'*

Which prompted the swift response:

Scargill: *'. . . now I'm not going to correct you again, I hope . . . If people misinterpret what we're doing the way you're doing, then clearly it's little wonder the British people don't know the facts . . .'* (He then proceeded to reiterate a point he had made earlier)

Interviewer: *'We'll deal with those points later . . .'*

Scargill: *'No, I'm, sorry, you'll not . . .'*

Interviewer: *'Mr Scargill, could you please answer my question . . .'*

Scargill: *'No, I'm sorry, you'll not deal with those points later in the programme, you'll either listen to what I've got to say or not at all . . .'*

Interviewer: *'We'll come to those in a minute . . .'*

Scargill: *'No I'm sorry, you can either listen to the answers that I'm giving, or alternatively, you can shut up . . .'*

Interviewer: *'We'll come to those figures later, Mr Scargill . . .'*

Scargill: *'No, I'm sorry, one thing you're going to learn is that on an interview of this kind, you're going to listen clearly to the things that I want to talk about . . .'* (this banter continued for some time, until:)

Scargill: *'Now are you going to listen?'*

Interviewer: *'No, can you please . . .'* (but his voice is drowned out by that of his guest)

Scargill: *'Then as far as I'm concerned we might as well pack up this interview . . . Now it's obvious you're not going to listen, and if you're not going to listen, lad, then there's no point in me talking to you is there, eh?'* (They debated this moot point for a time, until:)

Interviewer: (Exasperated) *'Mr Scargill, Mr Scargill, can you* ***please*** *answer the question?'*

Scargill: *'Now are you going to listen to my answers or not?'*

Interviewer: *'If you listen, if* ***you*** *listen to my questions and give answers to them; it's as simple as that!'*

Scargill: *'Quite frankly, either you're going to listen to my answers or not. And if you're not, then you're going to obviously make yourself look a complete fool . . .'*

Interviewer: (Pleadingly) *'Then why don't you give answers to the questions I'm giving, Mr Scargill . . .?'*

Scargill: *'You're either going to let me answer the questions in my way, or if you want, write the answers that* you *want on a board and tell people that you want me to answer those questions your way . . .'*

Interviewer: (Gathering about himself his last shreads of composure) *'Can you come to the point then, and answer the question?'*

Scargill: (Unrelenting) *'I can come to any point I want providing you'll shut up and let me answer, but if you won't shut up, then I can't . . . If you don't, then this interview is going to go on in this silly way as a result of your irresponsible attitude.'*

Interviewer: (Abandonedly) *'Let's move on to something else . . .* (Sigh)'

But that proved to be a vain hope, and, although the question had long since been forgotten, by the audience at least, interviewer and interviewee continued the same exasperating little dance for some time, with Mr Scargill repeating the same point again and again, and punctuating his interviewer's unwelcome interruptions with observations that his would-be interrogator was:

- Speaking as a representative of the Coal Board or the Tory Government.
- Trying to make himself a budding Robin Day (a senior BBC anchor man), which he followed through with stern rejoinder: '*. . . well, tha's not doing it wi' me, lad!*'.
- That his interviewer was an ignorant man who ought to have more sense.
- And that he ought to get out of the chair and let someone else sit there who *could* do the job.

Were his remarks justified? Judge for yourself. Full marks for persistence on the part of the interviewer, but perhaps that persistence could have been better placed in seeking answers to questions designed to elicit information rather than to invoke the other man's wrath. In the end it was a victory on points for Mr Scargill, but one which was unlikely to popularize either him or his cause or do much to enhance the reputation of live broadcasting.

Strangely though; however disastrous it may have sounded, it *did* make compelling radio . . .

Hard news

The hard news interview is usually short, to the point, and to illustrate a bulletin or news item. It deals only with important facts, or comment and reaction to those facts.

Let us set up a scenario to see how this and other types of interview apply:

> A cruise liner is in trouble 80 miles out to sea with a fire apparently out of control in the engine room. You have the coastguard on the phone and he is prepared to be interviewed. Once the name of the ship, the number on board, her destination, her point of departure, and the name of her owners are established for the cue material, the questions to the coastguard would be:
>
> - *How bad is the fire?*
> - *How did it start?*
> - *Has anyone been hurt?*
> - *How can the fire be prevented from spreading?*
> - *How safe are the passengers?*
> - *What about the crew?*
> - *Are they likely to have to abandon ship?*
> - *What steps are being taken to rescue them? etc.*

The answer which will illustrate the news will be the strongest to emerge from these key questions. Important facts and background will be given in the cue, while more detail and explanation will go into the programme-length interview of between two and three minutes.

There is no reason to settle for interviewing the coastguard if there is a chance of raising the crew of the ship by radio telephone. A first-hand account from the people at the centre of a story is always preferable, though here the crew would almost certainly be too busy fighting the fire to talk.

Informational

The informational interview is similar to the hard news interview, but need not be restricted to major stories. Informational interviews can be about *events* – something that is happening or about to happen.

It can also provide *background*. Returning to the cruise liner story, an interview could be set up with the station's shipping correspondent, who would probably be a freelance with specialist knowledge. He/she would be asked about the whole issue of accidents at sea, with questions such as:

- *What is the normal procedure for abandoning ship?*
- *How safe is this?*
- *How long before the passengers could be picked up?*
- *Would they suffer from exposure in these weather conditions?*

Broadening to:

- *Just how safe is travelling by sea these days?*
- *How does it compare with air travel? etc.*

Informational interviews go beyond the main point to explain the facts: the *how* and *why* of the story. As such they tend to produce better extended features than short bulletin items.

Investigative

The investigative interview aims to get behind the facts to discover what *really* caused events and sometimes what could be done to prevent a recurrence.

This kind of interview can run and run and often forms the basis of a documentary.

Assuming with the above story you discover there has been a recent spate of accidents involving cruise liners, and this is the second vessel belonging to that shipping line to have caught fire within three months; then your next step would be to raise this with the owners.

With investigative interviews it is only sensible not to put your prey to flight by scaring them off with your first question, so the interview would be conducted something like this:

- *How did the fire break out?*
- *How quickly was it discovered?*
- *Why weren't the crew able to control it?*
- *When was the ship last checked for safety?*
- *What problems were discovered then?*
- *How would you describe your safety record?*
- *This is your second liner to have caught fire in three months . . . how do you account for that?*

At this stage it is likely the interview will rapidly move from being investigative into the category below:

Adversarial

No one likes to be cross-examined or have his/her motives questioned, so frequently this type of interview can turn into a war of words between the two parties as the interviewer tries to get the other to admit to things that he/she really does not want to say. The interview might continue:

- *Some people might see two fires in three months as negligence on your part. How would you answer that?*
- *Would you agree that your safety standards need looking into?*
- *What plans do you have for improving those safety standards? etc.*

And if it turned out that the crew had been unable to control the fire because they had set sail five hands down owing to a severe outbreak of flu back in port, the right and proper questions to ask would be:

- *Why was the ship permitted to sail with too few crewmen to deal with an emergency?*
- *Some would say this action put your ship and your passenger's lives in jeopardy. How would you answer that?*
- *What disciplinary action do you plan to take against the captain who authorized the sailing? etc.*

But beware . . . The adversarial approach should never be seen to be a head-on clash between the interviewer and the interviewee. The reporter is representing the audience or speaking up on behalf of public opinion. Even the question above about risking the safety of passengers and ship begins: '*Some would say . . .*'

A head-on clash can have disastrous consquences and produce allegations of victimization and bias (see the interview with Arthur Scargill earlier in this chapter). And if this happens it can shift public sympathy away from the reporter and towards the 'victim'.

Adversarial interviews run the greatest risk of a libel suit. This is where a person who has had something damaging said about him/her seeks compensation in the courts. As a journalist opening your mouth before thinking could prove to be your costliest mistake.

By nature, the adversarial interview attempts to undermine or disprove an argument by direct and public confrontation. The atmosphere may get heated, but the professional should always resist getting hot under the collar. In the heat of the moment it is too easy to say something disparaging or harmful to an interviewee.

The adversarial approach comes and goes with fashion, but should only be used where appropriate. There is really no excuse for cross-examining a welfare organization about plans for a new orphanage, unless the proposal really *does* smack of corruption. If the adversarial approach is used indiscriminately it could provoke a backlash and more calls to curtail the freedom of the media.

Interpretative There are two prongs to the interpretative interview: the first is the *reaction* story – a response either for or against what has happened; the second is an *explanation* of events.

Both approaches offer a perspective on what has taken place, and put the event into context. By bringing an issue into the light it is possible to examine it more closely.

Reaction is frequently stronger and more effective when it comes from someone who is personally involved.

Analysis, *explanation* or *interpretation* comes best from an expert eye far enough away from the story to remain objective.

Our shipping correspondent in the example above fits that bill exactly. He/she could ask:

- *How will this accident affect public confidence in sea travel?*
- *Do the safety laws need tightening up? If so, how?*
- *What provision is there in maritime law for setting sail without an adequate or healthy crew?*
- *What cover does travel insurance offer passengers?*

Personal (Figure 15) This might be a short interview with someone well-known about themselves, or a longer, more inquisitive and intentionally revealing *personality profile*. Among the best of this breed is Radio 4's *In the Psychiatrist's Chair* which talks to well known people from different walks of life, and attempts to get beneath their skins to find out, not *what* they do, but *why* they do it, what drives and motivates them and what in their past has

Figure 15 Vietnam revisited. Location interview with a woman who was hit by napalm and survived. Personal interviews require sympathetic interviewers. Relaxing the interviewee and winning her confidence are essential (courtesy ITN)

made them the people they are today? In short, what makes them tick?

The interview is intimate and penetrating. To lower a person's guard to the point where they become vulnerable and yet still secure enough with the interviewer to answer questions such as '*Do you believe in God*?' and '*Have you ever wanted to take your own life*?', requires the interviewer to combine the insight of a psychiatrist with the empathy of a priest at the confessional. It can make fascinating listening.

Emotional

The emotional interview is an attempt to lay bare someone's feelings, to enable an audience to share in a personal tragedy or moving event. The emotional interview springs from the personal interview, above, and is perhaps the most sensitive area of reporting. It is dealing with a subject's inner self, an area into which the media too frequently trespasses uninvited.

Returning to our stricken cruise liner: time has passed, the fire has proved impossible to contain and the captain has been left with no option but to give the cry, '*Abandon ship*!'. Fortunately, rescue vessels were already at the scene and the passengers, bedraggled and nearing exhaustion, are starting to come ashore.

The reporter is at the quayside with the instruction to get the *human angle*.

Closing in on the first of the passengers, a woman who is weary but obviously greatly relieved to be setting foot on terra firma, he asks:

- *How does it feel to be back on dry land?*
- *Were you able to save any of your possessions?*
- *When did you first realize the fire was out of control?*
- *How did the passengers react to the news? etc.*

Mercifully, the reporter has remembered that the hackneyed and crass '*How do you feel*?' should only be asked to let us share in someone's relief or happiness, never their tragedy or misfortune. (See also privacy, page 167.)

For emotional interviews the rule is to tread carefully when your foot is on somebody's heart, and then only walk where you have been given the right of way.

Entertainment

The entertainment factor often plays a part in attracting and keeping an audience. The entertainment interview looks at the lighter side of life, the things that make us smile. If, on board the liner, a troupe of dancing girls had kept people's spirits up when the flames were spreading amidships by doing the can-can, then that is entertainment and the reporter who sneers at that angle is likely to get a roasting when he/she returns.

Actuality only

This is where the reporter's voice is removed from the interview, leaving only the interviewee. The technique is occasionally used to good effect in documentary or feature making, but is harder to master than it sounds.

The skill lies in building up a clear storyline which needs no narration to prop it up and in asking questions which prompt the interviewee to give all the information that would normally arise as background in the question.

Wrong approach:
Interviewer: *'Where were you when the fire broke out?'*
Passenger: *'At the bar.'*
Interviewer: *'Who told you?'*
Passenger: *'The steward.'*
Interviewer: *'What was your reaction?'*
Passenger: *'I didn't take it seriously. I thought they'd manage to put it out.'*

Better:
Interviewer: *'Could you tell us where you were when the fire broke out, how you got to hear about it, and what your reaction was?'*

Passenger: *'I was at the bar with half a dozen others, when the Steward came in and told us fire had broken out in the engine room. We didn't think much of it. We were sure they'd put it out. But we didn't know how wrong we were.'*

With this technique multiple questions are often required to get a good flow of answers. The interview will usually have to be worked out in advance with the interviewee, and several retakes might be necessary to get the important background while still sounding conversational and natural. (See also vérite page 103.)

Telephone or remote

Interviews may be carried out on the phone or with a subject who is speaking from a remote studio. Remote studios are linked to the mother station by cables, microwave or satellite, offering studio quality sound for radio, and combining sound with vision for TV. (See also page 237.)

The poor sound quality of phone lines mean phone interviews should be avoided where it is possible to record the interview or get the interviewee into the studio. Use a phone only if you have to, and then keep the recording as short as possible.

With our earlier telephone interview with the coastguard, a clip of that would be used for the bulletin, and, to produce a longer piece, this could be combined with narrative by the reporter to cut out as much phone quality material as possible. Few listeners will trouble to strain to hear what is being said.

Vox pop and multiple

Vox pop is an abbreviation of the Latin vox populi, or '*voice of the people*'. The vox is used in broadcasting to provide a cross-section of public opinion on a given subject. In the US it is known as the '*person in the street*' interview.

The technique is to get a broad mix of opinion and different voices. Alternate between male and female, young and old. Begin and end with strong comments and make good use of humorous remarks.

Shopping precincts make a happy hunting ground, and one radio presenter was known for his regular vox about topical items which he recorded each week with the same crowd at a bus stop.

Vox pops work best where the reporter's voice is kept out as much as possible. A single question should be asked, which is introduced in the cue, and the reporter asks that question of people in turn with the recorder on pause, flipping the pause off before they answer.

Variations in background noise can make editing difficult, but recording wildtrack and using fades and retakes can go some way towards compensating for the problem. (See editing, page 224.)

Returning to our running story, if the holiday booking season is at its height, our reporter could catch people outside travel agents, and after making introductions, ask them:

> *'There's been another fire on a cruise liner, and passengers have had to abandon ship, so how does that make* ***you*** *feel about travelling by sea?*

The *multiple* interview differs from the vox by taking a smaller number of selected extracts, often drawn from longer interviews and having the reporter link them together. This is known as a *package*. (See page 199.)

Our ship saga is ideal for such treatment. Excerpts from the coastguard and the ship's owners could be mixed with comment by the shipping correspondent and glued together with narrative by the reporter.

Grabbed

Our final category concerns interviews which people do not want to give but which reporters are determined to take.

These are usually short and may comprise only one or two brief comments or a terse '*No comment!*', which is often comment enough.

Grabbed interviews are obtained by pushing a camera or microphone under the nose of a subject and firing off questions.

Our reporter has caught sight of a smoke stained uniform. It is the captain coming ashore. He seems in no mood to answer questions. Rushing over, our reporter pushes the microphone towards him and asks:

> *'How did the fire begin?'*
> (The Captain ignores him and quickens his pace. The reporter pursues and repeats his question)
>
> Captain: *'It began in the engine room . . . overheating we think.'*
>
> Reporter: *'Why weren't you able to put it out?'*
>
> (No answer)
>
> Reporter: *'Could it be that there weren't enough crewmen on board?'*
>
> (Silence)
>
> Reporter: *'Why did you set sail without a full crew?'*
>
> Captain: *'No comment!'*
>
> (He is hustled forward and swallowed up inside a big black car with official number plates.)

The grabbed interview usually works best on camera, where, even if the subject says nothing, he can be watched by the audience and his reactions noted.

Frequently there are so many reporters that there is no chance to pursue a line of questioning. If you ask even one question at a free-for-all, you are doing well. Not that it matters a great deal; the mêlée and persistent refusals to answer add to the sense that here is someone with something to hide.

Grabbed interviews are often intrusions of privacy. It would be unwarranted to grab an interview with a widow after a funeral or anyone who is grieving or suffering. **Ethically, personal privacy should only be intruded upon where someone's understandable desire to be left alone runs counter to proper public interest**. That could be argued to be true of our captain. (See also page 167.)

On occasions grabbing interviews can do more harm than good. Royalty will understandably take umbrage – they will usually speak to the media by appointment only. Similar rules apply to heads of state or anyone to whom the station would rather not risk causing an offence. And as with the adversarial interview, there is always the risk of saying something libellous. Bear in mind that your unwilling subject may be only too happy to find occasion to sue you.

THE DISASTER STORY CONTINUES...

Having concluded our foray into the jungle of the interview, let us return to hear how Mr Scargill and his hapless interviewer are getting on. They are still at it...

Interviewer: *'Let's move on to something else... the meeting you're having tomorrow...'*

Scargill: *'No, I'm sorry, we're not moving on to anything until you let me put the point of view across on behalf of those that I represent.'*

Interviewer: *'I think you've put it over several times, Mr Scargill.'*

Scargill: *'... all I've done so far is to be interrupted by an ignorant man like you, who ought to have more sense...'*

Interviewer: *'Mr Scargill, we've... (sigh). Can we conduct this interview rather than having a slanging match?'*

Scargill: *'Well you started it, not me!... All that you're doing so far is to present a question and then conveniently ignore the point that I want to give by way of response.'*

Interviewer: (Struggling to get a word in) *'Let's move on to another question...'*

Perhaps it is not surprising the interview has turned out the way it has. If you can remember back to where we came in, it was with the statement that the miners were divided over following Mr Scargill, and a request that the fiery miners' leader *concede* that the strike was bitter and that '*like never before miner is pitched against miner*.'

You could hope for more success in arm wrestling a gorilla than in asking a determined and embattled interviewee whose reputation is on the line to *concede*.

Another moral of this tale might be that if you plan to fight fire with fire, then do not pitch a match against a flamethrower. If there is ever an occasion when interviewer and interviewee should be evenly pitted it is against one another in an adversarial interview.

There are signs that this interview may be just about to come to an end . . .

> **Interviewer:** *'It seems you're incapable of answering any questions, Mr Scargill.'*
>
> **Scargill:** *'It seems as though you're the most ignorant person that I've ever discussed with on radio. Now either you're going to listen to answers even though you don't like them, or you're not. It's entirely up to you.'*
>
> **Interviewer:** *'Mr Scargill, thank you for joining us and I'm afraid not answering any of our questions here in Sheffield this afternoon. This live interview with the miners' leader Arthur Scargill . . .'*
>
> **Scargill:** *'This live interview has been absolutely appalling as a result of . . .'* (He is faded out)
>
> **Interviewer:** *'Independent Radio News, it's 1.30!'*
>
> REPRODUCED BY KIND PERMISSION OF INDEPENDENT RADIO NEWS.

FIELDWORK

1 Open a file marked 'interviewing'. Keep one page for each of the twelve categories of interview above and others for notes. Watch a variety of different TV news, current affairs and magazine programmes and see if you can identify all twelve types of interview in action.

2 See if you can come up with some new categories. Watch and listen to interviews critically. Each time ask yourself whether it worked or failed, whether it was good or bad, and why. File any tips on technique you pick up.

3 If you are in a class, break into pairs, preferably with someone you do not know too well, and without any preparation conduct personality interviews with one another. Attempt to discover what makes your partner tick and find out something new about him/her. Aim to spend between ten and fifteen minutes on each interview. Afterwards, sum up in a couple of paragraphs to the class what you have discovered about your partner. If you are not in a class, find a willing subject and see how you get on.

4 That interview was conducted off the top of your head. Discuss with your partner how you could best prepare yourself and your interviewee for similar interviews in future.

5 Log every interview you do in your file in the appropriate category. Over a period of time attempt to cover all twelve categories of interview. Make notes of any difficulties you experienced doing those interviews and any helpful tips. Share your problems and advice with others and pool your knowledge.

8 Setting up the interview

News is often too immediate to allow detailed research, and news items are frequently too brief to warrant an in-depth approach. The average length of a bulletin clip on British independent radio is around 30 to 35 seconds – just enough for one or two succinct points. Even a three minute report (and many music-based stations keep interviews to *half* that length) can support only four or five questions.

Longer interviews are more frequently the province of speech-based stations and current affairs departments, though many regional TV newsrooms will produce a daily half-hour programme which takes longer items.

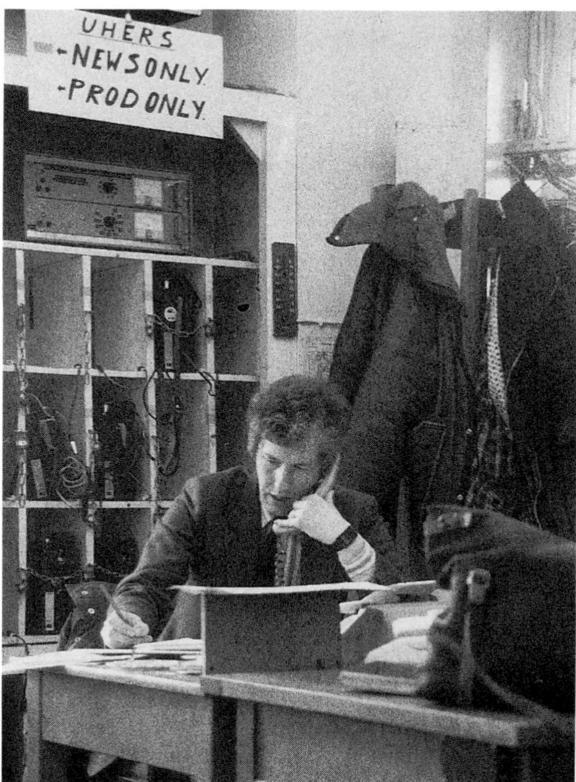

Figure 16 On the telephone . . . where most interviews begin. A few minutes spent setting up the interview correctly can save hours of time and much frustration later (Andrew Boyd)

Brevity is often cited as the reason why broadcast news is often shallow, tending to polarize issues into black and white for the sake of simplicity by removing all shades of grey. A common complaint is that broadcasters are content to deal with the *what* of the story, but seldom trouble to explain the *why* or the *how*.

BACKGROUND

But shallowness is no excuse for ignorance on the part of an interviewer. Reporters may not have time to gather background to a story, but they would be expected to carry much of that information in their heads.

Reporters should keep up to date with the stories their station is covering. Before beginning their shift, they should hear a number of bulletins, including those on rival stations, so they know what is happening that day and have a shrewd idea of the follow-ups they can expect to be given. They should also have read the local papers which have more space to give to background.

Reporters are often expected to be their own researchers constantly topping up their reservoir of knowledge about local news, so when they walk through the door and the editor says: '*Don't take your coat off . . .*' they know what to expect, and what to do next.

A PLAN OF CAMPAIGN – THE QUESTIONS

Familiarizing yourself with the story is step one. Step two is getting a clear idea of what to ask, which depends on the type of interview involved and its duration. (See the brief, page 31.)

One tip – if you are going out for a thirty-second clip, there is no point coming back with twelve minutes on tape. You would simply be laying up trouble for yourself; there will be twelve minutes to review and ten different answers to choose from. That takes time, and with hourly deadlines, time is one commodity the reporter never has to spare.

Five minutes beforehand spent thinking out the questions is worth half an hour's editing back at the station.

GET YOUR FACTS RIGHT

> Interviewer: *'Is this a plane that can run well on one engine?'*
> Interviewee: *'It runs best on one engine – that's all it has.'* – US TV

Before leaving the newsroom, make sure you have your facts right. There is nothing more embarrassing or more likely to undermine the reporter's reputation and that of his/her station than an ignorant and ill-informed line of questioning:

Reporter: *'Mr Smith, as hospital administrator, just how seriously do you view this typhoid epidemic?'*

Mr Smith: *'Hmm. I'm actually the deputy administrator, and two isolated cases hardly constitute an epidemic. Oh yes . . . and the name is* Smythe. *Now what was the question?'*

What chance of a successful interview?

Working to your brief, set up a chain of thought – a plan of campaign – by jotting down a few questions and arranging them in logical order. Sometimes the mind becomes clearer when its contents are spilled on to paper. Even if you never refer to your notes this can be a worthwhile exercise.

FIT THE BRIEF

Be mindful that whatever you ask has to fit the angle and length required by the brief and the result has to be relevant to your audience. Beware of leaping off at tangents that might interest you or a like-minded minority, but would be irrelevant to the majority. Keep to the point.

Let us take a bread and butter story and assume that the fire service has been called to a fire in an apartment block. It is serious and the flats have been evacuated. You go to the scene to talk to the chief fire officer. If your brief is to produce a thirty second clip then you have space for one line of questioning only. Human life is always more important than property, so your first question must be: *Has anyone been hurt?*

If the answer is *yes*, then the next question has to be *Who?*, followed by, *What happened to them?*, and that should be enough.

Whatever you do, do not follow the lead of one local radio reporter who began every interview regardless of the story with the same question: '*Tell me about it . . .*'. Leave that opener to doctors, psychiatrists and others who are paid by the hour.

CHECK ARRANGEMENTS

If time is of the essence, then no reporter can afford to waste it by heading the wrong way down a motorway or arriving at the wrong address. Arriving late for an interview only raises everybody's blood pressure. Check the arrangements before leaving and allow plenty of time to get there. Directions can be sorted out by telephone when the interview is being set up. At the same time you can get enough information to leave a brief story to tide the newsroom over until you return with your pictures or audio.

If you are working for radio, check your portable recorder before you leave. This is basic, yet often forgotten in the rush. One of my reporters interviewed a government minister then tried to play it back only to find there was no tape in the machine. Astonishingly, he agreed to wait while she returned to the station to get another reel and redo the interview. Another reporter grabbed a machine to cover a fire but found he could get no level on the meters. His batteries were not flat – there were no batteries in the machine. **Check it out before you take it out.** A comprehensive test takes less than a minute and can save hours. (For more details see portable recorders, page 214.)

Don't forget to take a spare tape and batteries.

APPROACH

Many young reporters, anxious to make a name for themselves, have to be reminded every now and again of the need not to promote their own careers at the expense of the station and its valuable contacts. Where the reporter comes face to face with the influential, want of a little wisdom can cause a great deal of damage.

It is old hat (but the hat fits too well to throw it away) to say that each reporter is an ambassador for his/her radio or TV station. How you look and conduct yourself can make or break a station's reputation.

Stations have different approaches to dress. Some permit an informal, even sloppy style, others insist on staff being suit-smart. First impressions matter. What your clothes and manner say about you in the first two seconds may affect the whole interview. A business suit might lose some interviews in a downtown area, where a casual style would be more credible, but if your news trade is with business people and politicians then dress to suit . . . in a suit.

How you deal with your contacts will have a lot to do with whether you keep them as contacts in the future. National reporters are often the bane of a local newsroom. Sometimes they don't seem to care whose toes they tread on as long as they get their story. As one local news editor put it: '*They don't have to live with their contacts . . . we do!*'

Pre-chat

> *'I must say, I get rather nervous before these sort of interviews, my particular fear is that I'll dry up.'* – MARK TULLY, BBC BUREAU CHIEF INDIA, ON HIS WAY TO INTERVIEW THE INDIAN PRIME MINISTER RAJIV GHANDI.*
>
> *'If they're frightened it's a matter of just talking to them beforehand, joking with them and putting them at their ease. Usually I say how I keep making mistakes as well, and then I fluff a question, and say, "I'm sorry about that!" Although you go in as a professional, you can't be too aloof, because people won't* talk *to you. It's got to be a conversation, and* you *have to start it.'* – ROB McKENZIE, PRODUCER/PRESENTER CAPITAL RADIO

Almost as important as the interview itself is the pre-chat. This is when reporter and subject establish a rapport, and the reporter sounds out the course he/she has charted for the interview.

Even if your deadline is only fifteen minutes away, your manner must be calm and relaxed, polite yet assertive but never aggressive. Approach is all-important. If the interviewee is inexperienced and nervous he/she will need to be relaxed and put at ease. Conversely, nothing is more unsettling than a nervous interviewer. Even if your adrenal gland is running riot, you must cover your trepidation with a polished performance.

A pleasant greeting, a firm handshake and a good deal of *eye-contact* is the best way to begin, with a clear statement about who you are and which radio or TV station you represent.

Eye-contact can work wonders for calming the other's nerves. A key contact at one radio station was the naval base's Port Admiral. Whenever it was necessary to interview him groans went up from the newsroom. He had an appalling s.s.s.s.stammer. Even a short bulletin clip would take an age to edit, and he could never be used for longer features. One day a

**See it for Yourself*, BBC, 1987

reporter discovered the knack of stopping that stammer. He fixed him in the eye and smiled all the time the admiral was speaking and the stammer just melted away.

Never rehearse an interview, just discuss it. Repeats of interviews are like second-hand cars – they lose their pace and their sparkle. Even nervous interviewees usually perform better when the adrenalin is flowing. Agree to a run-through only if you think there is no other way to calm your interviewee's nerves, but make sure your tape or camera is rolling. Then, if the 'rehearsal' goes well, you can ask the first few questions again when you sense they are into their stride and suggest dispensing with the retake. An alternative is to warm them up with some minor questions before getting down to the nitty-gritty.

Humour can effectively bring down the barriers, a joke or quip at the reporter's expense can often relax an interviewee and lower his/her defences, but obviously humour cannot be forced.

Beware also of putting up barriers. Even if you intend your interview to be adversarial, don't size up to your guest like a hungry lion to an antelope. To put it another way, every boxer knows that the best punches are delivered when his opponent's guard is down.

Body language

Body language is also important. The way we sit, how we cross our legs and arms, reveals a lot about how we feel. If your interviewee is sitting legs crossed and arms folded, then you know he/she is on the defensive and needs to be relaxed. If the reporter is cowering in the corner, while the interviewee is leaning back exuding confidence, then something has gone badly wrong indeed!

Discussing the questions

Once you have established rapport, done your spadework and checked the important facts, you are ready to draw up your plan of action before beginning the recording.

Be careful. Some interviewees, particularly those who have been 'caught out' at some time, may want to take control of the interview. Do not let them. If they say they will only answer from a set list of questions, then politely but firmly tell them you do not work that way – you prefer to be free to respond to the answers. If they request not to be asked a certain question then try to steer around that without making any promises. Conversely, interviewees may want to answer from notes or a script. Do not let them. It will sound 'read' and artificial. Reassure them they will come across better without them and that any mistakes can always be retaken. Discussing your first question may help to relax your guest and if the interview is more probing, that first question can be a dummy which you can edit out later.

If the interview is non-controversial and there are no conflicts of interest you can save editing time by outlining your questions and discussing the answers you are looking for. As Capital Radio's Rob McKenzie puts it: '*What I need is ninety seconds, so I will ask you these four questions, and your reply will be something like this . . . Yes?*'

This 'staged-managed' approach will only work where all the key facts of the story are clearly exposed beforehand and both parties agree on the angle. The biggest dangers here are reporters playing their aces before the interview begins or putting words into their interviewee's mouth.

At all times beware of conflicts of interest and be assertive but always courteous. Remember, *you* are in charge. The BBC advises its fledgeling reporters to adopt an attitude of 'informed naivete' – in other words, be a wolf in sheep's clothing.

If you are unsure about the subject it can help to let your interviewee chat about it beforehand so you can be clear you are heading in the right direction.

Beware of letting the pre-chat drag on for so long that the adrenalin dies and the conversation gets stale. It should continue just long enough to explore the topic, establish a direction and relax the interviewee.

THE QUESTIONS

(Figure 17)

> **Interviewer:** ***'Minister, why aren't you getting home to women?'***
> **Minister:** ***'Could you rephrase that?'*** – BRITISH TV
>
> ***'If I said that, I was misquoted.'*** – LORD HANSON ON THE WORLD AT ONE, RADIO 4

Our thoughts so far have been confined to the preparations for the match, the warm-up and the strategy. Now on to the tactics for the match itself – the questions.

There is more to the art of interviewing than developing the ability to engage complete strangers in intelligent conversation. **Good questions produce good answers.** The secret is to think ahead to the answers you are likely to get before asking your questions.

Using notes

Most interviewers would agree that preparing questions is constructive in planning the interview, but sticking closely to a list of written questions can be unhelpful during the course of the interview itself. The problems are:

- Eye contact is lost.
- When the interviewer is concentrating on the questions, he/she is unable to listen to the interviewee.
- Fixed questions make for an inflexible interview.

If you intend to use notes, use them sparingly. Write out the first question *only if you have to* to get the interview off to a good start. Complex questions are seldom a good idea, but if the form of words is critical then write the question down.

Write legibly. Preferably do not write at all – type. If you have to pause to decipher your handwriting you will lose the flow.

Perhaps the best compromise between maintaining rapport and keeping the interview on course is to make brief notes or headings of important points only. These should be sufficient to jog the memory without breaking concentration.

Figure 17 ITN reporter Jane Corbin conducts one of the last interviews with Mrs Indira Ghandi before she was assassinated (courtesy ITN)

Ask questions that will get answers

The *who*, *what*, *when*, *where*, *why* and *how* framework for writing copy applies equally to the news interview and the type of questions the interviewer should ask.

No reporter wants to be left with a series of monosyllabic grunts on tape, so questions should be carefully structured to produce good useful quotes rather than one word comments.

- The question *who* calls for a name in response,
- *What* asks for a description,
- *When* pins down the timing of an event,
- *Where* locates it,
- *Why* asks for an interpretation or an explanation,
- *How* asks for an opinion or an interpretation.

Questions beginning with these words will propel the interview forward and yield solid facts:

- '*Who* was hurt in the crash?'
- '*What* caused the accident?'
- '*When* did it happen?'
- '*Where* did the accident occur?'
- '*Why* did it take so long to free the trapped passengers?'
- '*How* did you manage to get them out?'

Yes/no questions

Inexperienced reporters often fall into the trap of asking questions that produce *yes/no* answers. They may come away with some idea of the story, but will seldom have anything on tape worth using.

Sometimes though, a yes or a no answer is required to establish a fact that will open the way for a new line of questioning:

Interviewer: *'In the light of today's street violence, do you plan to step up police patrols?'*

Police chief: *'No, we think that would be unhelpful.'*

Interviewer: *'Why?'*

Police chief: *'It could be taken as provocation, etc.'*

Less artful interviewers are sometimes tempted to ask a yes/no question in the hope that it will prompt their guest to do the work for them and develop a new line of argument:

Interviewer: *'Critics would say the plan to put a factory on the green land site is ill-conceived. Would you agree?'*

Developer: *'No, of course not. The design is modern and attractive and will bring many much needed jobs to the area.'*

That time the technique worked. More often than not, it does not:

Interviewer: *'Critics would say the plan to put a factory on the green land site is ill-conceived. Would you agree?'*

Developer: *'No.'*

Interviewer: *'Why not?'*

Developer: *'Well how could you expect me to agree to that... I'm the one who's building the darn thing!'.*

Using the question this way encourages a non-answer, or worse still, permits the interviewee to pick up on the 'yes' or 'no' in whatever way he/she wishes and head off on a tangent. The interviewer should always try to keep the whip hand.

Avoid questions that call for monologues

The opposite of the yes/no question, but which can have the same effect, is the question which is so wide its scope is almost unlimited:

Interviewer: *'As a leading clean-up campaigner, what do you think is wrong with porn shops and peep shows anyway?'*

Leave your tape recorder running and come back in an hour when she has finished! Pin the question to one clearly defined point:

'Whats the ***main*** *reason you're opposed to these porn shops?'*

Or: *'Which peep shows in* ***particular*** *do you want cleaned up?'*

Question scope is important. Make it too narrow and your interview runs like a car which keeps on stalling. Open it up too wide and it can run away from you.

Short, single idea questions

> Interviewer: *'Now obviously, er, Reverend, you don't like the idea of, em, these prep. schools being used as, em, fashionable schools for middle class parents, but, em, y... d-do you really think that i-i-it matters whether or not they* believe *– the parents themselves – in-in a Christian education as such. I mean, would you be happy if they particularly wanted and believed that the Christian, em, or th-the-the Anglic... the Anglican sort of education was right for their kids, would you like to see the church schools remain in that case, as long as you were convinced of their sincerity, rather than of the fact that they were doing it simply because it was a middle class fashionable thing to do?'*
>
> Reverend: *'That's a very good question. I don't know.'* – UK RADIO

If a question is to be understood by both the audience and the interviewee it has to be kept clear, simple and straightforward, unlike this example:

> Interviewer: *'Coming back to your earlier point about owners who get rid of their pets, don't you think there should be some kind of sanction, I mean, some sort of measure or something, against owners who dump their unwanted pets, as happens so frequently after Christmas, when they get given them as presents and find they didn't really want a pet after all?'*
>
> Animal welfare spokesman: *'Em, well, er, I'm not exactly sure what you've got in mind...'*

Cotton wool, by the sounds of it. Try:

> Interviewer: *'What penalty would you like to see against owners who dump their unwanted pets?'*

Keep the threads of the argument untangled and stick to one point at a time.

Progress from point to point

To maintain the logic of the interview each question should naturally succeed the previous one. If the interviewer needs to refer back to a point, this should be done neatly and followed through by another question that progresses the argument:

> Interviewer: *'Going back to owners who dump their pets after Christmas, would you like to see some form of penalty imposed against them?'*
>
> Animal welfare spokesman: *'We most certainly would.'*
>
> Interviewer: *'What have you got in mind?'*

Building bridges

Each question should arise naturally from the previous answer. If the two points are only distantly related the interviewer should use a bridge, as in the question above. Another example is this from interviewer Michael Parkinson, talking to Oscar-winning actor Ben Kingsley on Radio 4's

Desert Island Discs:

> Parkinson: *'Then I suppose after getting the academy award for best actor in **Ghandi** you must have been offered an enormous range of parts. What parts were you offered?'*

Avoid double questions

The interviewer should ask one question at a time, otherwise a wily subject will be able to choose which to answer, and which to ignore. Even the most willing of subjects may forget one half of the question:

> **Bad question:** *'What form will your demonstration take, and do you think County Hall will take any notice?'*
>
> **Better:** *'What kind of demonstration do you plan to put on?'*

Following the answer with:

> *'What effect do you think it'll have on the views of county councillors?'*

Keep the questions relevant

An interview is not a mental exercise. Like news, it deals with matters concerning real life. As we said earlier, one of the problems with talking to experts in any field, is they are liable to speak in abstractions or jargon. **The point of relevance to the audience is the point that needs bringing out above all.**

As with news writing, examples should be concrete and real. If you begin by asking how high inflation will rise, be sure to follow it up with a question about whether wages and salaries are likely to keep pace or what it will do to the price of bread.

If it is a question about inner city poverty, do not just talk about living standards, ask about the food these people eat or get a description of their homes.

Get away from the abstract and relate ideas to everyday realities.

Avoid leading questions

A leading question is one designed to lead interviewees into a corner and trap them there. More often it has the effect of boxing-in the reporter with allegations of malice, bias and unfair play.

Take the example of an interview with an elderly farmer who was seriously burnt trying to save his photograph album from his blazing house:

> Interviewer: *'Why did you attempt such a foolhardy and dangerous stunt over a worthless photograph album. Surely that's taking sentimentality* too *far?'*

This question, like most leading questions, was based on assumptions:

- Saving the album was stupid.
- It was dangerous.
- The album was worthless.
- The farmer's motive was sentimental.
- And that a sentimental reason was not a valid one.

But assumptions can prove to be false:

Farmer: *'My wife died three years ago. I kept all my most precious things together. The deeds to my house and all my land were inside that album with the only pictures I had of my wife. It was kept in the living room, which was away from the flames. I thought I had time to pull it out, but in my hurry I fell over and blacked out. Now I've lost everything.'*

The scorn of the audience would quickly shift from the farmer to the callous interviewer.

If somebody is stupid or wrong or to blame, draw out the evidence through polite and sensitive interviewing and leave the audience to pass judgement.

Bad question: *'You knew the car's brakes were faulty when you rented it to Mr Brown, didn't you? The car crashed, he's in hospital and it's your fault. How do you feel about that?'*

Better:

1 *When did you find out the car's brakes were faulty?'*
2 *'But later that morning, before the brakes could be repaired, didn't you rent it out to another customer?'*
3 *'Weren't you worried there could be an accident?'*
4 *'How do you feel now your car is written off and your customer, Mr Brown, is in hospital?'*

Expose the fallacy of an argument, not by putting words into a person's mouth, but by letting the evidence and his own words condemn him.

Leading questions are frowned on by the courts. The same should go for interviews.

Mixing statements with questions

Sometimes it is necessary to give some background information before coming to the question. The question and the information should be kept separate for the sake of clarity, and the question at the end should be brief:

First commentator: *'So, for the fourth time in a row the Lions have romped home with a clear victory, and are now standing an astonishing eleven points clear at the top of the table. Manager Bill Fruford, tell us, what's the secret?'*

Avoid statements posing as questions:

Second commentator: *'With me here is manager John Turnbull who's team's performance crumpled completely in the last five minutes, with the Lions making all the running over a dispirited side.'*

Turnbull: (silence)

Commentator: *'Mr Turnbull?'*

Turnbull: *'Sorry, you talking to me? What was the question?'*

When he passed the ball to the manager the commentator lost possession, but leaving go like that, especially after such a disparaging account of the team's performance, is leaving the commentator's own defences wide open. The manager could have said anything he wanted as no direct question had been asked of him. As it was, because of the phrasing of the question, the manager was not even aware the ball had been passed to him.

Beware of questions that would be out of date

If the interview is being pre-recorded, remember to say nothing that would render the item out of date. If the piece is to go out next Wednesday, avoid:

'Well, Mr Wilson, what's your reaction to today's events?'

Similarly, watch the changeovers from morning to afternoon, afternoon to evening, evening to night, night to morning. The safest position is to drop any time reference from a story or an interview. Broadcast news is about immediacy. Even an only slightly out of date time reference can make that news sound stale.

Avoid sounding ignorant

Always check your facts before you launch into an interview. Clear up details like the following during the pre-chat:

Interviewer: *'Mr Schaeffer, why have you decided to sack half your workforce?'*

Mr Schaeffer: *'They have not been sacked.'*

Interviewer: *'You deny it?'*

Mr Schaeffer: *'What has happened is that their contracts have expired and have not been renewed. And it's not half the workforce, it's 125 staff out of a total of 400.'*

Interviewer: (Sheepishly) *'Oh.'*

If you are not in the full picture, get filled in before the interview begins, but remember, as soon as you rely on your interviewees for background, you are putting them in a position where they can manipulate the interview to their advantage.

WINDING UP THE INTERVIEW

The words '*and finally*' are best avoided during an interview, as a point may arise which may beg a further question or clarification, and saying 'and finally' twice always sounds a little foolish.

Other phrases such as '*Briefly . .*' or '*One last point*' may also serve as wind up signals if necessary. Save your gestures and handsignals for experienced studio staff (Figure 18).

Finish strongly

An interview should go out with a bang and never a whimper. It should end in a way that gives the whole performance a bold and emphatic full stop.

Recorded interviews should not end with '*Thank you very much Miss Smith*'. Save your thank-yous for rounding off live interviews and handing back to a presenter.

Figure 18 *The Budget Programme.* One of the toughest jobs in radio – chairing a live, round-the-table discussion in the talks studio while news is still breaking. Split-second timing, a cool head and an ability to concentrate on several tasks at once are minimum requirements (Andrew Boyd)

If during a live interview a guest insists on going on over her time, then do not be afraid to butt in with a polite, '*Well, I'm afraid we must stop there,*' or '*That's all we've got time for, Miss Smith, thank you very much.*' And if she refuses to take the hint, it is the job of the producer to switch off the microphone and usher her out.

BEING INTERVIEWED YOURSELF: THE Q & A

Sometimes the tables get turned on reporters and they find themselves having to answer the questions. If they have been covering a major breaking story, such as an air crash or a gas explosion, they will have expert knowledge and the advantage of being available.

'Q & A' stands for *question and answer*. Reporters, hot foot from the air crash, may be invited to break into normal programming to give the audience a first hand account of events. If they have been covering the story live the station can cross to them at the scene for description as well as background.

The *questions* will be scripted by reporters. It would be pointless leaving the line of questioning to a music presenter who has little idea what has been going on, or ask them qustions they cannot answer.

The *answers* should not be scripted, though. Unless they were experienced actors their conversation would sound almost as artificial as interviewees who insisted on reading from a statement.

With unscripted pieces there is always a danger of repetition or hesitation. Beware of this. Under nerves, people often say too much or too little. Keep a check on yourself and say just enough to fill the allocated time with solid details and interesting information without resorting to filler, bulk, or repetition.

Introducing actuality

If the Q & A is with a radio reporter live at the scene, that reporter may want to introduce some actuality, such as an interview recorded earlier with a witness or an official. If you are using reel to reel tape, this should be rough-edited on the machine, cued-up ready to go and introduced in the same way as any news interview. For a smooth production, it would be better to have that interviewee beside you when you go live. (See also story treatment, page 200.)

FIELDWORK

1 Listen to (and record if possible) a number of interviews on radio and TV and list the questions that were asked in each.

What proportion of the questions were of the *who*, *what*, *when*, *where*, *why* and *how* variety? Do all the questions follow on from one another? If not, why not? Does each interview follow a logical thread? Where do you think the interviewer has deviated from his/her planned list of questions to pick up on one of the interviewee's answers? Can you pick out any *bridging* questions or *double* questions? Are there any *leading* questions? If so, how do you react to them? Are there any badly phrased questions? How would you rephrase them? Do the interviews finish strongly? If not, how could they have been edited to give them a more definite conclusion?

2 Below are four scenarios. Draw up a list of five questions for each which would adequately cover those stories:

- A fire in a hotel where three people are trapped.
- The announcement of a major new contract at a steelworks.
- The launch of an outrageous fashion range by a local designer.
- A blind man who is planning to climb a mountain.

3 Interview simulation: taking control

This is a power game requiring two players. One plays the reporter and the other the interviewee. The story is about a landlord who has bought houses that are due for demolition and is letting them to tenants who he is keeping in squalor for profit.

The story concerns eight houses in Bridge Street split into single and double rooms, some are in need of repair and all are badly inadequate.

The landlord, Albert Smith, is leasing the houses cheaply from the local authority and charging high rents. The tenants are mainly poor immigrants. A shortage of rented accommodation means they have to stay there or become homeless. They have complained about the squalid conditions which they say are to blame for the constant ill-health of some of their children.

The reporter's brief is to interview the landlord to expose what is happening and, in a manner that is both fair and reasonable, call him to account. The landlord's aim is to defend his reputation and show himself up in the best possible light. If the local authority accepts the case against him, he could lose his houses. The central plank of his defence is that the immigrants would be homeless without him, and he knows that if the local authority ruled his houses uninhabitable, they would then have the responsibility of housing the immigrants.

The reporter has one constraint upon him – if the landlord disputes any facts that are not included in this brief, the reporter must not be dogmatic about them.

Both parties should finish reading this brief and then re-read it. The reporter should then spend up to five minutes privately thinking up questions, in which time the interviewee should anticipate the questions that would be asked and prepare a defence.

The exercise is one of control. Both parties want the interview to go ahead, though both are hoping for a different outcome. Each should try to take charge and to bend the interview to his own purposes – one to expose the facts, the other to gloss over them and turn them to his advantage by making them seem more acceptable.

If you have recording equipment, record the interview. Conduct it preferably in front of a small audience of classmates who can later offer constructive criticism. You have fifteen minutes to conduct the pre-chat and the interview.

4 Afterwards discuss the interview. Who came out on top and why? How did the reporter attempt to expose the facts and how did the landlord try to cover them up? How did each side feel about the attempts to manipulate him during the interview? Were the right questions asked? How did you resolve differences in opinion about the facts of the story. What did the audience think?

5 Interview simulation: Q & A
There has been a serious accident on a main highway from town. Several cars are involved and some people have died. You are at the scene of the crash and your station wants to conduct a live interview with you about what you have seen. Imagine the scene and work out a scenario, then draw up a list of questions for the presenter. You should have enough material to stay on air for three minutes. If you are in a class, find someone to be the presenter and go ahead with the Q & A.

9 From 2 minute headlines to 24 hour news

> *'Give us 22 minutes, we'll give you the world'*
> – SLOGAN OF WESTINGHOUSE ALL NEWS RADIO

News programmes come in almost as many shapes and sizes as the people who present them, from two-minute headline summaries to 24 hours of non-stop news. As broadcasting develops new forms of expression and the choice of programmes continues to grow, news is having to be marketed in increasingly diverse ways to continue to win audiences accustomed to greater choice. With cable and satellite television has come greater specialization. Viewers can now stay tuned to one channel all day without glimpsing a headline, or watch wall-to-wall news if the fancy takes them. And as news programmes get longer, the distinction between news and entertainment becomes more blurred, with keep-fit spots, recipe slots and even horoscopes juggling for position amid the more usual news fare.

Figure 19 Reading the extended news summary at BBC Radio Solent (Andrew Boyd)

THE BULLETIN

In the UK, the brief news summary is known as a bulletin. In the US, *bulletin* may refer to a one-item snap of breaking news, while in UK terms, that would be known as a newsflash. The UK definitions apply here.

The bulletin is a snapshot of the day's news at a point in time and is usually on air from three to five minutes. Individual items are kept deliberately short – usually under a minute – so a good number of stories can be packed in. TV bulletins may be illustrated with film footage and stills, known as *visuals*, while radio bulletins may use voice reports and interview extracts (*actualities*). Or, the bulletin may be read straight without any illustrations, the technique favoured by the BBC World Service (Figure 19).

NEWS PROGRAMMES

News programmes usually aim to provide a broader view of the day's news, summarizing the best stories of the day, instead of the hour. Length usually ranges from 20 to 60 minutes. Items are generally longer and more detailed than those in a bulletin, and more sophisticated, using actualities or film footage, stills and graphics. Some shorter stories may also be incorporated to increase the breadth of coverage. If a programme is to gain audience loyalty, it will have to establish a clear identity and have a greater balance and variety of material than a bulletin. (See establishing programme identity, page 117.)

DOCUMENTARY

The documentary deals with a topical issue or subject in depth, and is less dependent on a *news peg* – some immediate and newsworthy occurrence taking place before that subject can be aired. Documentaries usually last between 30 minutes and an hour and will cover a single subject or a small number of issues.

Documentary styles vary from straightforward reportage to dramatized documentary and *vérite* techniques (also known as *direct* or *actuality* reporting). The *drama documentary* makes use of actors to reconstruct events and conversations. The use of drama inevitably requires a degree of speculation and is a further smudging of the margins between fact and fiction, producing what is sometimes disparagingly referred to as *faction*.

VÉRITE

Vérite techniques try to get as close to the untainted truth as possible, by doing away with the narrator, chopping out all the questions and linking the various interviews and actualities so it seem as though no reporter was present. The intention is to produce a purer piece of journalism, closer to reality for being untainted by the presence and preconceptions of the reporter. But this is, of course, an illusion.

The reporter's influence, though unseen or unheard, is perhaps greater than ever, for a good deal of skilful setting-up and manipulation is required to get the interviewees to tell the story so it appears to be telling itself, without requiring linking narrative. Interviewees have to be primed to provide answers that effectively encapsulate the unheard questions so listeners can follow the drift.

Where it succeeds, vérite paints a picture which is closer to the subject and more intimate, giving the impression of looking in on somebody's life unobserved. Where it fails, it can be both contrived and confusing and a self-inflicted handicap to story-telling. Vérite is best used where solid information is less important than atmosphere, such as a day in the life of an inmate at a prison, or this psychotherapy session below.

Psychotherapist: *'If you could place a flower on your mother's grave . . . what flower would you take?'*

Alan: *'A rose.'*

Psychotherapist: *'A rose. Well, let me give you a rose. Take it. What colour would it be?'*

Alan: *'Red.'*

Psychotherapist: *'Red. Take the rose in your hand. You're doing fine. Right? Come and place it. And if you could have been responsible for writing something on her tombstone, what would you have written?'*

Alan: *'I love and forgive you.'*

Psychotherapist: *'Just take this hand for a moment. I want you to be held in the way you were never held as a kid. No? You can't do that.'*

Alan: *'You're going to get me all lovey dovey and then they're just gonna kick me in the teeth.'*

Psychotherapist: *'What's your fear of being held, Alan?'*

Alan: *'. . . being loved, and having that love and trust thrown back in my face. And to hold people. You know, it must be lovely that. You know, to comfort somebody. I'd like it. It must be nice.'*

Psychotherapist: *'One of the things that came over in your work is that you have a lot of anger and a lot of hatred from what happened in your family. Where do you think that anger and hatred went?*

Alan: *'It went in myself. It's just filthy what I've done. I did worse by commitin' rape than what mum ever done to me. God knows what was goin' through my head that night. I don't know. I remember grabbing hold of her afterwards and cryin' and sayin' I don't know what's goin' on, what's happened. I'm sorry. There she is crying. I said, I didn't hurt you, physically, did I? Mentally I've hurt her; it was degrading. Been standing there for about 10 minutes cryin'. I was doin' the more cryin'. I was goin' mental. I just walked along the town for about two weeks like a tramp. I wouldn't sleep in a bed, slept under bushes, in parks, just drinking. Bad news.'* – *ACTUALITY* RADIO 4

This 'fly on the wall' method demands that highly intrusive equipment such as cameras become as inconspicuous as part of the furniture. The aim is to record an accurate 'slice of life', rather than the inflamed normality one might expect where the presence of crews and reporters must make interviewees feel like actors on a stage. To achieve this, crews may have to be present on location for long enough for their subjects to become acclimatized to them before filming can take place in earnest.

Radio scores heavily over TV here, being dependent on nothing more obtrusive than a reporter with a microphone.

24 HOUR NEWS

Perhaps the ultimate news programme is the 24 hour news channel gaining popularity on satellite and cable TV. Ted Turner was the first to go 24 hours with his Atlanta-based Cable News Network (CNN), which went on the air on June 1 1980. CNN provides round-the-clock news to many nations including the US, Canada and Australia and a special service to Europe. What was begun by the man who was dubbed, '*mouth of the south*' and who has been called the '*living embodiment of the new-media barbarism*'*, is now being emulated by others.

> ***'What CNN means by news is very different from what the BBC and ITN mean. On CNN, news, as well as politics, current affairs, and the "and finally" stories, means Hollywood gossip, sport, cookery hints, business, more business and Fitness Breaks with Jake. Muscle-bound Jake exercises on a sandy beach and exhorts viewers, "Don't quit!" Shadowed by a bikini'd blonde, he demonstrates his "one-arm dumbbell triceps extension workout".'*** – THE LISTENER†

But 24 hour news was on radio years before television jumped on the bandwagon. All-news radio is credited with making it's professional debut in Mexico in 1961, when the station XTRA in Tijuana began broadcasting a rip-and-read format which was later to spread to Chicago and be adopted and adapted by other networks.‡

The 24 hour news format has since developed a number of distinct styles: the magazine approach, which presents a variety of programmes and personalities throughout the day; and the news cycle, which repeats and updates an extended news bulletin, and lasts usually between twenty minutes and an hour.

The US Westinghouse format adopted a news cycle, with a constantly updated sequence of hard news repeated throughout the day, '*Give us 22 minutes, we'll give you the world*' was the slogan. Repetition was not thought to matter, because Westinghouse stations catered for an audience that tuned in for the latest news and then tuned out.

CBS stations extended that cycle to an hour to try to hold an audience for longer. National news could be taken on the hour, followed by local news, with traffic, sport, weather reports and other items programmed into the cycle, moving away from the extended bulletin feel to become a news programme. Programmes became double-headed for variety, and the style aimed to be warmer and more relaxed than the Westinghouse model.

* David Housham in 'CNN', *Broadcast* 4 October, 1985.
† Richard Gilbert in 'Satellite TV Supplements, *The Listener*, 16 October, 1986.
‡ Philip O. Keirstead, *All-News Radio*, TAB Books, 1980.

The other approach is the magazine style which builds programmes, such as phone-ins and discussions, on to a backbone of regular bulletins and summaries which run at intervals throughout. This is the philosophy used by LBC in London and transplanted to British breakfast television, albeit with a greater emphasis on entertainment. First attempts at commercial breakfast TV in Britain, which aimed at a hard news approach, proved disastrously unpopular, and a lurch towards light entertainment had to take place before a substantial audience could be won.

WEEI in Boston, which was formerly owned by CBS, is one of the few independent news radio stations operating in the US. Its format is mixed, switching from news cycle to magazine approach at different times of day. Overnight, it opts into the Cable News Network.

Annette Bosworth, assistant to the Vice President, News and Programming, describes the hourly news cycle: '*We have CBS news at the top of the hour for six minutes, then traffic and weather and a news summary – just local stuff – for about a minute or so, then we have a six or seven minute local package, some sport and a couple of features, and then we start all over again at the bottom – except at 30 the news package is seven or eight minutes long and involves both local and national news.*'*

WHO DOES WHAT?

The bigger the news organization, the more specialists it is likely to employ. Job titles and descriptions vary across organizations and countries, but the news process in radio and TV is basically one of getting the stories in, and putting them out. These two jobs are called *input* and *output*.

Network TV news

Input	Output
Input editor	Programme editors/producers
Home/foreign editors	Anchors/presenters/newsreaders
Reporters and correspondents	Journalists/writers
Camera crews	Film/cuttings librarians
Home/foreign assignments editors	Graphic artists
Operations organizer	Studio production staff
	Engineering staff

On the *input* side, stories come in from news agencies, with reports from international news services and material from freelances. Each is *copytasted* (scrutinized) by the relevant desk editor and potential stories are passed to the input (or intake) editor who will decide whether the station will commission them from correspondents or cover them itself. Assignments editors will detail reporters, correspondents and crews to those stories and the operations organizer will handle technical matters such as satellite booking and outside broadcast facilities.

Output is concerned with producing programmes from the material gathered. Editors and producers choose the items to go into their programmes. Jouranlists, writers or sub-editors write the stories and the pre-

* Ian Hyams, WEEI Video, 1986.

senters may rewrite some to suit their own style of delivery. Reports are enhanced with graphics and archive shots, and the studio production staff, led by the director, put the programme on air while the technical quality is monitored by the engineers.

This is a simplification, and in most organizations there is a degree of overlap between input and output. The hierarchy in the local radio newsroom may run as follows:

Local radio news

News editor
Duty editor
Sports editor
Programme producers
Reporters
Programme assistants
Support staff

This pattern will also vary. The news editor will be responsible for the running of the newsroom and its staff. A duty editor may be delegated to take charge of day-to-day news coverage. The sports editor feeds items into programmes and bulletins. Producers organize particular programmes, from commissioning items to overseeing their presentation on air. Programme or technical assistants operate the studios. Newsreading and presentation may be divided among reporters and producers. Support staff include the newsroom secretary.

FIELDWORK

1 Compare two radio bulletins – one a straight read, the other using illustrations. Which was the most interesting? Which told the news more succinctly? Did the actuality add to the story or could the newsreader have said the same things better? Which bulletin was the most memorable? Which did you prefer?

2 Listen to a radio documentary and a shorter radio feature. Apart from the length, what is the difference in the way they are constructed and the methods used to explain a story?

3 'Dramatized documentaries cheapen the news by mixing fact with fiction and information with entertainment.' Discuss.

4 If you can, compare the output of two 24 hour news stations using different formats. Listen or watch the news cycle run through twice. What changes were made in the second cycle? Which format did you prefer – news magazine or news cycle? Why? Which format would (a) pull in the biggest audience? (b) keep an audience for longer?

What are the advantages and disadvantages of a 24 hour news cycle over several short news programmes at fixed points in the day?

5 If you were given the opportunity to make a 30 minute fly-on-the-wall documentary, what subject would you choose, and why? Draw up a rough plan of coverage and think in detail how you would produce the first three minutes of the programme.

10 Item selection and order

> *'The finger that turns the dial rules the air.'* – WILL DURANT

In the world of the media the consumer is king, and today's audiences with remote control TV sets and radio tuners can pass judgement and verdict on a substandard programme or item in the time it takes to press a button. Greater choice and greater ease of making that choice have taken their toll on audience tolerance. Selection and comparison between broadcast news is now as easy as choosing a magazine at a news stand. More than ever the success of a programme will depend upon the producer's ability to select the stories the audience wants to see or hear – his news sense – and his skill in assembling those items into a programme.

The producer's first task is to match the coverage to the style and length of the programme. A two-minute headline summary may cover the current top eight stories, providing a sketched outline of events. A half-hour programme may go over substantially the same ground, but in more depth.

Researchers have found a surprising unanimity about what newsgatherers regard as news.* Importance, significance, relevance, immediacy, proximity, human interest and novelty, are all factors which go into the complex equation of news selection. (See item order below, and what is news?, page 3.)

'A FAIR PICTURE...' From the million words a day that spill into newsrooms such as the BBC World Service, programme makers have to select and boil down just enough to fill their programmes, which in the case of a three minute bulletin, may amount to little more than 500 words. But within these limitations, the aim is to provide an objective picture of the day's main news.

* See also Alastair Hetherington, *News, Newspapers and Television*, Macmillan, 1985, p. 4.

'I hope it's a fair picture. A picture of light, dark and shade, but as the end of the day it's a highly selective picture because we cannot be everywhere all of the time,' says Bob Wheaton, editor of the BBC's *6 O'clock News*.*

> ***'In a sense we put a telephoto lens to the world. We only show in close-up the things that are newsworthy, and they tend to be sad things. It is a fact of life that a lot of what goes into the news is gloomy and disastrous and sad . . . News judgement . . . is not a very precise science but it is the way in which journalists are trained to say this is an interesting story, it is relevant, we ought to tell the audience this.'*** – RON NEIL, EDITOR BBC TV NEWS†

To a degree, media feeds off media. Journalists as a breed are fiercely competitive. They scrutinize one another's programmes, grinding their teeth if someone's angle is better or their pictures are sharper, and if a rival comes up with a new story, then wolf-like (or lemming-like) they charge in packs towards it. As Bob Wheaton puts it, news judgement '*is born of journalism, of reading papers every day, reading magazines, or watch-in other television programmes.*'‡

ITN's *Channel Four News* has different priorities to most other British news programmes. *Channel 4 News* aims to get into the *hows* and *whys* behind current issues. Its brief is also to look in more detail at neglected areas such as medicine, science and the arts and to extend British television coverage of foreign affairs to the oft ignored and usually overlooked Third World.

> ***'Channel 4 News has a pace of its own in the sense that normally the first and second item can be quite long and there may be a third item, and then the "newsbelt" to pick up the pace. Then the idea is that you can settle down, feeling that you have been briefed on the stories of the day, and then, after the break, go into other subjects which are not part of the day's news.'*** – STEWART PURVIS, DEPUTY EDITOR, ITN§

The Channel 4 newsroom is unusual in that the whole production team is brought together early in the day to have a say in what goes into the programme. BBC and ITN conferences tend to be limited to the more senior staff.

On good days, where hard news abounds, media rivals will often run the same lead story. On quieter days, which produce fewer obvious headlines, it can look as though rival stations in the same city are reporting from different countries on different days of the week.

* *Inside Television*, BBC, 1986.'
† Ibid.
‡ Ibid.
§ Alastair Hetherington, *News, Newspapers and Television*, Macmillan, 1985, p. 195.

SECOND THOUGHTS

After their programmes, most large news organizations will hold a post-mortem to see what can be done to prevent mistakes recurring. Introspection can be useful in small doses, but too much criticism from above can stultify creativity, crush initiative, and instil a tendency to produce safe, but predictable, material.

The BBC, with its tiers of higher management and policy of 'referring-up' is renowned for its policy of rigorous self-examination. BBC news editors are still relatively small fish in a very large pond, ranking about fiftieth in the corporation's hierarchy and answerable to those above them for their decisions, and ultimately, their news judgements. ITN, which produces only news, has a smaller, and thereby less oppressive, hierarchy and gives its executives a greater say in their own decision making.*

ITEM ORDER

Harry Hardnose† is a typical (although mythical) news hack of the old order. He worked his way up to his position as a senior staffer in the newsroom by the sweat of his brow and does not plan to unveil the mysteries of his profession to every young upstart. If anyone asks about his news judgement, and few do, Harry simply points to his nose and sniffs, '*That's my secret.*'

But if the truth be known, Harry has neither the imagination nor the mental agility to explain the process of sniffing out and sorting out the news. For him it has long ceased to be the complex equation it once was. The myriads of baffling decisions and bewildering juxtapositions are now resolved in a moment, thanks to a mixture of pure instinct and neat whisky.

Harry is a 100 per cent proof hack. He does not *decide* what makes one story more important than the others, or which stories to run and in what order, he just *knows.*

Hard news is Harry's speciality. He calls it *information of importance to the listener*. Soft news is anything that is *interesting*, *entertaining* or just plain *juicy*. In the event, Harry leaves the decision making to his glands. The more juices a story stirs up and the harder it hits him in the gut, the higher he slots it in the bulletin.

Thankfully, old soaks like Harry are a dying breed. But he does have a point. News selection does become a matter of instinct. Academics cannot resist the temptation to reduce the decision-making process to a formula, but formulae work best with subjects less complex than the human mind, and belong in the sterile conditions of the laboratory, rather than the creative chaos of the newsroom.

> ***'Anyone who says you can make a journalistic judgement in a sort of sterile bath is talking bunkum, twaddle. You make a judgement because of your empirical knowledge store; you make it because of your family, because of the society in which we live.'***
>
> — PETER SISSONS, PRESENTER, *CHANNEL 4 NEWS*‡*

* Alastair Hetherington, *News, Newspaper and Television*, Macmillan, 1985, pp. 34–7.
† Creation of the cartoonist, Steve Bell. ‡ Alastair Hetherington, op. cit. p. 195.

The key factors in item selection are the story's *significance*, its *impact* on a given audience, its *interest*, *topicality* and *immediacy*. Most of these are related with a good deal of overlap between them.

1 The significance of the story

Harry Hardnose would tackle the issue of significance in its widest sense. '*Do we, or do we not, have a story*?' he would yell. '*This one'll rock 'em! Is there enough dirt here to get that £$@! out of office?*' The academic would put the same questions, though couched in less colourful language: 'How important is this story in global or national terms? In what measure does it reflect our changing times, and to what degree does the story speak of political change or upheaval?'

2 The material impact of the story

'*This'll hit 'em where it hurts!*' drools Harry. The question is, 'does the story materially affect *our* audience in terms of their earnings, spending power, standard of living or lifestyles?' Relevance is incorporated into this notion of significance and impact.

3 Audience reaction (the human interest factor)

When it comes to interest, Harry asks whether the story tugs at their hearts, causes them to suck in their breath, to swear or to smile. '*Blind nun on dope rescues dog from blazing orphanage*' is Harry's favourite story. He has already written it – now he is just waiting for it to happen.

More objectively, what strength of feeling is this story likely to provoke? It may not change the audience's way of life, but for it to be of human interest it should upset, anger, amuse, intrigue or appall them, or be about people who have a similar effect on them.

The *Wow!* factor comes in here, with stories about the biggest, smallest, dearest, fastest, etc., which are intended to surprise or astound the hearer.

4 The topicality of the story (the lemming factor)

As Harry would put it, '*Everyone else is flogging it, why the hell haven't we run it?*'

Has the story been in the public eye lately? If so, how largely has it figured? Linked to that is the immediacy factor.

5 The immediacy factor (the yawn factor)

Is it news just in? Is it a brand new story that has broken, or a new angle on one that is still running? Conversely, has it been running for long enough to reach the point of boredom?

If a story is getting stale, then by definition, it is no longer news. On the other hand a new item may breeze into the bulletin like a breath of fresh air. Its position may then be dictated by its freshness, especially when linked to topicality. In other words, if the bulletin is full of the latest hijacking, then news of a hostage release is fair bet for lead story.

Some news stations producing regular bulletins concentrate on providing a new-look programme every hour, in the hope that the variety will persuade the audience to tune-in for longer. Others will argue that listeners do not stay tuned for long enough to get bored with the same bulletin. They prefer to let the lead story run and run, albeit freshened up and with a change of clothes, until it is replaced by something of equal significance. Again we see a mix of entertainment values and news values in operation.

Where bulletins are revised substantially every hour, there can be a loss of continuity, and stories of real substance are likely to be knocked down simply because they are regarded as old hat. Some stations attempt to strike a balance by running extended news summaries at key points in the day, such as 1 p.m. when the current stories are shelved and the day's major items are dusted off and re-run according to their significance that day.

6 Sport/specialisms

'*Football results? – Bung 'em at the back of the bulletin.*'

If the practice is to separate the sports news or other speciality like financial news into a section of its own, then each story within that section will be prioritized individually and run together in order of priority. The exception is speciality stories that are significant enough to earn a place in the general run of news.

7 Linking items

'*Ah, return of the mini-skirt; record number of road accidents – I wonder?*'

Frequently items have linked themes or offer different angles on the same story. Splitting them up would be a mistake. They should be rewritten to run together.

8 Actuality/pictures

'*Strewth! Where'd you record this one, in a* ***bathroom?***'

Some stories may be illustrated, others may not. The addition of actuality or film, its length and quality may be extra factors in deciding where to place each item in the bulletin. It may be policy to spread illustrations throughout or to run only one phone quality item.

9 'And finally . . .'

'*Got a tickler here about some kid who tried to hold up a bank with a water pistol . . .*'

With items that are bright, frivolous, trivial and can guarantee a smirk if not a bellylaugh, common practice would be to save them for the end of the bulletin.

LOCAL CONSIDERATIONS

> ***'At Hallam, I aim for punchy stories that are not overdramatic with short cues and a mix of local and national stories. Delivery should be aggressive and confident, but not too speedy. Stories should be kept short, sweet and simple, and if a humorous item is included at the end of the bulletin, that's fine. I do not like to run gory stories at meal times, nor racy ones, such as sex court cases, when mothers and fathers may be sitting down listening to the radio with their children or even their grannies. We aim for a family audience.'***
>
> —JIM GREENSMITH, NEWS EDITOR, RADIO HALLAM, INDEPENDENT LOCAL RADIO STATION IN SHEFFIELD, ENGLAND

Local considerations may feature highly in positioning items in the bulletin. What may be of interest nationally is unlikely by itself to satisfy a local audience, so the relative weight given to national and local news will have to be carefully considered.

Audiences and their needs may change throughout the day. First thing in the morning, all viewers or listeners may want to know is: '*Is the world the same place this morning as it was when I went to bed; will I get wet when I leave the house, and will I be able to get to work on time?*'

Some of the most successful radio stations are based in big cities serving one clear community with a common identity. Others may serve regions with several small cities, a number of towns and many villages, so '*three people died today when a lorry went out of control in North Street,*' would leave half the audience scratching their heads about *which* North Street the newsreader was referring to.

How local is local? News editors may find the strongest news coming regularly from one location, but may have to consciously drop good stories for weaker ones from elsewhere to try to give an even spread of coverage.

FOREIGN COVERAGE

Central to the question of relevance is *proximity*. '*Is this story about me, about things happening on my doorstep, or is it about strangers 2000 miles away who I have never met and did not know existed?*'

Western news values are often insular and unfavourable to foreign stories unless they are about 'people like us,' as BBC TV news editor, Ron Neil, explains: '*Our research shows that people in this country would far prefer a preponderance of British news to foreign news. The judgement can only be what are the most relevant stories around in Britain today.*'*

All things considered, item selection and running orders will often be settled on nothing more objective than the gut reaction of journalists about the gut reactions they expect their stories to produce from their audience. In other words – impact.

PRODUCING A RUNNING ORDER

> ***'You never go into the programme at 6.30 am with a running order that stays the same throughout the show – ever. Always there are changes, sometimes the whole thing is rewritten. You're given a running order but you basically throw it away and just wing it throughout the morning.'***
>
> —JOHN HUMPHRYS, PRESENTER OF RADIO 4'S TODAY PROGRAMME.†

Many newscasters hold the bulletin running order in their heads – especially radio newsreaders who are operating their own studio equipment. Where a technical assistant drives the desk for the newsreader, he/she will usually want a running order listing the items and giving the durations, in-words and out-words.

Stations that produce longer programmes sometimes combine running

* Speaking on *Tuesday Call*, BBC Radio 4, 30 September 1986.
† *See it for Yourself*, BBC, 1987.

HALLAM TODAY

Guide Time	ITEM	RUNNING TIME	ELAPSED TIME
30"	Hallam Today Jingle	30"	30"
	Programme teasers (20 secs max. i.e. 3 teasers – 20 words each)		
2'30"	NEWS DESK & WEATHER	2'27"	2'57"
2'00"	MUSIC	2'10"	5'07"
2'30"	Intro and Billboard 1	2'42"	7'49"
1'30"	AD BREAK	1'10"	8'59"
2'00"	Intro and Billboard 2	2'15"	11'14"
2'00"	MUSIC	2'05"	13'19"
2.00"	Intro and Billboard 3	2'06"	15'25"
30"	Traffic	·25"	15'50"
1'00"	NEWS DESK	1'00"	16'50"
2'00"	Intro and Billboard 4	1'46"	18'36"
1'30"	AD BREAK	1'30"	20'06"
4'00"	SPORT AT 5.20 P.M.	3'47"	23'53"
2'30"	MUSIC	2'35"	26'28"
2'30"	Intro and Billboard 5	2'30"	28'58"
1'00"	Closing NEWS HEADLINES	1'02"	30'
	OUTRO		

Figure 20 Programme running order. The Item column gives the standard programme format which the producer works towards when compiling the programme. The Guide Time column gives the recommended times of each item. When all the items are in, the producer puts their exact durations in the Running time column. The Elapsed time gives the cumulative time of all the items which has to add up to thirty minutes – the duration of the programme. Music can be cut short or stretched out to make the programme fit to length (courtesy Radio Hallam)

order with format. A pre-printed sheet shows what kind of stories should go where, and approximately how long each should be. Using this modular approach, features are plugged in and replaced where necessary, but for items to be fully interchangeable they will usually have to be of a fixed length. The producer's job is to organize the coverage so suitable items of the right length are brought in, and then to make sure the programme goes out to plan (Figure 20).

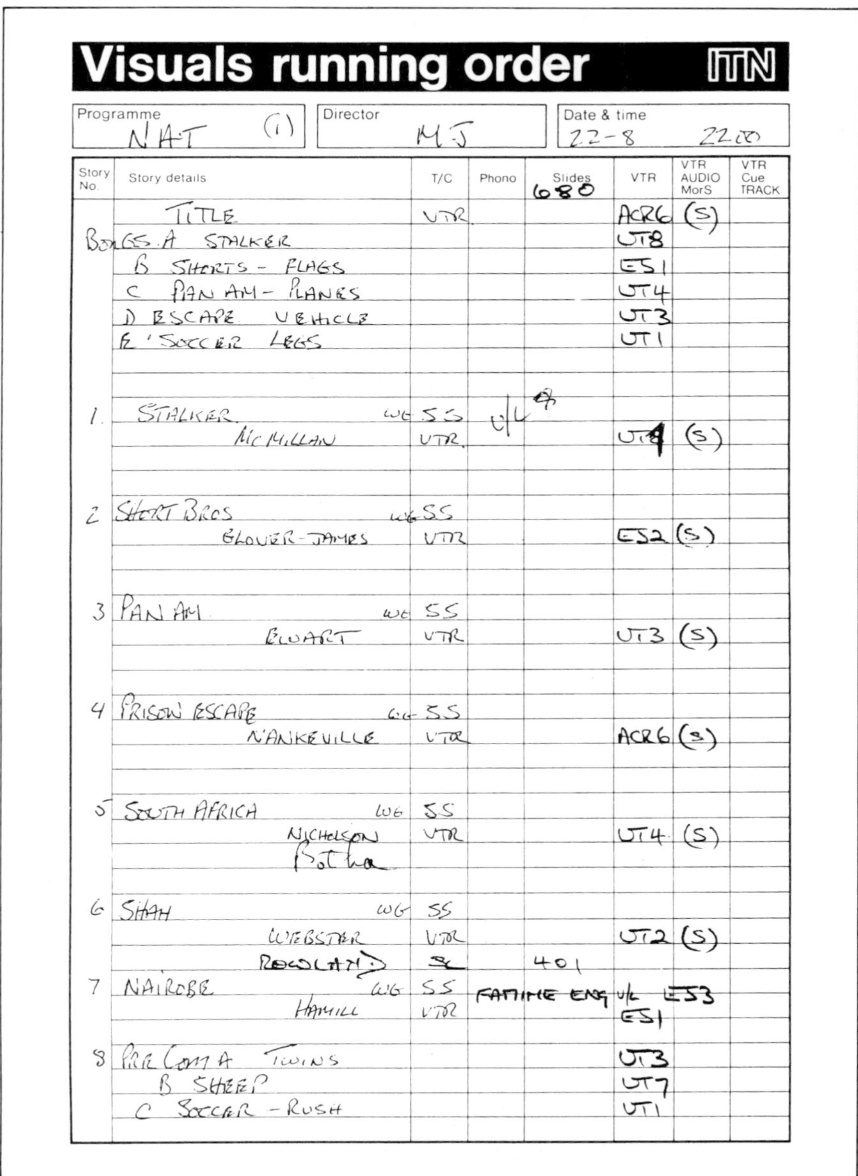

Visuals running order ITN

Programme: NAT (1) | Director: MJ | Date & time: 22-8 2200

Story No.	Story details	T/C	Phono	Slides 680	VTR	VTR AUDIO MorS	VTR Cue TRACK
	TITLE	VTR			ACR6	(S)	
BONGS	A STALKER				UT8		
	B SHORTS - FLAGS				ES1		
	C PAN AM - PLANES				UT4		
	D ESCAPE VEHICLE				UT3		
	E 'SOCCER LEGS				UT1		
1.	STALKER WG	SS	V/L				
	McMILLAN	VTR			UT4	(S)	
2	SHORT BROS WG	SS					
	GLOVER-JAMES	VTR			ES2	(S)	
3	PAN AM WG	SS					
	STUART	VTR			UT3	(S)	
4	PRISON ESCAPE WG	SS					
	NANKEVILLE	VTR			ACR6	(S)	
5	SOUTH AFRICA WG	SS					
	NICHOLSON Botha	VTR			UT4	(S)	
6	SHAH WG	SS					
	WEBSTER	VTR			UT2	(S)	
	ROWLAND	S		401			
7	NAIROBI WG	SS	FAMINE ENG		V/L	ES3	
	HAMILL	VTR			ES1		
8	PRE COM A TWINS				UT3		
	B SHEEP				UT7		
	C SOCCER - RUSH				UT1		

Figure 21 Visuals running order gives the order of stills, graphics and captions which are to be included in the programme and tell the director which machines will display those stills (courtesy ITN)

A completed running order may be an elaborate document, giving precise details of items, durations, ins and outs, or it may be a rough guide to what the producers and directors can expect and hope for in the next half hour. TV news has more than one running order to work with. With the list of programme items, which may be constantly changing, will be a list of the visuals that go with those items (Figure 21). TV directors driving programmes which rely on sophisticated production techniques and make increasing use of live reports will frequently have to 'busk' the order, working with a schedule that changes so often, it may never be produced in final form on paper.

FIELDWORK

1 What qualities do you think make a story big enough to run as a bulletin lead?

2 If you have access to a rip and read service take ten stories from the printer and select seven to make up a bulletin. (If you cannot get at any rip and read, cut the stories from a newspaper.) Then discuss how you chose the three to drop.

3 If the seven remaining stories are too long for broadcast or are written in a newspaper style, rewrite them for broadcast to a maximum of sixty words each.

Then working purely on instinct, rank those stories in order to compile a bulletin.

4 If you are in a class, switch your stories with those of a classmate and compare running orders. Now discuss your similarities and differences and see if you can agree an order between you.

5 Now listen to a five minute radio bulletin and assess the running order. In what order would *you* have run the items and why?

11 Putting the show together

ESTABLISHING PROGRAMME IDENTITY

> *'In the city of Boston there are 41 rated commercial radio station signals reaching the metro market and 6 or 7 FM educational stations, and the station that survives is the station that has a very clear identity, and that is what we have, there is only one news radio station in Boston, and that is WEEI, and our identity is widely understood.*
>
> – JOHN RODMAN, VICE PRESIDENT FOR NEWS AND PROGRAMMES, WEEI, BOSTON*

Every programme maker would be grateful for a guaranteed audience for his/her offering. Perhaps fortunately for the consumer there is no such thing. Where news stations and different news media compete, there can be no room for complacency. In the end, the best product should find the most takers – but only if that product is what the consumer wants.

Audience loyalty is important. Even where rival news programmes are broadcast at the same time and there is little to choose between their coverage, sections of the audience will have their favourite and will probably stick with it. They may like the style, pace and rhythm of the programme, or the way the sport, traffic and weather are put over. Or it may be the special features that match their own interests, such as fishing or business news. It could be that one programme offers more audience participation – phone-ins, or discussions. Or the audience may simply feel more comfortable with the presenters of one channel, finding them warmer, more cheerful and more 'like folks' than the 'cold fish' on the other side. Meanwhile, the rival station may pick up viewers for precisely the opposite reason – the audience preferring their more formal, authoriative style.

To a family at home, the presenters are like friends or acquaintances who join them in their front room for half an hour or more each day – longer perhaps than most real friends. Small wonder the choice of presenters is viewed with such importance.

Every producer's aim is to find a winning format and stick with it, in

* Ian Hyams, *WEEI video*, 1986.

the hope that the audience will do the same. But the familiarity factor can work against them. Even belated improvements to a programme that has been creaking with age will usually produce an audience backlash and – initially, at least – lose a number of viewers who were very happy with the product as it was. The art of maintaining audience loyalty is to find what the customers want, and give it to them – consistently.

WINNING AN AUDIENCE – THE OPENERS

> ***'What you decide to lead on is lent an enormous amount of importance. If you say [grave voice] "Good evening. The headlines at six o'clock, there's been a train crash in Scotland," then people will think, "this must be terrible, there must be lots of people dead." If, one or two stories in, you say [brighter, almost cheerful voice] "a train has crashed in Scotland," it's immediately a much lighter business.'***
>
> – BBC NEWSREADER, SUE LAWLEY*

The openers are designed to lure and capture the unsuspecting viewer. The first few seconds of a programme are all-important. During these moments the audience may be gained or lost. In television news, the openers will often be the most complicated and closely produced part of the programme. They will probably comprise a signature tune and title sequence, which may feature sophisticated computer graphics and a tightly edited montage of still and moving pictures. This may be followed by headlines or teasers – tersely worded five second tasters written to intrigue – perhaps each illustrated with a snatch of film showing the most gripping moments of action to come.

The openers, demanding quick-fire operation and split-second timing, may be the only part of a news programme, barring the individual items, to be pre-recorded, and this is likely to be done during the rehearsal shortly before transmission.

Radio news, which is spared the demanding third dimension of pictures, has an easier task. The programme may begin with a signature tune, voiced-over by an announcer, which is faded down beneath the voice of the newsreader, who may give the headlines in turn, each supported by a colourful or intriguing snatch from an interview or report to be featured in the programme. This list of coming attractions is known as the *menu*.

KEEPING AN AUDIENCE – HEADLINES AND PROMOTIONS

> ***'Television news is a marketable commodity, like peaches, computers, toothpaste and refrigerators.'***
>
> – CAROLYN DIANA LEWIS, AUTHOR, *REPORTING FOR TELEVISION*

Movie makers realized years ago that not even a blockbuster of a film can sell itself. For a movie to do well at the box office, it has to be promoted.

* *Inside Television*, BBC, 1986.

Trailers have to be produced capturing the best of the action and the juciest dialogue to show the audience the thrills in store. News producers are not beneath using the same techniques.

Headlines achieve two important functions: at the middle and end of a programme they remind the audience of the main stories and help reinforce that information. Reinforcement aids recall, and an audience that can remember what it has heard is more likely to be satisfied. At the beginning, the headlines hook the audience in the same way as the cinema trailer, and later serve to encourage them to bear with an item that may be less appealing because they know something better is on the way. During the programme, forward trails, such as, '*Coming up, Spot the singing Dalmatian, but first news of the economic crisis*,' do much the same job.

British television's *News at Ten* is broken by a commercial break, and the producer knows that his audience for part two of the programme must never be taken for granted. The first half of *News at Ten* ends on what are known as the *pre-commercials*. This group of three headlines before the break is regarded as vital for keeping an audience. '*These are probably more important than the headlines at the beginning of the programme*,' says producer Phil Moger:

> *'I'm terribly aware that come the break people are thinking, "Ah well, time to get ready for bed," certainly, "I'll put the kettle on," and that's well documented because electricity companies will tell you there's a surge during the centre break of* **News at Ten**. *I see my job during those three sentences before the break as getting them to come back and not make the tea or pull the covers down on the bed. I want them back to see something. The pre-commercials have to have something of weight, something for women and something for sport. That is my ideal pre-commercial.'*

When *News at Ten* first went on air, the art of holding an audience over a break had yet to be perfected and viewing figures dipped appreciably after the adverts. Good stories alone are no guarantee of an audience. Having the stories and persuading the audience to wait for them is the way to keep them.

ACTUALITY

> **1936 . . .**
>
> *'Members of your staff – they could be called BBC Reporters . . . should be held in readiness . . . to cover unexpected news of the day . . . a big fire, strikes, civil commotion, railway accidents . . . It would be his job . . . to secure an eye-witness . . . to give a short account of the part he or she played that day. In this way . . . the news could be presented in a gripping manner and, at the same time, remain authentic . . . Such a news bulletin would in itself be a type of actuality programme.'*
>
> – RICHARD DIMBLEBY, OUTLINING HIS PROPOSALS TO THE BBC'S CHIEF NEWS EDITOR*

* See also John Herbert, *The Techniques of Radio Journalism*, A & C Black, 1976.

. . . 1986

Lively inserts

RADIO TWO has begun inserting "illustrations" into its news summaries, such as extracts from correspondents' reports from around the world and on-the-spot recordings.

This is in addition to the use of such material in the main bulletins at 7 and 8 am, 1 and 5 pm and midnight.

Use of actuality, as it is called, will liven up the bulletins at a time when competition from day-time television is imminent, it is hoped.

Bryant Marriott, controller of Radio Two, said it had been a long-held ambition to illustrate the summaries which run from 6 am to 11 pm.

UK Press Gazette, 27 October, 1986

'Actuality is what makes radio bulletins come alive – use as much as possible.' – SIMON ELLIS, NEWS EDITOR, BBC ESSEX

It may have taken sections of the BBC half a century to take up Dimbleby's proposals above for illustrating the news, but actuality – interview extracts and on-the-spot reports – has for decades been a central feature of TV and radio news reporting world-wide.

Actuality is used to transport the audience to the scene, to hear the words as they were said, and to see or hear the news as it is actually happening – hence the term *actuality*. This is where broadcasting scores heavily above newspapers. If a single picture is worth a thousand words, what must be the value of moving pictures – and sound?

That said, there are still radio stations such as the BBC World Service which hold a substantial audience with a straightforward summary of the day's news untrammelled by actuality or so much as a hint of an illustration.

PICTURES

The supremacy of TV news suggests that moving pictures hold the greatest audience appeal, but the enduring attraction of radio must be due in no small part to the way in which radio stimulates the imagination of its audience, making radio listening a more active experience than the passive, attention-consuming pastime of watching TV.

Recent developments in TV news have had less to do with changing formats or presentation styles than the availability of faster and better pictures. Television is undergoing a continuing revolution. When TV news began, newsreel film, which could be weeks out of date, was superseded by film reports made the same day. Now the slow medium of film has given way to faster newsgathering using videotape and live transmission of pictures. Access to the action has been made easier by long-distance relay techniques and more portable and less obtrusive equipment. (See also gathering the news, page 275.)

Good pictures no longer simply illustrate the news – they *are* the news, and without pictures the event may not be reported: '*You don't want to look like a radio news bulletin which just has a newscaster sitting there. You rely on the strength of the pictures,*' says BBC TV news editor Ron Neil.*

* *Inside Television*, BBC, 1986.

The availability of pictures may decide whether a story is run or dropped, and the strength of those pictures will often determine its position in a bulletin. When mounted police charged picketing miners during the British miners' strike, this significant escalation of police tactics was reported prominently by the BBC and mutedly by ITN. BBC cameras recorded the incident, but ITN missed the charge, having been misinformed about where the main picketing would take place. The BBC headlined the charge to a background of pictures, while ITN, with nothing more than a reporter's account of the incident, left it out of the headlines and ran a shorter version of the story in the programme.*

GRAPHICS

> *'I put a tremendous emphasis on graphics. They are a marvellous asset in explaining things to people, so I always try to use a lot of them. You can spell out a story line by line: "SDP policy is . . .", and use graphics to explain complicated points: "the meltdown pattern is . . ." and so on.'*
>
> – PHIL MOGER, PRODUCER, *NEWS AT TEN*

TV graphics can do much to overcome the broadcaster's bete noir – the difficulty most listeners have in absorbing and retaining background information while continuing to take in a steady stream of facts. The context of the story can be explained by displaying and holding key points or quotes on the screen. Without this advantage, radio news has to resort to the old adage of KISS – *keep it simple, stupid.*

Radio producers will try to run an even spread of copy stories, illustrated items and voice reports, and may juggle the position of stories in the programme to try to achieve a pleasing variety. TV producers play the same game with taped reports, stills, graphics and to-camera pieces, working hard not to load the programme unevenly with too many static items or on-the-spot reports.

PROGRAMME BALANCE – BEING ALL THINGS TO ALL PEOPLE

Producers may not be able to please all the people all the time, but they do their best to please some of them some of the time and leave everybody satisfied. *News at Ten*, which is ITN's flagship, tries to cover all the important stories of the day, doing the job of a paper of record, and then includes human interest items to widen the appeal. One light story is usually placed in the first half of the thirty minute programme.

The aim is to satisfy a wider audience than any newspaper, embracing readers of quality and popular press alike. '*All the hard news has got to be in part one with a pop newspaper story before the break*,' says producer Phil Moger. '*Also it's quite a nice idea to give part two a bit of weight. The first item in part two is an extended news story, a featurette. I'd like the second to be a bit of an upmarket story.*'

The formula has improved since the programme's launch in 1967.

* Alastair Hetherington, *News, Newspapers and Television*, Macmillan, 1985.

Then editor, Geoffrey Cox, described the first two editions as having a '*jerky lack of rhythm . . . lumpy disproportion between items,*' and being '*ill shaped, broken apart rather than linked by the commercial break, and exuding . . . traces of lack of confidence.*'*

British regional TV news has faced criticism for being bland, dated and dull. Regional television owes it identity to its local news which often hauls in large audiences. But there have been complaints that programmes, which in some cases have changed little since regional television began in Britain, are beginning to creak.

> *'Too many of the programmes seem to have fallen into a dreary formula pattern, and there is a distinct danger of many of them becoming complacent and second-rate . . . reporting ranged from the merely satisfactory to the downright mediocre. Not enough care was being taken in assembling the programmes as a whole. There was little contrast in the length and variety of the items. Too much was routine, and frankly boring.'* – John Gau, Chairman of the Judges at the Royal Television Society's TV Journalism Awards

This broadside against regional news at what was supposed to be an award-giving ceremony was redoubled by a chairman of the judges, who said standards had been poor for years: '*There is very little sign of investigative reporting, and most of the items are the result of routine calls to the local police or fire station.*' The RTS called for '*real stories about social developments*' and wanted to '*jolt the regional teams into trying harder to dig up the significant stories in their areas, to find the original and telling angles, and to get in the questions that really count.*'[†]

Groupings and variety

> *'Television viewers need relief from sorrow, suffering, pain and hate. A steady drumbeat of tragedy tends to leave the viewer weary and exhausted. Thus, in a series of waves, the program reaches a climax of shock and woe, then eases off for something light and unchallenging, and then later, it returns to stories that are murderous or scandalous or worse.'* – CAROLYN DIANA LEWIS, REPORTING FOR TELEVISION

'*Programe feel*' is a key to the success or failure of a show. That feel is down to the rhythm, pace and variety of the programme as well as the substance of its reports, and that feel is enhanced by the way items are grouped together. Sport and other special interest features are often segmented together, and even world news or local news, if these are thought to hold only a secondary appeal, may be grouped in segments that are short enough to hold those in the audience who have tuned in primarily to hear something else.

* Geoffrey Cox, *See it Happen*, Bodley Head, 1983, chpt 41.

† From 'Rigor Mortis in the Regions', *The Sunday Times*, 8 March, 1987.

Story groupings may be broken down further by location or comparative weight. Some US radio stations operating an hourly cycle of news will divide the national and local news into major and secondary items and run the secondaries in slots of their own at fixed points in the cycle. These groupings of minor items will be kept short, with brief stories, and used almost as fillers to vary the pace between weightier or more interesting segments.

Segmenting can be counter-productive. Running all the crime stories together may lose their impact. It might be better to group them at intervals in the programme. Likewise, film reports or actuality with a similar theme, such as coverage of a riot and a noisy demonstration, are often best kept apart. Too many talking heads (dry, expert opinion) may also bore the audience.

During research for the British Independent Broadcasting Authority Dr Barrie Gunter discovered that an audience is more likely to forget an item when stories are grouped together. Two other researchers, Colin Berry and Brian Clifford, also identified a 'meltdown' factor, when similar stories ran together in the audience's mind. They placed a Mafia trial story in the middle of four foreign news items and then among four from the UK. Recall among the British audience was 20 per cent higher when the Mafia story was placed in the unusual context of UK news – normally it would be kept separate.*

> *'To a great extent the news is produced. It is not simply gathered in, written up, put in a certain order, slapped on the air and punched out. It is produced by things like headlines, signature tunes, stop-gaps in the middle where we give the stories coming up next, little quotes at the end of the* Six O'clock News. *We intend to make it both visual and entertaining and indeed to make you smile sometimes.'*
>
> – BBC NEWSREADER, SUE LAWLEY†

Beside all these considerations is one of taste. It may seem good for variety to follow a triple killing with Mimi the dancing dingbat, but the audience would not thank you for it. It would make light of a serious and tragic story. Juxtaposition requires a good deal of care, and to keep the audience informed about where the programme is going, transitions should be clearly signposted:

'International news now . . .'.
'Meanwhile, back home . . .'.
'But there is some good news for residents of . . .'.
'Industrial news . . .'.
'On the stock market . . .'.

* As reported in *UK Press Gazette*, 21 July, 1986.
† *Inside Television*, BBC, 1986.

Transitions, timechecks, thoughtful linking, and headlines, help to create programme feel and establish identity. They can be overdone.

Missed Connection

'Radio 4 has invented a kind of English not found anywhere else in the media: the radio link. This consists of taking two topics which have absolutely nothing in common and then finding a link between them, and the more tortuous the better.

One example comes from a presenter who was linking a murder thriller to a programme about cheese-making: "And from something blood curdling to something rather more milk-curdling. . . ."

What's amazing is that this sort of contorted thinking has not spread. It seems a natural way of doing the Radio 4 news headlines: "New controls were announced today by President Mubarak to bring tourism back to Egypt. And talking of pyramid selling, that's just one of the many financial devises that Mrs Thatcher promised this afternoon to examine more closely as she spoke in the mother of Parliaments. But it was the mother of Russian dissident Yuri Orlov who made the headlines in Moscow today with a brave declaration of liberty. A brave declaration of another kind was made by David Gower in Jamaica where England are only 346 behind the West Indies and their steaming attack, though steaming is hardly the word to apply to the weather which will continue cold and frosty. Now the news in detail . . .".' – MILES KINGTON IN *THE TIMES*

In radio, it is best to separate phone reports of indifferent sound quality to avoid testing the patience of listeners straining to hear above the interference on their car radios. Indoor and outdoor reports may be mixed, and extra variety can be added by using male and female co-presenters. Alternating stories between the two can lift a programme, and research suggests it helps viewers remember the items. But on a short programme, too many voices can have a ping-pong effect if each presenter does not have enough time to establish an identity.

The idea is to give a spread of light and heavy, fast and slow, busy and static, to get the most variety and interest from the material.

'When you are planning an hour-long news programme you have to keep things strong right the way through, rather than do what happens in a news bulletin, where you start with the most important and finish with the most trivial. It's got to have a strong beginning, to hold itself up in the middle and have a good end. I want a piece that people can remember.' – ROB McKENZIE, PRODUCER/PRESENTER CAPITAL RADIO

Figure 22 Sheila Mallet and Sim Harris double-head Chiltern Radio's main lunchtime news programme, *Chiltern Reports*. Many stations consider the male/female spread of voices ideal for double-headed presentation (Andrew Boyd)

Rhythm and pace

Rhythm and pace are as crucial to programme feel as the choice of items. The style of writing, speed of reading, pace of editing and length of each item determine whether the programme surges ahead or drags.

Individual reports should run to just the right length to hold interest, and leave the audience wanting more rather than wishing for less. Information also has to be presented at a pace which the slowest in the audience will be able to follow without frustrating the rest. The programme should be rhythmic, though with enough variety and occasional changes of pace to stimulate interest. Items should aim for a standard length, with none cut so short as to feel truncated or abrupt, and none allowed to run on to the point of boredom.

Where short news items are used, the overall rhythm of the programme can be maintained by grouping them in segments that are about the same length as a standard item, or by inserting them into the programme at regular intervals.

Where an item is less likely to be of prime interest to an audience, it will usually be trimmed shorter than the others, and positioned between stories which are thought to be popular and have been promoted as such. The aim is to tempt an audience to stay tuned for as long as possible and preferably longer than intended.

The importance of rhythm is even more closely observed in pop radio where news programmes belong in the context of a music show. The audience is conditioned to the rhythm of the three minute disc, so any single news item of over three minutes would feel as though it were dragging. Many news bulletins on pop stations are three minutes long. Stations that pump out fast, beaty, music to a young audience will often want their news to be the same – bright, youthful and moving along at a cracking pace. Radio 1's *Newsbeat* and Capital Radio's *The Way It Is* are followers of the fast and furious principle. The brisker the pace of the programme, the shorter the items should be, and interviews with people who are ponderous in their delivery should be cut even shorter to avoid dragging the pace.

FIELDWORK

1 Watch closely several news programmes on TV and radio, and reconstruct the format used to compile them. Note the balance and length of the stories and the use of headlines and pre-commercials. See how stories are linked and whether back announcements are used.

What gives these programmes their *feel?* Who are they aimed at and how could they be improved?

2 Set up a half hour news programme from scratch. Choose a target audience (family, young people, business people, community cross-section, etc.) and consider the kind of programme you want to produce. Think about the contents, pace, length of items and programme feel and draw up a brief setting out your plans. If you are in a class, work on this in groups of four.

3 Using the rip-and-read or copy from newspapers, find enough ideas for stories to fill your programme. Remember that length is a crucial factor. Decide the duration of your reports, then assemble those stories into a running order.

Write the cues to your stories in a style that is appropriate to the programme you have in mind. Decide whether your writing should be terse and emphatic, in a hard news style, or chatty and relaxed, to suit a more discursive feature style.

Think about the overall balance of your programme. Does it have a good blend of light and shade, serious and offbeat? Should you be running special interest items such as sport? Are the stories positioned to hold interest throughout? Is the first half overloaded with heavyweight items?

4 Now work on the headlines and linking. Set it up properly with headlines at the start and a summary at the end. Should you use full-length headlines or short teasers? Does your programme have a commercial break? If so write some pre-comms. If not, produce a menu in the middle saying what is coming up. Revise the cues where necessary to provide better links between stories. Consider whether back announcements would be beneficial.

If you are in a class, discuss your work with another group when you have finished preparing your programme and swap your ideas and criticisms.

5 If you have studio facilities, work in groups to produce actual programmes, using news from an agency feed or going out as reporters and getting your own.

12 Making the programme fit

Many programme makers will share the same bad dream – their show is either five minutes too short and grinds to a halt early, leaving a gaping hole before the next item, or it develops a will of its own, gathering momentum until it becomes an unstoppable juggernaut, overruning hopelessly and throwing out the programme schedule for the entire network.

In the business of news, live, late or untimed material is an everyday problem that can turn reality into a nightmare – if you let it. But the prospect of a programme running out of control is one that can be easily prevented with a little forethought.

Few news programmes can boast running orders that have every item buttoned up and timed to the second – news is not like that. Getting a news programme to run to time is down to forward planning and flexibility.

CUTTING

Where a programme is in danger of overruning and has to be cut, the incision can be made in a number of ways. The most drastic is to drop an item completely. Another way of saving time is to replace a longer item with a shorter one. Where only a small saving is required, trimming an item on air usually does the job.

The easiest way to do this is to cut something that is live. If reporters are conducting a live interview, they will be told when to wind-up by producers, who will also tell them the time they have remaining for the interview, and will count them down during the final moments. If they have fifteen seconds left and still want to pursue another point they may put their question in a way that makes their interviewee aware time is running out, such as, '*Finally, and briefly . . .*'.

Programme makers often include live material towards the end of a programme as a flexible buffer which can be compressed or expanded to fill the time. Where all the items are recorded and all are to be run, producers may be faced with the unenviable task of having to cut an item on air so it appears quite naturally to have come to an end.

This can be made far less fraught with a little help from reporters.

Before they finish editing the item, they should make a note of a place at which their story can be brought to an early end, along with the words before that point and the duration up to that point. This is known as a *pot-point*, and it gives the producer the flexibility to run the item in either its shorter or longer version. Cutting early is known as *pot-cutting*, and is made by either switching out the picture and soundtrack or physically stopping the tape machine.

> *...it was the worst massacre in Punjab since extremists began their campaign for an independent Sikh homeland – Khalistan – land of the pure.*
>
> *As bullets swept through the bus, passengers dived under the seats for cover. When the gunfire stopped, 38 had died and 23 were injured. The interior of the bus was covered in blood and glass.*
>
> *The driver later said that a car had pulled up in front of the bus and five youths had ordered him out at gunpoint. One of the gang then drove to a deserted spot four miles away – where the shooting began.*

POT: 'blood and glass'
DUR: 56″
OUT: 'shooting began'
DUR: 1′06″

The need to cut is not necessarily the fault of bad planning. Important late news arriving while the programme is on air may force another item to be cut or dropped.

In radio the process of cutting or filling is perhaps the simplest of all. Assuming a five-minute bulletin has a sequence of sport, an 'and finally' and weather at the end, which should only be cut if essential, the newsreader works out the combined duration of those items and deducts this from the total length of the bulletin. If they come to a minute and a half, then the reader has three and half minutes remaining for the 'meat' of the bulletin. If the programme started at 2 o'clock the newsreader knows that he/she has to begin the end sequence by three and a half minutes past 2. Watching the clock, the reader simply aims to come out of the main material as near to that time as possible, and any other stories that have not been read by then will have to be discarded. (See also Backtiming, below.)

Writing the weather or sport to flexible lengths, with paragraphs that can be kept in or cut, will allow readers to use these items to make any final adjustments so the bulletin comes out exactly on time. This way, late news can be slotted in without throwing the programme timing.

FILLING

Filling is a more serious problem than having to cut, because it implies the programme is short of good material and the producer has been failing in his/her job. Items should never be run simply as makeweights – every story should deserve its airtime. It is up to the news producer to make sure that on even the quietest news day there is enough good material to run, even if it means switching to softer stories.

Many newsrooms compensate for the ebb and flow of news by sending out reporters on slow days to produce timeless features that can be kept on the shelf and run whenever necessary. In theory, the day should never come when a gap appears in the programme, but if holes do appear, they should never be filled by running a story for longer than it deserves. Nor should they be plugged by second-rate items and limp ad-libs. A producer should always commission or have on standby a number of items as a safety net, especially when late pieces are expected that might not turn up on time.

Where the programme is slightly short of material, say when a feature has been dropped to make way for a late item, the filling is best carried out in the same way as the cutting – with live material. More short stories may be inserted into the programme, but in TV, even this requires forward planning to line up the relevant stills or graphics to accompany them. The easiest place to pad is in the live to-camera items such as the weather or sport. Scripts for these should incorporate a number of *out-points* where the presenter can finish early, as well as extra paragraphs which give interesting additional information but which will not sound like padding on the air.

Another way to take up slack at the end of the programme, is to promote items coming up in the next edition – but stand by for complaints if the station fails to deliver the goods the following night.

The last few seconds are usually filled with the goodbyes or *outs*. It is easy at this stage to be lulled into a false sense of security and to think the programme is over. Do not be fooled, many good programmes are ruined by ending badly. The most important 30 seconds of a show are at the beginning. Next come those at the end. The audience's lasting impressions will be gained in those moments. The start should persuade them to watch; the ending will persuade them to watch tomorrow – or try the other channel.

For this reason, relying on inspiration to provide ad-libs to fill the final half minute is about as foolish as risking running out of fuel in the last half mile of a motorway. The art of the ad-lib is to make scripted comments sound spontaneous, and many broadcasters who may appear to be masters of spontaneity will probably have scripted every pause, stumble, word and comma. Few things sound more forced and banal than the artificial exchange of unfelt pleasantries between presenters to pad out the last few seconds of a programme. (See also ad libs, page 141.)

If desperate measures are called for, then the producer may use music as a flexible bridge before the next item. This obviously works better in radio, while television's equivalent is to linger for an uncomfortable length of time on the parting shot of the weather forecast. Music during a programme can often be lengthened or shortened without it noticing – especially when there are no vocals – but the problem at the end of a programme is getting the music to end exactly on time and on a definite note.

BACKTIMING

The way to achieve a neat and definite ending is to *backtime* the music. Producers need to know the duration of the music – usually an instrumental signature tune – and they then count back on the clock from the second the programme is due to end to find the exact time the music should begin. At that moment, regardless of whatever else is going on in the programme, the music is started, but with the volume off or the sound mixer on *pre-fade*. (This means the audience cannot hear the music but the technical operator can.) As the presenter winds up the programme, the music is faded up beneath his/her voice, and fills the gap from the moment he/she finishes speaking, to end exactly when the programme is scheduled to stop.

Whatever steps are taken to cut or fill a programme, it should never be necessary to resort to the practice once rife within the BBC of playing for time by using dull and irrelevant public service handouts.

The golden rule is that the audience should never be aware that the programme before them is anything but the polished and completely professional product the producer intends. Never pad with second-rate material, never cut raggedly, and plan ahead so you never have cause to panic.

Endquote – From the Newsroom of BBC Ulster

'On Tuesday it was a quarter past five and we had 31 seconds for the entire programme. Everything else was still being edited.'

'What do you take for the ulcer?'

'Vodka – and lots of it.'

FIELDWORK

1 Whenever you produce programmes get into the habit of providing standby reports and scripted material to use as padding. Give opt-out points on the filler material.

2 Next time you make a tape or report, include pot-points, giving outcues and durations.

3 If you have access to studio equipment, practice backtiming and pre-fading signature tunes to get them to end exactly on time.

4 Even if you are not able to use a studio, you can practice pot-cutting by listening to news reports on the radio and hitting the off button when you think you can hear a suitable cut. With practice you will become reasonably competent at making clean cuts. The technique is to anticipate the end of a sentence.

5 Write up a weather report (taken from a newspaper or teletext) to run for exactly a minute. Script it so there are opt-outs at 30 seconds, 40 seconds and 50 seconds. The weather should be able to finish at any of those points and still make sense. Now try it with a sports report.

13 News anchors and presenters

Figure 23

'Voice is music and I think we respond much more than we realize to the music of the human voice.' – CHRISTINA SHEWALL, VOICE THERAPIST

THE TALENT

In showbusiness, actors and performers are known as the 'talent' – a label which has been transferred to the newsreaders and anchors of TV and radio stations.

Despite the hard work of the reporters, producers and other talented members of the news team, a station's reputation will stand or fall on the performance of these few front line people. A good anchor can boost a station's ratings while a bad one will send them crashing. Little wonder the Walter Cronkites of this world attract top salaries, and head-hunting to find the most talented and charismatic newscasters is rife.

The appetite for information continues to grow, but the way it is served up has had to adapt to today's fast food era. The old days of the announcer in his dinner jacket, proclaiming the news as one might announce the arrival of dignitaries at a state banquet have long gone. The years have seen deliberate attempts to lighten the news with greater informality. The battle for ratings has brought a babble of inane 'happy talk' to US TV. Even British television has unfrozen its stiff upper lip a little on its breakfast shows by substituting soft furnishing and baggy sweaters for solid desks and stiff suits.

Presentation styles differ between general programming and news. The more a programme aims to entertain, the warmer, friendlier and more relaxed its style will usually be, while news presenters tend to adopt a tone that is serious and more formal, in keeping with the weightier material of a bulletin.

Despite convention, the two approaches are moving closer together. Broadcast news is gradually becoming more personal and newsreaders more approachable and friendly. The authority is still there, but the mantle has been lifted from the schoolmaster and placed upon the shoulders of everybody's favourite uncle or wise friend. But the movement away from the more severe style of news presentation is still incomplete. Many exponents of the stern-faced, horn-rimmed spectacle brigade still bid us a fierce '*Good evening*' each night.

ANCHORS VERSUS NEWSREADERS

> *'In a word, an anchor has to have* ***believability****. The viewer has to believe what he is saying and that he understands its significance. One gets the impression that some British newsreaders have less understanding of their stories. When one sees a leading newscaster working on a TV quiz show and others doing fluff things, it's the sort of thing most American TV journalists who have any ambition would never do. The good ones see themselves as journalists first.'*
>
> —PAUL CLEVELAND, ASSIGNMENT MANAGER, ABC NEWS, LONDON.

The term 'anchorman' originated in America with Walter Cronkite. In the UK 'newsreader' or 'newcaster' is preferred, showing something of the difference in presentation styles either side of the Atlantic – styles which are emulated around the world.

Put simply, British newsreaders are seen as serious and slightly remote authority figures who would never allow their personalities to colour a news story, while US anchors are serious but friendly authority figures who comment on as well as present the news.

The term 'anchorman' suggests personal strength and authority, as though the bearer of that title, through a combination of experience, personality and charisma is holding the programme together and somehow grounding it in reality.

'Newsreader' has fewer personal connotations. The focus is off the individual and on to the news. 'Newscaster' suggests a benign oracle – an authority who has at his disposal privileged inside information which he will graciously impart to all who will sit at his feet to receive it. In the personality stakes, the newscaster is a step ahead of the newsreader, but still several paces behind the anchorman.

BBC newsreader John Humphrys, who presented the television *9 O'Clock News* before moving over to front the Radio 4 flagship, *Today*, is a slim, unassuming man with hair that has turned prematurely silver. He is against the whole idea of newsreaders being stars in their own right:

> *'It's difficult for a news presenter who becomes such a celebrity that he or she becomes the news. There is a danger you become a less effective newsreader when people are watching you to see whether you arch your eyebrows or how you say Nkomo. What you're paid to do is deliver the news. I don't like the whole personality cult. I'm just an ordinary, unexceptional guy who tries to read the news competently and not allow my character to intrude on it.'**

QUALITIES OF A NEWSCASTER

> *'On Radio 4 what we try to do is make sure that the professional voices . . . the announcers and the newsreaders . . . above all else speak with informed authority, and that means they must have credibility as far as the listener's concerned.'* – JIM BLACK, PRESENTATION EDITOR, RADIO 4

The ideal qualities for a newscaster or anchor have been variously listed as:

- Authority
- Credibility
- Clarity
- Warmth
- Personality
- Professionalism
- Good voice
- Good looks

In America with its Hollywood tradition, film star good looks coupled with paternal credibility often seem top requirements for the TV anchor. The degree of warmth and personality will depend on how far station style has moved towards the 'friendly' approach. In the USA the policy can sometimes seem to be, '*Smile, smile, smile*', while in the UK in particular, it can be, '*Scowl, scowl, scowl*'. In the UK credibility is everything. It seems the craggier and more battered the face, the more likely it is to present the news – unless that face belongs to a woman.

WOMEN NEWSCASTERS

When it comes to women presenters, TV stations might be loath to admit it, but the notion that sex appeal is paramount still seems universal.

ITN newsreader Julia Somerville sees no reason why middle-aged women should be kept away from the cameras:

> *'At the moment, the majority are moderately youthful – not too youthful, or they wouldn't be credible. But as we have craggy, seasoned, weathered, middled-aged men on TV, why can't we have some craggy,*

*'Who's the Man in the News,' *Sunday Magazine* 20 October, 1985.

> *seasoned, weathered, middled-aged women? Television... doesn't want glamour reading the news. What is far more important to people in a newsreader is trust.'*

The trend towards longer news programmes has resulted in the growing use of double-headed presentation, where newsreaders or anchors take it in turn to introduce the stories. Many programme makers believe a good combination is to put male and female presenters together.

MORE THAN JUST A NEWSREADER...

> *'I'm not interested in newsreaders – actors reading the news – it debases the news. Many of them don't know what the hell they're reading. When they interview somebody they read questions somebody else has written. That's wrong. The news ought to be told by journalists – they have more credibility.'*
>
> —HARRY RADLIFFE, LONDON BUREAU CHIEF, CBS NEWS

A TV news presenter is usually more than just a pretty face, and the popular misconception that an anchor simply walks into the studio ten minutes before a programme, picks up a script and reads it into a camera could not be further from the truth.

TV newsreaders will usually be seasoned journalists, who have graduated from newspapers and radio and had their baptism of fire as a TV reporter. Their move to presentation will have been as much for their proven news sense as for their on-screen presence.

Like most journalists, newsreaders will be news addicts, steeping themselves in stories throughout the day. They will be expected to be on top of the day's events and understand their background so that live interviews on current issues will pose no problem.

As the day progresses newsreaders will follow the material as it comes in and may offer their own suggestions for coverage.

> *'On big days you try to get in very early on the ground floor. You really need to be in the swim of things, in the full flow. It's important to be in on the discussions about who they plan to interview. Then people give all the reasons for the interview and that helps you about the line you should take.'* – Channel 4 Presenter Trevor McDonald

Where stations run several news programmes a day, newsreaders will work with teams to update their show and help establish its own clear identity. Part of that process will be rewriting stories to suit their individual style.

In radio, what scores is a clear resonant voice that conveys authority: In fact, the voice can often belie the looks. One British newsreader who sounded broad-shouldered, seasoned and darkly handsome on air, was in the flesh short and with a glass eye.

Radio news presenters can have a variety of different tasks, depending on the size and location of the station. In smaller outfits in Australia and the US, radio news is often read by disc jockeys, who tear the copy from the rip-and-read and have to undergo an instant personality change from purveyor of cosy banter to confident, well-informed bearer of tidings of significance. Their schizophrenia may then be made complete by having to read the commercials. To cap that, they may have to double as an engineer or technical assistant.

Some bigger stations hire presenters simply for their news reading abilities; while others look for journalists who read well on air and can double as roving reporters after their show is over.

Most radio stations will expect their news presenters to be able to at least re-write agency copy. The bigger, more news-orientated stations will expect much more besides, and British radio will usually insist that newsreaders are experienced journalists who can turn their hand to a variety of tasks, including live interviews.

PROFESSIONALISM

> *'I'm not particularly interested in pretty faces or pretty voices. I'm much more interested in credibility. An anchor should have worked as a reporter and know what a story is about.'*
>
> —JUDITH MELBY, NETWORK PRODUCER, CANADIAN BROADCASTING CORPORATION
>
> *'Authority is not a sound. Authority is a state of knowing what you are talking about and being able to explain it convincingly and readily to somebody else.'*
>
> — DAVID DUNHILL, BBC VOICE TRAINER AND FORMER NEWSREADER.

Credibility and authority – qualities every newsreader needs – are derived largely from personal confidence. That the newsreader knows what he/she is talking about should never be in question.

When cracks appear in the confidence and hesitation creeps into the delivery the newsreader's credibility can quickly go out the window – often closely followed by the newsreader. Such is the price of stardom in a business where consistent credibility and a flawless delivery are minimum requirements for a person whose performance has such a direct bearing on programme ratings – and profits.

Professionalism comes from having a cool head and plenty of experience. But it means more than remaining unruffled when all around you are behaving like headless chickens.

Consistency in presentation is vital, irrespective of whether you got out of bed the wrong side, or whether you slept at all last night; whether your curry is giving you heartburn or your wife has just left you.

Professionals hang up their personal life with their coat when they arrive for work and only take it up again when their work is over and they head for home. Along with their troubles, professionals hang up their bias, their background, their politics and their prejudices.

No one can be truly free from bias, but professionals have a duty to see their work is as free from prejudice as is humanly

possible. This can only be done by recognizing where personal preferences, opinions and prejudices lie and compensating for them by being scrupulously fair to the opposite viewpoints whenever they appear in the news.

Radio newsreaders have to purge every trace of bias from their voice. The TV newsreader's task is more difficult: the face, which could betray an opinion at the speed of thought, must remain objective throughout.

VOICE (Figure 24)

Adverts for jobs in radio frequently call for a newsreader with a '*good microphone voice*.' This usually means a voice that is reasonably rich, crisp and resonant and free from obvious impediments, such as a hare lip, stammer or a lisp – what BBC voice trainer David Dunhill describes as, '*a voice with no pimples*'.

There is still a preference (or prejudice) within the industry for male voices reading the news. The widely held belief is that they carry more authority, and that female voices can sound high pitched and irritating through the tinny speaker of a transistor radio. But this does not account for the fact that women now outnumber men in British local radio.

REPORTER

Radio Northampton

Are you a young ambitious reporter with at least three years' journalistic experience? If so, Radio Northampton has a vacancy that may interest you. The work is primarily reporting, interviewing, bulletin writing and newsreading. Good microphone voice and current driving licence essential.

We are an equal opportunities employer

BBC LOCAL RADIO

Figure 24

Should that trend develop, conventions about broadcasters' voices may change.

Voices that would not fit the 'good microphone voice' description are those that are piping, reedy, nasal, sibilant, indistinct or very young sounding. Newsreaders with accents that are not local to a station may find it difficult to persuade news editors to take them, on the grounds that their out-of-town intonations may not find favour with a local audience.

Accents can also be a problem in network radio. One Radio 4 presenter's clear Scottish accent brought in an unrelenting stream of vitriolic hate-mail. Ideas about the 'suitable broadcast voice' differ: '*For every newsreader the public adores, there is another public which hates that one*,' says David Dunhill.

> *'I'm not sure there is such a thing as a good microphone voice. Obviously the voice should be comfortable to listen to, friendly and clear, but I don't think it should be a special kind of voice with a special vocal quality.'*

Minor speech impediments such as weak 'Rrs', or 'THs' that become 'Vs' may be barriers to an otherwise promising career. Professional voice training may sort these problems out, and voices that are thick and nasal may be improved by medical treatment to the adenoids. With effort, voices can sometimes be lowered to give an impression of greater authority – Margaret Thatcher's is one in question. In the long run, most voices sound richer and wiser as their owners get older.

Another essential quality in a newsreader is the ability to *sightread*. For some people, the seemingly simple task of reading out loud can prove impossible. Not everyone has the ability to read ahead, which is essential for a smooth delivery, and for them sightreading can mean a staccato stumbling from word to word, losing the flow and sense of the item. It can trouble people who are dyslexic or have to read in a foreign language. Some may have this problem without even realizing, as few people are frequently called on to read out loud. For many, their last public performance might well have been at kindergarten.

FIELDWORK

1 Make a study of three different newsreaders. Award marks out of ten for *authority*, *credibility*, *clarity*, *warmth*, *personality*, *professionalism*, *good voice*, and for TV, *good looks*. Add the scores and see which newsreader comes top in your estimation. Was this the newsreader you preferred anyway? Do your scores agree with those of your classmates? Discuss any differences.

What do *you* think are the most important qualities in a newsreader? Why?

2 How would you define *professionalism*, and how would you know if it was missing?

3 Do you think newsreaders should be more or less formal in their styles? How would this affect the credibility of their presentation?

What do you think gives a newsreader his/her authority?

What effect do you think would be the effect on the ratings of 'middle-aged, craggy-faced' woman newsreaders?

4 Do you prefer single headed or double headed presentation? Why?

5 Record yourself reading a number of news stories from the rip-and-read, teletext or newspapers. How do you sound compared with professional newsreaders? What is the difference and how could you improve?

If you are in a class, take turns to read a number of stories in front of your classmates and give your honest and constructive appraisals of one another's style. Discuss to what degree authority, credibility, clarity, warmth and personality are present, and how each of you could improve your styles.

14 'On air!'

PERFORMANCE

Newsreading is the point where the business of information and the game of showbusiness meet. How glitzy or glossy the presentation will depend on how far the TV station has travelled down the road to entertainment. But even among the 'heavy' set of newsreaders most outwardly disdainful of TV's gloss and glamour, the act of being oracle to more than a million viewers will always have something of the ego trip about it... however hard they may try to deny it.

TV presenters have to live with fame, but while being a public figure may massage the ego when the public is on your side, that same fickle audience will be as quick to complain as they are to compliment, not only if your performance begins to falter, but if they do not like the cut of your suit or the shape of your tie.

Figure 25 Programme presenters must have their wits about them – in radio, presentation can mean operating a control desk, cueing tapes for broadcast, reading scripts and conducting live interviews – there is no room for mistakes (Andrew Boyd)

TV presenters should never let their dress sense get in the way of their news sense. Says BBC newsreader Sue Lawley: '*If you have a funny haircut or too low a blouse or something that's too dramatically fashionable people will say, "Look at her, what's she got on? Gosh!" Then they are looking at her and not listening to what she is saying.*'*

Newsreader John Humphrys was once voted Britain's best dressed man, though he says he is not interested in clothes. As though to make the point he turned up for the award at London's smartest hotel wearing a £50 suit. He later admitted to Woman magazine, '*Mind you, all the smartness on the* 9'O Clock News *was only from the waist up – I was my typical scruffy self below the desk!*'

Conservative without being frowsty is probably the safest dress style to aim for.

Similarly, presenters' mannerisms can sometimes draw more attention than the stories they are reading. Leaning back or forward, swaying from side to side, scratching the nose, licking the lips, blinking hard or waving the hands about, are all tics which the budding anchor may have to iron out by patient practice in front of a mirror, or better still, a video camera, before risking his/her reputation before an audience.

PRESENCE

In the hot seat of the TV studio, with flooding adrenalin and a wildly beating heart, the newsreader may find it difficult to remember that real people are sitting the other side of the screen anxious to hear what he/she has to say. The camera, lights and other paraphernalia can seem as impersonal and uninviting as a dentist's chair. But the newsreader has to screw down the lid on his/her panic and somehow dismiss all that hardware. **The camera must cease to be a single staring eye set in a metal face, and become an acquaintance or friend. You would not talk *at* a friend, so you should not talk *at* a camera. Speak *to* it. It likes you. It is on your side. But what you say and the way you say it will need charisma and the force of confidence to carry through the lens to the viewer the other side. This is the x-factor that marks out a good newsreader. It is called *presence*.**

> *'Sometimes you are verging on hysteria. I always take a deep breath before the camera comes on to me. The first time I ever went into a TV studio to do a live broadcast my teeth were chattering. I said to the presenter, who'd been doing it for 15 years, "You must feel quite calm by now." He replied, "Dear boy, the day you come in here without any nerves is the day you'll stop doing it because you'll have lost your edge." I know he was right. You have to feel the adrenalin pumping.'*
>
> – BBC NEWSREADER, JOHN HUMPHRYS†*

Adrenalin can be a problem – either way. The first-time presenter may have to fight to bring it under control. The old stager may have to fight to keep it going. One radio newsreader used to deliberately wait until the last

**Inside Television*, BBC, 1986.
†'Who's the Man in the News?' *Sunday Magazine*, 20 Oct 1985.

moment before hurrying into the studio. Often the disk jockey would have fired the seven second signature tune into the bulletin before the newsreader had even sat down. All this was to keep the adrenalin going. Not recommended. Brinkmanship can, and does, lead to disasters on air. But a steady stream of adrenalin, always under control, could be the mystery ingredient behind that all-important and indefinable commodity – presence.

GETTING THROUGH TO THE AUDIENCE – RAPPORT

> *'When I'm on air, I often imagine I'm talking to my own sister or a friend.'*
> — BBC *WOMAN'S HOUR* PRESENTER, SUE MACGREGOR

BBC trainees are sometimes given the following pearl of wisdom:

Information + Presentation = Communication

Successful communication is largely a matter of presentation, and that depends on the way the copy is written, and the way it is read. Good newsreaders are ones who establish rapport with their audience.

Such rapport defies satisfactory definition. It is a kind of chemistry that exists between newsreaders and their audience. Where it is present, both presenter and audience are satisfied. Where it is absent, the information seems to fall short and fail to connect, and the presenter, cut off behind a barrier of electronic hardware, will usually be aware of the fact.

BBC trainer Robert McLeish says rapport is established by '*thinking outwards*.' Voice trainer David Dunhill calls this '*radio reaching out*'. Trainee newsreaders are encouraged to '*bring the script to life*,' to '*lift the words off the paper*,' to '*project their personalities*,' to '*establish a presence*' or to be '*up-front*'. But rapport begins with never regarding a mass audience as simply that. Each listener is an individual who has invited you into his/her home. You are a guest; an acquaintance or even a friend, and you have been welcomed in because you have a story to tell.

Newsreaders, particularly in radio, can easily forget about the audience. Cocooned within the four walls of the studio, they may begin to sound as though they are talking to themselves. They are going through the motions, their concentration is elsewhere and their newsreading will begin to sound stilted, sing-song, and insincere.

The solution to strident anonymity or mumbling into the microphone is to remember that you are not reeling off information or reading from a script, but *telling* someone a story.

Radio newsreaders have an added disadvantage. In normal conversation, the person you are talking to will be able to see your face. Your expressions will reflect your story. If it is sad, you will look sad, if it is happy, you will smile. Your hands may do the talking for you, gesticulating and adding emphasis. You may have a tendency to mumble but people will make up with their eyes what is missed by their ears by watching your lips.

Now imagine you are talking to someone who cannot see your lips, your eyes, or your hands. That vital part of your communication has gone. This is how it is in radio. This handicap is overcome by working to put into your voice all the expression that would normally go into your face and hands.

A word of warning – overdo the intonation and you will sound as though you are talking to a child, and talking down to the audience is something no newsreader will get away with for long.

KNOW YOUR MATERIAL

> *'Liverpool... About 500 people, or 500 – I think that should be half a million people rather – were treated for broken arms and ribs... No, heh, sorry... 500 people were treated for broken arms and ribs, hysteria and bruising after half a million screaming fans gathered outside an official reception to see their FA cup winning heroes – Almost a disaster!'* – UK RADIO

Confidence comes from experience, from being in command of the bulletin and thoroughly familiar with the material. Inexperienced newsreaders should spend as much time as possible reading and re-reading the stories *aloud* so when they go on air they are on familiar ground. This also highlights phrases which clash and jar, mistakes, unfamiliar names that need practice, poor punctuation and sentences that are impossibly long. All these problems are easily missed by the eye, but are likely to be picked up by the voice.

Many newsreaders rewrite their stories extensively to make certain the style suits their voice – the best way to be familiar with a story is to write it yourself.

> *'The essence is to get over what you understand to be the truth of the matter, and the essence of that is to completely understand what you're reading before you open your mouth. Provided you understand it your listeners will understand it. One does hear a lot of reading where there's a great deal of wrong stressing and it just shows that the person hasn't comprehended what they're reading.*
>
> *'Intelligence in reading is very important, because the listener has only one opportunity to hear what you are saying; he can't turn back the page to read a difficult sentence again, as he can with a paper.'*
>
> – JOHN TOUHEY, BBC WORLD SERVICE NEWSREADER

AD-LIBS

Few professionals rely on ad-libs to see them through a programme. Back-announcements, station identities, comments and seemingly casual links are usually scripted. When the programme is running against the clock, a live guest is settling down in the studio to be interviewed any moment *and* there is a constant stream of chatter in your ear from the control room, even the snappiest quips and witticisms thought up before the show tend to be driven from your mind. The best way to avoid embarrassment is to script *everything* barring the timechecks, and even these should be handled with care.

'*It's thirteen minutes to two*' is the sort of phrase a presenter can take for granted, but try glancing up at a clock yourself and giving an immediate and accurate timecheck and you will see how difficult it can be to get right. From the half past onwards, the timecheck can involve some tricky mental arithmetic. Special presenters' clocks are available – at a cost – which display the time as it would be said: '*thirteen minutes to three*'. Even distinguished broadcasters who have fallen foul of the timecheck might consider this money well spent.

> *'The time is six o'clock. Good evening, this is Jon Snow with the news. I'm sorry, the time is half past six, and this is Jon Snow with the local news, but first, a look at the headlines . . . half past five! – I'm sorry; very confusing clock on the wall, here.'* – UK RADIO

Always engage your brain before putting your mouth into gear – *think before you speak.*

After newsreaders have rehearsed the bulletin, they should try to insist on a few minutes peace and quiet before the programme to read it through again, though in TV this can be a vain hope.

In the end, performance is everything. What would you prefer to hear – a newsreader stumbling through an unrehearsed bulletin bursting with up-to-the-minute stories and failing to make sense of it, or a smoothly polished delivery of material that may be ten minutes old but makes complete sense?

THE GATE

Some newsrooms operate a gate to give readers a chance to compose themselves. This is a bar on new copy being handed to the newsreader later than five or ten minutes before a bulletin. Old hands may scoff at this – they can pick up a pile of scripts and deliver them sight unseen without batting an eyelid, but for the less experienced reader, a gate can make the difference between a smooth performance and wishing the studio floor would open up and swallow you.

MAKING A SWIFT RECOVERY

> *'The worst disaster that ever happened to me was when I was smoking during a news bulletin and set my script on fire. I tried waving it about but it only made it flame up more. We got it out somehow, but it was a bit distracting. I dare say anybody listening attentively will have realized something had gone a bit wrong. I don't think I said anything; just carried on in the British tradition.'* – DAVID DUNHILL

When things go wrong, the anchor or newsreader is expected to stay cool and professional. Whatever the ferment beneath the surface, no cracks must appear in the calm exterior. The coolest recovery on record was probably that of a wartime BBC announcer who pressed on with his script after a bomb fell on Broadcasting House.

'*I always think of a fluff as a kind of small microbe*,' says David Dunhill, '*Once it gets in and gets you, you will go on fluffing the rest of the bulletin*.' The answer is to immediately and completely dismiss the mistake from your mind and focus your total concentration on the rest of the bulletin.

Most fluffs occur when newsreaders are expecting trouble, like a difficult foreign name, or when they have already fluffed and their mind is sidetracked. The irony is that the difficult name is usually pronounced flawlessly, while the reader stumbles over the simple words before and behind it in the sentence.

> ***'A flash from Washington... the House of Representatives Jurish... Judiciary Committee, which is considering, em, a, the impeachment of President Nixon has voted umanimously... unanimously to call Mr Nixon as a witness. Of course, whether Mr Wick... Nick... Wixton... winwhether Mr Nixton... Ahh! (tut) Sorry about this! (laugh) whether Mr Nixon will agree is quite ano-nother matter.'*** – BRITISH RADIO

'*When a programme has been tricky and you think you have done it reasonably well, that's a very exhilarating feeling*,' says newscaster Trevor McDonald. '*But there are times when you know you haven't done awfully well and you feel really bad about it and wish you could go home and forget it, only you can't. My own mistakes always loom much, much larger in my own mind. When I talk to people about them, they haven't noticed them sometimes, but even the little mistakes always loom. You have to aim for perfection. There's no other way*.'

Perhaps it is this striving for perfection and quality of merciless self-criticism that turns a broadcaster into a top professional.

The art of the accomplished recovery is to prepare for every contingency.

The worst mistake any presenter can make is to swear on air – *do not even think it*, otherwise you will probably say it.

The commonest problem is the taped report that fails to appear. The introduction has been read, the presenter is waiting, and – nothing. Next to swearing, the broadcaster's second deadliest sin is dead air. Silent airspace is worst on radio. On TV, viewers can watch the embarrassed expression on the presenter's face.

If an item fails to appear the radio presenter should apologize and move smartly on to the next. In TV, presenters will usually be directed what to do by the control room. Up to three seconds of silence is the most that should pass before the newsreader cuts in. Novices often make the mistake of pausing for ten or more seconds in the hope that the technical operator will find the fault and cure it.

The problem can be compounded by confusing the audience with technical jargon like: '*I'm sorry, but that cart seems to have gone down.*' Or, '*We don't seem to have that tape/package/insert.*' Practice what you are going to say when something goes wrong until it becomes almost a reflex action.

When that report eventually does arrive, the audience will have forgotten what it is about and the presenter should re-introduce it by re-reading or paraphrasing the cue.

Where readers stumble over a word or phrase, they should judge quickly whether to repeat it. If the sense of the item has been lost, by saying, for instance, '*Beecham pleaded guilty to the murder,*' when he pleaded *not* guilty, then the sentence should be repeated. Avoid the cliché, '*I'm sorry, I'll read that again*' – '*I'm sorry*' will do. If the mistake is a minor one, let it go. Chances are the audience will quickly forget it, whereas drawing attention to it with an apology may only make it worse.

'Ronald Reagan is alive and well and kicking tonight, one day after the assassination attempt, just two and a half months into his pregnancy...'
– US TV

'Police are finding it difficult to come up with a solution to the murders... the commissioner says the victims are unwilling to co-operate.'
– US RADIO

'Well, the blaze is still fierce in many places, and as a result of this fire, two factories have been gutted and one homily left famless.'
– AUSTRALIAN RADIO

'One of three Labour MPs who just returned from Afghanistan... has now said he'd seen very few Soviet troops and control of the city was clearly in Afghan hounds – hands!' – BBC RADIO

'Following the warning by the Basque Separatist organization ETA that it's preparing a bombing campaign in Spanish holiday resorts, British terrorists have been warned to keep on their guard... I'm sorry (chuckle) *that should be British* tourists...' – UK RADIO

'The... company is recalling a total of 14,000 cans of suspect salmon and fish cutlets. It's believed they're contaminated by poisonous orgasms.'
– AUSTRALIAN RADIO

'And now here's the latest on the Middle East crisis... crisis... Lesbian forces today attacked Israel. I beg your pardon, that should be Lesbanese... Lebanese. (laughter)' – ANON

CORPSING

Newsreaders face few greater threats to their credibility than that of corpsing on air. Corpsing may not be a literal occurrence but it can feel much the same. It means to dry up, grind to a halt, or, worse, burst out laughing.

These are signs of nervousness and panic. Such laughter is seldom sparked off by genuine humour; it is the psyche's safety valve blowing to release tension that has built up inside the reader. Anything incongrous or slightly amusing can trigger it off.

The audience does not always see the joke, especially when the laughter erupts through a serious or tragic news item. Where professional self-control is in danger of collapsing, the realization that untimely laughter can bring an equally untimely end to a career and that a substantial part of the audience may write you off as an idiot unless you pull yourself together, can often have the same salutary effect as a swift sousing with a bucket of icy water.

Self-inflicted pain is a reasonable second line of defence. Some presenters bring their mirth under control by resorting to personal torture, such as digging their nails into the palms of their hands or grinding the toes of one foot with the heel of the other. A less painful way to prevent corpsing is to not permit yourself to be panicked and pressurized in the first place.

> ***'Finally, the weather forecast. Many areas will be dry and warm with some sunshine... It actually says shoeshine on my script, so with any luck, you might get a nice light tan.'*** – BBC RADIO

RELAXATION

The key to the confidence that marks out the top-flight professional is the ability to be in command, and at the same time relaxed. This can be a tall order under deadline pressure and the spotlights of the studio.

Tension can manifest itself in a number of ways, especially in novice newsreaders. The muscles of the neck and throat may tighten to strangle the voice and put it up an octave. Their reading may also speed up. Stretching the shoulders and arms like a cat before relaxing and breathing deeply will often reduce this tension. (Note: Do this *before* you go on air!)

Another problem is that beginners can sometimes – literally – dry up. Tension removes the moisture in the throat and mouth and it becomes impossible to articulate. Relaxation helps and a glass of water – sipped slowly to prevent the splutters – will usually be sufficient to moisten the lips, mouth and throat.

A word of warning – drink nothing containing sugar or milk. Hot, sweet coffee is *out*. Milk and sugar clog the palate and gum up the mouth. Alcohol should be avoided for *obvioush reashonsh*.

The same goes for eating food just before going on air. A bolted sandwich before a bulletin can undermine the coolest demeanour. Stray particles of bread and peanut-butter lodged in the molars are a sure way of turning on the waterworks and leaving the newscaster drooling with excess saliva – and there is always the risk of going into the bulletin with a fit of flatulence or a bout of the hiccups.

Tiredness can also ruin otherwise good newsreading. Broadcasters often work shifts and may have to cope with irregular sleep patterns and, for early birds, semi-permanent fatigue. Weariness can drag down the muscles of the face, put a sigh in the voice and extinguish any sparkle. Gallons of black coffee – without sugar – may be one answer, limbering up the face by vigorously contorting the lips, cheeks and mouth may be another. But do not let anyone catch you doing that on camera, unless you want to end up on the Christmas collection of out-takes.

FIELDWORK

1 Think back to your study of different newsreaders (Chapter 13). Which had the most presence? Is this the one who scored highest on your list? How do *you* define presence?

How successful were those newsreaders in establishing rapport with their audience? Do you think rapport is conscious or unconscious? How would *you* go about establishing rapport?

If you are in a class, prepare and read a bulletin out loud and get votes out of ten for *presence* and *rapport*. Ask your colleagues to try to define why these factors were present or absent in your reading.

2 Practise reading bulletins on tape and listening back to find ways to improve your powers of communication. Remember that communication is not so much technique as a state of mind.

3 If you are in a class, swap a bulletin you have written with one of your neighbour's. Now read it out loud without checking it through or even glancing at it beforehand. Did you have any problems? What with? Why?

Does the copy need rewriting to suit your reading style? Rewrite it then read it through once for practice and then out loud for real. What difference did being familiar with the copy make?

4 Plan what you would say if (a) a taped report went down on air; (b) the wrong tape was played after your cue; (c) the next item went missing.

Practise some impromptu timechecks throughout the day. Glance up at the clock and immediately say the time out loud. Which is easier, before the hour or after the hour? How long does it take for the time to register accurately once you have glanced at the clock? Remember to always allow yourself that much time before starting to give a timecheck.

5 Practise the relaxation exercises outlined in the chapter and see if they help you. If not, develop your own that will.

15 Newsreading mechanics

SPEED

The acceptable pace of newsreading, like hemlines, seems to go up and down with fashion. My first attempt at newsreading was giving the headlines at the end of a half hour radio programme. I was told to go at it as fast as I could and duly complied. That evening, still flushed with pride and wonder, I asked a friend what she had made of my debut as a newsreader. '*Couldn't understand a word of it* she said, with characteristic bluntness, '*you were gabbling*.'

The right reading pace is one which is comfortable for the reader, clear to the listener, and which suits the station's style. That could be anywhere between 140 to 220 words per minute. British TV usually favours three words per second, or 180 wpm, which is a natural and pleasing pace which loses none of the urgency associated with the news.

Three words per second is also a handy formula for timing a script – a twenty second lead becomes sixty words, a thirty second story is ninety words, and so on.

The ultra-slow 150 wpm, which finds favour on and off in America and on foreign language stations, permits a delivery which is almost Churchillian in its portentiousness, and highly persuasive. It is the pace popularized by broadcasting giants like Edward R. Murrow who critics used to say took ten seconds to get through his wartime dateline: '*This . . . is . . . London*.' The BBC's World service, aimed at an audience for whom English is a foreign language, paces itself at between 140 and 160 wpm.

Pace is less important than clarity, and an aid to clear reading is to pause. The pause is a cunning device with many uses. It allows time for an important phrase to sink in and for the hearer to make sense of it; it permits a change of style between stories; it can be used to indicate the beginning of a quote, and it gives newsreaders time to replenish their oxygen supply.

BREATHING

Newsreaders, like swimmers, have to master the art of breath control. Good breathing brings out the richness and flavour of the voice.

First you have to sit correctly to give your lungs and diaphragm as much room as possible. The upper half of the body should be upright or inclined forward, with the back slightly arched. Your legs should not be crossed.

Air to the newsreader is like oil in an engine. Run out of it and you will seize up. The aim is open the lungs and throat as widely as possible, so breathing should be deep and from the belly instead of the usual shallow breathing from the top of the lungs. *Never* run into the studio. Breathless readers will find themselves gasping for air or getting dizzy and feeling faint.

> *'One of the golden rules is to never run before a news bulletin. I went downstairs – it was a very long way down – and I sat there with two minutes to go and suddenly realized to my horror that I had left all the national and international rip-and-read upstairs, and so I stupidly ran. I got into the news, and of course I couldn't breathe. Panic makes it worse and it was – GAAASP! – like this all the time and I felt absolutely awful, I just wanted to die and I had to pull out after two minutes. It must have sounded dreadful. Fortunately none of my immediate bosses were listening or they would have rocketed me sky high and quite rightly.'*
>
> —PENNY YOUNG, NEWS EDITOR, BBC RADIO NORTHAMPTON

Newsreaders should take a couple of good breaths before starting and another deep breath between each story. They can top up at full stops (periods) and paragraphs, and, faced with long sentences, can take shallow breaths where the commas should be. Better to rewrite the story; but where time does not allow, sentences can be broken up with a slash to show readers where they can safely pause while still making sense of the copy:

> *'The editor of the Nigerian magazine* ***Newswatch*** *who was killed by a parcel bomb / has been buried today. Dele Giwa had a reputation as an investigative journalist / who was not afraid to run stories which might prove unpopular with the military government. He'd been interrogated by the security services only days before his death / and an hour before the bomb went off / a senior security official had rung to ask for his address. The security services deny any involvement in his killing.'*

The pauses help the listener make sense of the copy by dividing the sentences into *sense groups*.

Breathing through the mouth permits faster refuelling than through the nose, but newsreaders should beware of snatching their breath. Gasping can be avoided by opening the mouth wider and taking the air in shallow draughts. The general idea is to avoid making a noise like a parched Australian swilling down a tube of his favourite amber nectar.

PROJECTION

There are different schools of thought about whether newsreaders should project their voice or talk naturally. In television a conversational tone is more appropriate to the illusion of eye-contact with the audience, and projection matters less because television audiences offer more of their undivided attention than radio listeners.

Radio presenters have to work harder. They should project just enough to cut through distractions and get attention. Overprojected newsreading makes the listener want to back away from the set or turn the volume down. Under normal circumstances there is no need to bark out the story like a war correspondent under crossfire. If radio broadcasters can picture themselves at one end of an average sized room with a couple of people at the other end whose attention is divided between chores and listening to what they have to say, their projection will be about right.

Radio newsreaders' voices often have to cut through a lot of background noise before reaching the listener, especially if they are being heard on somebody's car radio or in a living room full of hyperactive two-year olds. **Yelling is not the way to make sure every syllable is heard – clear diction is**. All too often newsreaders can be heard running words together, swallowing the ends of words and leaving sentences trailing in mid-air because their attention has already drifted on to the next story. Newsreaders' eyes cannot move from the page and neither should their minds. There should be a kind of magnetism between the mind and the script if they are to have any feel for the copy and sound sincere about what they are reading.

EMPHASIS

Copy should be read aloud to establish which words should be given extra emphasis. These are usually the key words and descriptions. For example:

> *'The PENTAGON has REJECTED calls to pull US WARSHIPS out of the GULF. Earlier, the SOVIET UNION said IT would withdraw its OWN fleet if the US, BRITAIN and FRANCE did the same.'*

These words can be capitalized, as shown, or underlined. Some readers favour double underlining to highlight different degrees of emphasis.

Shifting the position of the emphasis in a sentence can completely alter its meaning and tone. This can have a dramatic effect on the story:

> *HE said their action had made a walkout inevitable.*

Stressing the word *he* may suggest there are others who might disagree with this statement.

> *He SAID their action had made a walkout inevitable.*

Emphasizing the word *said* casts doubt on the truth of the statement, implying there are grounds for disbelieving it.

> *He said THEIR action had made a walkout inevitable.*

The speaker now sounds as though he/she is pointing a finger in accusation at another group of people.

> *He said their action HAD made a walkout inevitable.*

This has an intriguing double-meaning. Does *had* suggest the possibility of a walkout was true earlier, but is no longer the case, or is the stress on *had* a rebuttal, as though denying a suggestion that the action would not lead to a walkout? Think about it. The answer would probably become obvious from the context, but it highlights the importance of the newsreader having a clear understanding of the item before attempting to read it on air.

A common failing of untrained newsreaders is to imagine that due stress and emphasis means banging out every fifth word of a story and ramming the point home by pounding the last word of each sentence. This is about as elegant as a tap-dance in jackboots. Each sentence must establish its own rhythm without having a false one stamped upon it. Stress exists not to make the copy punchier, but to bring out its meaning.

PITCH

As well as having rhythm, the voice also goes up and down. This is called *modulation*, or pitch, and some readers who are new at their business or have being doing it too long can sound as though they are singing the news. The voice goes up and down a lot, but in all the wrong places. Voice trainer David Dunhill describes this as, '*Redolent of an air hostess telling me to fasten my seat belt or extinguish my cigarette.*' Modulation can add interest to the voice and variety to an item, but random modulation coupled with universal stress can make an audience grateful for the commercial break.

> Sentences usually begin on an upward note, rise in the middle, and end on a downward note. These are known as uppers and downers. But what happens to the downers when the last word belongs to a question?

Read this sentence yourself to find out.

These uppers and downers are signposts to the listener. They subconsciously confirm and reinforce the way the sentence is developing and help convey its meaning.

MICROPHONE TECHNIQUE
(Figure 26)

The important things to avoid with microphones are *popping* and *paper rustle*. Popping occurs when the mouth is too close to the mike and plosive sounds, such as Ps in particular, produce distortion. Radio newsreaders can tell this is happening by listening to themselves on headphones, and can prevent it by backing away or turning the mike slightly to one side.

Different microphone effects are possible. The closer the mike is to the mouth, the more of the voice's natural resonance it will pick up. Late night radio presenters use the close-mike technique to make their voices sound as sexy and intimate as someone whispering sweet nothings into your ear. Where a voice is naturally lacking in richness, close mike work can sometimes help compensate.

Conversely, standing away from the mike and raising the voice can make it sound as though the presenter is speaking live on location – useful for giving a lift to studio commentary over outdoor scenes or sound effects.

Figure 26 *'One should sit in a reasonably upright way with one's face towards the microphone. A lot of people I've noticed tend to drop their heads over their scripts, so the soundwaves from the mouth are reflected rather than going directly into the microphone. Always address the microphone properly. Breathing should be from the diaphragm and one should not make a noise. You hear a lot of heavy breathing and that should be avoided. Instead, take a controlled intake on breath at the start of each item,'* John Touhey, BBC World Service newsreader (Andrew Boyd)

Most directional mikes will give their best results about 15 cm (6 in) from the mouth.

The microphone, being closer to the script than the reader's ears, will pick up every rustle and scrape of the page, unless great care is taken in moving the paper. Use thick paper which does not crinkle, or small pages which are less prone to bending.

The best way to avoid paper rustle is to carefully lift each sheet, holding it in tension to prevent it bending, and place it to one side. To cut any noise that even this might make, lift the page while it is still being read and place it down *after* you begin reading the next item. The sound of your voice will drown out any paper rustle.

USING THE PROMPTER
(Figure 27)

(Credits roll . . . ***Police 5*** *with Shaw Taylor.)*
'Good evening. One of the most difficult crimes to detect is that . . . (pause) *committed by a stuck autocue.'*

'Autocues can make or break you in a live programme'.
—BRITISH NEWSREADER ANNA FORD

'The most important thing with an Autocue is to make sure that you check it. The operators are very good, but everybody's human. Words can be misspelt, words can be left out.'
—ANDREW GARDNER, UK NEWSREADER*

**It'll Be Alright on the Night*, London Weekend Television

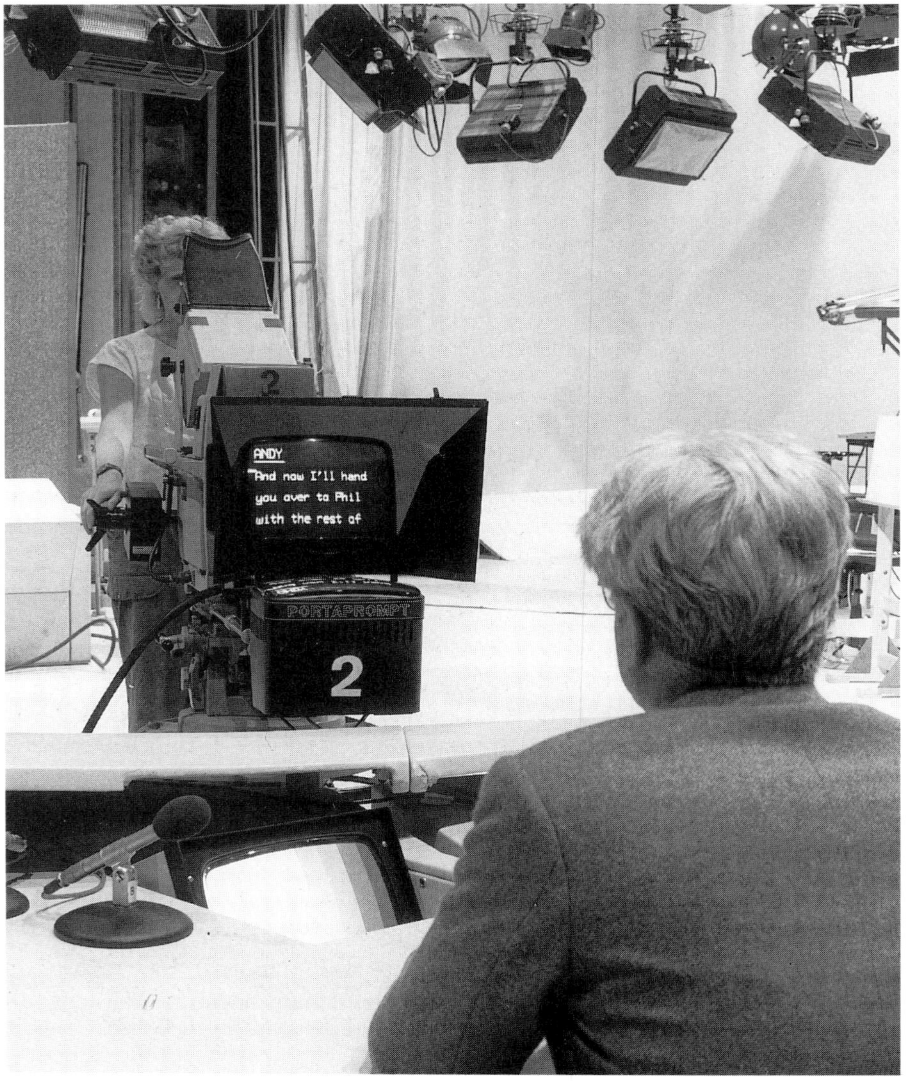

Figure 27 The studio teleprompter. The aim is to give the impression of eye contact with the viewer (courtesy EDS Portaprompt)

Many TV stations use devices to project the script on to glass in front of the camera so presenters can give the impression of eye contact with the viewer as they read the news. (See also prompting, page 333.)

The intention is to make it seem that they know their material off by heart and are simply telling the story to the audience. What frequently spoils the illusion is the way some newsreaders stare woodenly into the camera, as though trying to make out a spot on the end of the viewer's nose. Worse still is when they screw up their eyes to peer at some mis-typed or corrected word on the prompter.

How often do you see newsreaders with their faces frozen in a permanent scowl of concentration, eyebrows never moving, as though glued in position or permanently carved in an unnatural and ingratiating arch across the forehead? If the camera is the newsreader's best friend, then the prompter has to be seen as the smile on your best friend's face, and responded to as such.

But newsreaders cannot afford to relax *too* much – they may destroy another of TV's illusions. Many TV stations display computer pictures or stills in a box or window to one side of the newscaster. To the viewer it appears to be behind the reader, but often the reverse is true and readers who are prone to fidget are liable to disappear behind the window.

Stations which do not use prompters put an even greater strain on their readers. Somehow, presenters are expected to give a flawless delivery of the script in their hand while looking up at the camera to keep eye contact with the viewers. Compromise is the best that can be hoped for. Readers will have to look up at the camera as much as possible without losing their place on the script or forgetting the words that follow. Where the bulletin is broken up with pre-recorded items, the reader can use the pause to refresh his/her memory about the next story.

Eye-contact with the viewer should be re-established at the beginning of each item, because the first few words and the expression on the newsreader's face sets the scene for the story. This is where memory comes in. If you can remember the first line of each story, then eye contact can be achieved. Similarly, you should cultivate the habit of scanning ahead and fixing the next half-dozen words in your mind. It can be good to glance down at the script when reading a quote. This tells the audience that you are concerned with getting your quotes right.

NOISE, NOISE, NOISE

One blight TV newsreaders have to live with is the constant babble of noise injected directly into their ear through the earpiece, which keeps them in touch with the control room. Into their ear comes not only their countdown but everything said to the cameracrews, videotape operators, graphics operators, caption operators, etc. Putting it mildly, it can be a distraction:

> *'You've got to develop a split brain to be able to read the news and listen at the same time,' says* John Humphrys. *'When I say,' "Here's a report from Beirut," they have to start the machine rolling with the report on it five seconds before it comes on, otherwise the picture doesn't stabilize and the sound's wonky. So I have a countdown going on in my ear, and I have to make sure my last word finishes on zero.*
>
> *'Inevitably, things go wrong. I'm saying, "Here's a report from Beirut" and someone starts screaming in my ear, "It's not ready yet!" Once, something went wrong with the countdown three times in succession and I lost my cool and said on air, "I wish someone would tell me what is going on".'**

* 'Who's the Man in the News?' *Sunday Magazine*, 20 October, 1985.

BRINGING THE STORY TO LIFE

Once a script has been written and handed to the newsreader it becomes his/hers alone. The reader must identify with the story and transform it from being mere words on a page. The copy has to be lifted off the paper, carried through the microphone, transported over the airwaves, and planted firmly in the listeners' imagination. And that is done by *telling a story*.

The test of whether communication has taken place is audience reaction. A news story should produce a response of pleasure or pain. If you were to tell a friend about a family illness, you would expect him to react. If he listened to you with a deadpan expression and turned away unmoved, you would wonder whether he had heard you right.

News should be the same. The audience will response to you as they would to an actor on stage. As actors strive to give life to their lines, your task is to bring your copy to life. Newsreaders' talents lie in perfectly matching their tone to the storyline. Skilfully done, this makes the story more accessible by signalling its meaning, significance, importance and relevance – the emotions in the voice reflecting in part the emotional response that the story should produce in the hearer. For most experienced newsreaders this process is automatic, but for many new to the business it is a skill that has to be learned.

The skill lies in the subtlety of the storytelling. If newsreaders were painters, they would use watercolours and washes, never lurid oils. Histrionics over the airwaves will result in the listener diving for the off-switch. Only a ham goes over the top and a poor actor fails to do justice to the script. This is the task of the newsreader – to do justice to the script.

A simple tip – when you are happy, you smile, so when you smile, you sound happy. If a story is lighthearted, then crack your face and smile. But if the news is grave, then the newsreader could do little worse than to sound as though the unfortunate victim has just won the pools. Hearing, '*Four people have died in a pit disaster*,' read by someone with a broad grin is not only embarrassing, it is insulting. If you want to convey gravity, then frown. If the story is sad, then look sad.

One way to spare yourself from reading with a gleeful grin what turns out half way through to be an obituary is to make some indication of the tone in which the copy should be read. It can be helpful to draw a suitable face at the top of the page (Figure 28).

If the newsreader assumes that expression, then the tone should be just about right.

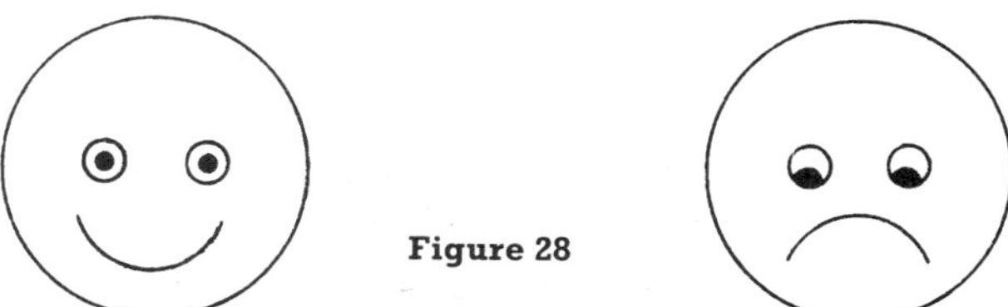

Figure 28

'Take care of the sense and the sounds will take care of themselves.'
– LEWIS CARROLL

FIELDWORK

1 Practise sitting correctly to read some copy. Make sure you take plenty of air, but not so much that you have to strain to hold it. Now read the copy into a recorder and hear how you sound. Try different postures to see which gives you the most air and feels the most comfortable.

Go through that copy again, marking it for breaths and then read it to see if that helps you.

2 Ask someone to time you reading an item of copy that is more than 230 words long. Get them to stop you after exactly a minute and work out your reading speed by counting how many words you have read.

3 Record yourself reading again and practise removing scripts that have been read without making a sound. Also try different amounts of projection to see which sounds best and underline difficult stories for emphasis to see if this helps you.

4 If you have access to a TV studio with a prompter, practise reading to camera. Avoid staring at it and practise animating your features while still keeping a natural expression.

5 Try reading out loud the stories below and bringing them to life by stressing the correct emphases and using the appropriate tone. Then, just for fun, try some of them in a tone that is totally unsuitable, and see how ridiculous they sound.

'Three people have died in a highway pile up on the outskirts of Boston.'

'A Lancashire window cleaner has won almost half a million pounds on the football pools.'

'Good news for industry... the latest figures show a major upswing in trade.'

'Unemployment is getting worse... the Government has just announced a sharp rise in the numbers out of work... and more job cuts could be on the way.'

'New Zealand's longest surviving heart transplant patient has just celebrated her golden wedding anniversary.'

'But despite all efforts... there were no survivors.'

'The blaze tore right through the warehouse, exploding tins of paint and showering flaming debris into the air. The building was completely gutted.'

'Jonestown's new civic offices are due to be completed tomorrow... at a cost of eleven million dollars.'

'Ratepayers say they're disgusted at what they describe as a huge waste of public money.'

'The strike call went out and the members obeyed it... despite warnings the company would fold as a result.'

'Lucky, the black and white kitten's done it again.... Determined not to live up to his name, he's got himself stuck up his owner's oak tree, and firemen have been called out to pull him down... for the fourth time this week.'

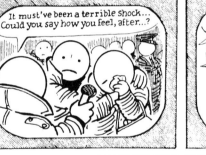

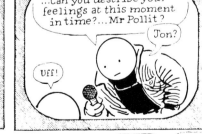

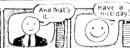

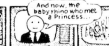

We bring you — live, from the scene of the tragedy.....
Good evening
...And now, back to Jon Pollit, live, from the scene of the tragedy...
NEWS
...No further casualties...
...but any minute now...
...more of the relatives of the dead & injured, who witnessed this terrible tragedy, will be leaving the building....
Ah...Excuse me...Mrs Baker is it?... Mrs Baker, excuse me...
...this must be a very distressing time for you...could you say something about your feelings at this mo...
It must've been a terrible shock... Could you say how you feel, after...?
...Mrs Baker, ...could you?
Mrs Baker...
You, sir, how do you...?
Sir?
Sir?
How do I feel?
Oarf!
That's how I feel!
Can we have a close-up on this?
Uaff!
Uff!
Mr Pollit?
Jon?
Oof!
This must be a very distressing moment for you...
...Can you describe your feelings at this moment in time?... Mr Pollit?
Jon?
Uff!
And now, the baby rhino who met a Princess...
And that's it...
Have a nice day!
© Posy Simmonds 1986
Figure 29

16 Power, freedom and responsibility

POWER

> *'Television is credited . . . with almost superhuman powers. It can – they say – start wars, and it can sap the will to continue those wars. It can polarize society, and it can prevent society talking sensibly to itself. It can cause trouble on the streets.'*
> – FORMER BBC DIRECTOR OF PROGRAMMES, BRIAN WENHAM
>
> *'There is a weird power in a spoken word . . .'* – JOSEPH CONRAD
>
> *'I know that one is able to win people far more by the spoken than by the written word, and that every great movement on this globe owes its rise to the great speakers and not to the great writers.'*
> – ADOLF HITLER IN *MEIN KAMPF*

Framed, and hanging in a prominent position on the wall of a commercial radio station is a poster depicting a wild-eyed, battle-dressed revolutionary clutching a microphone and shouting slogans across the airwaves.

The caption informs: '*Any budding Che Guevara will tell you the most powerful means of communication.*'

Come the revolution, every radio and TV station becomes a strategic target. The poster may have been aimed at advertisers but its message is universal: even in peacetime, whoever controls the media has the whip hand in the war for people's hearts and minds.

> *'It's a frightening thing with television that we have this enormous power,'* says Phil Moger, producer of ITN's ***News at Ten***. *'I don't think we should ever forget it.'*

No wonder that media control, its accountability, impartiality, and the vexed issue of censorship, have featured so largely in debate – where such debate is permitted – in recent years.

At the heart of the issue is the question of who should hold the reins – the government or the broadcasters. A free media is one which has its first responsibility, not to politicians, but to its audience. Whether the media uses or abuses its liberty will determine the esteem in which it is held by those it serves. That esteem may prove decisive in whether the balance eventually tips towards freedom or control.

REGULATION

British radio and TV operate under more restrictions than their newspaper counterparts. Newspapers can back which political party they choose, but broadcasting is required by law to be impartial and balanced.

The purpose laid down for the BBC was that it should inform, educate and entertain. For BBC and independent services alike, a premium was placed on the breadth and quality of programming. The BBC is governed by Royal Charter, and independent television and radio by the IBA Act. BBC funds are provided by a licence fee which is set by the Government, so it is the party in power which controls the purse-strings.

The IBA awards franchises to radio and TV stations which it has the power to remove. The IBA in turn is licensed by the Home Office and key members are appointed by the Home Secretary. So once again, the party in power has the final say.

At the time of writing there are plans to expand and partially deregulate the commercial radio sector and to shift control to a different body, but one which again would be appointed by the government.

In the USA the regulatory body is the Federal Communications Commission (FCC). This is composed of seven Commissioners who are appointed by the President. The FCC holds a looser rein over radio and TV than its counterparts in the UK, but also issues, renews and has the power to revoke licences. The FCC has no power to censor station output and has no direct control over networks.

Many US stations also subscribe to the voluntary code of the National Association of Broadcasters which attempts to maintain standards of factual, fair and unbiased reporting, as well as balance and good taste.

Complaints from listeners and viewers also play their part in shaping output. In Britain, the Broadcasting Complaints Commission adjudicates on complaints from individuals who believe they have received '*unjust or unfair treatment*' or '*unwarranted infringements of privacy*' by the media.

Australian broadcasting is regulated by the Broadcasting Act and overseen by the Australian Broadcasting Commission and the Australian Broadcasting Tribunal, which are statutory bodies.

'INDEPENDENCE'

> ***'There can be no higher law in journalism than to tell the truth and shame the devil... Remain detached from the great.'***
> — WALTER LIPMANN, US JOURNALIST
>
> ***'Reporters are puppets; they simply respond to the pull of the most powerful strings.'*** — LYNDON B. JOHNSON, US PRESIDENT

In Britain the Government can step in to prevent a programme going out on air. The Home Secretary has the power under the licence granted to the BBC to require the corporation not to broadcast a programme. The IBA has similar powers over 'independent' broadcasting.

Several major questions lie at the heart of the censorship issue:

- *By censoring what we see or hear, is the government exercising commendable responsibility in sparing less well educated viewers from 'harmful' opinions they may not have the mental capacity to judge for themselves?*
- *Or, is the Government displaying a paternalistic arrogance that underestimates and patronizes its citizens?*
- *Is it wise and responsible government to ensure that a tool as powerful as the media is used as a positive force for social control, national development and the common good?*
- *Or is political censorship simply a cynical way for the government to preserve its power by silencing the more outspoken voices of opposition?*

These questions come down to the right or otherwise of a government to decide for us what we can or cannot hear.

Government interference in British broadcasting is well-documented. In 1986 alone, attacks upon the BBC included the following:

- Conservative MPs took libel action against the Corporation over a Panorama documentary which portrayed them as extremists.
- The Conservative Party Chairman publically accused the BBC of bias and unprofessionalism over its coverage of a US bombing raid on Libya.
- A programme in the aptly named *Secret Society* series, about plans for a British spy satellite was deemed to be in breach of the Official Secrets Act and was banned. Special branch raided BBC premises and took master tapes, documents and notes.

Days after the Special Branch raids Alasdair Milne, Director General of the BBC, was asked to resign. Before long, most of his top management had also been removed.

But censorship and government interference is no more rife in Britain than in many other nations. Britain's 'half-free' press, as it has been called, has a good deal more freedom than its counterparts under some regimes where freedom of speech is something it would be wiser not to discuss.

CENSORSHIP IN DEVELOPING NATIONS

> *'Freedom of information is a fundamental human right and is a touchstone of all the freedoms to which the United Nations is consecrated, and that freedom implies the right to gather, transmit and publish news anywhere and everywhere without fetters.'*
> — UNITED NATIONS RESOLUTION 59, PARAGRAPH 1
>
> *'In developing countries we cannot have a free-wheeling press. It might be too deceptive and people would get too excited. People here have not yet developed the critical sense to judge stories without being unduly influenced or distracted.'* — INDONESIAN GOVERNMENT OFFICIAL*

*'Indonesia dangerously still the same', *UK Press Gazette*, 12 May, 1986.

Many developing and totalitarian nations see the issue of media control in a different light to the West. Their governments often seek to use the media as an instrument of social control, education and national development.

In areas of political instability governments will attempt to exercise control over the media, which would otherwise become a powerful rallying point for the opposition. Failure to do so, it is argued, could lead to destabilization in a country which may already be suffering from unrest, famine, political or religious strife.

For broadcasters in nations governed by a single party system with no concept of a loyal opposition, the task of providing an unbiased and factual account of events can be fraught with danger.

> ***'In the last ten years 60 journalists, most of them radio reporters, have been assassinated by the secret police. This fear has led individual journalists to self-censorship. Investigative journalism is almost impossible in Guatemala.'*** – JOURNALIST JULIO GODOY*

In one year alone, thirty journalists were killed worldwide (half in the Philippines), 109 imprisoned, thirteen held hostage or disappeared, and seventy-six bombed, beaten, wounded or interfered with. Increased censorship was reported in Zimbabwe, South Africa and areas of South America, while censorship was relaxed to some degree in Nigeria and South Korea.†

THE MYTH OF OBJECTIVITY

> ***'The BBC has no editorial opinions of its own. It has an obligation not to take sides; a duty to reflect all main views on a given issue.'***
> – BBC NEWS GUIDE
>
> ***'The very selection of the news involves bias, there is some bias in every programme about public policy; the selection of the policy to be discussed and those to discuss it means bias.'***
> – *NEWS AT TEN* NEWSCASTER SIR ALASTAIR BURNET‡

Contrast the statement above of how things *ought* to be from the BBC with the statement of how things probably *are* from one of Independent Television's leading figures.

Complete impartiality is like perfection; an ideal for which many will strive but none will wholly attain. Even the most respected journalist can only be the sum of his/her beliefs, experience and attitudes, the product of his/her society, culture and upbringing. No one can be free from bias,

* 'Guatemala: Freedom of the Press or Freedom to Oppress?', Links 28, 1987.
† Freedom House, Annual Report, 1985.
‡ Richard Spriggs Memorial Lecture, 1970.

however hard he/she may try to compensate by applying professional standards of objectivity; for objectivity itself, subjectively appraised, must by nature be an unreliable yardstick.

The journalist's duty is to recognize the inevitability of bias without ever surrendering to it.

The BBC World Service claims to deal with the problem of personal bias through a combination of professional integrity and an exhaustive system of checks and balances.

> *'People do have their politics, quite definitely, but they are very good at keeping them out of the news,'* says BBC External Services assistant editor, James Edwards. *'They'd never get through anyway, because there are too many checks and balances, too many people asking questions. There is a dual personality which says, "I'm an observer, this is not me talking politics, just me talking about things from both sides. I'm not directly involved, I'm merely telling you what is happening".'*

The process of eradicating bias begins by recognizing that every argument has at least two sides and that the truth probably lies somewhere between them. The journalist must stand back and view the argument from all sides, before scrupulously drawing out the key points to produce as full, balanced and impartial a picture as possible in the time available.

And here is another of the journalist's dilemmas: that there is never enough airtime to paint the masterpiece he/she would wish. Even the fullest report of an issue can be at best a sketch, and at worst a caricature, of events.

Opinion and comment

> *'The first law of journalism – to confirm existing prejudice rather than to contradict it.'* – ALEXANDER COCKBURN

American broadcasting has a tradition of fine commentators: seasoned journalists who tread the margins between factual information and reasoned opinion.

The path was established by men like Edward R. Murrow, who did much to haul America out of the destructive introspection of the McCarthy era, with its fanatical witch-hunts against public figures with real or imagined links with Communism.

The British news tradition tends to shy away from the projection of personality, preferring to aim for the factual approach that permits viewers and listeners to make up their own minds on an issue.

Times change and there are signs that the pendulum may be swinging towards a more personal style of *telling*, rather than announcing, the news. This can be seen most clearly where factual reporting crosses over into interpretation and analysis which is often presented in a personal way by the reporter.

Campaigning journalism

> *'Traditionally the reporter is supposed not only to refrain from comment but also to speak in neutral tones, never giving any intimation of his feelings. Any flicker of emotion would signal both an intellectual loss of self-control and violation of the sacred code of objectivity.'*
> – *MEDIA WEEK* MAGAZINE

Campaigning or committed journalism, must by necessity be biased journalism, yet it has its place. In 1983 a report by Michael Buerk of the BBC on the famine in Ethiopia was credited as opening the eyes of the world to the crisis and leading to an unprecedented flood of relief for the stricken region.

Media Week magazine described the Buerk report as '*unashamedly emotive*', and quoted from Edith Simmons, Press Officer of UNICEF (UK): '*It seems as though he was no longer merely reporting, but actually experiencing something.*'

It then quoted Norman Rees, ITN's chief assistant editor: '*In scenes of great tragedy and conflict a reporter has to be touched by what he's seeing. I don't think the reports would be as valuable if we didn't get a feeling of involvement and concern on behalf of the reporter.*'*

IMPARTIALITY UNDER FIRE
(Figure 30)

The strongest test of media impartiality comes at times of internal division or external conflict. Nothing nails colours to the mast more quickly than a good old-fashioned war.

> *'The BBC's independence has been challenged at critical times: at the time of the General Strike in 1926, during Suez, over Northern Ireland in the 1970s and again during the Falklands Conflict. It is a principle that has always survived.'* – BBC NEWS GUIDE
>
> *'The most pressure I have ever been under was certainly during the Falklands war. Communications were controlled by the Ministry of Defence and this meant they effectively had us by the b***s because they could cut the line of communications with our correspondents unless we toed the line and agreed to delay stories. On some we delayed for as long as 24 hours. I don't think it is anything we would ever agree to again, with hindsight.'* – BBC EXTERNAL SERVICES SENIOR DUTY EDITOR TONY DUNN

During the Falklands war, a BBC *Panorama* presenter was removed after presenting a programme which ran interviews opposing the British military action. These were not with adherents of underground organizations or unhinged and irresponsible fanatics, but with elected members of the British Parliament: MPs.

* Quoted in 'It takes six minutes of TV to make something happen', *Media Week*, 8 March, 1985.

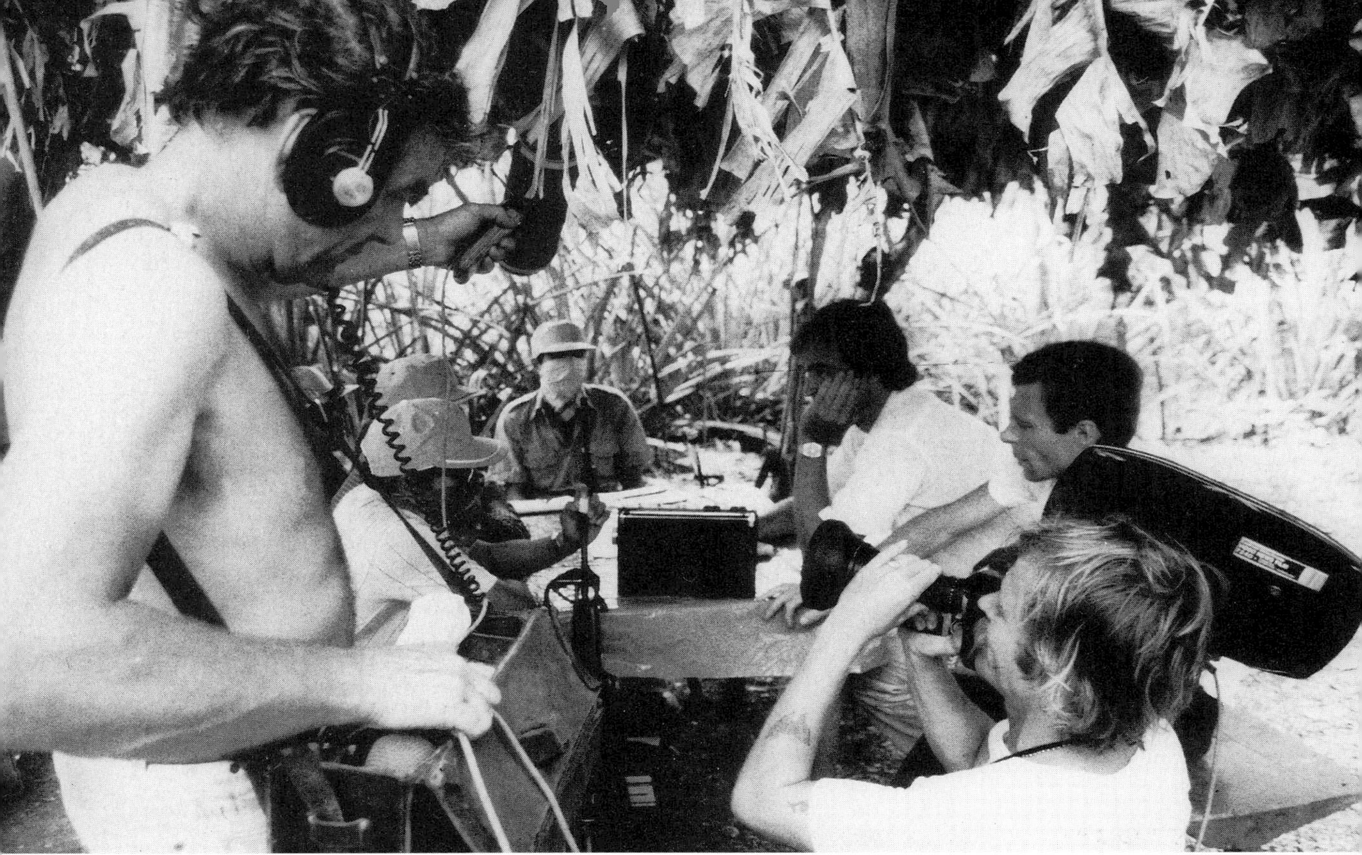

Figure 30 War reporting in Central America. When do freedom fighters become terrorists? (courtesy ITN)

RESPONSIBLE REPORTING

Reporting disorder

It is possible for the very presence of reporters and camera crews to create news by making a tense situation worse.

Demonstrations have been known to liven up at the first sign of a camera, and there will always be those who see the presence of the media as an essential weapon in their particular propaganda war. It can be difficult to distinguish where coverage of an incident becomes incitement. Many reporters, including this one, must have been tempted to ginger up coverage of a demonstration by encouraging the crowd to start chanting as they begin their live report.

Another danger in the presence of the cameras is that they may be seen to be legitimizing or endorsing what is happening and encouraging that to continue. And as every cameraperson will know who has ever had a good shot laid to waste by kids cavorting and yelling, '*Hi mum*!' the mere presence of a lens can bring out the performer in most of us.

The media is not always welcome where there is disorder, especially when it is coupled with violence and crime. The presence of a camera or recorder on the streets may be seen as a threat by those who fear identification if the recording is turned over to the authorities.

During one wave of riots in Britain a reporter was killed, another slashed across the face with a knife, TV crews were stoned and charged by

Figure 31 Where do camera crews stand on the question of bias? This crew faces the acid and petrol bombs behind British army lines in Londonderry. If they switched sides they could find themselves in the firing line for rubber bullets or worse. Wherever they stand, someone will accuse them of bias ((courtesy ITN)

mobs and many other reporters were attacked. John Downing, *Daily Express* photographer, said there was a good reason for the violence against the media: '*rioters . . . see us as an arm of the police, because newspapers are giving away pictures taken at the riots to the police.*'* Under the Police and Criminal Evidence Act British police have the right to requisition unpublished pictures which might be useful in evidence.

Camera bias
(Figure 31)

This spiral of distrust tightens if camera crews are forced to retreat to the safety of police lines to film disorder, as happened increasingly during the year long miners' dispute in Britain. One TV crew, which went into Markham Main colliery with the agreement of the miners' union, was '*set upon, punched, kicked, and told that if they didn't get out they'd have the living daylights beaten out of them.*'†

Forcing the cameras to shelter behind police lines inevitably produces a

* 'Why journalists are targets for the rioters', *UK Press Gazette*, 9 December, 1985.
† From *News, Newspapers and Television*, Alastair Hetherington, Macmillan, 1985, p. 265.

distorted, one-sided view of the action which will see the other side as the aggressors, resulting in accusations of bias.

Camera bias can be present even in run-of-the-mill industrial relations. If striking workers are filmed as an unruly mass blocking the roadway and management are interviewed in the calm sanctuary of their offices, the impression will be that management represents the virtues of order and reason, while workers are seen as the forces of disorder.

The camera may also distort the news by highlighting the point of action: a three-hour demonstration by 100,000 passes peacefully until a group of twenty trouble-makers throw beer cans and stones at the police. The skirmish lasts eight minutes before police drag the culprits off into waiting vans. A forty second film report on the evening bulletin includes twenty seconds on the disturbance. The impression is of a largely violent demonstration. The only way to compensate for the contextual distortion is to stress the relatively small scale of the incident. (Figure 32).

Unfair film editing

SIR — It is said that the camera cannot lie. It can and does.

There was an unfortunate example of this in Newsview on BBC Two on Saturday evening, October 4. As this was a clip from BBC TV programmes earlier in the week it had had even larger audiences.

We were shown Eric Hammond on the Electricians' Union making a cheap jibe at the expense of Arthur Scargill, who, he said, was trusted on the issue of nuclear energy as much as a £6 note. Then viewers saw and heard uproarious applause from the delegates. This was followed by Ron Todd of the Transport Workers calling for the phasing out of nuclear power.

The truth is that Hammond received hardly any applause at all. The massive cheers were during Ron Todd's speech. I know because I was in the conference hall.

FRANK ALLAUN

Figure 32 *UK Press Gazette*, 3 October 1986

Distortion

Prevailing news values can sometimes be a distorting mirror on the world. Decisions about what to cover are made with one eye on the clock and the other on audience appeal. They may be made by news editors away from the scene or live-action cameramen in the heat of the moment. They are always made under pressure.

Four common causes of distortion were isolated in a British working paper on the media. Professor Denis McQuail gave them as*:

- Emphasis on action, conflict and personalities,
- Selection of particular events and themes for coverage, especially disorder and upheaval,
- Labelling or stereotyping in the reporting of sections of the community such as minority groups and women,
- The snowball effect where the media covers a story because the media is covering the story.

* Adapted from working paper No. 2, HMSO, 1976, p.5.

Sensationalism

The reporter's hunger for a good story with upbeat actuality can lead down the road to sensationalism, especially on a thin news day when the editor is scouting for a strong lead. The easiest solution is the unethical one which is to 'hype' a story and blow it up out of proportion. Thus a suggestion that overtime might be cut at a local steelworks unless more orders can be found becomes, '*Jobs threat as steelworks grinds to a halt*', and so on.

Unless the facts are permitted to speak for themselves without embellishment, fact gives way to fiction as the story is inflated until it can stand up as a headline. Making something out of not very much can easily give way to making something out of nothing.

Good taste

> ***'Good taste . . . means having a decent respect for our listeners. We cannot, and should not, shield them from the realities of life. But we do our best not to cause any listener unnecessary anxiety, shock or mental suffering, any parent or young child needless embarrassment or offence.'*** – BBC NEWS GUIDE

The same radio and television programmes can reach a mass audience of young and old, educated and ignorant and can span widely differing cultures. It is inevitable that sooner or later an item which appeals to one section of an audience will offend another. The journalist must consider whether the significance of that item will outweigh the offence or embarrassment it may cause.

Clearly a news item which pokes fun at minority groups or deliberately shows them in a bad light would be in poor taste. So would graphically detailed accounts of violent or sexual crimes which could upset young children.

With newspapers and magazines, parents have a chance to veto what their children may read. But with daytime TV or radio news, by the time they realize the item is inappropriate, it is already too late and the damage is done. So the onus is on the broadcaster to use sensitivity in selection.

One stomach-churning example from radio is the story of a seaman who had to be airlifted from his ship after an injury to his hand turned gangrenous and became badly infected. One of the rescue crew who winched him to safety told reporters he had seen maggots crawling out from under the man's bandages.

A vivid account of the rescue with a full description of the seaman's hand was broadcast repeatedly over the breakfast period and into the mid morning, before the managing director of the radio station phoned the newsroom to withdraw the story because it had put him off his breakfast and was threatening to deter him from lunch as well.

OK, I confess, the story was one of mine, but in the newsroom environment it can become easy for reporters, who, hour by hour, are soaking up stories of the worst of life's excesses, to

overlook the effect of their words on the feelings of their audience. All these second-hand horrors can have a numbing effect. It can be easy to forget that every tragedy has a person at its centre.

Young reporters may feel that it is their mission to '*tell it like it is*' and give the audience real life in the raw, but few audiences will thank you for constantly and gratuitously rubbing their noses in the gutter of life.

> *'If somebody gets his head blown off, I personally would be quite happy to show it – because that's what happens when somebody gets his head blown off. I don't want to put gratuitous violence on television, but I think sometimes we err too much on the side of good taste.'*
> – HARRY RADLIFFE, BUREAU CHIEF, CBS NEWS
>
> *'We would exercise restraint at the point of showing a mangled body. We would show bodies under sheets and bloody sheets covering the body, but we would not show the body. Violence is around us every day. You don't really need to show those pictures to get across the violent nature of a story.'* – PAUL CLEVELAND, ASSIGNMENT MANAGER ABC NEWS
>
> *'We had a film about Greenpeace and the whaling in the Faroes. I saw the News at One version which had already been hugely sanitized and I couldn't even take that. I can't think of anything I've ever seen that was so absolutely horrifying – literally a sea of blood and knives. So when we came to the* News at Ten *version we had literally a tithe of what was there.*
>
> *'You've got to tread this fine line of not bowdlerizing it to the extent that it's all so pleasant. It's a matter of degree, suggestion and hint.* Don't dwell. *The difference between getting it right and getting it wrong may be about a second.'* – DAVID NICHOLAS, EDITOR ITN

Privacy (Figure 33)

At times of tragedy the media is frequently accused of preying on distressed victims by subjecting them to a further ordeal by camera. That was the criticism levelled after coverage of the Zeebrugge ferry disaster in which 187 died.

> *'Many from the national media didn't give a damn. The story meant everything to them. They thought nothing of arguing, bribing, cajoling – even lying. There had already been a number of incidents with reporters and photographers scuffling with relatives in hospital wards. At the height of the disaster more than 1000 journalists were in Zeebrugge – most of them hunting in packs. They pounced on anyone who offered even the slightest hope of giving them a new angle. There are times when, like all decent, honest journalists, I felt ashamed to be counted among their number.'* – JOHN HAMMOND, NEWS EDITOR*

* From 'Ashamed of the Press,' *UK Press Gazette*, 23 March, 1987

Figure 33 Should cameras intrude on personal grief? The Zeebrugge ferry sinking *(left)* cost 187 lives. Grieving relatives were pursued by newsmen *(right)*

When freezing sea water cascaded through the open bow doors and capsized the cross-channel ferry Herald of Free Enterprise, the media descended in droves. The ship, which was later designated a mass grave, became a magnet for camera crews and reporters. Many European stations pulled no punches in their coverage, while British audiences were mercifully spared the shots of floating corpses being hauled out of the water.

But many survivors were seen as legitimate targets by camera crews from all nations who shot them being taken sodden, bedraggled and bewildered into ambulances and coaches; shots which also showed the anger and frustration of some who clearly regarded the presence of the cameras as unwelcome and intrusive.

The coverage produced an outcry from some quarters. Clare Jenkins, an outraged viewer and journalist herself condemned the reporting on the BBC programme *Network*:

> *'The competition – for the first picture, the first on-the-spot report, the first interview with a survivor – is so fierce that better judgement and finer feelings are often steamrollered. A lot of reporting rightly focused on the possible causes of the disaster, but far too much went into useless voyeurism that neither helped nor informed. Relatives who had just identified their loved ones were forced to face the further ordeal of running the gauntlet of prying cameras.'*

For TV editors the dilemma is weighing up the right to personal privacy against the demands of legitimate public interest while avoiding the trap of voyeurism:

> ***'Disasters are stories about human grief and it would be wrong in the coverage of any disaster, in fact it would be distortion, not to show the grief, but our rule is that one shows the grief and one doesn't dwell on it.'***
> **– NORMAN REES, CHIEF ASSISTANT EDITOR, ITN***

* From *Network*, BBC1, 21 April, 1987.

INTERNAL PRESSURES ON REPORTING

Resources

In a radio newsroom that is squeezed for staff, the only stories that will be chased are those that will yield an acceptable result within the available time. News that is too far away or would need too much digging might be dropped by smaller newsrooms in favour of more accessible material. And even when the story gets back, there is no guarantee it will be ready in time to get the position it deserves in the bulletin.

Lack of space is a major constraint. A three minute bulletin contains fewer than 550 words – a single page of a broadsheet newspaper will hold ten times as many – yet the bulletin is supposed to cover all the important news stories.

A half-hour news programme may comprise ten or fewer features with a sprinkling of short copy stories, yet is expected to offer information, comment and analysis on all the major events in the world that day.

Faced with a gallon of news to squeeze into a pint pot of a programme, many news editors may find themselves tempted to limit coverage to the bare facts which can be told quickly, and duck analysis and explanation, which require context and take longer.

Selection

Lack of space forces the problem of selection. A highly visual item such as a spectacular carnival would look better on TV and so would be more assured of a place than a more significant story about increasing delays for elderly patients awaiting replacement hip joints. The more visual an item, the more likely it is to be covered on television.

The addition of good pictures or a snappy interview may also lift a story in the running order – sometimes beyond its merits. The bulletin order will also be influenced by the need to spread the illustrations evenly throughout.

Pressures of ratings

> *'People who defend pure journalism are operating in a world that's unrealistic.'* – NEWS CONSULTANT STEVEN MEACHAM*

An uneasy alliance exists between the drive for profit and the quest for news on any commerical station that depends on ratings for its survival. When profit motive replaces news values there is pressure to pander to the lowest public taste for fear that audience and advertisers alike will desert unless the station delivers only the goods that the mass market will buy. And that pressure spills over into the newsroom.

A growing trend from America, now casting a dark shadow across both sides of the Atlantic, is for commercial stations to employ news consultants to pep up the audience figures.

Among their sweeping changes has been the introduction of 'happy

* Anne Karpf, 'News with the miracle ingredient,' *The Guardian*, 22 July, 1985.

talk' where the news is sugared with folksy chatter by presenters about their pets and kids. News stories have been squeezed to a ninety seconds maximum, and actualities cut back to around ten seconds.

Outspoken critic of the consultants, Ron Powers, protests that news is being treated like any other commodity:

> *'the news . . . can be restructured, improved, smoothed out, bolstered with miracle ingredients, and topped with a hearty rich flavour that the whole family will enjoy. Finger-lickin' good'**

The dilemma for journalists is that while news consultants may not be improving the quality, they *are* pushing up the ratings.

Pressures of advertising

With the financial benefits of advertising come new pressures. It takes a strong-willed head of sales to let a business person storm out with a hefty advertising budget unspent because the station intended to carry an unfavourable news item about his/her company.

That will would have to be iron indeed if the amount at stake would make the difference between profit and loss or survival and shutdown for a struggling commerical station. Independence depends greatly on a news editor's ability to withstand pressure and maintain his/her integrity.

Many commercial stations have a policy of not permitting news staff to read adverts on air. Their concern is that linking journalists, who are supposed to be impartial, with advertising, would compromise the authority of the station's news service.

The advertiser's hope is that viewers will receive what is being said about the product with the same unquestioning trust they gave to the news – only now the scripts flow from the pen of the ad man whose sole concern is persuasion, not information.

THE LAW

Libel

The biggest legal trap facing many journalists is the law of libel. This differs in detail from country to country but has its similarities. In Britain, a libel is defined as the publishing of anything that would:

> *'Expose a person to hatred, ridicule or contempt, cause him to be shunned and avoided, lower him in the estimation of right thinking members of society generally, or disparage him in his office, profession or trade.'*[†]

British libel laws also hold a reporter responsible for broadcasting a libellous statement made by somebody else. So, if a council leader gave you some dirt on the leader of the opposition, *you* could be sued for libel, for putting those words on air.

Without some protection investigative journalism and court reporting would be impossible. In Britain, the main defences are complex and provide a lucrative field for lawyers. In essence they are that the report was true, or offered a reasonable opinion based on facts that were true, or

*Anne Karpf, 'News with the miracle ingredient,' *The Guardian*, 22 July, 1985.

[†] L.C.J. McNae, *Essential Law for Journalists*, Butterworth, 1985.

that it was protected in law by privilege, which covers reporting of Parliament, courts and public meetings.

In addition to the man-traps of libel there are laws governing court reporting, confidentiality, copyright, race relations, privacy, official secrets and other areas, which make reporting a minefield for the ignorant.

Safe and successful reporting requires a thorough working knowledge of the law that allows journalists to push their reporting to the brink of legality without falling into the chasm.

Anyone planning a career in journalism should ensure they receive a thorough training in media law. Failure to do so could, in the worst extreme, leave you bankrupt, imprisoned and with a shattered reputation.

NATIONAL UNION OF JOURNALISTS' CODE OF PROFESSIONAL CONDUCT

1 A journalist has a duty to maintain the highest professional and ethical standards.
2 A journalist shall at all times defend the principle of the freedom of the press and other media in relation to the collection of information and the expression of comment and criticism. He/she shall strive to eliminate distortion, news suppression and censorship.
3 A journalist shall strive to ensure that the information he/she disseminates is fair and accurate, avoid the expression of comment and conjecture as established fact and falsification by distortion, selection or misrepresentation.
4 A journalist shall rectify promptly any harmful inaccuracies, ensure that correction and apologies receive due prominence and afford the right of reply to persons criticized when the issue is of sufficient importance.
5 A journalist shall obtain information, photographs and illustrations only by straightforward means. The use of other means can be justified only by overriding consideration of the public interest. The journalist is entitled to exercise a personal conscientious objection to the use of such means.
6 Subject to justification by overriding considerations of the public interest, a journalist shall do nothing which entails intrusion into private grief and distress.
7 A journalist shall protect confidential sources of information.
8 A journalist shall not accept bribes, nor shall he/she allow other inducements to influence the performance of his/her professional duties.
9 A journalist shall not lend himself/herself to the distortion or the surpression of the truth because of advertising or other considerations.
10 A journalist shall neither originate nor process material which encourages discrimination on the grounds of race, colour, creed, gender or sexual orientation.
11 A journalist shall not take private advantage of information gained in the course of his/her duties, before the information is public knowledge.
12 A journalist shall not by way of statement, voice, or appearance endorse by advertisement any commercial product or service, save for the promotion of his/her own work or of the medium by which he/she is employed.

> *'Broadcasters should be encouraged to practise self-discipline and self-regulation in areas such as codes and standards, on the basis that increased responsibility is a concomitant of increased freedom.'*
> —FEDERATION OF AUSTRALIAN BROADCASTERS

FIELDWORK

1 Who has the last word on what is broadcast in your country, the Government or the broadcasters? Is this healthy? Discuss.

Find out how the system of regulation works and what offences might cause broadcasters to lose their licences.

'The purpose of the media is to: "disseminate objective information, exert constructive social control, channel peoples' aspirations, permit communication between the government and the public, and to mobilize the community in the process of nation building." Should the media be used in this way as an instrument of 'positive propaganda?' Discuss.

2 '***The notion of an impartial and independent media is a myth.***' Discuss.

What personal biases and preferences are you aware of? Privately jot down your political position (left, right or centre), your religion, and the class, caste, or status of your parents. Now consider how those factors have influenced your thinking on a number of issues, for instance, whether you are for or against abortion, nuclear weapons, capital punishment, censorship.

Do you think it is necessary to attempt to be objective in the way you present issues that you hold strong personal convictions about?

Think of a subject you do feel strongly about. If you had to cover that issue how would you attempt to deal with your personal bias?

3 A passenger plane has crashed thirty miles away in a built up area killing and injuring most of those on board and several on the ground. How would you cover the story for local radio while minimizing concern in the local community? Who would you talk to and what would you ask? What information would you need?

4 You are a news editor on a commercial radio station. Your bulletin includes a good story about a video rental chain that has been raided by the vice squad, who removed obscene videos. The company is owned by a major advertiser with the station who threatens to withdraw his account unless you drop the story. The sales director tells you not to run it. What would you do and how would you defend your actions? If you are in a class, role play the discussion with another student playing the sales director.

Supposing you discover that your radio station is losing money and the loss of this account could mean redundancies or cuts in the news service? Does that make any difference to your actions? Justify your decision.

5 Look through the NUJ code of conduct. Do you agree with everything it says? Do you think it leaves out anything? Do you think any of those rules may be difficult to work out in practice? Why?

Part Two

RADIO

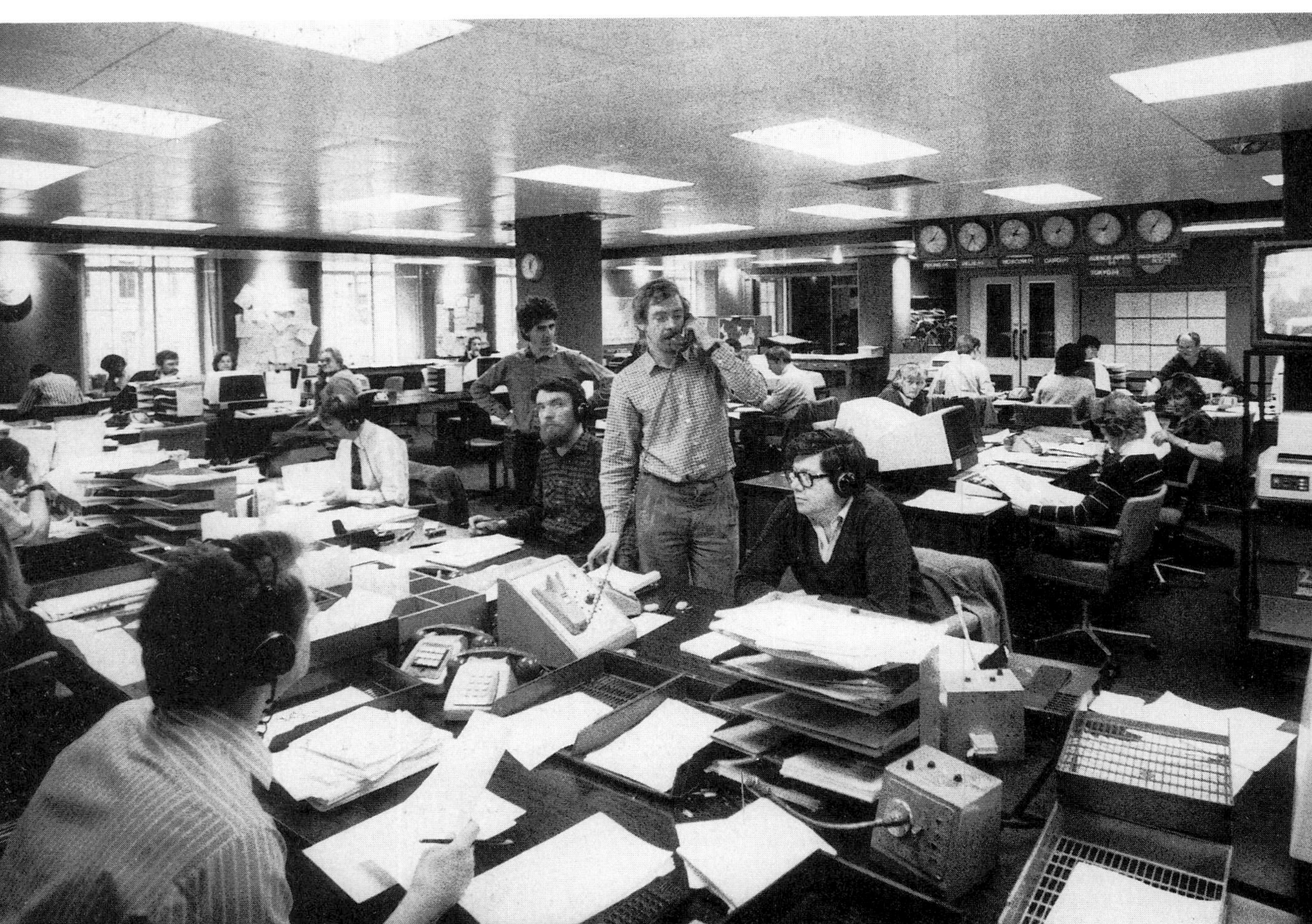

Figure 34 The cavernous newsroom of the External Services, the biggest in the BBC and one of the largest to be found anywhere – *'you are at the centre of world events, you know everything that is going on'* (courtesy BBC External Services)

17 The best of British

Wherever you live, the chances are you will be able to listen to the BBC World Service. It is one of the giants of broadcasting and enjoys an unparalleled reputation. For the purposes of this book, it provides a global point of contact with British radio. This chapter offers an insight into the way the World Service works.

> *'It is some years now since the sun finally set on the British Empire. And yet, in one respect this country still does rule the waves – the air waves. The BBC's External Services, with more than 100 million listeners around the world, has achieved a reputation for political independence and reliability that gives it a stature no other national radio can match.'*
> – *THE WASHINGTON POST*

The sun may indeed have set on the British Empire, but that is easily forgotten from within the magisterial headquarters of the World Service, as the stirring strains of *Imperial Echoes* herald the start of another *Radio Newsreel*. If you lean back, half shut your eyes, and let the newsreader's well modulated and oh-so-British intonations wash over you, the world is much as it was between the two world wars and the Empire Service is still in its heyday.

As you pass through the impressive portals of Bush House bearing the legend, '*To the Friendship of English Speaking Peoples*', and step along the pale, travertine-clad corridors and up the wide and winding staircase, the effect is reminiscent of an art-deco hotel or once elegant gentleman's club. Only when you enter the doors of the newsroom on the fourth floor does elegance give way to utility. The brown carpeting, battered wooden desks and ochre columns give a worn but comfortable air, like a faded easy chair or battered pair of slippers.

This is the largest newsroom in the BBC and one of the biggest in the world. The staff of 120 are at the hub of every international event of any consequence. Dominating proceedings is an elevated bank of clocks giving the current time in Peking, Delhi, Moscow, Cairo, Buenos Aires,

Figure 35 A million words a day pour into the newsroom from news agencies all over the world. In the quest for accuracy no story is run without first being confirmed by another agency (Andrew Boyd)

Tokyo, Washington and New York – a constant reminder that this is a 24 hour service reporting from and to every corner to the globe (Figure 35).

The task of this enormously productive news processing plant, is to take the mass of raw material coming in and refine, reshape and rewrite it into 350 stories of global news that are broadcast daily from the building.

An estimated millions words a day spill in on agency tapes. Reuters, PA, AP, UPI, AFP, pump out their information on colour coded paper which instantly identifies the source. The BBC's General News Service adds domestic copy, and the Corporation's Monitoring Service, which listens to major radio and television broadcasts in more than 120 countries, passes on its selection of the world's most important stories.

'Sometimes the news affects you, but it's the excitement *of the whole thing, the* excitement *of being at the centre, and that's one of the first things that strikes you here. You're at the centre of world events. You know everything that's going on.'* – ASSISTANT EDITOR, JAMES EDWARDS

'If you wander around the studios of Bush House for a couple of hours, you find it an amazing cross between the Tower of Babel and the United Nations on a good day.'
– JOHN TUSA, MANAGING DIRECTOR BBC EXTERNAL BROADCASTING*

* *See it for Yourself*, BBC, 1987

Seventy-five voice dispatches are filed daily by the BBC's world-wide network of correspondents from every international trouble spot and scene of upheaval. Bulletins go out on the hour 24 hours a day. From some fifty studios programmes criss-cross the globe with broadcasts in thirty-seven languages – a total of 734 hours a week of news and general programming. In addition, the news is rebroadcast by stations in fifty countries – the 1300 GMT bulletin alone in twenty countries, including Canada, Australia, the West Indies and Hong Kong.

Keeping up with the information is a major task, says assistant editor James Edwards:

> *'Trying to keep on top of the news is like climbing up a mountain that's terribly slippery. You never get to the top. Even when you're very close to it, you just keep slipping back again. If you can manage to stand in the same place then you're almost ahead of the game.'*

Unlike most others this is a newsroom without reporters. The journalists in the field are the stringers and foreign correspondents. The few specialists dealing with Commonwealth, economic, political, defence and EEC affairs occupy a small room the other side of the staircase. The newsroom is almost exclusively the enclave of sub-editors.

The style is solid, factual information which is meticulously checked and double checked for accuracy.

THE SERVICE

A nine minute bulletin of world news is broadcast at intervals, interspersed with shorter news summaries. Foreign correspondents' reports are featured in the four fifteen-minute *Radio Newsreels*. Three half-hour editions of the news magazine *Newsdesk* are produced, as well as five five-minute bulletins called *News About Britain* (NAB). NAB with its warts-and-all approach to the UK, has occasionally brought the External Services into conflict with its paymasters, the British Foreign Office.

The enormous task of translating bulletins into thirty-six languages, is undertaken by ten different language services, grouped under three broad headings: European, Latin American and the 3As, which comprises the African, Arabic and Asian services. Each employs academics, journalists and experts from many nations to translate, modify, adapt and scrutinize every word to be sure it satisfies the External Services standard of total accuracy. They do not always succeed. Sometimes the translation can go embarrassingly wrong. '*Public house*' has been translated as '*brothel*', '*taking stock*' as '*raiding cattle*'; and '*coaches telescoped*' as '*coaches hurled so far away that one could see them only through a telescope*'.

THE SYSTEM

At the top sits the editor, who with his deputy and managing editor is in charge of strategy and planning. Day-to-day responsibility for the newsroom falls to the assistant editor. He takes the helm over a twelve-hour shift and the guiding hand in his absence is that of the senior duty editor. Coverage at home and abroad is organized by the news intake editor who allocates correspondents.

The BBC's domestic service has correspondents in the world's major capitals. External Services broadcast their reports and plug the gaps in coverage with their own correspondents.

The backbone of the operation is the news bulletin produced by the central writing unit on which every bulletin in every language is based (Figure 36).

Each story from the teleprinters is passed to the central copytaster who hands potential news items to the senior duty editor. News for the foreign

```
              0C4 1453 16/02/87        LINES : T=12  P=12       1454

                      =1500 CENTRAL BULLETIN=
                             16/02/87

SENIOR DUTY EDITOR:      BARNY MASON

CENTRAL DUTY EDITOR:     JOHN BAMBER

 1   C64         (0008)   1300 TOP
 2   C71         (0017)   1430 MOSCOW CONFERENCE
 3   C45         (0012)   0900 SOVIET DISSIDENT
 4   C63         (0013)   1230 WAR CRIMES TRIAL
 5   TO COME     (0009)   1530 OCCUPIED TERRITORIES
 6   C68         (0011)   1400 GEMAYEL - THATCHER
 7   C59         (0013)   1200 PHILIPPINES - MILITARY
 8   C70         (0011)   1430 BANGLADESH STRIKE
 9   C50         (0009)   1000 LAMBSDORFF
10   C57         (0010)   1130 GREEK STRIKES
11   C73         (0011)   1500 CHAD BOMBING
12   C66         (0012)   1300 TAIL
                                                 LINES 125
ALSO AVAILABLE:
--------------

13   C72         (0008)   1500 INDIAN SHOOTING
14   C61         (0005)   1230 INDIAN SCHOOL DEATHS
15   C62         (0007)   1230 EEC OIL TAX
```

Figure 36 Central Bulletin running order

services passes through the regional desks. The regions have the freedom to expand on the basic details given in the central bulletin, but normally news is selected on the basis of the *guiding formula* – the news of the world as seen from London.

> *'Looking at the world as a whole, we select what we in London consider to be the most significant, important and interesting events of the day. And we apply this formula to all bulletins (except two or three specialist ones) in all languages. It follows that in most cases our lead story and other major stories will be the same whether we are broadcasting to Pakistan or to Peru. When there is no strong lead and a wide choice of other stories, there are likely to be variations in the make-up of bulletins. And of course there will always be very considerable variations in regional stories, chosen to cater for the interests of a particular audience.'* – BUSH HOUSE NEWSROOM GUIDE

'*All the running orders are decided in the newsroom*,' says news editor Terry Heron, now retired. '*this way we can make sure we speak with more or less the same voice*.'

Mr Heron rejects any suggestion that cultural imperialism may be at work: '*The regions are quite content, indeed relieved, that the editorial decision making process is focused in the news department, because then they are sure the BBC speaks with one editorial voice and has one stamp of journalism*.'

INDEPENDENCE

'We have no pressures, no advice, no guidance at all *from the Foreign Office,'* says Terry Heron. *'The last thing the Foreign Office wants is to be involved with us and the last thing we want is to be involved with them.'*

External Services cost the British Foreign Office around £120 million pounds a year. That might sound a lot, but it is less than £1 per listener *per year*.

> *'We are funded by the Government, yet we are independent of it. This piper (the Government) does not call the tune. Very wisely so. If he did, people would not stop to listen.'*
> – JOHN TUSA, MANAGING DIRECTOR, BBC EXTERNAL BROADCASTING, TO THE COMMONS SELECT COMMITTEE ON FOREIGN AFFAIRS
>
> *'Impartiality means that in any conflict or dispute we always try to report the views of both sides . . . We do this whether Britain is involved or not; and if it is a domestic dispute, whether the Government is involved or not.'* – BBC PRESS OFFICE

THE NEWSROOM CONFERENCE

In a 24 hour newsroom the development of stories and spread of coverage may appear to be a seamless robe, but the threads of each newsday are taken up at the 9.45 am news conference chaired by the editor. The computer-produced news diary is a focus for discussion, and senior management, representatives of foreign services and home based correspondents offer their ideas in turn. Below is a portmanteau of extracts from a number of such meetings.

> *'We've got 50 feared dead from a bus which plunged into a river in Bangladesh... we've got that from two agencies. The Soviet/Afghan talks opened in Moscow today... we'll be seeing if any statements come from there. In Africa, Sudan is issuing a statement saying they're not helping the guerillas in Uganda. Chad has issued a statement saying their soldiers were involved in fighting yesterday... that's only on one agency at the moment.'*
>
> *'Beirut... it's a bit difficult to tell, but it does look as though it's building up again, though Reuters is a lot more excitable than others there.'*
>
> *'And once again there's no food in the refugee camps?'*
>
> *'Yes.'*
>
> *A pause, then the news editor observes: 'Our bulletins were full of blood last night... rather self-indulgent I thought... all those people running around with severed limbs.' Some nod. Others smile wryly. The point is taken and the focus of attention shifts to another corner of the room.*

The newsroom conference is a seismometer of world events. Every shift in policy, political upheaval or movement of troops is registered and analysed and its intensity measured on the newsroom's equivalent of the Richter scale. The severity of the crisis can also be gauged by the World Service audience which rises dramatically wherever there is tension.

After the conference the editor briefs the heads of the language services and the talks and features departments. The service heads then hold their own departmental meetings attended by representatives of the newsroom.

THE STORIES

All news copy is dictated to copy typists and keyed directly into the computer. As well as being faster, the theory is that dictating the stories produces them in a way that suits the patterns and rhythms of speech.

Once on terminal, the draft is revised by the sub or duty editor. Revisions – 'mods' – can be printed to order. Stories can be adapted to suit different regions and whole bulletins can be rewritten in a matter of minutes.

News stories are measured by lines instead of the more usual word count. A line contains an average of ten words, and World Service newsreaders estimate they read between thirteen and fourteen lines per minute (130 and 140 words per minute) – slow compared to other British newsreaders.

1 2 3 4 5 6

C58 1142 16/02/87 LINES : T=10 P=10 1142

7 =1200 BANGLADESH STRIKE= 8

A half-day strike called by opposition parties in Bangladesh has brought the capital, Dhaka, almost to a standstill and disrupted life in several other cities. Opposition leaders said the strike was part of their campaign for greater democracy in the country. In Dhaka, and in the port cities of Chittagong and Khulna, the streets were virtually deserted; shops, offices and banks were closed, as were schools and colleges. The strike went off without any serious incidents, but police in the town of Rajshahi in west Bangladesh say they fired teargas to disperse a group of students who set up a road-block.

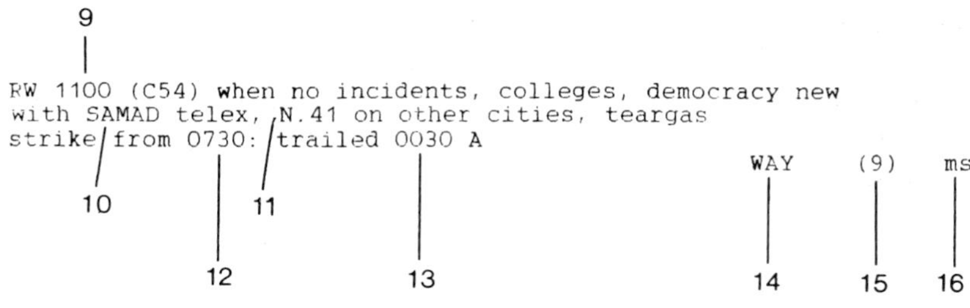

9

RW 1100 (C54) when no incidents, colleges, democracy new
with SAMAD telex, N.41 on other cities, teargas
strike from 0730: trailed 0030 A

WAY (9) ms

10 11 12 13 14 15 16

Figure 37

1 C shows the story was produced by the central writing unit and the number indicates that it was the fifty-eighth to be written since midnight
2 Time the story was entered into the computer
3 Date
4 Total number of lines in the story as counted by the computer
5 Total number of lines on that page
6 Time received by the stencil cutter
7 Time of next half hour point after story was written
8 Catchline (slug)
9 Shows it was a rewrite of story number fifty-four which was produced for 11 o'clock
10 Name of stringer
11 Number of the telex received from that stringer
12 Time first news of the strike was received
13 Time of first story indicating that the strike would take place. 'A' sources the trail with the African, Arabic and Asian service
14 Name of the writer
15 Number of lines in the story, according to the typist. (Unlike the computer, the typist has discounted the last line because it is only two words)
16 Typist's initials

The system for marking up copy is more elaborate than for almost any other radio station. Each story is numbered for rapid recall on the computer. To make sure every detail can be traced back to source, all the key points are listed at the foot of the copy with the times they were received by the newsroom. To help with rewriting the story, the time code indicates how old that information is so the writer can decide which points to keep and which can now be dropped. The time of the original is then prefixed with RW for rewrite. Every new story carries a list of sources that have been used (Figure 37).

ACCURACY

> *'Accuracy is obviously of first importance. If we get things wrong, if we are careless or ignorant or naive, our credibility is damaged. That is why we have a newsroom which puts every story through a process of briefing, scutiny and revision at various levels of seniority. Accuracy is so vital that though we like to be fast, if possible first, with the news, if there is any conflict between accuracy and speed, accuracy must always come first.* – BUSH HOUSE NEWSROOM GUIDE

The World Service will never run an agency story unless it can be confirmed by an independent source. Even then the newsroom may be cautious. Intake editor Peter Brooks describes this as the *two-source rule*:

> *'We need reports from two agencies, or an agency and a freelance before we will run the story, and we actually watch to make sure the freelance hasn't filed to the agency as well, to be certain we've got it right. The exception is correspondents' reports which are accepted as trustworthy. We also want to check we've got our names, facts, and figures right. Everything we write is checked by many people round the building who know far more about the subject than we do.'*

The exhaustive system of checks and balances is also intended to prevent hoaxers or propagandists pulling the wool over their eyes. Says assistant editor, James Edwards: '*One of the things people ask is "Aren't you going to be tricked and bamboozled into putting out propaganda?" And the answer is, if you are inexperienced, yes. But we are not inexperienced, so virtually nothing ever gets out that is deliberately misleading.*'

RADIO NEWSREEL
(Figure 38)

Few things could be more typically British than the signature tune which heralds each edition of *Radio Newsreel*. In 1939, the HM Royal Airforce Band recorded a rousing number and christened it with what was even then the unashamedly nostalgic title, *Imperial Echoes*. The tune was adopted as the signature of *Radio Newsreel* which began broadcasting reports by BBC foreign correspondents during the Second World War.

The word 'newsreel' also casts a backward glance, and the presentation style, without a hint of actuality or a single interview, harks back to the days before portable tape recorders paved the way for illustrated news

Figure 38 (*top*) Two minutes into another edition of *Radio Newsreel*. Compared to a TV control room, the studio has the hushed air and unhurried manner of a library reading room. (*middle*) Producer Hans Bremer (far right) checks the progress of his programme with newsreader John Touhey (through the glass) while one of the two studio managers keeps an eye on the levels. (*bottom*) The other studio manager laces up the tapes in order and fires them on cue (Andrew Boyd)

programmes. Even the very proper intonations of the newsreaders are reminiscent of a bygone Britain:

> Continuity: *'BBC World Service. In a few seconds we have an edition of* Radio Newsreel *at 15 hours. Then at 15.15 in our series* Not So Long Ago *we look back to events in the early 1950s and specifically the Anglo Iranian oil crisis, 1951–54 . . .'.*
>
> (Greenwich Time signal: PIP, PIP, PIP, PIP, PEEP!)
>
> Narrator: *'15 hours Greenwich Mean Time. BBC World Service presents* Radio Newsreel.
>
> (signature tune: *Imperial Echoes)*
>
> *'And first the main points of the news. In Moscow, Mr Gorbachev has accused the United States of trying to scrap the 1972 treaty on anti-ballistic missiles . . .'.*

The atmosphere in the radio studio is more relaxed than anything you will find in TV. Instructions are infrequent and considerably less terse:

> Producer: *'Right, we're coming out of this one early, because we're not really convinced about the end part. About the third line from the bottom on the first page, on the words, "this immediate response", then it's Goodman next.'*

The process of putting out the programme is simplicity itself compared to TV and the chains of communication in the studio are short. Only six people are directly concerned with getting the programme on air. The newsreader sits in the studio, separated by glass from the producer, two studio managers and the production secretary. The *Radio Newsreel* duty editor has put the programme together and drawn up its running order and the producer is responsible for making it happen on air.

The studio manager (panel) operates the mixing desk, putting the reader and tapes on air and watching the levels. Behind her is the studio manager (tapes) who threads the correspondents' reports on the tape machines and plays them on cue. On the far left is the production secretary who checks the timing.

Compared to many other radio stations, the programme style is basic and the studio overstaffed. Common practice on smaller stations is for a single technical assistant to operate the studio mixer and the tape decks. More sophisticated programmes than *Radio Newsreel* are often entirely self-operated, with the presenter (who may double as the producer) operating all the equipment and combining that with live interviews.

The fifteen minutes of *Radio Newsreel* allow the BBC's foreign correspondents to go into greater depth on the day's major stories than in a news bulletin. The average length of each report is 1 minute 25 seconds. Correspondents phone in from around the world and their reports can be recorded automatically in a number of locations throughout the BBC.

In typical belt and braces fashion, reports are transcribed and copies given to producers and studio managers. Edits are marked on those scripts in pencil and cuts made by bringing down the volume on the panel. The reading speed is slow enough to permit clean edits on air without having to resort to cutting the tape.

Radio Newsreel and an extended magazine programme, called *Newsdesk*, are broadcast seven times a day across the world, and rebroadcast many times including on some public service stations in the USA. *Radio Newsreel* also produces two editions of *World Round-Up* for Australian and New Zealand domestic radio.

The decision not to include illustrations and interview extracts is deliberate: assistant editor James Edwards: '*There are no tapes because we think the best way of telling people the news is simply and straightforwardly. We've always thought that and we still do. And if you live abroad you want to turn on the news and just hear a straight report of what's happened.*'

When the original recording of *Imperial Echoes* wore out, a new version was commissioned which was less portentious, and some thought almost whimsical. '*And there was a flood of letters saying, "We can't stand that tune. Give us back our original!" We ran this new tune for six months or so and then a studio manager, rummaging through an antiques shop found a pristine 78 of the original signature tune, so back it came. Young people may say, "Cor, that's old fashioned," but people like it. It's distinctively BBC, it's distinctively British.*'

FOREIGN CORRESPONDENTS
(Figure 39)

The BBC employs about thirty full-time foreign correspondents and commissions stories from 100 freelances. The job of foreign correspondent is one of the most coveted positions in journalism and no easy option.

> ***'The BBC is listened to very widely and has a left-over image of being the great colonial institution which is both admired and resented at the same time, so they pick you up on the slightest thing and deeply resent anything they regard as unfair coverage.'***
> – JOHN RHETTIE, BBC CORRESPONDENT, SRI LANKA

One of the hardest jobs can be reporting from a country with a divided community – whatever is said about one side is likely to be regarded as unfair by the other. John Rhettie's reports from Sri Lanka have resulted in a row in Parliament, a Moslem MP threatening to knock his teeth out and a veiled threat of deportation, which he describes as typical of the pressure on BBC foreign correspondents in particular who insist on their right to make independent assessments.

There is no short-cut to becoming a foreign correspondent. Would-be roving reporters are expected to join the BBC and work their way upwards.

For foreign nationals hoping to work from their own countries, limited

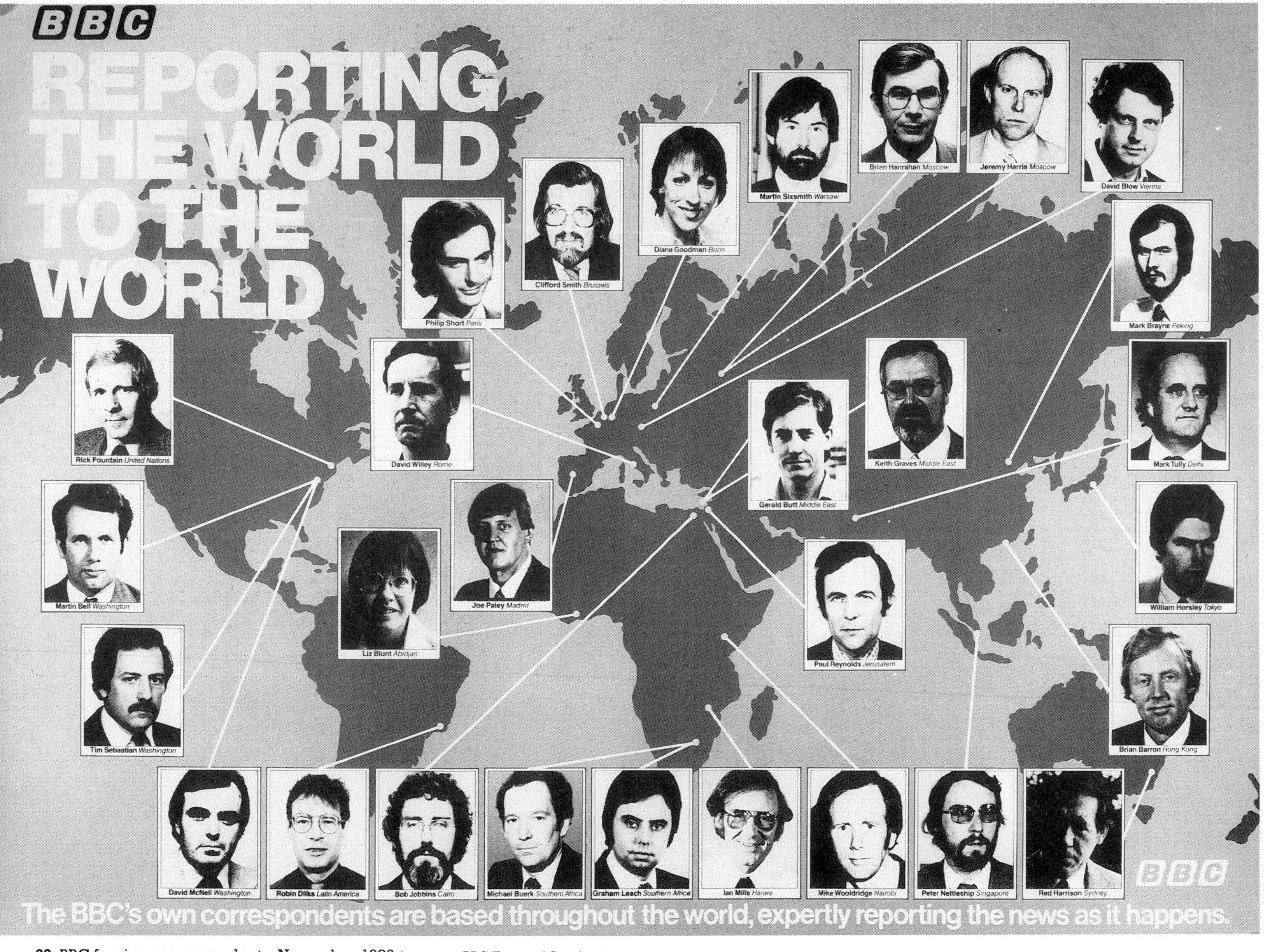

Figure 39 BBC foreign correspondents, November 1986 (courtesy BBC External Services)

opportunities may exist as stringers. The BBC occasionally recruits nationals with a proven track record in journalism and an expert knowledge of their country's affairs.

Sensitivity, a sense of humour and a touch of aggression head John Rhettie's list of qualities for a foreign correspondent:

> *'If you combine aggressivity with humour you can get a long way; if you're just aggressive you can put people off, but you have got to be a bit pushy. It requires an immense amount of energy, and you've got to do your homework – that's absolutely vital. You've got to know the situation, the people you're dealing with and have your communications set up in advance.'*

SPONSORED STRINGERS

As well as foreign correspondents, the BBC has a corps of sponsored stringers. These are staff journalists who satisfy their wanderlust by taking unpaid leave to work as correspondents abroad. The Corporation keeps their jobs open and pays them for each item or report it broadcasts. BBC fees would make a slender living so they are allowed to file to other news organizations as well.

The system is a useful safety valve. The BBC holds on to and develops its talent, extend its eyes and ears abroad, and when the stringer returns, increases its pool of knowledge and expertise in the newsroom.

NEWSREADERS

World Service newsreaders are neither trained journalists nor simply actors chosen for the rich, resonant quality of their voices. High on their list of qualifications comes a detailed understanding of world events and fluency in foreign languages, as newsreader Lawrence Reeve-Jones explains: '*As I read I'm consciously looking for names. I scan the next line, usually right up to the full stop. If I see a name which is unknown to me in the language in which it is written, I will probably take it very carefully. People are very sensitive about the pronounciation of their names.*'

The BBC has a pronunciation unit to advise newsreaders, which produces an index of names and places. The most unfamiliar may be spelled phonetically.

The pace of reading is slower than the domestic service and newsreaders sound more detached, perhaps even aloof from their stories. Their voices are also more typically British than their counterparts:

> *'Some of us are conscious that the World Service sounds possibly rather old-fashioned,'* says Lawrence Reeve-Jones. *'In the past it's been probably a public school voice – not too Guard's officer throaty, and not too camp – what they call* received pronunciation. *It is an educated voice with no local vowel sounds intruding.'*

THE WAY AHEAD?

The colonial image of the World Service is under review with the aim of rejuvenating the output to take it beyond the year 2000.

'*It does sound a bit dated*,' admits former news editor Terry Heron, '*We are identifying certain old-fashioned habits and making recommendations to change some of them. The concern is that the younger audience will not listen to us unless we are more in tune with the kind of life they lead.'*

For similar reasons, inroads are also being made into television. '*The BBC is perhaps the best news gathering organization in the world. So to restrict that to radio in the year 2000 and beyond would be inadvisable, because people will be watching more and more television,*' believes Mr Heron. '*One letter from Turkey said, 'With great regret, I am writing to tell you I am no longer going to listen to you in the evening, because electricity has just been supplied to my village and we all watch the communal television set.*' I have had similar comments from the subcontinent.'

The World Service dream is for a 24 hour TV channel, but the initial target is for four half-hour programmes a day, offered to TV stations on condition that the news is to go out in its entirety, uncensored, or not at all.

For the time being at least, the World Service can perhaps be summed up by one of its signature tunes – *Imperial Echoes*. It is as old-fashioned as a vintage Rolls. The accuracy of its craftsmanship and attention to detail are second to none. And it is every bit as British.

> ***'I remember being in the port city of Matadi in what is now Zaire, in what was then an exceedingly dangerous time. With a British cameraman, I was holed up in a hotel, feeling urgently the need to know the situation elsewhere in the country, where a revolution was going on. "the neat trick," he said, "would be to dial the Beeb." We located an ancient shortwave radio. The BBC told us that the Congolese armed forces has threatened to shell and destroy a hotel in Matadi. It was the one in which we were listening to the broadcast. We left. The hotel was promptly shelled and destroyed. Naturally, I have since had a certain affection for the BBC.'*** – CHARLES KURAIT, CBS NEWS

FIELDWORK

1 If you can, listen to the BBC World Service news and compare its style and content with your domestic radio service and describe the difference.

2 The guiding formula is that World Service news is the news of the world as seen from London. Is that obvious from listening to it? Supposing it was the news as seen from your country or nearest large city. What difference would that make?

How do you react to this guiding formula? Do you welcome it or regard it as an imposition of a set of news values that do not agree with your own? Discuss.

3 What system does your local radio newsroom use to review stories and check them for accuracy? How does it compare with the extensive checks and balances of the external services?

Do you believe that checks and balances in the newsroom can eliminate biased reporting? Give your reasons.

4 Listen if you can to an edition of *Radio Newsreel* and write down your comments. Does the style appeal or is it too old-fashioned? How could it be improved?

Do you find the correspondents' reports lively or dull? Would they be improved by adding extracts of interviews and actuality or would this detract from their authority?

How do you think the World Service could modernize its image and win a younger audience? Discuss your plans and proposals for revamping the service.

5 '*BBC External Services are funded by the Foreign Office so any attempt to provide independent coverage is compromised from the start.*' Discuss.

Do you think BBC foreign correspondents are impartial or do you find their reporting biased? Give some examples and discuss.

Suppose you were setting yourself up as a foreign correspondent in the country of your choice. How would you establish yourself and what contacts would you make?

18 Story treatment

> *'You can be working on three or four major stories a day with little research backup. You go in and you do your three and a half minute interview, pick out your twenty seconds of actuality, do a voice piece, and at the end of the day you've got to say well, actually, I've just skimmed over a number of issues.*
>
> — IRN PARLIAMENTARY CORRESPONDENT RICHARD BESTIC

There are many different ways to present a news story for radio from the simple copy story to the full-blown documentary. Television and radio techniques differ because of the use of visuals, but in many respects are similar in the way they package information as news. This chapter explores the different treatments radio gives to news. The newsroom described below and the characters within it are entirely fictitious.

It is a quarter past two on a quiet summer afternoon in Surrey, England. The only news worth reporting is that it is hot. The Guildford

Figure 40 Reporting for radio – on location for the BBC Bengali Service (courtesy BBC External Services)

newsroom is raking through the embers of the day's stories and wondering what to resurrect from the breakfast show to flesh out the five and six o'clock news programmes. The phone rings. Three hands grab for it but only the news editor's practised reaction connects. Relief is at hand. News has broken. News editor Ian Hinds is grilling the caller with all the zeal of the Spanish Inquisition:

'***When*** *did this happen? Just* ***now? How*** *many dead!? Are you* ***sure****?* ***Where****. . .? Outside Guildford station!!?'*

Fuelled by adrenalin, the news machine leaps into life. A story that develops quickly with new information coming in is known as *breaking news*, or a *running story*. Below are the various treatments that a fictitious radio station might give to this equally fictitious – but feasible – story of a train crash at Guildford.

NEWSFLASH (BULLETIN US)

News editor Ian Hinds lingers on the phone for only as long as it takes to check the details, then bashes out a few lines on his typewriter. Next he strides across to the studio, moving quickly, but not so fast as to become breathless, and glancing to check the on-air light is off, he bursts through the soundproof double doors, informs the presenter he has a newsflash and parks himself in the chair in front of the guest microphone.

As soon as Hinds is in place, the presenter dips the record he is playing, and says, '*And now over to our newsroom for an important newsflash*,' before firing an urgent five second jingle (sounder) and opening the microphone for Hinds:

> *'Two trains have collided just outside Guildford station, killing at least three people, injuring others, and leaving several more trapped in the wreckage. The accident, which happened in the past half hour, involved the delayed 1.51 from Guildford and the 1.18 from Waterloo. The names of the casualties and the cause of the accident are not yet known. The police are setting up an emergency phone number for relatives. We'll be bringing you that number as soon as it is announced.*
>
> *'That newsflash again . . . Two trains have collided outside Guildford station, killing three, and leaving others trapped and injured. More news on that crash as we get it.'*

The presenter fires another jingle, thanks Hinds on air and puts on another record, this time something more downbeat in keeping with the sombre news.

By now, Hinds is already back in the newsroom badgering British Rail for that emergency number, while the newsroom secretary is tasked with making sympathetic noises to clear the switchboard which is already getting calls from anxious friends and relatives of passengers.

Holding on for British Rail, whose press office is permanently engaged, Hinds barks out instructions to his team of reporters, which has been galvanized into action. One is on to the police, another is alternating between the fire brigade and the hospital and a third has already filed the story to the network newsroom in London.

The opposition station output is being played through the newsroom loudspeakers and Hinds permits his team a moment's self-satisfaction when they hear their rival's newsflash go out on air – four minutes after their own.

Just then the British Rail number comes through on the telex. Hinds holds the line to the press office in case they have more information, and toys with the idea of a second newsflash, but quickly drops that in favour of extending the headlines on the half-hour which is now less than three minutes away.

The newsflash is news at its most immediate, and highlights the task that radio does supremely well – getting news on air almost as quickly as it happens, and sometimes while it is still happening.

During the newsflash Hinds takes care to give the accurate departure times for the trains to limit needless worry from friends or relatives, and at the end repeats the information for those who may have missed or misheard it, at the same time seizing the opportunity to promote his station's news output. Listeners are left in no doubt that if they want to catch the latest on the crash first they should stay tuned to Surrey Radio.

Now Hinds has to make sure he and his team can deliver that promise.

HEADLINE

The story makes the lead on the headline round-up on the half hour. A headline is usually a brief summary of the main points of the story, and is seldom longer than four lines, or forty-eight words. In the case of the train crash, Hinds dispenses with convention and gives a fuller version. His second headline is more typical.

> *'A train crash at Guildford this afternoon has killed three passengers and injured four others. Several more are feared trapped in the wreckage. Rescue workers are now at the scene, about a mile north of Guildford station.*
>
> *'Both trains were travelling on the northbound line and collided head-on. They were the London-bound 1.51 from Guildford and the 1.18 from Waterloo. The names of the casualties are not yet known, but police have set up an emergency phone number for relatives to call for details. The number is 01.000.0000. That number again . . . 01.000.0000.*
>
> *'Train services between Guildford and London are suspended until the track can be cleared. More news on the rail crash as it comes in.'*
>
> *'The rest of the headlines now:*
>
> *'Plans for a 10 million pound office block in Woking have come under fire . . . Opposition councillors say Woking is already full of empty offices and the fifteen storey building would be another white elephant and unnecessary eyesore in the town centre.' Etc.*

Headlines (or *highlights*) are often read at the start of a major bulletin or news programme to signpost the news and encourage the audience to keep listening. They may be given again at the end to recap on the major stories, or, as in the case above, be read on the half past or quarter hour in lieu of a longer bulletin.

COPY STORY

This is an amplified version of the four line headline, giving the story in more detail, but without an accompanying interview (actuality). Copy stories are usually short – about twenty to thirty seconds, depending on house style. Stations which run 'straight' bulletins comprising only copy stories may run items up to double that length. Hinds' first 'headline' on the train crash was really a copy story.

Normally on a major story a voice report or interview extract would be used, but the briefer copy-only form comes into its own when:

- The story is breaking and no interview or fuller account is yet available.
- There is not enough time in the bulletin for a more detailed report.
- A fuller account or interview has already been used, and a shorter version is required to keep the story running without it sounding stale.

VOICER OR VOICE REPORT

Reporter Julian Alleck is driving to the scene in the radio car, with a helper, known as a gopher, to hump the equipment and set up the interviews, but there is some doubt whether he will be there in time for the three o'clock news. The other reporters are on to the police, fire brigade and British Rail to get information and try where possible to record interviews on the telephone.

With more information coming in, Hinds is not prepared to settle for a repeat of the copy story at three o'clock, so he asks a reporter to draw the facts together and turn it into a voice report.

GRINDLE/OWN   19.8   14.55   TRAIN SMASH

'The death toll in the Guildford train crash has now risen to four, and rescue workers believe more people could still be trapped in the wreckage of the two commuter trains. Lesley Grindle has the details . . .

CART: Rail smash
DUR: 40″
OUT: was to blame

'Less than an hour ago the 1.18 from London smashed head-on into the delayed 1.51 Guildford to Waterloo train just outside Guildford station. Four people died in the forward carriages, including the two drivers. Nine others are known to be injured, two seriously. Rescue workers say several more are still trapped in the wreckage and they're using cutting equipment to try to get them out.

'The names of the dead have not yet been released, but the police have set up a number which relatives can call for more details. It's 01.000.0000, that's 01.000.0000.

'The cause of the crash is still uncertain, but BR says early indications are that points failure may be to blame.'

As soon as the voicer is recorded, it is filed to network for inclusion in the national news on the hour. Some stations take this live, piping it in along a circuit. Others prefer to compile and present their own bulletins using a mixture of national and local news. This is a *newsmix*. As well as offering a live news service, the network newsroom sends out component stories of the bulletin individually. Cues and copy stories are sent along a teleprinter, and interviews and voicers along an audio circuit where they are re-recorded by the individual stations. (See also pages 26, 202.)

Voice reports offer an explanation of a story as well as additional details, and they permit a change of voice from the newsreader. They can also offer interpretation and anlaysis by a specialist, such as a sports editor or financial correspondent. In this way the voice report can express an authoritative opinion which would be inappropriate coming from the mouth of a newsreader.

Voicers are either recorded or read live, and are usually made at the stage where the information has outgrown a copy story, but where no actuality is yet available. They should be well researched, balanced, authoritative, crisply written and well-read. They would usually run from 25–35 seconds, excluding the cue, and longer in the case of a major breaking story.

The first paragraph of the voicer is known as the *cue* or the *lead*, into the report. Most stories which use an illustrative interview or voice report require a cue.

Above and below the cue is a set of information about the story. This is the *marking-up*. Most stations will have their own ideas about how this should be done. (See also pages 54, 181.)

What Hinds wants most of all for the bulletin is the live report from the scene, but in case this is not produced in time, the voicer above has been recorded to provide *holding* material, which can be used as a fall-back or substitute.

Holding material can take the form of a copy story, voicer or interview. Good holding material has prevented many a last-minute crisis and loss of face.

TEASER OR TASTER

It is now five seconds to three and Hinds is seated in the newsbooth to read his five-minute bulletin, a mixture of local and national news. As the news jingle is playing, he is hoping that one of the other interviews planned will come up trumps in time for this bulletin.

He begins with a set of teasers:

'A train crash at Guildford claims four lives... passengers are still trapped,'

'Inflation is on the up again,'

'Councillors are gunning for Woking's white elephant,'

'And in sport, Big Bobby quits for first division soccer.'

Urgent, present tense and very brief, the teaser is an enigmatic abbreviated headline used at the start of a bulletin or news programme to act as a lure by giving a taste of the story to come and teasing the audience into listening on to find out more.

A collection of three or four teasers is called a *menu*. It serves the same purpose as the menu in a restaurant – to whet the appetite.

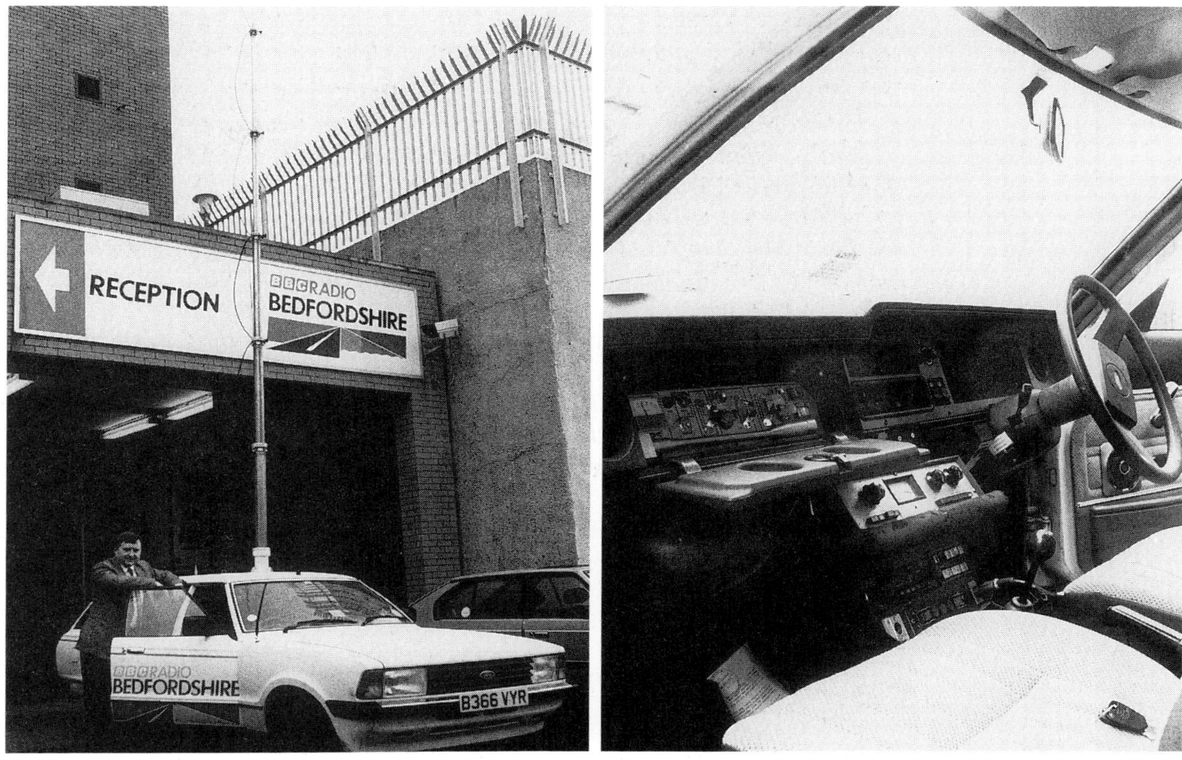

Figure 41 (*left*) The radio car with its tall pump-up aerial acts like a mobile studio for sending on-the-spot reports back to the station. (*right*) The idea is to keep the operation as simple as possible so that even the most non-technical of reporters can cover a breaking story without having to bring an engineer along to press the buttons (Andrew Boyd)

VOICE REPORT FROM THE SCENE
(Figure 41)

It is now 3.02. Less than five minutes ago, the radio car pulled up as close as it could to the crash, and reporter Julian Alleck spanned the last 50 metres by running a flying lead from the car with a microphone clipped to the end to bring him even closer to the action.

Alleck's brief is to go live into the 3 o'clock news with a minute long report. After snatching a few words with a British Rail official and a fire officer, Alleck contacts the newsroom on the radio car's *talkback* and says he is in position. In as few words as possible, Lesley Grindle gives him the latest information, gained over the telephone, and Alleck stands by to go live. Through his headphones he can hear the station output. Hinds has begun reading the bulletin, and the voicer by Grindle on the crash is going out on air.

Thirty seconds later he can hear Hinds finishing the story he is on and beginning the cue:

> *'As you heard just now, four people have died, and the number of injured is now up to twelve. More passengers are still believed to be trapped in the wreckage of the two trains which collided head-on on the*

northbound line just outside Guildford station. Julian Alleck is there now and describes the scene . . .'

'The picture here a mile up the line from Guildford is one of devastation. The two trains are twisted together beside the track and firemen and rescue worker are cutting open the wreckage to free any passengers who are still trapped.

'For reasons that are not yet clear, both trains were on the northbound line when they hit head-on. Their front carriages were torn from the rails by the impact, and are now lying locked together. Both drivers were killed in the crash. It's known that two passengers have also died, both on the London train, where firemen with cutting equipment are now working.

'The remaining five carriages of that train have also overturned and are on their sides, while all four coaches of the Guildford train have concertinad together in a zig-zag off the track, but are, remarkably, still on their wheels.

'Ambulance crews say they've taken twelve other passengers to hospital where they're being treated for injuries, and are now standing by while rescue workers continue to cut open the wrecked carriage, to search for any others who may still be on board.

'British Rail officials are inspecting the damage, and though they won't say for sure, early indications suggest that points failure might be to blame.

'This is Julian Alleck returning you to the studio.'

Back at the radio station Hinds picks up from him:

'And we'll be interrupting normal programming to bring you more news from the scene of that rail crash just outside Guildford as the information comes in. To repeat what we said earlier, all rail services between Guildford and London are suspended until the track is cleared.

'Meanwhile, in the rest of the news . . .' Hinds continues the bulletin.

Alleck's voice report, hastily set up with precious little time for preparation, concentrated on describing the scene for the listener. He has placed himself close enough to the action to pick up the sounds of the rescue operation, yet not so close as to interfere with the work of rescuers. His live report has stimulated the imagination by adding colour and description to the more factual studio voicer that was broadcast earlier in the bulletin.

On the spot reports can be made by cellular phone, radio telephone, regular phone, radio car or by a special studio quality line called a circuit.

The voicer from the scene gives more opportunity for descriptive, accurate and up to the minute reports than is possible with a studio voicer. Given time Alleck would have liked to include live or pre-recorded actuality, such as an interview with a survivor or rescue worker. His next task will be to gather more facts and get hold of the chief fire officer or a Southern Region spokesperson and have them standing beside him so he can interview them when he next goes live, or to record interviews with them which can be played during his live report. The main difficulty with such interviews is that it may not be possible to edit them on location, so there is little leeway for mistakes.

Alleck ends his report by handing back to the studio. Another common way to wrap up is to give a *standard outcue (payoff)* like this: '*Julian Alleck, Surrey Radio, at the scene of the rail crash, Guildford.*' The standard outcue (SOC) is more than simply a neat way to round off a report, it promotes the fact that the radio station has a reporter at the scene and heightens the impression of the station's news power.

In this case, the newsreader, Hinds, follows the live report with a *back announcement* (back anno). This is a further piece of signposting and promotion, letting the audience know that if they stay tuned they will hear more on the story.

If Alleck had had more time to take in the situation, Hinds could have conducted a *Q & A* (question and answer session) with him, interviewing him live about the story to get more details. To make sure the reporter is not caught out by a question for which he does not have the answer, he will usually provide the list of questions for the presenter to ask. This helps the flow without removing the impression of spontaneity. (For more on the Q & A see page 99.)

INTERVIEW

Radio stations frequently interrupt their schedules to provide on-the-spot coverage of major breaking news, and Alleck is asked to give his next live report as soon as he has enough information.

By 3.15 his gopher, a student who is getting work experience in the newsroom and hoping to break into radio, has come up with a witness to the crash. The woman was out walking her dog along a footpath less than 300 metres from the collision. She is shaken, but seems almost relieved to be interviewed and unburden herself of the things she has seen.

Alleck weighs up whether she is too unsteady to be interviewed live, but she is intelligent and articulate, and he thinks with careful handling she will cope. He decides to take a chance. Raising the studio on the radio car's talkback he tells the producer of the afternoon programme to stand by. He scribbles a cue on his notepad and dictates that to a journalist who has been summoned to the studio. As soon as it is typed, the producer tells him to stand by to go live, and moments later, the presenter is reading the cue for his second report.

'More news on the Guildford train crash now. If you've been listening in, you'll know that two trains have collided just outside Guildford station on the London line, killing four passengers and injuring others.

'Our reporter Julian Alleck is at the trackside, and he's been joined by Mrs Petra Cavanagh from Guildford, who saw the crash when she was out walking her dog near the railway line . . .'

J.A. *'Mrs Cavanagh, can you describe what happened?'*

Mrs C. *'Yes* (County accent), *I was walking Lucy, my Dalmatian, along the footpath, quite close to the track really, when I saw the London train coming, some way in the distance. At the same time I could hear another train behind me. I didn't think anything of it because the railway line has two tracks at this point, and . . . and one just assumes, of course, that the trains are on different lines.*

'Then the northbound train passed where I was standing and gave a terrific blast of its hooter; then there was a frantic squealing of brakes and I . . . I suppose I realized then, just . . . before they hit, that they were both on the same line. It was really quite appalling. One could do nothing to stop it.'

J.A. *'What happened when they collided?'*

Mrs C. *'Well, you understand, I . . . could only see the back of the Guildford train, but there was a simply dreadful noise, like a . . . like a shotgun going off by one's ear, then the train seemed to lift for a moment, and, very slowly it seemed, the carriages began to come off the track, one to the left and one to the right, until they came to rest. One was just rooted to the spot. I mean, one couldn't believe one's eyes.'*

J.A. *'What did you do next?'*

Mrs C. *'Well, I . . . I suppose one should have run to the nearest house and called for an ambulance, but, er, the extraordinary thing . . . that, er, that didn't enter my mind. I ran to the train, and when I got there I realized how much more badly damaged the other train . . . er, the southbound train, that is . . . was, if you follow me.'*

J.A. *'Can you describe what you saw?'*

Mrs C. *'It was really rather too horrible. The, er, the two front coaches were crushed together, very badly; I pity anyone who was inside. The other coaches were on their sides. From farther back passengers were opening the doors and starting to clamber out. The side of the train had become the roof, as it were. They were having to jump down on to the track from quite a height. Some of them were quite badly hurt. It's a wonder nobody was electrocuted.*

'I must confess, I'd been standing there feeling quite sick, and when the people started to come out, I remembered myself, tied Lucy up so she wouldn't wander on to the track, and set to helping the people down.'

J.A. *'How long was it before the ambulances arrived?'*

Mrs C. *'I really can't say. We were all so busy just helping people out. Others had come by then, from the homes nearby, and I sent one of them back to fetch blankets and another to get some ladders. I can't say I noticed the ambulances arrive.'*

J.A. *'Thank you. Mrs Petra Cavanagh who organized the rescue from the trains until the emergency services could arrive.*

'The death toll from the crash currently stands at four, but amazingly, only twelve people seem to have been seriously injured. If the same accident had happened in the evening rush hour, those figures could have been far worse.

'As I speak, rescue workers are checking the wreckage of the for-

ward coaches to see if anyone is still trapped. It looks as though the line will be out of action for quite some time.

'This is Julian Alleck at the scene of the train crash in Guildford.'

'Thank you Julian. And we'll be going back to the scene of that crash, I'm sure, later in the programme.'

Julian's next live report comes at twenty to four. By then two more passengers have been freed from the wreckage, both seriously injured, and rescue workers are satisfied that no one else is trapped. Work is going on to clear the line. The newsroom contacts Alleck to tell him the British Rail press office in London is now investigating the possibility that a points failure was to blame for routing the southbound train on to the northbound line. But at this stage, BR will not be interviewed about it. The news editor wants Alleck to get hold of a British Rail official at the scene and put the question to him live. This Alleck does, but the official is, understandably, not very forthcoming.

The interview adds more depth, permits a further exploration of a story and gives an opportunity for informed comment. Standard radio news interviews vary in length depending on house style. Between ninety seconds and about three minutes is almost standard, though those on extended news programmes may run a little longer. Live interviews, which are seldom as concise as edited ones, may also be longer.

NEWSCLIP

The most newsworthy quote from an interview is frequently edited from it to provide a short illustration to go with the story in a later bulletin. This would be about the same length as a voicer – usually 20 to 35 seconds – and is known as a *clip*, *cut* or *insert*. Clip or cut because it is an extract cut from an interview, and insert, because it is inserted into the bulletin. The cue will give the facts of the story, and the insert will develop them with explanation or comment.

Surrey Radio's 4 o'clock news is due on air shortly, and Hinds, ever eager to keep one jump ahead of the opposition, is extending the bulletin to make way for another full report from the scene.

Alleck's report will incorporate clips from the interviews with the witness and railway official. These are being edited by journalists in the newsroom from recordings of the two live interviews. These are known as *ROT's* (recording of/off transmission). The edited clips will be played in from the studio.

In addition, Alleck is asked to do a short live interview with a rescue worker. The report is complicated by playing in items from two separate locations and the timing is crucial.

PACKAGE

The 4 o'clock programme begins with a menu headed by the following teaser:

'The Guildford train crash . . . Four die, twelve are injured . . . British Rail say points failure is to blame . . . a witness describes the crash . . .'

After the rest of the menu, Hinds begins the lead story:

'British Rail say a points failure may be to blame for the train crash outside Guildford this afternoon which killed four and injured fourteen others. Four people were trapped in the wreckage and had to be freed by firemen with cutting equipment.'

'The 1.18 from Waterloo collided head-on with the London bound 12.55 from Portsmouth Harbour minutes after it left Guildford station. Both trains had been routed on to the same line.

'For the past hour and a half rescue teams have been working to free passengers trapped in the wreckage and efforts are now being made to clear the line. Our reporter Julian Alleck is at the scene of the crash . . .'.

(Live)

'The combined speed of the two trains was thought to be in excess of seventy miles an hour. The impact twisted together the front carriages of each, killing the drivers instantly. Firemen with cutting tools are still trying to separate the trains. In all, six passengers were trapped in the front compartment of the London train. Two were killed in the crash and the other four were pulled out injured, but alive.

'Mrs Petra Cavanagh from Guildford saw the crash happen:

(Tape)

'The northbound train passed where I was standing and gave a terrific blast of its hooter; there was a frantic squealing of brakes and I . . . It was really quite appalling. One could do nothing to stop it. There was a simply dreadful noise, like a shotgun going off by one's ear, then the train seemed to lift for a moment, and, very slowly it seemed, the carriages began to come off the track, one to the left and one to the right, until they came to rest. One was just rooted to the spot. I mean, one couldn't believe one's eyes.

'It was really rather too horrible. The two front coaches were crushed together, very badly; I pity anyone who was inside. The other coaches were on their sides. From farther back passengers were opening the doors and starting to clamber out. The side of the train had become the roof, as it were. They were having to jump down on to the track from quite a height. Some of them were quite badly hurt. It's a wonder nobody was electrocuted.'

(Live)

'In charge of the rescue operation was chief fire officer Tony Stims, who's with me now. Tony, how badly injured were the trapped passengers?

'Several of them were quite seriously hurt. Lucky to be alive I would say. I'm surprised only two passengers died in the impact and more weren't badly injured.'

'Was it a difficult operation, freeing them?'

'More delicate than difficult, OK, obviously we had to take a lot of care with the cutters that we didn't injure anyone further.'

'You're trying to separate the trains now and clear the track. How do you plan to do that?'

'Well, we've had lifting gear standing by for the past forty minutes, but we couldn't use it until we were sure everybody was out of the train. The first thing we want to do is haul them off the track, so the railway boys can get the trains running again.'

'How long will that take?'

'Half an hour. Maybe more, maybe less. Difficult to say.'

'Thank you. Chief fire officer Tony Stims. British Rail are launching an inquiry into this accident, but say their first indications are that points failure may be to blame. This was confirmed earlier by their spokesman here at the scene, John Turbot:'

(Tape)

'Obviously we're investigating; it could only really be points failure, beyond that I can't say at this stage.'

'You mean a faulty points operation directed the London train on to the wrong track?'

'It's still too soon to be sure but that appears to be correct, yes.'

'How could that happen?'

'Well that's what we've got to find out. It's really a matter for an inquiry.'

'Do you suspect an equipment failure or an operator error?'

'I'm sorry but as I've already said, that's a matter for an inquiry.'

'Has the problem now been rectified?'

'Yes.'

'Then you must know what caused it.'

'We've got a good idea, yes, but as I told you, it's for the inquiry to make the final decision.'

'Four people have lost their lives this afternoon. If you're planning to open the line again today, what assurances can you give commuters that the problem has been solved and won't happen again?'

'Well let me correct you. We intend to get the trains running but on adjacent tracks which were not damaged in the accident.

(Live)

'British Rail spokesman John Turbot. Services between Guildford and London are expected to resume within the next hour.

'This is Julian Alleck, Surrey Radio, at the scene of the Guildford train crash.'

(Back in the studio)

'And police have issued a phone number for anyone who may have had a friend or relative on either of those trains, it is . . . etc.'

As soon as the bulletin is over, Alleck checks on the talkback that the package was successfully recorded back at the station, then files again his last paragraph substituting a network outcue for the Surrey Radio tag.

The station will switch the outcues and then send the package via a circuit to the network newsroom. It will be Surrey Radio's fourth item on the crash to be sent 'down the line'. Alleck has given the train's correct origin as Portsmouth Harbour to broaden the information for a wider audience.

From its London base, the network newsroom will send the item back along the contribution circuit for distribution to the other local stations in the network.

Alleck's piece with its three inserts is more sophisticated than the basic package, which usually comprises a cue and a couple of short interviews. These are wrapped up in the reporter's own words, which are grouped before the first interview, between the interviews and usually after the last interview. These are known as *links*.

Packaging is useful for presenting a balanced account of two sides of an argument and for permitting the use of more elaborate production techniques to include sound effects or music. (See also page 230.)

Unlike the standard interview, where the focus is on the interviewee, the package sets up the reporter as raconteur and guide. The cue presents an overview of the story and the reporter's first link adds flesh to that and provides an introduction to the first interviewee.

The middle link allows the reporter to summarize any important points that have been left out, and to tie what has just been said to the second interview, which he then introduces.

The final link is used for summing up the two arguments, adding important details, and pointing the way forward for the story, in this case by referring to the time it will take to restore train services.

A strength of the package is that you can use extracts of interviews which have been boiled down to their essential information. Contrast the edited interview with Mrs Cavanagh with the original live version with her. The edits have been made to focus on the description of the collision and to eliminate unnecessary information and verbal tics.

MINI-WRAP

While Alleck is filing his report, the network intake editor is on to the newsroom asking for an update on the story. He wants a shorter version for the bulletin, preferably wrapped (packaged) and with a maximum duration of forty seconds, which coming from network with its appetite for news fast and furious, is quite a concession.

No sooner has Alleck finished filing his package than reporter Phil Needle is on the talkback passing on network's request.

Alleck decides to give it the full treatment, and solicits the help of Needle to further edit down the interview clips to cram something of all three into the report. In vain, Needle protests about squeezing quarts into pint pots, but Alleck will have nothing of it.

Ten minutes later Needle is on the talkback again offering fifty seconds, and Alleck sends him away with a flea in his ear. After two more hatchet attempts, they manage between them to concoct the following report:

ALLECK/OWN 19.8 16.38 CRASH/NETWORK U.D.

'British Rail say points failure may have been to blame for this afternoon's rail crash outside Guildford which claimed four lives and injured twelve.

'This report from Julian Alleck at the scene of the crash . . .

REEL: CRASH/NETWORK UD
IN: 'The crash happened . . .'
OUT: SOC
DUR: 40"

'The crash happened after the Waterloo train was accidentally routed on to the same line as the train from Portsmouth Harbour. Mrs Petra Cavanagh saw it happen . . .

'There was a frantic squealing of brakes and a simply dreadful noise. The two front coaches were crushed together; I pity anyone inside. The side of the train had become the roof. Passengers were having to jump down on to the track from quite a height. It's a wonder nobody was electrocuted.'

'Six passengers were trapped and had to be cut free, but two were already dead. Chief fire officer Tony Stims was in charge of the rescue:'

'Several were quite seriously hurt. Lucky to be alive. I'm surprised only two died in the impact and more weren't badly injured.'

'British Rail are investigating. Their spokesman John Turbot:'

'It could only really be points failure, but it's for the inquiry to make the final decision.'

'This is Julian Alleck, Network Radio, at the Guildford train crash.'

All reference to the track being cleared has deliberately been left out, as the position by 5 o'clock could well be different. Up-to-date facts can be added nearer the time and included in the form of a back announcement.

The wrap works out at nearer forty-five seconds than forty, and to boil it down that far has required some 'creative' editing to cut the actuality while still making sense of the narrative. The piece is already sounding slightly breathless and disjointed, and with time creeping up towards the bulletin, they decide to call it a day and give the duration as 40 seconds, hoping nobody in network notices the deception.

Sometimes people can be *too* clever with mini-wraps, and when Needle plays the edited version to him down the talkback Alleck is forced to concede that perhaps it does sound a little garbled in places, but his satisfaction at having crammed three pieces of actuality in forty seconds (or so) overrules his other sensibilities, and anyway, there's no time now to mess around with a remake.

Meanwhile, back in the newsroom, Hinds has just listened to a recording of the opposition 4.30 bulletin and is having convulsions. They have got actuality with one of the survivors from the hospital, and his own staff reporter, Lesley Grindle, whom he had sent there to do the same has just rung in to say she is terribly sorry, but she had forgotten to load any tape on her recorder. After some choice remarks, Hinds slams down the phone and, clutching his head, finds some consolation in the thought that Alleck at least has done a decent day's work.

In the corner another phone is ringing. It is the network intake editor. His tone is sarcastic. '*About that mini-wrap. Great,* ***if you can follow it****. Any chance of a remake? And could you cut it down a bit?*'

Out on the railway line at Guildford, somebody's ears are burning . . .

FIELDWORK

1 Open a file for each type of story treatment. Then listen to a news bulletin that uses illustrations and actuality clips and list the story treatment given to each item (*headline, copy, story, teaser, etc*).

Then do the same with an extended news programme. Make notes on stories that fit the various categories and see if you can pick up tips about technique or learn anything about the pitfalls. Keep listening until every category is covered.

2 Go back to Alleck's live interview with Mrs Cavanagh. Without looking at the edited verison, show how you would cut it to reduce it to a thirty-five second newsclip. Type out the quotes you would leave in.

What good material do you feel you have had to cut out to get it down to length?

Now do the same with the Turbot interview.

3 Take a news story from a newspaper and produce from it a *teaser, headline, copy story* and *voicer*.

If you are in a class, all work on the same story and then compare your different versions. Have you all agreed about what to leave in and what to take out? Discuss your differences and see if you can come to some agreement.

4 Now take a newspaper story which quotes two sides of an argument and write it up as though you were doing the script for a package. Include cues and links, and extracts from the interviews. Keep the whole package down to 2 minutes 30 seconds (at 3 words per second).

Now cut the package to 1 minute 30 seconds.

Do you find it difficult working out what to leave out?

Now turn it into a mini-wrap of just 40 seconds (120 words).

What do you think of mini-wraps? Do you find them slick and professional or do you think they can sometimes be too clever? Do they tell you more or less than you would find out from a voicer or newsclip?

5 '*Editing distorts what people say by focusing in on only what the journalist wants them to say. To be fair, peoples' comments should not be edited.*' Discuss.

How can you avoid distorting what someone says when you edit their interview?

19 Principles of recording

Figure 42 BBC war correspondent Michael Reynolds, reporting from liberated Venice in 1945 using a 'portable' disc recorder (courtesy BBC External Services)

The recording business has come a long way since 1898 when Valdemar Poulsen first captured sound on piano wire fixed to a hand-turned drum. Developments with wax drums and discs followed, though even through the Second World War poor quality recordings were still being made on wire which could only be edited by knotting the ends and melting them together.

But there was a surprise in store for the Allies. When American troops liberated Paris they burst into a radio station expecting to find an orchestra in full flood, only to discover the Germans had found a way to record music on tape with a quality of reproduction previously undreamt of. Tape was here to stay!

In the post-war years bulky recorders went on a reducing diet, and stereo sound made its debut in the mid-1950s. Ten years later Philips introduced the device which was to revolutionize sound recording – the compact cassette – and Ampex cracked the problem of recording visual images on tape. The videotape recorder (VTR) was born, and soon to go down the same road as audio tape with the videocassette recorder.

The computer age brought the next leap in quality. Digital tape and laser discs are being used increasingly in the world of broadcasting, but both are being surpassed by digital recordings stored directly in computer memory.

Further developments and miniaturization have made it possible for today's reporters to move unhampered to the forefront of breaking stories and send back live studio-quality reports.

TAPE

If at the turn of the century anyone had dared suggest that lengths of rust-coated plastic would one day carry sounds and images which could be transmitted across the globe, no one would have taken him seriously.

Yet recording tape is basically just that – polyester ribbon covered with ferric oxide. This is cut into different widths to form the basis of most standard reel-to-reel, cassette or videotape.

Sound quality varies with the metal coating on the tape. Ferric, or iron oxide, is the most common, while chrome, pseudo chrome and metal tape offer higher quality at a higher price.

The metal is coated on one side of the tape in the form of fine magnetic needles, which are glued to the plastic film with a binding agent and polished.

Reel-to-reel tape is still standard in radio stations because it provides high quality sound and is easy to edit. It usually comes on reels of 5, 7 and 10.5 in (12.7, 17.8, 26.7 cm) in diameter.

Different thicknesses are available. Thinner tape offers longer recording times because more can be wound on the reel, but it is prone to stretching and that stretchiness makes it harder to edit.

A rule of thumb is that recording quality improves with the quantity of tape used. So the wider the tape and the faster it travels, the better the reproduction.

Tape speed is usually 7.5 in (19 cm) per second, though 15 ips (38 cm) may be used for better quality. Standard tape width for sound only is usually a quarter of an inch (6 mm).

Cassettes use narrower tape and operate at the slower speed of $1\frac{7}{8}$ ips (4.7 cps). This means a drop in quality, especially at higher frequencies.

As a result, high-speed reel-to-reel recordings usually sound brighter, clearer and richer than those made on cassettes. But cassette and sound technology has improved to the point where the difference is harder to distinguish.

Videotape is being used increasingly to record sound only. The tape heads on a video recorder rotate at high speed, which has the same effect as moving the tape extremely rapidly past the recording head – the quality of the recording improves.

Chiltern Radio in Dunstable pioneered the use of videotape in British radio by using it to record and broadcast late night music programmes. The five-hour tape was set up to fire adverts and announcements automatically so the station could operate unmanned overnight.

Reclaiming tape

Edited reel-to-reel tape can be reused, providing there are not too many splices, but care should be taken not to mix different sorts of tape on the same reel, as recording machines are usually set up to work effectively with one kind of tape only.

Tapes can be wiped clean by passing them through a powerful magnetic field which destroys the magnetic pattern the recording has made. This is done by placing the tape in or on a *bulk eraser*. If these are used incorrectly a regular swooshing noise will be left on the tape (Figure 43).

Bulk erasers are powerful electromagnets, so reporters are advised to keep mechanical watches well clear. Journalists have also discovered to their horror that the bulk eraser can wipe clean the magnetic coding on their credit cards!

Figure 43 The bulk eraser is a powerful electromagnet which wipes the magnetic pattern on the tape – make sure you take your watch off before using it and keep any credit cards well clear! (Andrew Boyd)

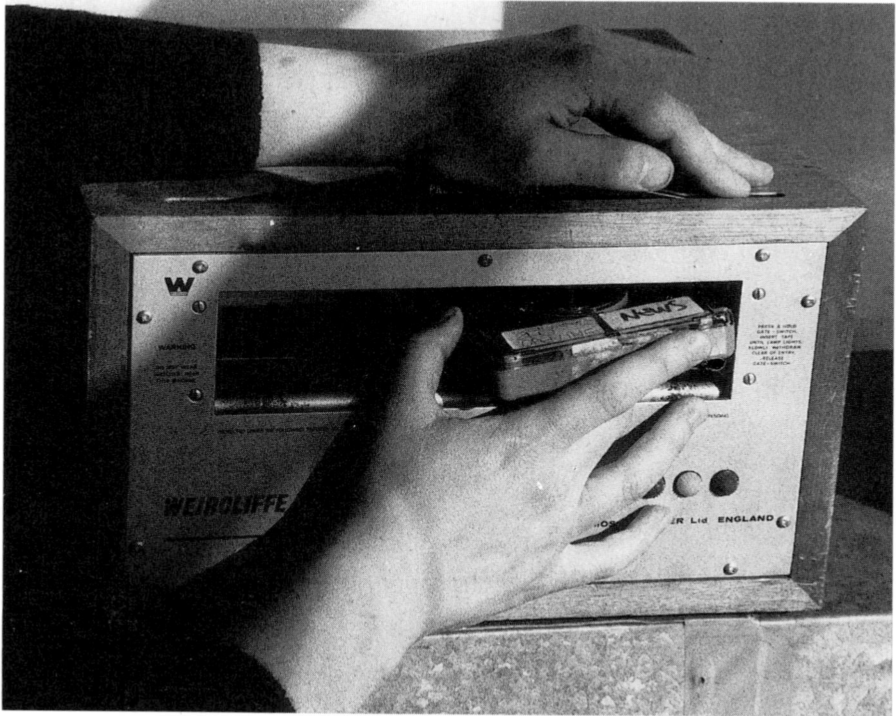

Care of tapes

Tapes should be wound evenly on spools and kept in boxes to keep dust at bay. These should be stacked vertically to prevent damage to the edges of the tape and the spools.

Tapes should also be kept clear of loudspeakers, television sets, bulk erasers, and anything that will give off a magnetic field.

CARTRIDGES
(Figure 44)

Cartridges offer a faster, easier way of playing recordings on air than using reels of tape which have to be laced-up by hand on playback machines.

Cartridges (or carts) are plastic boxes containing endless loops of tape of different durations, such as forty seconds for short news items, or three and a half minutes for longer features.

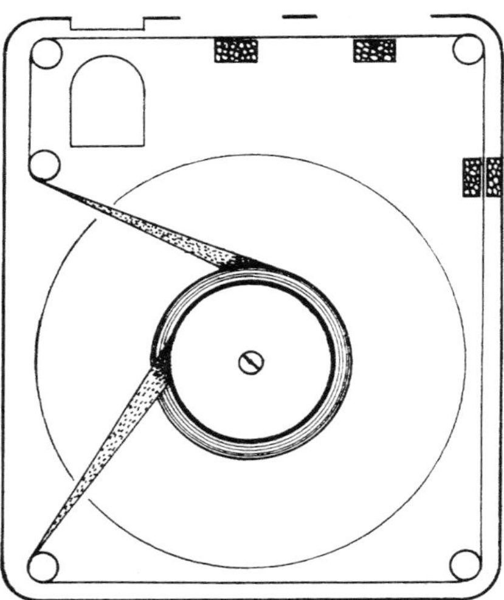

Figure 44 Cutaway of a tape cartridge. The tape runs round in an endless loop. The machine stops automatically when it reads an electronic pulse at the start of the recording. Without this pulse, the machine would play the recording over and over. When it stops, the cartridge is *cued-up* and ready to be played again

The cart is inserted into a recording machine. When the record button is pressed an inaudible electronic marker, known as a *cue pulse*, is placed on the tape. To begin the recording you press the start button and to end it you hit the stop button. If you press the start button again, the loop will continue until it reaches the cue pulse when it will stop automatically. It is then *cued-up* ready to be played.

A secondary pulse may be added at the end of the recording. This puts some types of cart machine into fast-forward and re-cues them more quickly. Tertiary pulses may be used to trigger off a second cart or other item of equipment.

Cart recordings that are no longer required are bulk-erased and used again.

The quarter inch tape, which is graphited for dry lubrication, is joined in a loop by a short length of splicing tape.

Cartridge machines don't have erase heads, so it is *vital* to bulk erase a cartridge before you record on it, otherwise the old recording will also be audible.

Pros and cons of carts

Advantages

- Carts have made it faster and easier to play adverts, announcements, jingles (sounders) and short items.
- High quality carts are often used instead of discs for playing music. Radio Mercury in Crawley, was one of the first British radio stations to transfer its playlist to cart.
- Carts can be labelled and stacked in racks which makes them more accessible than reels or discs.
- Carts are self-cueing and do not have to be rewound like tapes.
- Carts are easy to use, so radio newsreaders can present programmes without the aid of a technical operator. This is known as *self-opping* (self-operation).
- Carts are faster and easier to play than tapes, and have opened the way to highly illustrated news bulletins. Interview extracts and voice reports are recorded on cart. Newsreaders plug them in to the slots in the order in which they will be played. When one has finished, they simply swap it for another. (See also pages 236, 237.)

Disadvantages

- Flexibility has its price:
- Recordings have to be re-recorded (dubbed-off) on to cart, and this usually results in a drop in quality and an increase in tape noise.
- Each time a tape is played some of its magnetic coating wears away and there is a gradual fall off in quality. Like the brakes on a car gradually wearing out, the driver may not notice the deterioration until the day his/her foot hits the floor and the car fails to stop.
- Carts are expensive and the tendency is to keep using them until they break. This can result in tired carts producing muddy-sounding items.
- A cart machine may occasionally run slightly past its cue pulse, cutting off the first syllable of the first word on the recording. This is known as *clipping*. This gasp of sound is transferred to the end of the loop, and there is a danger that it may be heard on air while the cart is rewinding.
- Reels of tape are made ready (cued-up) by hand so the operator can check he/she has the right tape by listening to the first few words and matching them against the words given on the cue sheet. The tape can be wound back in a moment but if operators want to check the first words on a cart they will have to run the cart all the way through until it re-cues.
- Sometimes presenters stop carts and remove them before they have had time to re-cue. As a result, when they are played in the next bulletin all that comes out on air is silence.

Digital carts

Digital carts do away with most of the disadvantages of ordinary carts and increase their flexibility.

They offer the same plug-in-and-go ease of use, with greater quality. More than thirty cuts can be held on a single cartridge and the machine can be programmed to select the order in which to play them. So all the clips in an extended news bulletin can be kept on one cartridge. (See also Digital recording below.)

PRINCIPLES OF RECORDING

Sound

Sound is created by vibrations in the air. The faster the air vibrates, the higher the sound will seem to the hearer. The speed of these vibrations is known as their *frequency*, and frequencies are measured in *hertz*. One thousand hertz is *kilohertz*. Human speed spans a range between around 50Hz to 6Khz. The deeper the voice, the lower the frequency. The human ear can hear sounds from about 16Hz to 18Khz.

As well as being high or low, sounds are loud or quiet. Their loudness, or *sound pressure level* (SPL) is measured in *decibels*. The higher the decibel number, the louder the sound. Speech rises to about 70 decibels. A gunshot would approach 130db and would cross the listener's threshold of pain.

How recordings are made

Microphones convert sound into an electrical signal. This varies in relation to the sounds being picked up by the mike.

The signal is boosted by an amplifier and passed to the *recording head* of the tape recorder. An electromagnet then converts it into a magnetic current.

As the tape runs across the head, the magnetic current arranges the metal particles on the tape into a pattern which varies with the sounds being recorded.

When the tape is played back the operation works in reverse. The magnetic pattern on the tape is converted back into an electrical signal at the *playback* head which is boosted through an amplifier and converted back into sound through the loudspeakers.

Tape heads

Tape recorders have two or three heads. The first to come in contact with the tape is the *erase head*, an electro magnet which wipes out old recordings before the tape reaches the *recording head*. Some machines may use a third head for *playback*, while others combine record and playback.

Tracks

Some machines record across the whole width of the tape. This is a *full* or *single track* mono recording. Others use the top half of the tape only, which means the tape can be turned over and recorded on the other side. This *half track* recording is also mono. (Turning the tape over and recording on both sides makes it impossible to edit the original because any cuts would go through both recordings.)

Stereo recordings, which separate sounds on to different tracks to be played back through two loudspeakers, are made by recording one sound source on the top track and the other on the lower track. This is *half track stereo*.

Many domestic reel-to-reel machines use *quarter track stereo*, which permits the tape to be turned over and used on the other side. Cassettes use a similar system but the layout of the tracks is different.

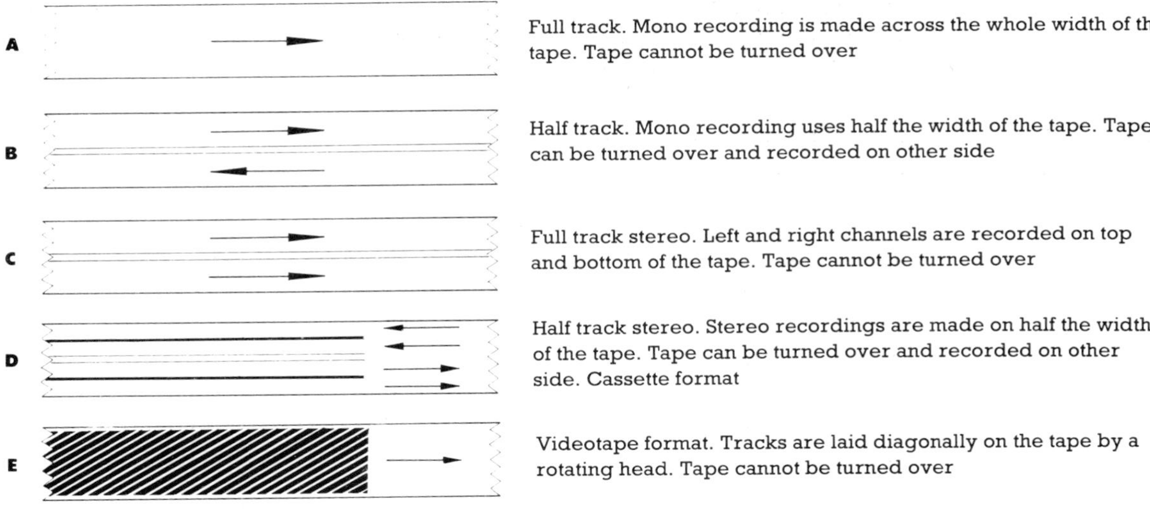

A
Full track. Mono recording is made across the whole width of the tape. Tape cannot be turned over
B
Half track. Mono recording uses half the width of the tape. Tape can be turned over and recorded on other side
C
Full track stereo. Left and right channels are recorded on top and bottom of the tape. Tape cannot be turned over
D
Half track stereo. Stereo recordings are made on half the width of the tape. Tape can be turned over and recorded on other side. Cassette format
E
Videotape format. Tracks are laid diagonally on the tape by a rotating head. Tape cannot be turned over

Figure 45

Tapes recorded on some types of machine may not play back successfully on others using a different system (Figure 45).

Video recording

Videotape recorders work differently again. The recording head is circular and revolves very quickly to allow more information to be put on tape to incorporate colour pictures as well as sound.

Digital recording

Tape is a noisy medium. If you take a brand new blank tape and play it back, you will probably hear a hiss. This *tape noise* is present all the time on playback.

Digital recording does not suffer from tape hiss and distortion. It converts the signal into pulses of binary code which are put on the tape or disc. Once encoded, the original sound is effectively locked in and cannot deteriorate, even after playing many times. Unlike a conventional (*analogue*) recording, this code cannot become corrupted by hiss, hash, distortion or wow and flutter (alterations in tape speed).

On playback, the binary code is decoded and turned back into a signal. As long as the code can be read the playback will be as close to the original as the hi-fi will allow. Digital techniques mean the machinery, not the tape, has become the limiting factor in the quest for audio perfection. Copy after copy can be made without any loss in quality.

Digital recordings can be stored on tape, laser disc or computer hard disk. Computers can hold a radio station's entire playlist of music or a day's programming. Audio can be edited on computer and items programmed to be played on air in any order. (See also the touchscreen studio, page 241.)

Bias

Early tape recordings were subject to serious distortion and noise until a recording made by chance near a radio transmitter produced a better result. The transmitter's high frequency signal had been picked up by the recording head of the tape recorder and distortion was reduced as a result. This accidental discovery was incorporated into recorder design and is known as *bias*.

Equalization

Bias had the unfortunate side-effect of causing a loss in high frequency, which meant a tailing off of higher sounds. To compensate, the recorded signal can be adjusted on playback to boost the high frequency. This is known as *equalization*.

Tapes which have different bias settings require different equalization (EQ) settings for playback. Bias and EQ can be altered by switches on the tape recorder or are adjusted automatically by the machine. Equalization affects playback only and has no effect on recording.

Noise reduction

Most unwanted tape noise is in the high frequency range. If you turn down the treble most of it will disappear, but so will many of the high notes.

Noise reduction systems drown out the hiss by boosting sounds in the high frequency range during recording. The high frequency is reduced on playback to its normal levels and the hiss is reduced with it. The most commonly used types of noise reduction are the Dolby B or C systems, which are incompatible.

Types of microphone

There are three main types of microphones: *ribbon*, *moving coil* and *capacitor*.

The ribbon type, which is one of the most expensive, has a *diaphragm* of thin aluminium foil which is vibrated by the sounds around it like an ear drum. It moves within a magnetic field to create a signal.

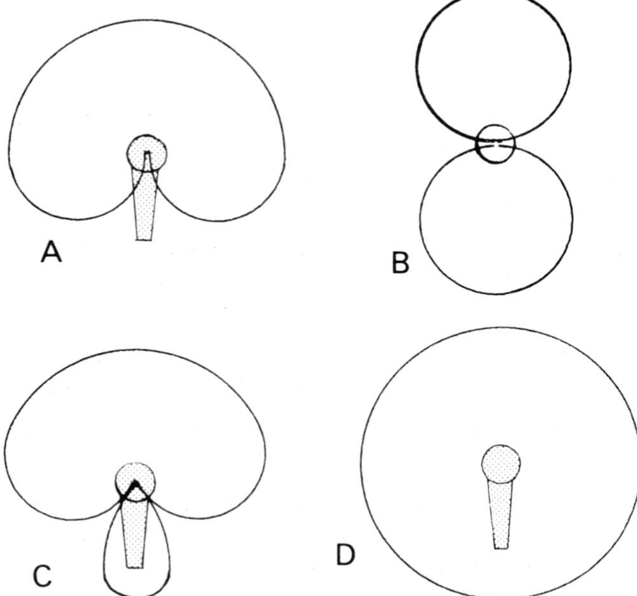

Figure 46 Microphones are sensitive to sounds coming from a specific area around them. This is known as their *directivity pattern*, which varies according to mike type:
A Cardoid
B Figure of eight (top view)
C Hyper cardoid
D Omni-directional
Ribbon mikes with their figure of eight pattern are useful for interviews which can be conducted at a table either side of the mike. Omni-directional mikes pick up the least sound from handling, but because they pick up all round they can draw in unwanted background sounds

The moving coil, or *dynamic* type, has a wire coil attached to a diaphragm which also vibrates in a magnetic field.

In the *capacitor*, or *condenser* type of microphone, the diaphragm is replaced with the plate of an electrically charged capacitor. These microphones require an electric current, which is usually supplied by a battery (Figure 46).

Ribbon mikes are *bi-directional*. They respond in a figure of eight, picking up voices on both sides. They are often used to record studio interviews or discussions and are placed on a stand or suspended from the ceiling. Most varieties cannot be used out of doors, as any wind will blow against the ribbon creating a whooshing noise.

A specialized version of ribbon mike is the *lip mike* which is used by commentators. These respond to nearby sounds only and are held against the mouth.

There are two types of moving coil microphone. Some pick up sounds all round. These are *omni-directional*. Others pick up from in front of the microphone only. These are *uni-directional*. Their pick-up pattern is described as *cardioid* (heart shaped).

Radio reporters use hand-held microphones of either type. Some mikes are unsuitable because they pick up movements made by the hand. This *handling noise* is kept to a minimum in broadcast-standard mikes.

Stand-mounted uni-directional microphones are usually favoured by newsreaders.

Capacitor mikes vary in their response pattern. These are commonly used in television clipped to a tie or hanging from a *lavalier* or cord.

By using two tie-clip mikes with a stereo recorder you can avoid having to wave a microphone under a subject's nose. This is useful for longer interviews or where the interviewee needs to be put at ease.

FIELDWORK

1 If you have cartridges available try making a recording on one which has not been bulk-erased. Play it back and hear how it sounds.

Now take that same cart and stand it on a loudspeaker for a few minutes before playing it back. Does it sound different? In what way? Why?

2 Make a recording on another cart and put it very quickly in and out of the bulk eraser. Play it back and describe how it sounds. Experiment with using the bulk eraser until you find the most efficient way to wipe a cart clean.

3 If you have access to different types of tape machine, make a recording and try playing it back on a machine with a different format. How does it sound?

4 Which would you prefer to work with, carts or reels? Discuss the advantages and disadvantages of each.

5 Which kind of mike would you use for the following situations: reading the news; street interviews; interviewing one person in a talks studio; interviewing three people in a talks studio, or an in-depth personality interview in someone's home?

20 Using portable recorders

> *'In my opinion, the most dangerous machine of them all is the microphone.'* – BBC PRESENTER ESTHER RANTZEN

Portable recorders fall into the reel-to-reel or cassette variety. Each has its pros and cons:

REEL-TO-REEL VERSUS CASSETTE: ADVANTAGES AND DISADVANTAGES

Recording quality

- Reel machines may offer superior quality reproduction with reduced noise.
- Cassette reproduction is usually considered adequate for broadcast speech. Their quality is constantly being improved.

Portability

- Reel machines are usually larger, heavier and sometimes bulky.
- Cassette recorders are smaller and lighter and sometimes tiny. Useful for discreet recordings.
- Tape reels can be bulky to carry.
- Cassettes are light and small. An hour's tape can easily fit into a pocket.

Editing

- Reels may be edited directly from the machine, or on the machine itself.
- Cassettes require dubbing – re-recording on to reels of tape – before they can be edited.

Durability

- Reel-to-reel recorders are usually built tougher to be more durable. Their size also makes them easier to service.

Cost

- Reel machines and tapes are expensive and tapes usually have to be bought from a specialist.
- Cassette machines are cheaper and cassettes are inexpensive and readily available.

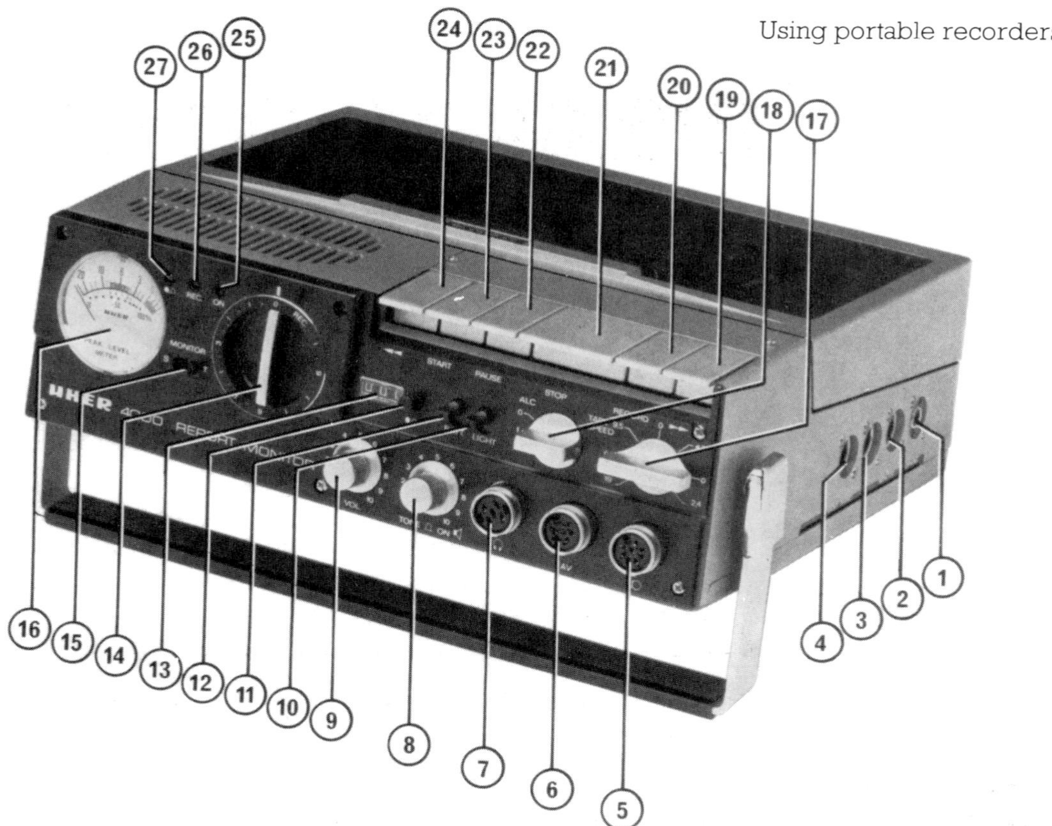

Figure 47 UHER 400 report monitor portable reel-to-reel recorder (courtesy UHER)

1 Headphone socket for monitoring recordings
2 Monitor socket for connection to an external amplifier
3 Battery charger or remote control socket
4 Radio phono socket for connection to a tuner or amplifer
5 Microphone input. The Uher microphone has a remote control switch which can stop and start the tape
6 Audio visual socket for controlling synchronized sound and film
7 Second headphone socket (to accommodate phones with a different type of plug)
8 Tone control and loudspeaker cut. (Pull out knob to shut off machine's speaker)
9 Playback volume control
10 Light. Illuminates recording meter when depressed. One press turns the light on for fifteen seconds. Two presses will keep the light on constantly. Another two presses will extinguish the light.
11 Battery level check. If the needle on the meter remains in the green area when this is pressed, then the batteries are charged.

The battery level button should be kept down for a number of seconds in case there is any fall off in after the initial meter reading due to weak batteries

13 and 12 Tape counter and reset button. When an interviewee comes up with an important point, the reporter can jot down the number shown on the counter so he/she can quickly rewind to the right place afterwards
14 Recording volume control. (Also known as the gain control)
15 Level monitoring switch. This can be switched to show the signal being recorded on the tape, known as the source (S), or the signal being played back from the tape (T)
16 Recording level meter. Also indicates battery condition
17 Speed selector. 19 cm is equivalent to 7.5 ips. This is the Uher's fastest speed and provides the best quality recording. The selector knob also switches on the machine. 0 is the off position
18 Automatic level control (ALC). There are three settings.
0 = off; 1 = fast; 2 = slow. (See Recording, below)
19 Fast forward. (Not for use in recording)
20 Record key
21 Stop key. This halts the tape transport and takes the machine out of its current mode (playback, record, etc.)
22 Pause key. This pauses the tape transport, while leaving the machine in its current mode
23 Start key. This puts the Uher into playback. To make a recording, start and record keys must be activated simultaneously
24 Fast rewind
25 Green Machine-on indicator
26 Red recording indicator
27 Yellow Audio visual indicator

Reel-to-reel: The Uher

A common workhorse in many radio stations is the *Uher* recorder. This is a German made, high quality, battery-powered unit, capable of excellent reproduction, which is built like a tank and is almost as heavy.

Notes to BBC trainees laughingly describe the bulky Uher as the reporter's '*radio notebook*.'

It is powered by five 1.5 volt batteries or a rechargable power pack, and can also be connected to a car battery (Figure 47).

Recording on the Uher.

The principles here apply to most reel-to-reel machines.

Lacing up the tape (Figure 48)

Take a full 5 in reel of tape and place it on the left-hand spindle of the machine. Then place an empty *take-up* reel on the right.

Each spindle has a device designed to grip the reel firmly. This has three prongs and is called a *mandrel*. Before you can put the reels in place, you will need to line up the top and bottom halves of the mandrel. The reels can then be placed on the spindles. The top mandrels should then be turned to grip the reels. You could now hold the tape recorder upside down and shake it (not recommended!) and the reels will not fall off.

Next, pull some 10 in of tape from the full reel and draw it around the

Figure 48 Uher tape recorder laced up and ready to go. A common mistake for beginners is to forget to lace the tape around the take-up roller on the left (Andrew Boyd)

roller on the left of machine, which holds the tape in tension, and insert it vertically into the threading slot.

The free end of the tape should then be inserted into the slot on the empty take-up reel, leaving about a quarter of an inch exposed above the slot. Any more and the end will brush noisily against the tape cover during recording and playback.

Holding the exposed end of the tape, turn the reel anti-clockwise to take up one complete winding of the tape. Take care not to twist the tape in the threading slot. Then take up any slack.

Making a recording

1 Before taking a tape recorder out in the field or beginning a recording always check its battery strength.

This is done on the Uher by depressing the button (11) and reading the meter (16). The needle should rest in the green area marked on the dial.

2 Plug the microphone into its socket (5 or 7).

3 Cut the loudspeaker by turning the volume control to zero or pulling out the tone knob.

4 Take a recording level. The ALC (18) should be set at zero, and the monitor control (15) set to S, for source. With the pause key (22) down, the record and start keys (20 and 23) should be pressed. The level can now be set on the meter (16) by speaking into the microphone at the same volume at which the recording will be made.

The needle should approach the red section at the loudest sounds. It should not go into the red. The setting can be adjusted using the gain control (14).

The farthest point the needle reaches is known as its *peak*. If the needle goes into the red, the recording level is set too high, and the recording will distort. If it registers too low, the recording signal will be weak and the tape will sound hissy. (This is known as *signal-to-noise ratio*.)

5 Set the tape counter to zero.

6 Flick off the pause key (22) and check the tape is turning.

7 To be certain the tape is picking up the signal, switch the monitor button to T (tape) and check that the meter (16) is showing a good level. You are now recording!

Automatic level control versus manual

Recordings that are made at too high a level (volume) can distort. Automatic systems keep signals below that level, but when they fall too low they cut in and boost them upwards.

On the Uher, you can set the ALC to react either fast or slow. Uher recommend fast (1) for speech and slow (2) for music. These settings may not be ideal in all circumstances, so experiment with non-vital recordings.

If you switch the ALC off (0) and use the machine on manual you will have to monitor the levels to make sure the needle does not rise into the red, which would create distortion, or fall too low, which would give a poor signal-to-noise ratio.

Adjusting the recording levels manually gives you more control and creative freedom. You can use your professional judgement to choose settings to perfectly match different circumstances, instead of passing control to the machine, whose systems were designed to cope with ideal conditions. To look at it another way, how many racing cars do you know of which use an automatic gearbox?

Another drawback to some ALC systems is the problem of surge, or *pumping*, which can happen when there is a pause in speech and the ALC hunts for sound to boost the levels. If there is a lot of background noise, such as traffic, or clattering in a noisy canteen, the ALC will surge this forward whenever the person speaking into the microphone pauses for more than a moment.

Sometimes it is also possible to hear an ALC system stepping in to hold back the volume of a recording, because the level will dip momentarily.

None of these problems can occur with a manual recording that is correctly monitored, but having to monitor levels means your attention is divided between the recorder and your interviewee. Using ALC means you can save your concentration for the interview.

Cassette: The Marantz
(Figure 49)

Another industry standard portable recorder is the American made Marantz, which uses cassettes.

The Marantz Model CP230 is considerably cheaper than a Uher and, in common with other professional cassette recorders, has a number of special features.

Figure 49 Marantz CP230 portable cassette recorder with rechargeable battery roll in the foreground (courtesy Marantz Audio UK)

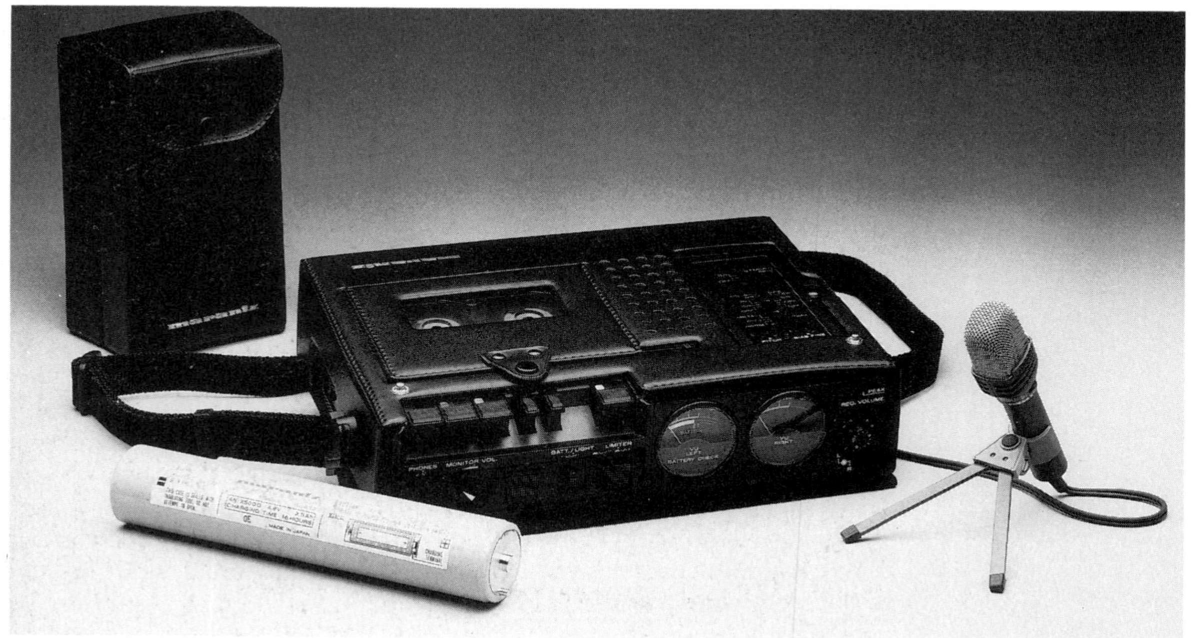

It has a *tape selector* to set the correct bias and equalisation for the cassette tape. *Normal* is used for ferric oxide tapes, *Cro2* for chromium dioxide and similar, and *metal* for metal tapes.

Two noise reduction systems are incorporated, *Dolby* and *DBX*, and a *MPX* filter is built-in to remove signals which might cause interference when recording from FM radio.

A red LED (light emitting diode) shows recording peaks. This reacts more quickly to changes in signal than the VU (volume unit) meter which shows the average recording/playback level and not the peaks. (Engineers frequently refer to VU meters as *virtually useless* meters).

A memory rewind button stops the tape when it has rewound to 999 on the counter.

There is a fine bias adjustment to match bias to individual tapes (best left alone).

A pitch control allows fine adjustment to tape speed. This works only in playback and can be useful for listening quickly to a recording or to help compensate during dubbing for batteries that were running flat. (Use only in an emergency.)

A limiter acts like an automatic level control to prevent loud recordings from distorting, but unlike ALC, it does not boost low recording levels. Levels should be set with the limiter *off*.

The Marantz is a stereo machine, but mono recordings can be made by switching the microphone mode to mono.

Unlike the Uher the Marantz has an automatic shut-off feature, which turns the machine off when the end of the tape is reached (Figure 50).

Figure 50 Nagra SNN miniature tape recorder – reel-to-reel quality at cassette recorder size (courtesy Kudelski)

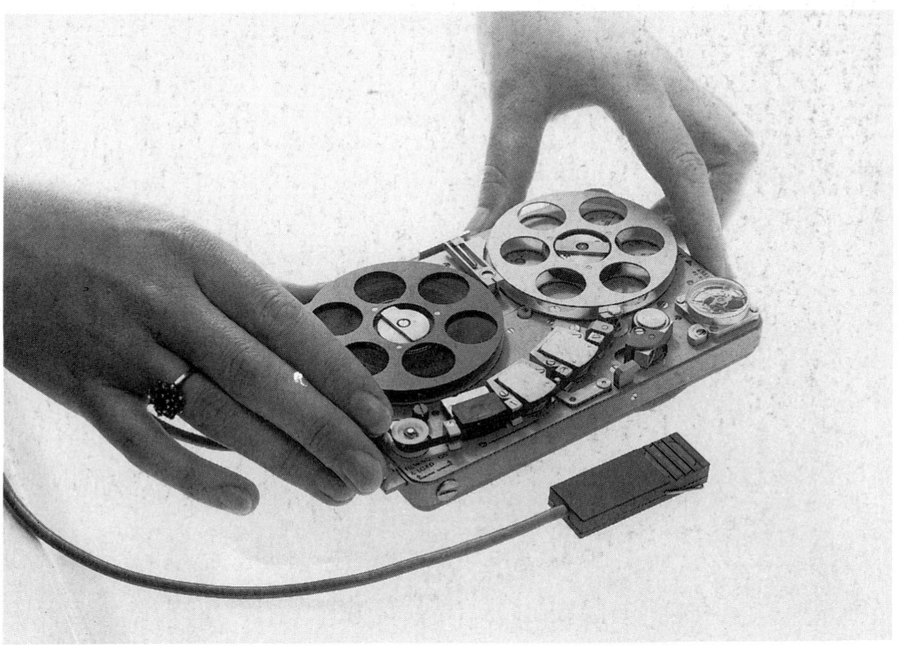

Figure 51 Mike handling. Take up the slack on the cable and grip the mike lightly
(Andrew Boyd)

If you want to preserve a cassette recording from being accidentally recorded over and erased, break off the two safety tabs on the back edge of the cassette with the end of a screwdriver or ball point pen. If you cover these holes with sticky tape the cassette can be recorded over again.

BEFORE THE INTERVIEW

The way you hold a microphone, even the way you sit or stand to conduct an interview, can have a crucial effect on the quality of your final recording.

Mike handling
(Figure 51)

Seemingly inexplicable clicks and bumps on a recording can often be traced to handling noise from the microphone.

Hand-held mikes should be gripped firmly but not tightly and fingers should be kept still, as any movement can often be picked up as handling noise.

If you have a ring on your microphone hand, remove it before the interview, as mikes are particularly susceptible to the small scraping sounds that a ring might make. Also remove any bracelets.

Take up any excess slack in the mike cable by looping it around your hand. This prevents loose cable bumping against the floor or furniture which can cause clicks.

It is important *not* to stretch the cable so tightly that you tug at the connection into the tape recorder or the point where the cable enters the mike. These two electrical connections form the weakest part of the cable. It is easy to cause an electrical click on the recording or damage the connection by pulling at the lead.

Lining up the victim

Uher recommend holding their own microphone 30 to 51 cm (12 to 20 in) away from the mouth, but some other microphones work better at closer distances. The only sure way to get the best performance is to experiment.

You will need to stand or sit with the mike held at an equal distance between yourself and your interviewee, unless one of you has a louder voice, when you will need to move the mike until the levels are balanced.

Setting up the room

Not all rooms are ideal for interviewing. Bare walls and wooden surfaces can produce a 'bathroom effect'. This can sound worse on tape than it did to you at the time, because the ear compensates for its surroundings. If the room is likely to echo, ask to do the interview somewhere else.

Failing that, if you close the curtains and both stand to do the interview facing into them, that can help dampen down reflected sound.

If there are no curtains, standing and facing into a corner of the room will cut the echo a little, and close mike operation will help some more.

Draping coats over the backs of chairs will provide a screen which will also help to dampen reverberations.

Never record across a table. You will have to stretch too far with the microphone and risk one of you being off-mike; the polished surface will reflect some sound back in the form of echo, and if your recorder is on the table the mike will pick up the sound of its motors or the tape turning. Perhaps just as important is the fact that if you are stretched out in supplication across your subject's executive desk you can hardly be seen to be in control of the interview! Pull your chair round and sit next to her.

Dealing with distractions

If there is a phone in the room, ask if it can be taken off the hook to prevent it ringing, and if there is noisy air conditioning, ask if that can be turned off during the interview.

The mike is more conscious of distracting noises than you will be. While you are concentrating on your interview, the mike will be getting on with its job, which is to pick up any sounds in the room.

If your interviewee has beads which rattle or a nylon coat which rustles, ask her to take them off. The same goes for papers which flap, or a clip-board which gets between the person and the mike. Few interviewees ever complain about being asked to disrobe (within reason!) if they are politely but clearly told why. Make a joke of it if it helps.

The level check

Next, you need to take your levels and arrange yourselves in a sensible recording position. One problem with the hand-held mike is that the user needs to invade the other person's body space to get a decent signal. A comfortable distance for normal conversation is with faces several feet apart. To record an interview without having to keep moving your mike arm, you will have to shorten that gap to a foot or less.

In body language terms, this invasion of space only takes place naturally when people are fighting or being intimate, so expect some natural apprehension on the part of the interviewee and to feel uncomfortable yourself at first. At this point, plenty of confidence, a little charm, a ready smile, well brushed teeth and a good deodorant are the reporter's most valuable assets.

Are you sitting comfortably?

Before you make your check make sure you are both sitting as you will be during the interview and that your interviewee is comfortable. Then get both your voices on tape. Ask your interviewee something about herself which is irrelevant to the interview to help her relax, like where is she going on her holiday, what does she think of the weather, or does she have any hobbies? Avoid stock questions like: '*What did you have for breakfast?*' An experienced interviewee will be bored stiff with that one.

Once you have taken the sound check and adjusted the levels make sure you listen to it back. A twitching meter is not always proof a recording is being made.

Beware of stuffing the microphone under the interviewee's nose. If it is that close she is likely to go cross-eyed, and an out of focus microphone windshield looks remarkably like a balled fist and has about the same effect on composure. Tuck the mike under her chin and out of direct line of vision.

Logging the tape

Before you begin your questions, log the tape. This is a simple precaution in case the tape gets lost, mislaid or confused with another. Give the name of the interviewee and the time and date: '*Interview with John Smith, April Fool's Day, Whenever.*'

Once the interview is over, wind the reel off and put a sticky label on it with your name and the subject.

Maintain eye contact

While the recording is under way, do not keep glancing at the recorder or your notebook; this can be disconcerting for your subject and can break the rapport you have established.

A video of journalism students recording an interview revealed how little real communication there was once the all-important eye contact had been broken. One student divided his time between looking at the recorder, fiddling with the levels and trying to read his spidery handwritten questions. As soon as he looked away, his interviewee's eyes also wandered and before long the interview had drifted off the track as concentration was broken.

Adjusting levels

Once you have set your levels you should not need to adjust them on your recorder. Compensate for small changes in volume by moving your mike. This takes practice.

If your interviewee leans backwards or forwards, feel free to break off the interview and politely explain that she must sit as she was when the level check was made, or volunteer to retake the level with her sitting in her new position.

Never nod instructions or gesticulate at interviewees, it only confuses and worries them. Stop and explain the problem (unless you are live!).

After the interview, always remember to check the recording has come out before leaving your interviewee. A quick retake there and then can save a lot of embarrassing explanations later. (For the journalistic considerations of the interview, see interviewing, page 75.)

FIELDWORK

1 Practise using your portable recorder in different circumstances on manual and on automatic level control. Listen back and describe the differences.

2 If you have a Uher with two automatic settings, try using them both under different conditions and compare results.

3 Now use the portable first in a room with soft furnishings, such as living room, and then in one without and compare the results. Have you picked up more echo from the unfurnished room?

If there are curtains in that room, draw them and make your recording speaking into them. Does it make a difference?

4 Find a willing partner and practise your microphone technique. Move gradually towards your partner into your normal interviewing position and ask him/her to tell you exactly when you begin to get too close for normal comfort. Did you also start to feel uncomfortable at that point? Practise your technique and ask your partner to suggest ways you could make this invasion of privacy less intimidating.

5 Decide on a subject to interview your partner about and ask him/her to play the part of the inexperienced and awkward interviewee, by shuffling, moving around and coughing, etc. For your part, attempt to keep control in as pleasant a way as possible. Then, without comment, swap round and repeat the exercise. Then discuss what you learnt and advise one another on how you could have best dealt with that situation. Did you keep up the eye contact?

21 Editing

Few raw interviews appear on air without some form of editing – live interviews are the obvious exception. But where an interview has been pre-recorded, and time permits, the reporter will usually want to tighten it up, and trim it to the required length.

Just as important is editing out irrelevant questions and statements to throw into focus those that are newsworthy. You may also want to alter the sequence of questions and answers to point up a strong angle that emerged during the interview.

Finally, recordings are usually fine-edited to give them polish by removing hesitation, repetition and intrusive background noise, such as a passing lorry, or a phone ringing.

Figure 52 Editing a report in a mixing studio. Interviews, sound effects, links and music can be combined to produce a professional package (Andrew Boyd)

Editing has four main functions:

- To reduce length,
- Remove unwanted material;
- Alter the sequence of recorded material;
- Permit creative treatment.

If your brief is to get a three minute interview with a Maori leader about his claim to land rights and you return with seven minutes on tape, then, unless the material is stunningly good, four minutes will have to go.

The best part of the interview may be at the beginning, so the last four minutes can be chopped.

Or the best parts could be the answers to the first, third, fifth and seventh questions, so the others will be edited out.

On second thoughts, those answers might sound better in a different order, so the unwanted sections should be cut out and the rest edited into a different sequence.

Lastly, you may want to add a creative touch by beginning the item with a piece of Maori tribal music. This will have to be blended in afterwards to fade under the opening words of the tribesman. This is known as a *cross fade*.

Similar principles apply to editing for television, although the process is complicated greatly by the addition of pictures. Unlike radio, TV editing is not usually carried out by the reporter or producer but by a professional VT (videotape) editor. (See also a story is born, page 256.)

STUDIO TAPE DECKS

High technology newsrooms may be equipped with computer-controlled editing suites, such as those in television, but most still make do with cheaper, tried and tested, reel-to-reel decks that allow tapes to be edited by hand. These range from big, robust, trolley mounted machines such as *Studers*, *Otaris* and *Ferrographs*, to the smaller *Revox*. Allowing for various degrees of sophistication, the method of operation is usually similar (Figure 53).

Studio tape decks work in broadly the same way as the smaller *Uher*, (described on page 216) but accept longer tapes on 7 or 10.5 in (17.8 or 26.7 cm) spools.

It is important not to mix different sizes of spool on the same machine, as this would create unequal tension on the motors. If a 5 in spool on the left was threaded to a 10.5 in reel on the right, the tension could be great enough to slow the playback to a halt. Two 5 in spools should be used instead.

These are usually made of clear plastic and known as *cine* spools. 10.5 in reels are usually aluminium and known as *NAB* reels. These have a circular hole at the centre, and are held on the spindle of the tape machine by a metal or plastic *hub*, which grips the reel in the same way as the mandrels on a Uher. (See lacing up the tape, page 216.)

Studio editing machines often incorporate a timer, which is invaluable for editing. These also work on fast forward or rewind for rapid timing.

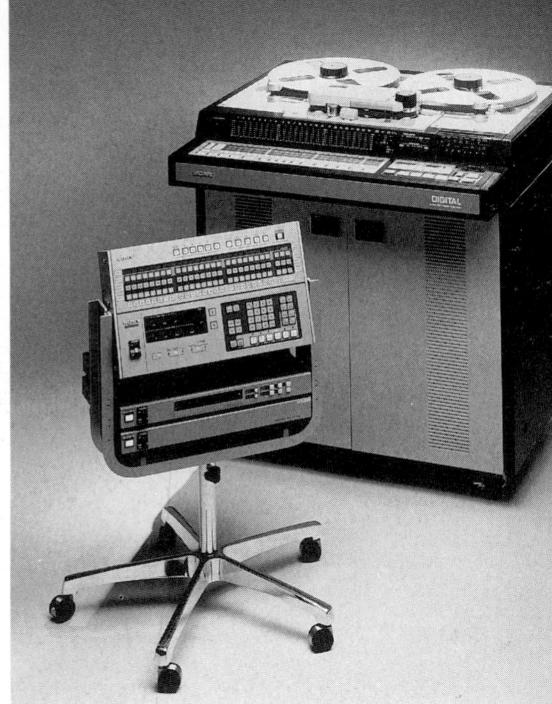

Figure 53 (*left*) The Studer tape deck is the standard workhorse in many British radio stations. It features a counter for timing tapes and a built-in editing block for manual cutting and splicing. This machine is stereo (courtesy FWO Bauch Ltd, Studer Agents) (*right*) Digital technology is fast taking over in the studio, offering superior reproduction, computerized tape-handling and a sound quality that will not deteriorate over generations of recording (courtesy Sony Broadcast Ltd)

MARKING AND CUTTING

Tapes can be edited on location, on a specially equipped portable recorder, but this is a fiddly exercise and at best imprecise, so most editing is carried out back at the radio station either by dubbing electronically on equipment similar to that used in television, or more commonly, on large reel-to-reel machines where the *tape path* is exposed for easy editing.

Most studio tape machines have an *edit* mode, which permits the user to stop the tape while it is still in play and turn the reels by hand. The tape is then moved backwards and forwards against the playback head while listening with headphones to find exactly the right place to make the edit.

Editing involves chopping out the unwanted passages from an interview, and joining together the rest. The cuts are made during pauses either side of the unwanted section.

The tape is then marked on the playback head with a *chinagraph pencil* and put on an editing block, where it is cut with a razor blade. The two ends of the tape are then joined together with *splicing tape* (Figure 54).

Where possible, master recordings should be preserved intact for reference and dubbed on another reel for editing.

Always think twice before discarding unwanted portions of tape. Your producer may ask for a longer version, which would mean reclaiming some of the edited sections. If in doubt, save all the out-takes. Number them and hang them up out of the way with splicing tape with a brief note

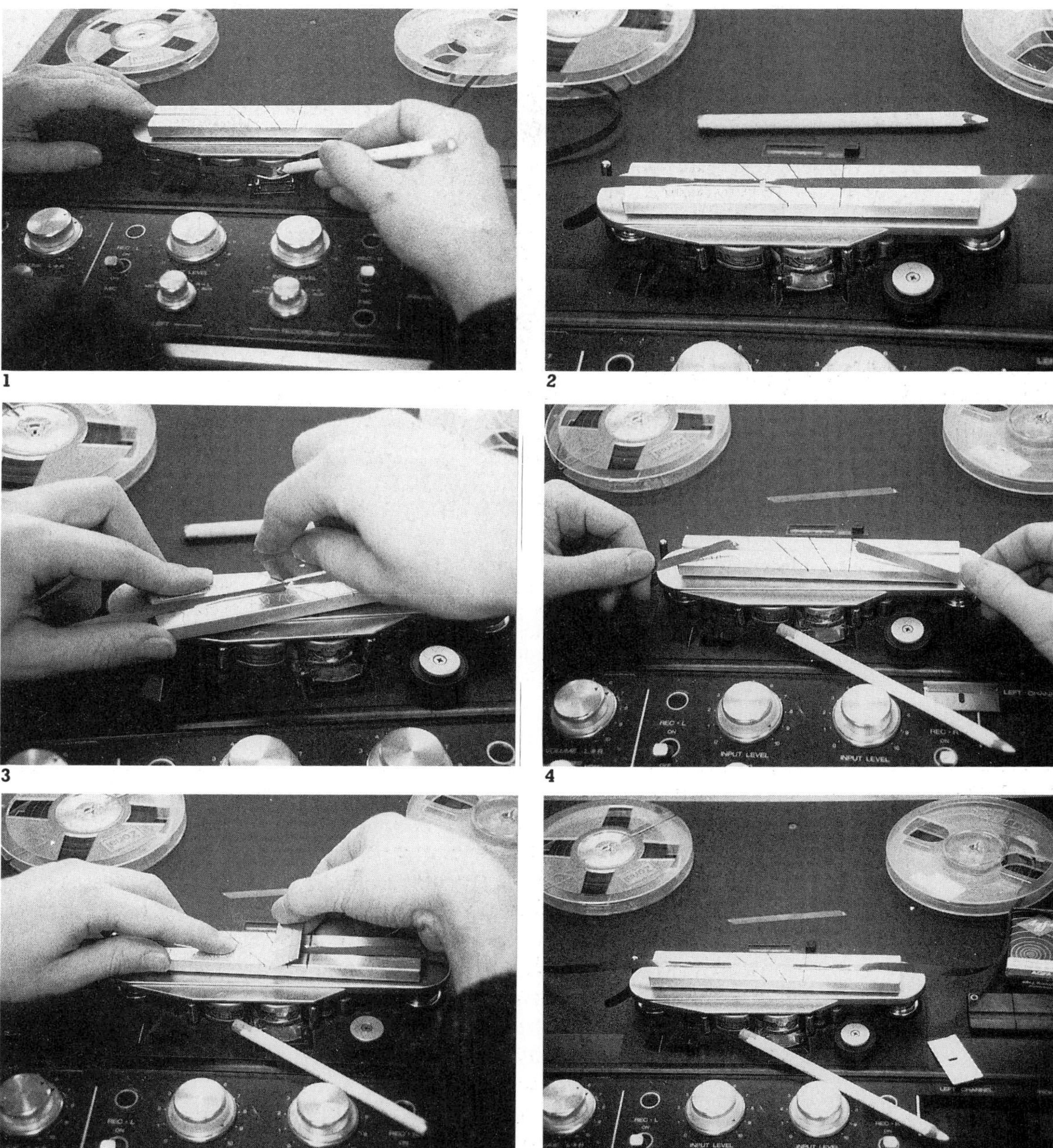

Figure 54

1 The portion to be edited out is selected and marked with a chinagraph (grease) pencil
2 The mark is placed over the cutting slot on the editing block. The vertical cut is used for tight (close) edits, but the angled slots permit a stronger edit
3 The unwanted section is cut out with an open razor blade or a splicing machine
4 The two ends are then butted together on the block to be joined. The unwanted portion – in this case a slight hesitation during an interview – can be seen above the editing block in the picture
5 Take a short length of splicing tape and make the edit
6 The final edit. The reel of splicing rtape is on the right (Andrew Boyd)

of what each numbered section contains, or simply save them on a separate reel. One length of tape looks remarkably like another and there are more productive ways to spend time than scavenging for a vital snippet in the mound of discarded tape across the newsroom floor.

THE EDITING BLOCK

Most editing blocks have three cutting positions. The widest angle produces the strongest edits. Joining the tape at an angle means the edit is unlikely to split open as the tape passes through the machine.

Sometimes the pause where the edit will have to be made is very fine, and there is little space between words to make the cut. Here, one of the other slots on the editing block should be used to make the cut at a sharper angle.

The higher the speed of a recording, the easier it is to edit, as the pauses take up more space.

LEADER TAPE

Different coloured plastic tape is used to mark the beginning and end of a recording. This is called *leader tape*. About 16 in (40 cm) is joined to the start of a tape and used to lace it up on the studio machine for playback.

Coloured leader tapes give different information to the tape operator. Leader codes vary. In independent local radio in Great Britain, the leader code usually follows the traffic light pattern; green for go, red for stop. Green is placed at the start and red at the end. In the BBC, tapes usually begin with yellow leader and go out with red. Stereo tapes begin with red and white striped leader.

Where several tapes are joined on a large reel this is known as *banding*, and three seconds (22 in) of yellow or white leader is used to separate each *band*. Leader tape cannot be recorded over, so any leader *must* be removed before using the tape again otherwise there will be gaps in the recording. Many good interviews have been ruined by small strips of leader which went undetected because the reel was not examined. It is not always possible to see strips of leader by looking at the reel. If in doubt, check by spooling it through on the editing machine at high speed.

The edited tape is cued-up on the playback machine by hand, by positioning the join between the tape and the leader to the left of the playback head. The start of the recording should be about $1\frac{1}{2}$ in (3.8 cm) to the left of the playback head, rather than actually on it. This compensates for any tape snatch when the machine is put into play.

DUB EDITING

Recordings made on cassette have to be dubbed on to reel before they can be edited. The cassette recorder should be rewound to the moment before the section begins and put on pause and play. To make the dub, the reel-to-reel machine is put into record and play and, at the same moment, the cassette is flipped off pause. The reel should be stopped the moment the chosen part of the recording has been dubbed across.

With precision equipment it is possible to dub edit a piece entirely without having to carry out fine editing with a razor blade, although great care and split-second timing are required to achieve a noiseless and natural sounding edit. Remote starts where one machine controls the other and computerized editing techniques make this increasingly possible.

'YOU CAN'T SEE THE JOIN . . .'

The principle of editing is simple, but the practice takes longer to master. The art is to leave the finished tape sounding completely natural, as though nobody had come within a mile of it with a razor blade. A good edit should be like a good wig. The join should be invisible.

The first rule of editing is that the finished product must make sense. Hacking sentences in half and joining non-sequiturs is not editing a tape, it is butchering it.

Secondly, the editing must be in sympathy with the subject's speech patterns. A good edit will never leave the voice dangling on a rising note, as the sentence will sound unfinished and unnatural; instead the edit should be made during a pause and following a natural downturn in the voice. Commas, full stops, and other punctuation points form natural pauses and are usually the best places to make the cut.

Where exactly the edit is made within that pause is also important. A pause of a fifth of a second will be 1.5 in (3.8 cm) long on a tape running at 7.5 ips (19 cm). The pause will end with an intake of breath before the next sentence. The edit should be made *after* that breath, but in the split-second before the speaker starts to utter the next word.

That breath will then sound as though it belongs to the word after the edit. In other words, you cannot hear the join.

Obviously the final word on the tape should not be followed by a pause and a breath, as this would sound as though the speaker had been cut off in full flow!

The following shows how a reporter would edit a section to produce a thirty-second clip. The words in capitals are the ones the reporter will keep, while the rest are edited out. Read the whole passage though, then just read the words in capitals.

Editing a thirty second bulletin clip

Reporter: *'OK. So what we need now is for you to explain that again on tape, but we'll have to tighten it up a little, otherwise it'll be too long to get into the bulletin. So . . . we're recording – what will you be telling the council?'*

Councillor: *'Well, when we get together tonight, what I'll be wanting to know is / WHY WEREN'T RESIDENTS TOLD THEIR HOMES WERE LIKELY TO FLOOD AT HIGH TIDE? / I mean, nobody had any idea this would happen, / WHY DID THE PLANNERS LET THIS DEVELOPMENT GO AHEAD IN THE FIRST PLACE, FOR GOODNESS SAKE? / I mean, this is what we pay them for isn't it? / WHY WEREN'T THE NECESSARY CHECKS MAKE – AND / who is going to pay for it? – That's the important one, / JUST WHO IS GOING TO PAY FOR THE DAMAGE? ONE THING'S FOR SURE, IT SHOULDN'T BE THE RESIDENTS, AND THEY'RE THE ONES WHO ARE HAVING TO PAY RIGHT NOW. / The . . .'*

Reporter: *'Have you . . . ? Sorry . . .'*

Councillor: *'No, go on.'*

Reporter: *'What I wanted to ask was / HAVE YOU ANY IDEA HOW MUCH THE FLOOD DAMAGE WILL COST TO PUT RIGHT?*

Councillor: *'THOUSANDS. HUNDREDS AND THOUSANDS OF POUNDS. CARPETS, WALLPAPER, FURNITURE, WHOLE HOMES ARE RUINED, AND ALL BECAUSE SOME FEATHERBRAIN DIDN'T STOP TO THINK ABOUT THE HIGH TIDES. IT'S NEGLIGENCE, AND SOMEBODY SHOULD BE SACKED.' /*

UNETHICAL EDITING

Care must be taken with editing not to distort the meaning of what has been said. Selective, careless or unscrupulous editing can make someone appear to be saying something completely different, and the easiest way to fall into that trap is to take a qualified statement and to harden it up into something stronger than the speaker said or meant.

Reporter: *'Are you in favour of the death penalty?*

Interviewee: *'That's very difficult to say. / YES... / I suppose so, under certain circumstances, but it's an awful thing to take a life, whatever that person has done. When you're dealing with / MURDERERS AND RAPISTS WHO WILL PROBABLY KILL AND RAPE ALL OVER AGAIN AS SOON AS THEY'RE RELEASED... / I don't know, maybe / THEY SHOULD BE EXECUTED. / But there are always those who are genuinely sorry for what they've done and are serving their time – while there's life there's hope. They might change. But it's the others, / THE MANIACS AND FANATICS WHO CAN'T STOP KILLING – THEY'RE A MENANCE TO US ALL, / but, on the other hand, that's what prisons are for, isn't it?'*

If you read only the words in capitals the statement becomes a strong and unqualified call for the death penalty. But taking the answer as a whole, that is not what the interviewee was saying.

Selective editing like the above is never ethical, and could never be justified, but reporters are often faced with having to shed some of the context and qualifications to get the audio down to length, and the decisions about what to cut are usually made against the clock. Where this happens, the story should be explained more fully in the cue or accompanying narrative. Your reporting skills will often mean your explanation will be more concise and economical than that of your interviewee, but the intention should always be to give a fair, accurate and complete picture of what has been said.

MIXING

For more sophisticated productions, one sound source can be mixed with another to achieve a blend. Returning to our interview with the Maori, the tribal song may be blended to fade into the background as he begins to speak and dipped down until it eventually disappears.

To do this, you would need three tape recorders and a mixer. One tape deck would have the Maori interview, another the music (which could be on disc or cart instead) and the third deck would record the combination of the two, which would be blended through the mixer.

Mixers can range from small boxes with a few controls to contraptions with a mind-boggling array of switches, sliders and knobs that look as intimidating to the uninitiated as the flight deck of a jumbo jet. Do not be put off – the idea is basically simple.

A mixer takes two (or more) sounds and allows you to blend them together as you wish. To do this it needs *inputs* to receive the signals, and *gain* controls to adjust their volumes. Meters display the volume levels, and a main gain sets the final level of the combined signal. When you have balanced the result to your satisfaction the signal is sent through the outputs to another tape deck or on to air.

And that is basically it, although sophisticated mixers also have a variety of extra controls for fine adjustments. Larger versions are used as the main *control desks* in radio stations to put programmes on air. Other versions mix and edit television programmes or produce music master tapes. (See also the studio, page 235.)

The volume on a mixer is set by a circular dial (*pot*) or, more commonly, a *slider* (fader) which is easier to use. The fader is usually pushed up to turn the volume up, and pulled down to turn it down. Nothing could be more logical; except the BBC decided to install the faders the other way up on its Mark 3 and Mark 4 control desks, so instead of up for up, it is down for up and up for down.

The most plausible explanation offered for this oddity is that the presenter or producer could push a conventional fader up by catching it with his/her shirt cuff.

SETTING LEVELS

The operator of the mixer, control desk or panel, rides the levels to maintain a consistent output. The sound should not be allowed to rise so high that it distorts, nor dip too low, or to surge and fall. Some desks have automatic level controls or compressors built into them to keep the sound output at an optimum, but running the desk on autopilot stifles any crea-

Figure 55 Setting the levels on the PPMs

A $5\frac{1}{2}$ is the usual peak for speech

B This stereo meter has two coloured needles to show the different peaks for the left and right channels. Music has a wider dynamic range than speech and sounds louder to the ear, so to avoid blasting the audience levels are usually turned down to peak at $4\frac{1}{2}$

C Speech over the telephone loses much of its dynamic range. It sounds quieter than normal speech and can be difficult to hear. Levels should be boosted to $6\frac{1}{2}$ to compensate

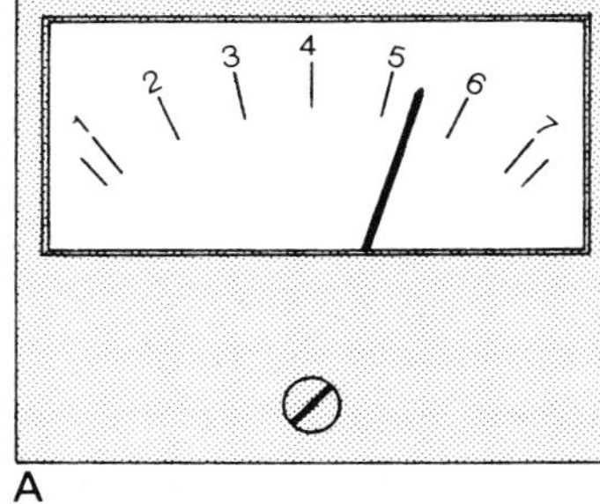

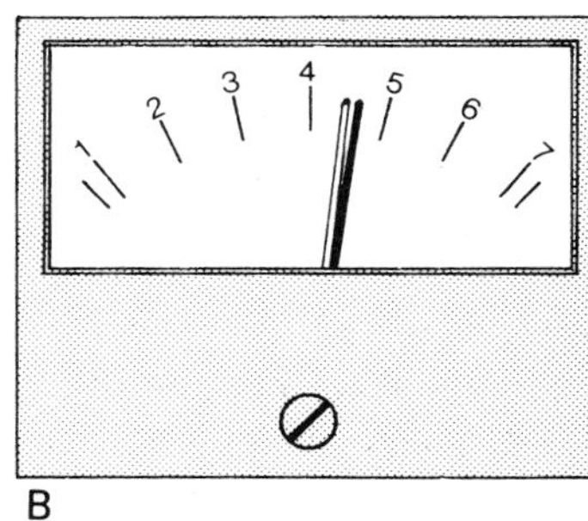

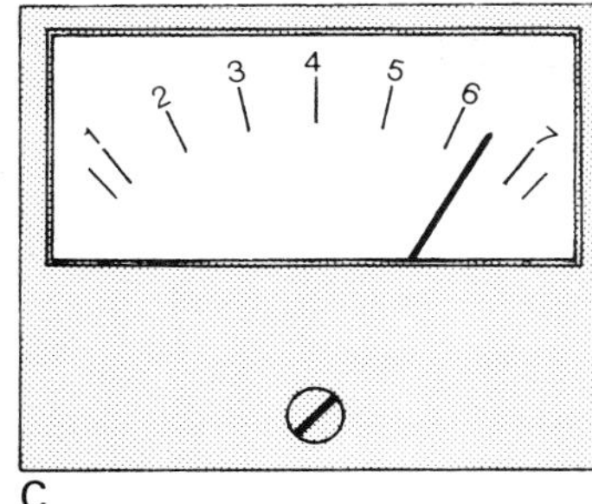

tivity. It can be a bit like holding every conversation at shouting pitch (see also page 217).

Levels are usually set on a *PPM meter* (peak programme meter), which registers the peaks of output but has a dampened action to stop it fluctuating wildly like a VU meter. This makes it easier to use (Figure 55).

TYPES OF FADE

Different fades can achieve a variety of effects.

Pre-fade

This is not really a fade as such, but a means of monitoring the tape or disc by listening to it play without putting it on air.

Most mixing desks have pre-fade buttons which send the sound from the source being monitored to one ear of the headphones, while the other ear can continue listening to what is going on air.

This enables presenters to cue discs or tapes while others are still being played. Also, when a local station is opting into the network news, the producer will pre-fade the network to make sure it is being received before crossing over on cue.

Cross fade

This fades up one source as another is faded out, and is commonly used to mix music or sound effects with speech.

Fading down and fading up

This is where one source is faded out and another faded in after a very short pause. This is useful where there are two sounds that would jar together if crossfaded, such as two pieces of music in different keys.

Pot-cut

This means closing the fader rapidly to cut short an item. Care must be taken to 'pull the item out' very quickly and at a natural pause in the speech, otherwise the words will be clipped or trail off.

This is made easier by reporters marking *pot-points* on the cue sheet telling the technical operator where the item can be cut early, and what the last words are before that point.

Fading in and out

When a sound effect or piece of music is to appear in a recorded item of speech it must be faded in and faded out gradually, or the join will show. Ideally, the listener should be aware of neither its coming in nor its going out (Figure 56).

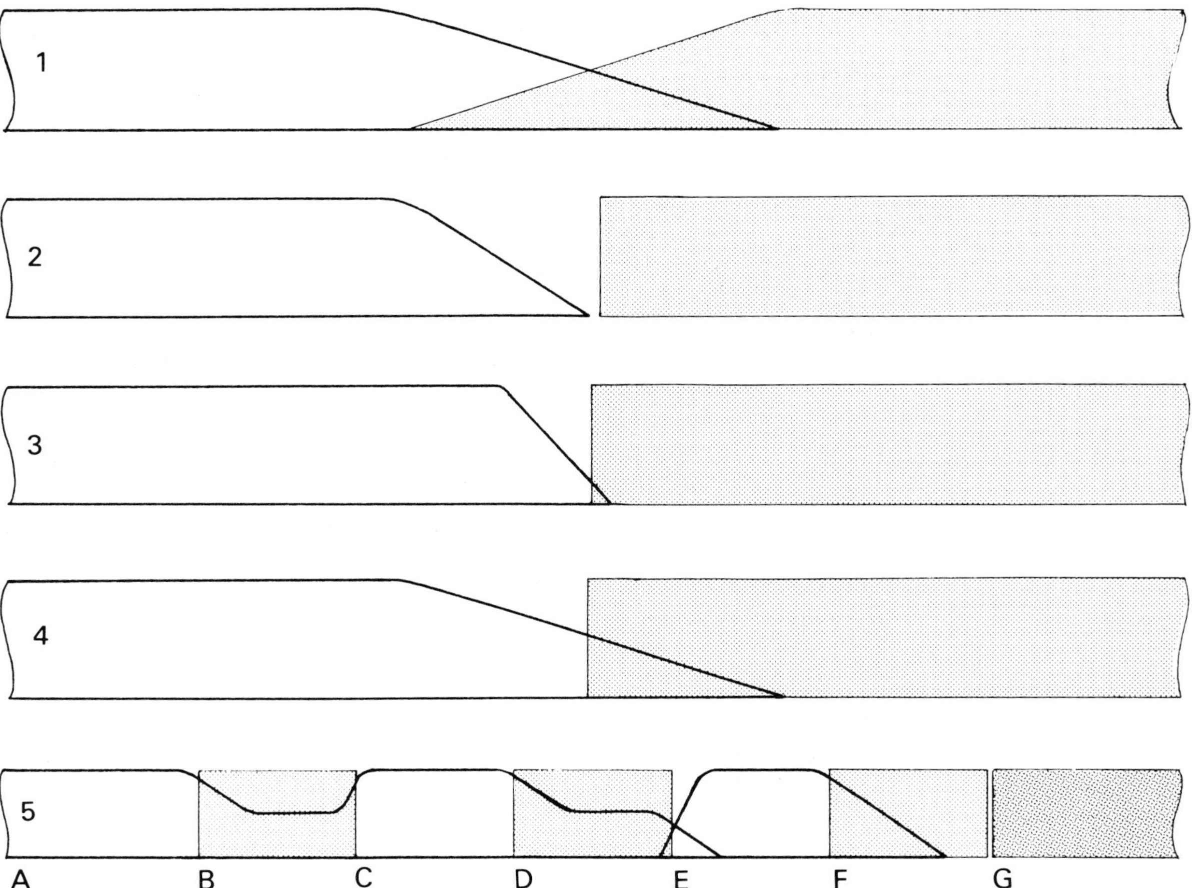

Figure 56

1 Crossfade. Where one item is faded out and another is faded in at the same time. (For example music giving way to sound effects)

2 Fade. The first item fades out completely before the other begins

3 The first item fades out quickly and the next begins sharply while the first is still dying away

4 The first item is faded out gradually, continuing to fade while the other begins. (For example music under speech)

5 SIGNATURE (DIP) *'It's 4 o'clock and this is Money Talks with Andrew Barlow. Good afternoon.'*

SIG. (DIP) *'Today, new claims of insider dealing on the stock market and the companies that are cashing in on the Aids scare.*

STAB (FADE) *But first, the budget, and the question today that everyone is asking – will he, or won't he cut the tax? Etc.'*

'. . . could push share prices to an all time high, as Peter Loyd has been finding out from the City.'

BUDGET/LOYD *'The market has been in a bullish mood today in anticipation of those tax cuts. Shares have risen, and look set to . . . etc.'*

The illustration represents the opening sequence to *Money Talks*. The signature tune (a) dips beneath Barlow's introduction (b) but does not disappear, bubbling underneath to re-emerge during a pause (c) and dipping again beneath the menu (d). It then crossfades into a stab (e) which brings the signature sequence to an end. Barlow introduces the first item (f) which then begins (g).

FIELDWORK

1 Record a song and try editing out one verse of it so you cannot hear the join. Try first with the angled cut on the editing block, and then with the vertical cut. Which was easier? Why?

Now record that song at 15 ips and do the same. It should be much easier to edit. What makes the difference?

2 Take an interview or programme you have recorded on cassette and choose a suitable clip for a bulletin. Now try dubbing that on to a reel-to-reel machine and making a clean edit without cutting the tape. Use the pause to control when to stop and start. Practise until you get it right.

Then add a second clip to the end of the first by dubbing. Can you hear the join? Do you find it difficult to produce clean edits this way? Would you prefer to edit like this or with a razor blade? Why?

3 If you have access to a computer-controlled editing suite, take two copies of an interview and edit one *by hand* before making the same edits to the other electronically. Compare the two techniques. Allowing for the fact that you were more familiar with the tape the second time, which process was quicker, which was easier, which gave you more control, and which did you prefer?

4 Take an interview you have made that could be improved by adding suitable music at the start. Practise using a mixing desk to crossfade that music beneath the interview. How long should the music run before being faded out? How loud should it be so it does not drown the interview or disappear too soon? What happens if you crossfade singing under speech?

5 Go back to the heading 'unethical editing.' How would you produce a fifteen second clip from the interview on the death penalty to give an accurate reflection of the interviewee's views? Write out your new version of the clip.

22 The studio today and radio tomorrow

Radio stations often have a complex suite of studios, each equipped to perform a different function.

ON-AIR STUDIO

Programmes are presented from the main on-air studio. Stations will usually have two identical on-air studios in case one develops a fault.

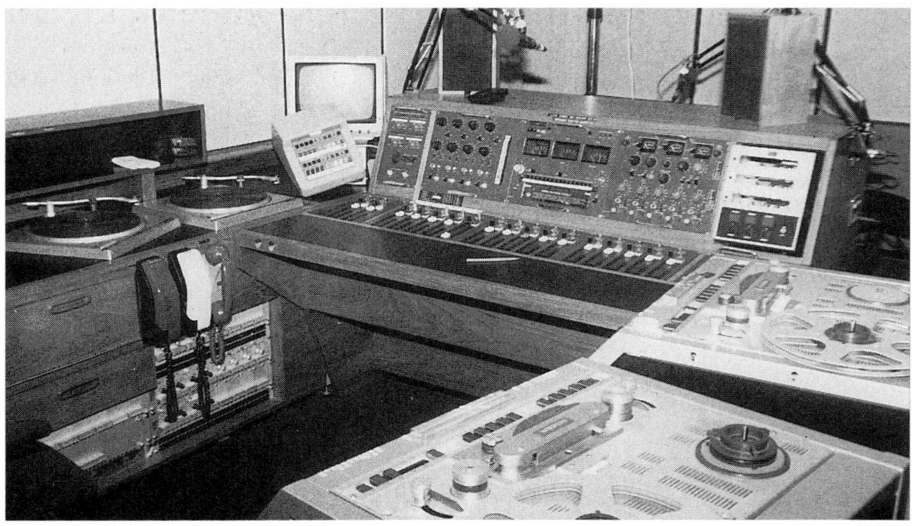

Figure 57 (*above*) BBC Mark 3 control desk with grams and tape decks at BBC Radio Bedfordshire. (*right*) The on-air studio at Chiltern Radio, a British station in the independent radio network. The control desk is simpler and less cluttered than that used by the BBC. Commercials are kept on scores of cartridges – six are lined up in the machine (left) ready to go (Andrew Boyd)

Standard equipment includes a control desk; two or more record decks; two or more tape decks; several cart playback machines; cassette machine; monitor loudspeakers; telephone; talkback system, which is a form of intercom; presenter mike and possibly other microphones; studio clock with on-air lights, and in commerical stations, cart racks for adverts.

Other features may include a compact disc player and videocassette recorder, and a visual display unit linking the studio with the newsroom for information such as headlines and the weather.

Commercial stations will have a separate studio complex to make adverts. This usually has a comprehensive mixing desk and adjoining talks studio.

TALKS STUDIO

The talks studio is an acoustically treated room for interviews and discussions. Guests sit around a circular or hexagonal table with a hole in the middle for microphones. (See also page 99.) The talks studio usually has a visual contact with the main studio through a large glass window (see figure 58).

THE CONTRIBUTIONS STUDIO

The news may be read from the on-air studio or a contributions studio. For the former the newsreader hands the technical operator (TO) the carts or tapes and possibly copies of the script. The reader can then concentrate on the presentation, while the TO plays in the audio.

Figure 58 The talks studio has a visual link with the main studio through a large glass window. The producer (right) can speak to the presenter via the talkback. The control desk is a BBC Mark 1 (Andrew Boyd)

Figure 59 Newsbooths are designed so reporters can present their own news programmes without technical assistance. Peter Heaton-Jones operates a simple mixing panel (left) while reading the cue to an interview. The moment he finishes the cue, his right hand will fire the cart containing the interview. The big meter in the centre of the stack helps him adjust the levels (Andrew Boyd)

Newsreaders sometimes operate their own studio equipment while they are reading the news. This takes place in a small contributions studio, with a simplified control desk, which is sometimes called a *newsbooth*. Audio inserts will usually be on cart (Figure 59).

Interviews and reports to the main network station will be sent from the contributions studio.

REMOTE STUDIOS

Some radio stations serve areas which are too large for reporters to be able to cover a story and get back in time for the deadline, or for guests to be willing or able to travel to the station to record an interview.

Recording everything by phone is quick and cheap, but at the expense of quality. *Remote studios* are a better solution. These are often small rooms rented in well-placed larger buildings such as city hall. They contain a microphone, mixer and possibly a tape deck. The remote studio is connected to the radio station by a studio quality line which is rented from the telephone company. Guests can go there to be interviewed and reporters can use them to send reports.

RADIO CAR

Radio cars are essential news gathering tools for on-the-spot coverage of stories such as fires, demonstrations, or live events.

The car will contain everything you need to send back a studio quality recording from the scene. This includes microphones and plenty of cable, often a sound mixer, a talkback system to base, and a UHF or VHF transmitter with a telescopic mast to beam the report back. (See also page 195.)

OUTSIDE BROADCAST VEHICLE

A development of the radio car is the outside broadcast (OB) vehicle, which has sophisticated equipment to mix complete programmes on location and send them out live. These are used for roadshows, large scale outside broadcasts, or live concerts.

CELLULAR TELEPHONE

> *'We can record an interview from down a sewer pipe, in the middle of a field or up a mountain, and send it back from anywhere in the world. It's like having a mobile studio available to you.'*
> — PENNINE RADIO NEWS EDITOR, GERRY RADCLIFFE

These portable battery-operated phones have opened the way for greater flexibility in news coverage. Reporters no longer need to be tied to the radio car to send back a live report.

It also means news editors can keep in touch with journalists and redirect them to cover breaking stories without having to wait for them to call in first.

For sports coverage the reporter is no longer rooted to the press box with its phone but can commentate from anywhere around the pitch or ground.

During one football match in Bradford, thick fog descended until spectators could see only half the pitch at a time. But the match could be followed by listening to Pennine Radio which had a commentator at each end of the pitch sending back reports on cellular phones. When one lost sight of the ball, the other simply picked up the commentary where the first left off.

By linking cellular phones to tape recorders, recorded interviews can be sent back from remote areas. The only drawback is that reports are in phone quality.

TELEPHONE REPORTS

For reporters out in the field without a radio link, the callbox or borrowed telephone becomes a tool of the trade.

Portable computers are being used increasingly to file copy back to base. Instead of dictating their story down the phone, reporters connect their computer to the phone via a modem which speeds the report back to base almost instantly.

More commonly, telephones are used for sending back location reports which are then recorded at the radio station. But you can also send recorded actuality over the phone, by connecting your tape recorder to the receiver with a pair of crocodile clips or a special lead that plugs into the phone socket (Figure 60).

A lead is plugged into the line-out socket of the tape recorder and crocodile clips are connected to metal tabs inside the telephone mouthpiece – only try it on phones that are meant to come apart! For phones which plug into wall sockets, the report can be sent by using a telephone coupler unit and connecting the tape recorder to the spare socket with a special lead.

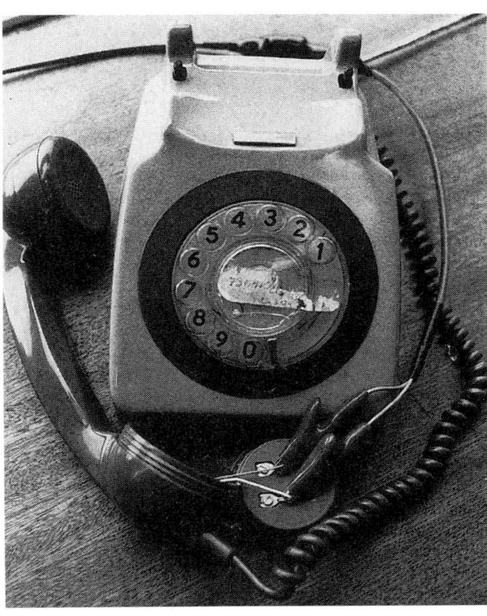

Figure 60 Croc-clipping. Tape recordings can be sent back to base along a phone line by connecting a lead from the tape recorder to the telephone mouthpiece (Andrew Boyd)

With a little practice it is possible to incorporate a recorded interview into a live report made on the phone. Interview extracts and linking narrative can be edited by the reporter back at base and played on air well before the reporter has had time to return.

Radio journalist Chris Rider was covering a royal visit. The Queen was opening a country park:

'The only available phone was in a small corridor. I was in the process of croc-clipping my report when a voice behind me asked, "What are you doing?" I turned round and it was the Queen. She was on her own. I stopped the tape recorder and said, "I'm sending this tape to a radio station in Portsmouth." Just then I heard a protesting and squawking at the other end of the phone; a voice said, "Why have you stopped sending?" I said, 'Well, I'm talking to the Queen actually." This very disbelieving voice said, "Yeah, yeah, sure you are. Wind it up and do it again." I was trying to smile at the Queen and at the same time tell the newsdesk to shut up! In the end I put my hand over the squawking and left them to it. I was explaining to the Queen how you croc-clipped when the doors burst open and two very worried security men ushered her swiftly away, giving me some very furtive glances. I think they must have thought I had some dubious device attached to the telephone. At least the Queen had a minute's lesson in how to croc-clip – though it's not a skill I think she would use too often.'

For foreign correspondents, whose lifeline is the telephone, it is essential to use telephone lines that are as free from crackles and interference as possible. Telephones use a narrow waveband, so the voice sounds thin and reedy. To help compensate, a variety of devices can be coupled to the phone to boost the signal and make the voice sound fuller.

Reporters who are calling back to base may want to avoid constantly feeding a callbox with coins by reversing the charges (making a collect call). Telephone systems differ, but often a reverse charge call will have a set of pips in the background and may be interrupted by the operator. You should politely ask the operator to remove the pips and not to interrupt the call. Phonecards, which work like credit cards and allow cashless calls to be made at a callbox, are another way of avoiding the coin-in-the-slot syndrome.

Telephones are also commonly used to record interviews with guests who are unable to come in to the studio, or on occasions when the station cannot spare the reporter to go out. These are recorded through a *telephone balance unit*. This allows you to use a microphone to record your voice in studio quality, and to adjust the levels to prevent your sounding louder than your interviewee.

Phone conversations can also be recorded by attaching an *induction microphone* to the phone and plugging it into a tape recorder. This provides a useful record of the conversation, but the quality can be indifferent and the levels are unbalanced.

Ethically, a person should always be told when their conversation is being recorded. In the USA, it has been a legal requirement to send a regular bleep along the line to show the interviewee that he/she is going on tape. The bleep, which was produced by a machine, could be turned off once the interviewee was told he/she was being recorded or was appearing live on air.

Phone levels

Recording levels for telephone reports need to be boosted slightly to compensate for the poor quality telephone line.

The phone is unable to convey the full tonal range of the human voice so the ear will perceive the thin-sounding recording as being quieter than normal and listeners will have to strain to hear unless the levels are adjusted. (See also page 231.)

Another way to improve the quality, is to put the signal through an equalizer on the mixer. Some of the hiss and hash can be filtered out, and the range of the signal can be boosted to make it sound fuller and clearer.

OBSCENITY BUTTON

Telephones are used for *phone-in* discussions where listeners call in with their questions and comments to a panel of experts in the studio. Here there is an even greater hazard than the faint phone line – the probability that sooner or later a listener will swear, blaspheme, or utter a libel on the airwaves. The presenter's last line of defence is the obscenity, or profanity, button.

As soon as a caller says anything which is seriously offensive, the presenter presses the obscenity button, and the offending comment never reaches the airwaves – even on a live programme.

This works because the programme has been put into *delay*. The show is being recorded and played back seven seconds or so later. The delay is carried out electronically, by putting the programme through a *digital delay* unit which stores the programme in its computer memory before playing it back seven second later, or by recording the programme on a *tape loop* which gives a seven second pause before the recorded programme reaches the playback head of the machine.

When the presenter presses the obscenity button, the programme is snatched out of delay and a seven second jingle is fired automatically. When the jingle finishes, the programme reverts to being live, and the profanity has, hopefully, been bottled up in that seven second segment which never went on air.

To put it back into delay, another jingle is fired and a fresh loop is set up, or, if digital delay is being used, the unit gradually puts the programme back seven seconds by adding an extra tiny pause to the recording every time it detects a gap in the speech, until the programme is fully back into delay.

THE TOUCHSCREEN STUDIO (Figure 61)

Technology is in use today which makes the most modern conventional radio studio look as out of date as a steam engine. Gone is the mixing desk and in its place is the computer screen. Gone are the faders, buttons and controls. Now to turn on a microphone, fade down a tape, play a record or fire a cart, all you have to do is touch the screen.

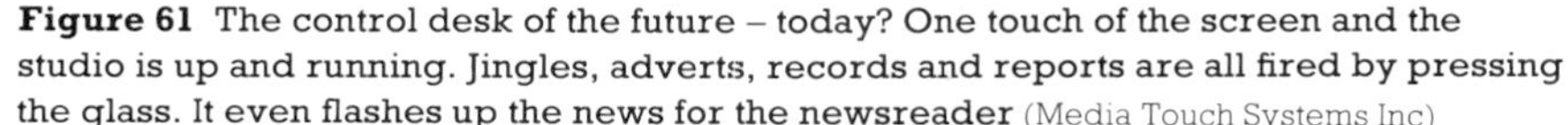

Figure 61 The control desk of the future – today? One touch of the screen and the studio is up and running. Jingles, adverts, records and reports are all fired by pressing the glass. It even flashes up the news for the newsreader (Media Touch Systems Inc)

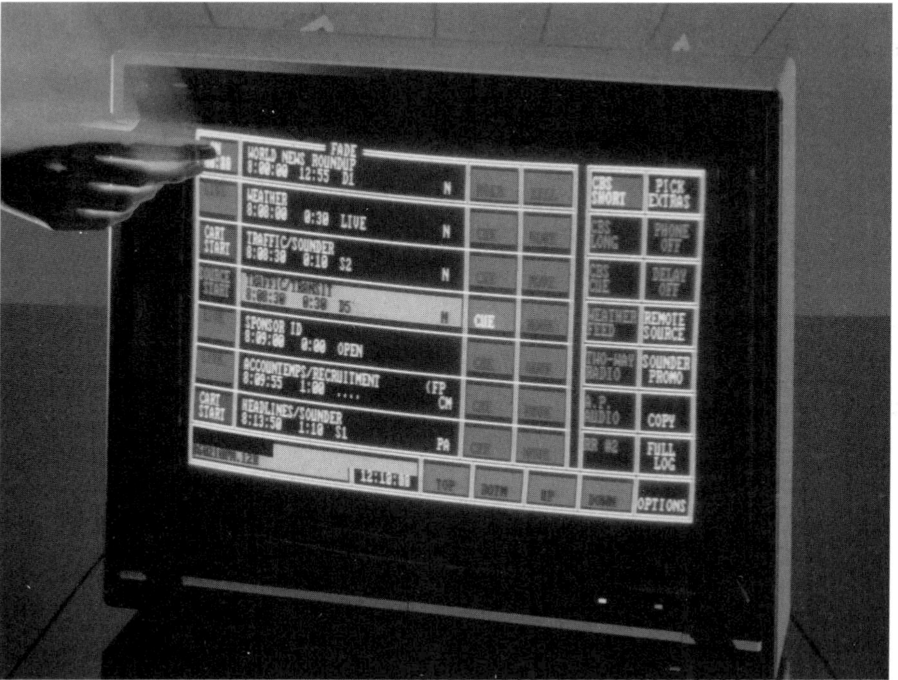

> *'The computer-driven system allows the presenter to switch microphones on and off; run audiotapes for news inserts and commercials; switch in and out of network feeds, live traffic reports, business reports, sports forecasts, and even control building security after business hours . . . The touch screen system eliminates the distractions of operating a sound mixing desk, allowing the presenter to provide a smooth presentation with no sacrifice of production quality . . . The system goes one step further because it runs the station as a totally automated facility overnight.'* – INTERNATIONAL BROADCASTING*

WEEI in Boston (USA) is credited with being the first news station to operate the system, which can also display entire news bulletins to be read from the screen and automatically provides a legal printed record of programming for the Federal Communications Commission. In the event of an unscheduled interruption, such as a network newsflash, the entire programming schedule can be recalculated to make up for lost time – at the touch of a screen. It even works out which adverts were played, and when, and automatically bills advertisers for the airtime. The broadcast studio might never be the same again.

TOMORROW?

How far technology will go is anyone's guess. Indeed, the days of tape may already be numbered as digital storage systems become more sophisticated.

Bulky reel-to-reel portables are on their way out. In their place are coming digital audio tape recorders. A cassette the size of a matchbox can record hours of superb quality material. Rewinding the entire tape takes only seconds, and editing with a rusty razor blade is becoming a thing of the past. Edits can be programmed on computer, as with videotape.

But even this technology is likely to be rendered obsolete almost immediately. Tiny, solid-state recorders, the size of a notepad, with no moving parts and using no tape at all could be just around the corner. These will save sounds (even pictures, one day) in tomorrow's successor to the microchip memory.

Digital delay devices with enhanced memories could one day save hours of editing by squeezing or stretching programmed undetectably until they come out at exactly the required length.

Fully automated programming is already possible. Digital audio equipment can store a full day's output on hard disk. It can also hold more than a thousand adverts, jingles and announcements that would previously be kept on cartridge, offer flawless playback quality, instant selection, be programmed when to fire them on air and offer editing accurate to 1000th of a second. Record play lists, many of which are already being chosen by computers programmed to the tastes of the target audience, can be stored in computer memories and revised in moments.

*From 'At the touch of a screen', November, 1986.

The information explosion is certain to lead to more radio output and a greater spread and specialization of coverage. Deregulation will speed that on its way. This could mean an explosion in smaller stations, as envisaged for the UK, each catering for different interests and sections of the community.

Remote-control radio receivers with pre-tuned channels will do away with old-fashioned dial twiddling and make it quicker and easier for listeners to find specific programmes, breaking the habit of staying tuned to one station. Wider use of the VHF waveband will mean a big improvement in radio reception and more widespread use of stereo programming.

Car radios are already available which can scan the airwaves and home in on localized traffic reports, and radio teletext is another new technology option which has made its debut. Radio by satellite promises another explosion in the quality and quantity of radio broadcasting.

In radio newsrooms, in the short term, suspicion towards existing 'new' technology is likely to gradually subside as radio realizes, however reluctantly, that it must move with the times. 'Faithful' old typewriters will be slung out (at last!) and word processors, where they have not already made an appearance, will come in, linked to the newsroom computer.

In the short-term computerized editing will become a common feature, provided it comes down in price sufficiently to suit radio's low budgets. Even relatively unsophisticated tape decks will feature more computerized functions. More widespread use will be made of existing technologies such as videotape and computer-controlled multi-track recorders for everyday sound recording and broadcasting.

Computers will also increasingly take over the scheduling of adverts and the split-second firing of jingles, ads and information on cart. Cart quality will improve by switching over to digital technology.

At network level, satellites will become the fashionable way to link up stations, and the agonies of waiting for the network headlines to trickle out on yesterday's slow speed printers will finally be over, as high speed printers take their place or the copy is fed directly into the newsroom computer.

It will not all be good news. One disadvantage will be that the network newsrooms will be free to redouble the amount of unintelligible material they send out to the regions, rendered all the more undecipherable as human error is superseded on a grand scale by gremlins in the computer.

If telephone technology improves to the state where conversations sound as clear as those carried out face to face, radio reporters may find themselves tied to the newsrooms to conduct their interviews. Not only would this be dull and have a terminal effect on reporters' expenses, it could mean a drift towards smaller newsrooms.

Whether this vision of 'Utopia' eventually becomes reality will depend more on iron will and hard cash than hardware. Union agreements will have to be renegotiated and manufacturers persuaded that radio is sufficiently lucrative to draw them away from their single-minded pursuit of television technology. As ever, cash is the ultimate carrot.

Even newsreaders whose position may seem unassailable, could one day find themselves victims of the microchip. As technology becomes steadily more sophisticated tomorrow's audiences might be tuning in to hear the news read flawlessly with wit, warmth and urbanity in a pleasing regional accent – by newsreaders with no moving parts. It could be sooner than you think!

> **'Voila – the computer speaks'**
>
> The world's first computer newscast was broadcast by Ottowa radio station CKCU-FM. Students from the Carleton School of Journalism programmed the DEC computer to read the news in a voice that was 'remarkably close to that of a human,' according to reports. The DEC can read the news in no fewer than seven different voices, each of them adjustable for pitch and resonance.
>
> Tutor George Frajkor said his talking computer could one day put newsreaders out of business, '*The newsreader can be replaced by anyone, putting the newscast back in the hands of the working journalists who write it... Voila, the computer speaks.*'*

FIELDWORK

1 If you have access to a studio and a newsbooth, prepare a bulletin with inserts and present it firstly with a technical operator at the control desk, and then entirely by yourself in the booth. Do you prefer to drive the news yourself, or be driven? What are the advantages and disadvantages of each type of operation?

2 As eye contact is so important in interviewing, what difficulties would you expect conducting an interview with a guest who is miles away in a remote studio?

If you are in a class, simulate those difficulties by devising a scenario and conducting an interview with a classmate *back to back*. Do not forget, he/she will need advice on how to use the microphone, how to sit, and how to turn on the equipment.

3 If you have access to the necessary equipment, practise sending a recorded interview down the phone by croc-clipping.

Now try packaging that interview on location by writing a cue and links, and sending it back *in the correct order* along the phone line. Think how you would do it beforehand, then experiment. (*Hint* – use a microphone.)

4 Make a phone interview and balance the levels until they are equal. Now play it back and listen with your eyes shut. Whose voice sounds loudest, yours or theirs? Practise balancing the report so both voices *sound* as loud as each other.

5 Talk to a journalist and a presenter and ask them how they imagine the radio station of tomorrow will look. Are they for or against new technology? Ask them which devices that have yet to be invented would make their jobs easier and more efficient.

How do *you* see the radio station of tomorrow?

*Derived from 'Voiced by Computer', *UK Press Gazette*, 6 June, 1986.

Part Three

TELEVISION

Figure 62 Behind the scenes in the news studio – bristling with equipment, lights and personnel. The floor manager (third from right) gives newscaster Leonard Parkin the countdown for the next edition of *News at One* (courtesy ITN)

23 Independent Television News

Figure 63 Two of ITN's senior presenters, Alastair Burnet and Sandy Gall behind the *News at Ten* desk
(courtesy ITN)

'News at Ten tries to give a big audience at the end of the day the news of the day, and not just the news as it may end up in the history books, but the sort of news about the Royal Family or showbusiness or sport that people would talk about in the building site or canteen the next morning.' – ITN NEWSCASTER SIR ALASTAIR BURNET*

Independent Television News (ITN) ranks beside the BBC in the UK's superleague for TV news. Since its first broadcast in 1955, ITN has had a history of innovation, producing the nation's first half hour and fifty minute news programmes and first home-produced satellite news.

* From *The Making of ITN*, ITN video.

No two organizations are identical. TV news is evolving as rapidly as new technologies – and union rules in some cases – will allow. This chapter offers an insight into how ITN works. Other TV stations will do things *their* way. Equipment, methods and terminology will differ, but they will also have much in common. The following chapters attempt to hold to that common ground without claiming to provide an exhaustive account of the working practices of every TV news organization.

GETTING THE NEWS

Every news organization performs two basic tasks: getting the news in, and putting it out – *input* (intake) and *output*.

On the input side, *newsdesk* selects the stories and assigns the reporters, and *assignments* looks after the camera crews. News from overseas is handled by the *foreign desk*.

After input has chased the stories, it passes them to the output desks – in ITN's case, one for each of its five news programmes. In charge of each desk is the producer who compiles the programme.

ITN seldom has to follow a cold trail for news, as agency wire services feed stories and pictures from around the world. *Copytasters* scan those stories and pass on any that are worth following. (See also page 106.)

Reporters and crews are on standby ready to be assigned at short notice. ITN has more than thirty crews to provide coverage seven days a week, fifty-two weeks a year. Where extra crews are required, freelance cover is brought in.

The basic crew comprises a cameraperson and recordist. A lighting electrician will be sent if required, but will travel to the story separately.

Being a TV reporter is seldom as glamorous as some might believe. Newspaper journalists can draw on their imaginations to describe a scene, but TV reporters are tied to the camera, and that can mean doorstepping a VIP's house all day for one vital picture.

THE BEST AND WORST OF TV NEWS

'The worst of it is being stuck in London, shunted around from one silly story to another, standing outside somebody's door in the pouring rain, from four in the morning till eight at night with no return for it, or doorstepping the TUC while some big industrial debate is going on and doing absolutely nothing for most of the day. Then in ten minutes you may suddenly get three or four people rushing out of the building and you have to try to grab them and interview them and they may just shake their heads and walk away, and you're left kicking your heels and thinking, that was a wasted day.

'The best of it is that you can go out on a story of national importance, spend all day on it, edit it, put your words to it and voice it up, and when it comes across as you wanted it to and people take notice of it, you have that feeling that some part of what you've put over in your minute and a half will stay in their minds and they'll have a better idea of what's going on.' – ITN REPORTER KIM SABIDO

For researching facts or checking information, ITN's news information department keeps cuttings, reference books and background on a myriad of subjects.

To back up those facts with pictures, the library keeps a store of thousands of slides and agency photographs as well as original footage from camera crews. Each item is cross-referenced on computer so reporters can quickly draw on a wealth of previously recorded material to illustrate their reports.

Stories can be made clearer by illustrating them with electronic graphics, produced by machines like the VT80 – ITN's ingenious adaptation of a knitting pattern machine. This has been programed with maps of virtually anywhere in the world which can be recalled at the touch of a button. It can also produce graphics.

The regular Eurovision link with broadcasting organizations throughout Europe offers three exchanges each day at noon, 3 and 5 pm (British Summer Time). The link-up is co-ordinated from Geneva and Brussels. Rival broadcasters in the same country are not permitted to filch one another's material. The foreign desk monitors the link to see what is on offer and news is paid for on a curious pro-rata system – the more TV sets in the country, the more that country pays.

The agency Visnews provides a good deal of the BBC's foreign coverage, while ITN draws on the resources of WTN (Worldwide Television News). ITN is in partnership with ABC of America, and they co-own WTN with Channel 9 in Australia. ABC and ITN supply one another with pictures and reports from their own countries.

Freelance crews are kept abroad to provide exclusive stories, but for long running reports ITN will send its own crews. A major difficulty in the satellite age is that if a government disapproves of reports being made about its country it can easily deny access to the satellite to prevent the story getting back.

To overcome this, ITN was the first British station to use its own portable satellite dish which can be transported to remote areas where it would otherwise not be possible to relay the story back.

Multiple deadlines have put an end to the old practice of bringing back reports by hand. To save time they are sent by satellite or microwave link, or by cable or microwave from a nearby regional TV studio. Only if the report is made almost on the station's doorstep will it be taken back by the crew or despatch rider.

Increasingly, reports are transmitted live from the scene by electronic news gathering (ENG) crews or outside broadcast vehicles, and portable editing equipment means items can be put together on location and sent back rapidly. This has been made possible by replacing film with videotape – a change for the better, according to John Flewin, input editor of *Channel 4 News*:

> *'In the days when we used film we would have to get it back here to be processed before we could even see it, let alone get a knife into it.'* Edited reports can now be completed within an hour. *'If you're up*

against time you can do it in ten minutes. It may not be such a good product but we can get it on air.'

THE EDITORS

The day begins for the duty news editor at the crack of dawn when he switches on his bedside radio to find out what has happened in the world while he has been sleeping. National newspapers and breakfast TV complete the picture before he turns up at ITN at 7.30 to begin what could well be a 15-hour day. Sanity is preserved by a shift pattern which provides for frequent days off.

The editor will have begun to plan his coverage the previous day, with help from the forward planning desk. He will know how many reporters are on duty, what stories some have been assigned to, and how many crews are available at ITN's London base and around the country. '*As he gets new information and different angles he must play that team like pieces on a chessboard*,' says John Flewin.

A list of prospects for the day will feature the news stories ITN knew in advance were happening, such as the announcement of unemployment figures or an election. By the time the news editor arrives, coverage of those will be under way. Phone calls to regional TV stations to check their prospects will swell the list further (Figure 64).

hulme Mon Aug 18 10:04 page 1 Status READY

1986 SLUG
HOME PROSPECTS MONDAY, AUGUST 18.

Reporters: Lloyd-Roberts; Roman; Sheriden; Draper (L). Home Affs: Cullen.
Ind Corrs: Smith; Webster. Pol Corrs: Rose.

HEALEY: Robert Healey appears in court at Stockport charged with the murders of his wife and stepdaughter. MacMILLAN ENG ex GTV.

EALING: Police question commuters at South Ealing station about the disappearance of Sarah Lambert. Her office is also open today and there is a chance her parents will be travelling up to see the police. Also possibility of a re-construction at noon plus interview with the other girl offered the job. LLOYD-ROBERTS

NIREX: NIREX contractors turn up at three sites:- Fulbeck in Lincs; Killingholme, Humberside and Elstow, Beds. Pix from YTV; CTV and Anglia. SHERIDEN

RABIES: Zambian woman believed to be suffering from rabies is in a Portsmouth hospital. How is she? Has she been in contact with anyone else? STEVE HARRIS ENG

CATHOLICS: Short Brothers investigate alleged threats against Catholic workers at the predominently Protestant aircraft factory. Its also the highest level of attacks on Catholic homes in 17 years GLOVER-JAMES ENG

RESULTS: 7,000 Scottish schoolchildren are given "no award" result in their exams. This is because the teachers" strike meant they did not do enough work for annual assessment. We talk to kids, teachers, parents and unions. CULLEN

TELETEXT: IBA to award franchises for radio teletext. This will allow the active businessman to keep in touch with what's going on in the financial markets etc. HATFIELD

Possibles and Watching: Thatcher moves in?
Ulster grand prix - GLOVER-JAMES ENG.
... stacking - THOMPSON.

Figure 64

The mailbag will be sifted by newsroom assistants and secretaries and the forward planning department will be notified of details in the post about coming events. In the newsroom, every item of news entering the building can either be monitored on computer or listened to discreetly through personal earpieces.

Once the news editor has allocated reporters to stories he then has to 'sell' his ideas to the producers of the different news programmes, each of which may have his/her own view about how to run the story.

Meanwhile the foreign editor is running up a large phone bill checking his reporters and contacts overseas. Later he will watch the early Eurovision link to see what stories are on offer.

Both editors need to have a clear idea of the day's coverage by 10.30 when the first morning conference takes place in the teak-panelled office of the editor-in-chief, which serves as the threshing floor for ideas. Suggestions are pooled and thrashed out, with the editor-in-chief acting as chairman and referee and checking that the stories fit ITN's style.

> *'What has served us well is hard news, unvarnished and attractively packaged offering good quality information. Tonight's news lead could be an interesting new translation of the Bible or a kidnapped girl in Surrey – as long as it's news.*
>
> *'I always like to think we are in serious popular journalism, not popular serious journalism. There are Times [newspaper] households and Sun [newspaper] households. We go into the Times and Sun households – into some extraordinary households. We know we are watched in the Palace at 10 o'clock and in parlours at 10 o'clock, so we have to be knowing and well informed to the considerable number of people who know more about a story than we do, and not condescending to those who know less.'* – DAVID NICHOLAS, EDITOR IN CHIEF, ITN

THE PRODUCERS

After running through their prospects, the home and foreign editors throw it open to the producers of different news programmes to make their bids for items. There are five programmes to fill: *News at 12.30*, *News at 5.45*, *Channel 4 News*, which goes out at 7 o'clock, *News at Ten* and *Superchannel News* plus a five-minute headline summary at 10.25 am. *Channel 4 News*, which is longer, offers more background analysis, so will usually run the story in more depth and look into the *hows* and the *whys* behind it. *News at 12.30* is the first programme on air, so the most pressing questions for that producer will be, 'how *quickly* can we get the story?'

With up to five programmes to feed, each story might have to be covered five different ways by the same reporter. Each producer will want the reporter's sign-off line to mention the name of his specific programme – and that can mean recording the last section of the commentary five times.

News at Ten is ITN's flagship. The producer – the output editor – will have come to work around 10 am. His is a short day – only about 13 hours. He is a sort of sheep-dog-cum-shepherd, who attempts to round up the individual items and pen them up inside his programme:

A day in the life of a News at Ten producer

7.45 am	Get up. Listen to *Radio 4*, read popular and quality newspapers.
9.55	Arrive for work. Check wire copy.
10.30	Conference with editor in chief.
11	Produce draft list of prospects – only half may end up in the programme.
12.30 pm	Monitor BBC news/*News at 12.30*
1.30 to 2.15	Eat sandwich at desk. Think of ideas for graphics.
2.30	Discussion with scriptwriters and graphic artists. Allocate stories. Revise running order.
5.15	Consult editor over possible running order.
7	Meeting with personnel involved in programme.
7.30	Revise running order.
8	Give running order to the programme director. Look at every story that is to be put on air.
10	Supervise programme transmission in control room.
10.30 pm	Off the air.

– NEWS AT TEN PRODUCER PHIL MOGER

Figure 65 Countdown to a programme . . . producer Phil Moger (left) hammers out the final details in the last minutes before the next edition of *News at Ten* (courtesy ITN)

It is now five past seven. Less than three hours to *News at Ten* and the programme is shaping up nicely. The Young Conservatives have stepped out of line again and embarrassed the Party faithful by launching a scurrilous attack on a Tory senior statesman. Unless something bigger breaks, this will be the lead.

Phil Moger has gathered his clutch of writers, reporters, editors, illustrators and newscasters, and, under the soft newsroom lights amid the intermittent chorus of cheeping computers, he is chairing the regular evening briefing to whip the programme into line.

Moger's background is working-class popular journalism. He talks fast, grafts hard and is very much in control. He bangs his ideas out with a mixture of sardonic street savvy and newsroom shorthand. His energy appears to be boundless. He believes his lead story calls for some context and that is what he gets.

'We're going to try to flesh out the story a bit, by looking at the trouble at last year's Young Conservative Conference. It looks like it's going to be top of the show at the moment, so that's what we'll do.'

There are no complaints, so Moger moves to item two. This is a story about airborne early warning radar for Britain. Home companies hope to fight off foreign competition by offering a system based on obsolescent aircraft. Moger, always with an eye for the visual, is anxious to illustrate the story further with graphics.

'OK. Katie – Mark Webster put that together, and the VT80s you've been doing are in the lead-in. I've got another idea with the VT80 that will fit your script – it's planes coming across the screen with a radar. Nice and simple, and it'll look sexy, so we'll go for that: VT80 plus Webster ENG.'

VT80 is a graphics machine; ENG refers to a videotape report, and 'sexy' is newsspeak for the attractive properties of a programme item rather than the curvaceous qualities of a person.

'Robin. Paisley – OK? I don't think we're hitting it hard enough about what Paisley actually says about the coppers, you know what I mean? There are three points he makes and I think we ought to see them on Aston somewhere along the line, Yeh?'

Aston is a machine that puts writing on the screen. Moger favours written quotes to drive home the point of the story. Next, a missing woman who may have been kidnapped by a sex attacker. This one gets the full Moger treatment:

'. . . it all gets a bit mysterious, and the police are saying that she may have had lunch with this guy; i.e.: she knew him. So it gets more interesting. Can we pull some library stuff of outside the house – GVs? I think it might be an idea for whoever gets the story to do a map of the lead-in, a pukka street map to show where the house was and where she was last seen, and I think we also need three nice supers on his moving picture, Paintbox, whatever, Yup?'

GVs are general views, lead-in is the written cue to a story item, supers are the names and titles superimposed over the picture and Paintbox is a graphics machine. And so the briefing continues, in the language of the cogniscenti, with each contributing as he sees fit, until no team member is left in any doubt about what he/she has to do.

Late news comes that the Soviets have issued an exit visa to an important dissident. *News at Ten* has been full of Soviet stories lately and Moger clutches his forehead in mock-agony. His histrionics elicit laughter from the assembled team.

'Incredible. Vodka on the house tonight folks! OK, let's get going and thanks very much.'

GETTING THE PROGRAMME ON AIR

With programme planning now well advanced, the task of making it happen on the air falls to the director. He/she is responsible for blending the different camera shots, graphics and reports that go to make up the programme.

There is a brief rehearsal at 9.40. Whether *News at Ten* bears more than a passing resemblance to that depends largely on late reports still coming in.

In the studio the newscaster can hear everything going on in the control room through the earpiece. This constant chattering into the ear can be a blessing or a curse. ITN newscaster, Trevor McDonald: *'One night I was interviewing an anti-apartheid spokesman and there was a great shout in the control room. For a moment I didn't know if I was interviewing the wrong guy so there was a long pause while I decided how to phrase the question. I have been reading the news for years and I still have a little jolt when somebody shouts.'* On some TV stations the newscasters can hear only the director's comments, but despite the drawbacks, McDonald prefers to do it ITN's way and have all the voices coming into his ear: *'At times you can almost hear the genesis of decisions of change. You can sometimes hear the producer say softly to the director, through whom all instructions must come, "I'm thinking that we have to make a change in story 15," and you mentally gear for it. So the change when it comes is not sudden. Anything that gives you that few seconds warning is good. I'd be very worried if I couldn't hear what was happening. I'd feel cut off.'*

'Stand by VT1, EJ1 . . .'

'. . . three, two, one, zero.'

'On air.'

It is 10 o'clock. The opening sentences of the programme – the 'bongs' – still fall between the chimes of Big Ben as they have always done and require the same special handling to make sure they fit, as Sir Alastair Burnet explains:

*'It's rather like having to write a headline in a newspaper: you're under discipline. You've got to get it into nine words – three seconds – and I think in the end that makes it punchier, better, and more memorable.'**

* From *The Making of ITN*, ITN video.

Electronic journalism and the satellite age have pushed deadlines back to the very last minute of the programme. Producers, presenters, reporters and directors have never been more tested than they are today, and more is to come. ITN offered Britain its first popular news service. *News at Ten* was the nation's first half hour news programme. *Channel 4 News* made room for analysis by extending the airtime to fifty minutes. The challenge now facing the programme makers is to push back the frontiers in the most complete way possible, by further dismantling the borders between news and current affairs, even national boundaries – with round the clock 24-hour news by satellite.

FIELDWORK

1 Arrange to visit a TV station and watch a news programme being prepared and going out on air.

2 During your visit work out how news coverage is organized and who decides what to cover and what to run.

Is there any arrangement for pooling reports with other stations?

How are reports sent back to the newsroom from location?

3 Do you think it is a good idea for newsreaders to hear everything going on in the control room through their earpiece? What problems do you think it could cause?

4 Simulate wearing an earpiece by listening to a talk station on the radio through headphones and reading out a news story on tape at the same time. Listen to the result. Did your newsreading suffer at all? Did you find it difficult to concentrate?

5 What effect do you think expanding the length of news programmes has had on coverage? Is longer news necessarily better news? Discuss.

24 A story is born

PANNING FOR GOLD

> *'When heatwaves come to scorch the streets*
> *And humid is the long-drawn day . . .*
> *The editors in huddles go*
> *And to the cameramen declare:*
> *"Quick! To the zoo, for we must show*
> *Some pictures of a polar bear."'*
> – HARRY IRVING PHILLIPS

It is August. The silly season. Parliament is on holiday with most of the nation's other newsmakers. It is traditionally the time of year when the bottoms of barrels are soundly scraped by newsrooms digging for raw material.

The 3.45 planning meeting at ITN is peopled by apologetic producers and disgruntled news editors, gathered to pick through the prospects for the following day. Any nuggets are few and far between.

The biggest running story is the deputy chief constable accused of bringing the police force into disrepute. His hearing is due in two days time, and the policeman says he will not talk until then. Fools' gold.

Drugs – a pop star appears in court on heroin charges; a trading standards officer warns car firms of the latest method of fiddling speedometers and it is Slimmer of the Year time – again. The woman has gone from 19 stones to 9 in a year. Her long-suffering fiancé of fourteen years has decided he can now marry her. 'Before and after' pictures are available. All that glisters may not be gold, but on a day like this the story has a certain attraction . . .

With the exception of a gas blast in Kensington – one person still trapped – it is back to sifting through the same old silt: Ulster; the follow-up to a story about nuclear dumping, and the England cricket team practising in the nets.

'And that's it.'

Looks of resignation are exchanged across the editor's office. It is a scene repeated in almost every August editorial meeting in almost every newsroom around the country.

'Foreign?'

All aspirations shift to the foreign editor.

'There's nothing definite for tomorrow.'

All hopes are pinned on getting an interview with a mountaineer recovering in hospital after the rest of his team died attempting to climb K2 in the Himalayas. Hard news and human interest rolled into one. But there is no guarantee the hospital will permit that interview.

'Is that all you've got?'

'Mmm – very quiet.'

'Gosh.'

This is the raw material of four programmes and two hours of news. Nobody is happy, but nobody is tugging at his hair. In the news business, stories have a habit of turning up when they are least expected – even in August.

The news editor for the production unit chips in. Her department deals with backgrounds and specials – in-depth work which can have a spin-off into news.

'Can I come up with a suggestion for the next couple of days?'

Indeed she can.

'It's on refugees, the Danish Prime Minister said today that Denmark and West Germany are taking more than their fair share. There are 10 million refugees in the world. Europe took 170,000, and the Sudan, a really poor country, took 300,000. The United Nations' High Commission for refugees thinks there's going to be another financial shortfall because of the emergency in Africa. They'll give us an interview. We also have a map of where all the refugees are in the world, and we can obviously use library pictures. It's not the hardest story, but it is current.'

The idea is received with relief and gratitude. The meeting ends, and the United Nations spokesman is booked for an early interview the following morning.

THE INTERVIEW

'He's late. He was booked for 10; the crew were booked for 10, but because of the bomb explosion, we've lost the crew.'

It is five to eleven. Reporter Michael Sheridan is clearly hassled. His report on the worsening refugee situation was not required for another two days, but a thin news schedule has brought it forward. The item is now wanted for *News at One**, and the discovery that yesterday's gas explosion was in fact caused by a bomb has meant the re-assignment of his camera crew. Instead of an in-depth report Sheridan is left with a rush job. And the interviewee from the United Nations has still not turned up.

'***He's here***'. The production unit news editor perks up. *'We'll do it in the Boardroom. We'll need a crew.'*

The interviewee is grateful for the opportunity to put his case. There is a record number of refugees and the money has run out.

Downstairs in the boardroom the pre-chat has begun: *'I'll ask you: "How serious is the problem? Is it getting worse? And what are you trying to achieve now?"'*

The interviewee looks a little uncertain. He has never been on camera before. The reporter's bedside manner is impeccable. Assurances, dis-

*Since then ITN has brought the deadline forward – the programme is now *News at 12.30*.

Figure 66 (*left*) Sheridan briefs the interviewee about the questions, with the camera in placing looking over his shoulder (*right*). The interview gets under way. The United Nations representative (*left*) listens while a question is put to him by Sheridan (*second from left*). To the right are the cameraman, recordist and lighting technician. Three lights provide even coverage. Barn doors direct the spread of light, and the beam from the left-hand lamp is spread by diffuser (Andrew Boyd)

pensed on scores of previous occasions, still sound fresh, polite and professional:

'*Basically you say whatever you want, but the more concise, direct and simple your points, the more effective they will be.*'

By now the crew have arrived and are setting up. Two chairs are arranged face to face and the reporter and his interviewee take their seats. Three 800 watt 'red-head' lamps are set up. One is the *key*, for the main lighting, another is the *fill*, to fill in the shadows – this has a diffuser over the lamp – and the third is the *backlight* to eliminate shadows from behind.

The camera, an ENG machine, which records on videotape, is mounted low on a tripod pointing over the reporter's shoulder and into the face of the interviewee. Sheridan holds a white notepad in front of the camera which the operator focuses on to adjust the colour balance. There is a problem with the lighting. Part of the background wall is not properly lit. Adjustments are made to the *barn doors*, hinged flaps on the lamp which can be adjusted to broaden or narrow the beam of light. Reporter and interviewee are fitted with tie-clip mikes and the recordist makes a sound check to balance the levels. It is now 11.17. Setting-up has taken less than 10 minutes. The interview begins (Figure 66).

Questions quickly move away from those outlined in the pre-chat as the reporter picks up on interesting points and develops them by firing new questions. Today's story is angled on the need for money, but Sheridan has to do a second story tomorrow, focussing on the problem of piracy at sea, so he asks some extra questions to cover that as well. Eight minutes after the opening question Sheridan winds up and calls to the cameraman, '***Two-shot, please.***'

Lights are rearranged and the camera is taken from its tripod and held on the shoulder as the cameraman moves round to take a shot of reporter and interviewee facing one another. Sheridan explains that this is known as the *establishing two-shot* and may be used at the start of the interview to set the scene of the conversation.

This completed, Sheridan tells the cameraman, '*I just need some noddies,*' and switches chairs with his interviewee. The camera is repositioned to record his face in profile while Sheridan, now looking at a blank wall, goes through a curious and almost comic routine of nodding, blinking and putting his head to one side and then the other, as though concentrating deeply on his interviewee, who is by now already over the other side of the room and preparing to leave.

These *noddies* or *cutaways* are the glue which joins different sections of interview. If you remove the middle of an interview and join the front and back together, the join would almost certainly show as a jump. Between the two shots, the interviewee may well have moved in his chair or tilted his head, so the cutaway is placed in between to disguise the join. (See also cutaways, page 293.)

This done, Sheridan bids his guest farewell and makes his way to the editing suite, where he will compile his report. The videotape, meanwhile, has been boxed and labelled and is taken to film traffic to be logged and recorded before being returned to the reporter for editing.

COMPILING THE REPORT

In the editing booth, Sheridan types his report into the computer. He is aiming for 1 minute 45 seconds, and library footage of refugees and the interview he has just completed will be fitted round the script. With him is a tape editor and a researcher who had been collecting archive shots for the longer production which had been planned. While Sheridan keys in his script, the editor runs these tapes through at high speed to search for suitable pictures to illustrate the report. (Figure 67).

The footage, on a mixture of high quality one inch tape and ENG cassette, has been called up from the film library by keying the word 'Refugees' into the computer database. All recent footage of refugees, plus a printed description of every shot on the tape is provided by the library in a matter of minutes, saving much precious time in pre-selection.

Elsewhere, a graphics operator has already been instructed to provide a map of the world showing the refugee hot-spots and a News at One writer is producing the *lead* (or *cue*) for the story, which the newscaster will read to introduce the item.

Time is short, and the aim is to have the graphics sequence recorded and incorporated into the package. The original plan was to draw a map of the world on one graphics machine, and as each trouble-spot was highlighted, a second, more sophisticated machine would add a still picture of refugees in that area, bringing the picture up from a dot on the map to fill a window on the screen. The two images would have to be mixed in a studio, and studio time is, as always, in short supply. Sheridan's time is also running out. He opts for the simpler solution of using just one graphics machine. A straightforward map will have to suffice.

'*I've got six different tapes with refugees from Sri Lanka, the Berlin Wall, lots of Sudan stuff, and some El Salvadorean refugees in the Honduras,*' the researcher explains. In moments, the Sudan pictures are flashing at high speed across the monitors as the editor searches for the right shot to fit the brief. Meanwhile, Sheridan has completed his script and the Basys computer is printing out several copies, one of which is rapidly despatched to the operator of the electronic graphics machine who is creating the map.

Then a picture is spotted of a solitary naked child walking dejectedly away from the camera into a barren wasteland. It is powerful and evocative – an ideal shot to lead into the report.

'*I think for the second shot we need close-ups of starving kiddies.*' The words

Figure 67 Visnews cameraman Mohammed Amin whose report on the plight of the starving in Ethiopia brought a flood of famine relief from the west. Shots are chosen for maximum impact to bring home the reality of the suffering (courtesy Visnews)

Figure 68 Sheridan (right) runs through his script with the videotape editor in the editing suite. Note the countdown clock on the centre monitor and the timecode displayed on the right-hand screen. Any changes to the script can be made on the computer (right) (Andrew Boyd)

may sound callous, even brutal, but the intention is to encapsulate the plight of the refugees in an image that will get right to the heart of the matter, and for many in the well-fed North, there is no more powerful image than that of a starving child.

Sheridan times his script while the two shots are assembled electronically and timed on a counter measuring hours, minutes, seconds and frames. (Figure 68)

'*We need a headline for this*,' says a face at the door. A seven second shot is required for the headlines at the start of the bulletin.

Sheridan acknowledges the request but is too tied up to deal with it at the moment. He checks the story lead on the computer to be sure that lead and script flow together without unecessary repetition.

At the touch of another button he summons the programme running order. His story is scheduled seventh. '*That means we have effectively till 10 past one to finish it, but we must treat the deadline as one o'clock.*'

Archive footage, which is still spinning away on the Videotape Recorder (VTR), reveals another haunting shot of a circle of Africans mourning a dead relative lying at their feet.

Sheridan times the next section of his script, and this visual sequence is then edited to precisely fit that timing. The sequence is advanced frame by frame until a suitable point to begin is located. An electronic pulse marks the section at its start and end and it is dubbed on to the master tape, under the control of a computer.

The tape recorders need a little time to get up to full speed, so both machines are automatically wound back to around 10 seconds before the first marker. Then the computer sets the tapes running. The instant the marker is reached the master tape is switched into record, and then off again at the end of the sequence. The operation produces flawless edits and is carried out automatically once the computer has been told where to make the joins.

Sheridan calls the graphics operator assigned to the report on the talkback and reads the next section of his script over the microphone. The map is to illustrate concentrations of refugees and the graphics operator has already been told which nations Sheridan intends to mention. Each time he names a country, the operator triggers a pre-programmed special effect which highlights that nation. The sequence is added to the master tape.

Sheridan relaxes visibly. '*We've broken the back of it.*' He is no longer at the mercy of interviewees who are late, camera crews who have been called out on other assignments, and studio bookings which may not be available until the last minute. There is a lot more to do, but it is all in hand. All, that is, except more pictures of refugees for the next sequence.

'*What we need now are* ***real*** *crowds.*'

Suffering, such as that endured by refugees, will always have a human face. An audience may struggle to comprehend even a hundred deaths, but will relate in a moment to a single hungry child or a small group of grieving relatives. But the refugee problem is vast, and having touched people's hearts with its reality, it now falls upon the reporter to explain its magnitude. '*Did you see any crowds on the tapes?*'

'*We've got crowds behind barriers in Berlin,*' comes the reply.

'*Yes, but are they* ***starving*** *crowds?*'

It is a rhetorical question. Some East Berliners might be classed as would-be refugees, trapped behind an iron curtain. But while they might get conscripted into the army, at least they are not at war. They might occasionally have to queue for food, but at least they will get fed. The focus of this report will be on those who are fleeing for their lives.

'*We'll take another look at Pakistan.*'

But before they do that, a spin through a tape on Thailand reveals thousands of refugees on the move, wading through rivers and climbing up banks.

'Do we have a crowd, or do we have a crowd?!'

The editor winds the tape back and forth with the joystick on the edit controller, freezing the frame and going into slow motion where a closer look is required.

A head appears round the side of the booth and patiently inquires, '*You haven't managed to sort out a headline, have you?*' Sheridan assures the writer he is giving it his best consideration. She leaves, apparently satisfied. Sheridan times the next section of his script. '*Nine seconds.*' Nine seconds of pictures are chosen and added to the master tape. Sheridan reads the script once more over the sequence to check the timing is good. It is.

The digital counter on the screen reads 00.06.08.17, corresponding to hours, minutes, seconds and frames. The master tape was started at 00.05, so the length of the report so far is one minute eight seconds and 17 frames. On British TV there are 25 frames a second, so the report is up to nearly 1'09".

Having given a brief overview of the refugee problem, Sheridan turns to his original interview with the United Nations representative. The tape is loaded and wound back to the question about fund-raising. The answer is timed at about 1'02". Too long. Only the second half is chosen.

A revised running order for the programme is handed round the door. The top stories have changed but Refugees is still seventh.

The interviewee's answer breaks into two sentences. Sheridan decides to take the whole of the second sentence which is a comment on the record number of refugees. The interviewee has a habit of blinking hard, and the editor takes care not to start or end on a frame which shows his eyes closed. the electronic markers are placed, and the shot dubbed on the master tape.

Sheridan plans to follow it immediately with the part of the interview about fund-raising, but before that can happen, a 'noddy' has to be added to cover the join between the two sections of interview. A suitable shot of Sheridan nodding gravely, recorded at the end of the original interview is found and then dubbed over the last few seconds of the master tape, where the interviewee is talking about the scale of the refugee problem.

The editor adjusts the sound mixer to make sure the soundtrack is not recorded over, otherwise the noddy would rub out the last few seconds of the interviewee's comment.

Sheridan then runs through the tape of the interview until he finds the answer about the UN's public appeal for cash and this is dubbed across on the master. The sequence is played back, revealing Sheridan nodding, then more of the interviewee. The join is completely undetectable and a viewer would have no cause to imagine that both statements had not been said together in the original interview.

A final shot of refugees is required to provide a suitable backdrop for Sheridan's last comment which will end the item. Pictures of a mother weeping inconsolably with her child are found and added. She is a refugee from Afghanistan. The image cuts to another of a seated and broken figure staring lifelessly into the distance.

Next comes the search for the headline shot that the writer has been agitating over. The opener of the naked child walking into the wilderness is the first choice, but that is found to be a second too short. ITN's headline shots for the one o'clock news have to be seven seconds long. Another image, and one almost as powerful is selected to run as a taster for what is to come.

Now the *supers* have to be worked out. These are the captions which appear over the pictures to say where each place is and who is talking. The writer is at the door again and Sheridan gives her a list.

All that remains now is to lay the soundtrack.

Sheridan goes into an adjoining commentary booth where there is a

Figure 69 Narrative is dubbed over the pictures in the commentary booth adjoining the editing suite. Note the monitor, microphones, headphones and timecode reader (centre) (Andrew Boyd)

monitor to view the assembled report, a microphone, a set of headphones, and a talkback unit. He reads part of his script while the editor takes a soundcheck. '*OK. We're happy.*' (Figure 69)

The tape is wound back to the opening frames which show a clock counting down from five seconds. When the hand reaches zero, the picture of the child walking into the wilderness appears on monitors in the editing and sound booths. Sheridan gives the image a moment to register and then begins his script. At the sound of his voice, the editor dips the background sound on the tape so Sheridan can be clearly heard.

All goes well until the cue into the United Nations man. Sheridan's voicer overruns by a second and cuts across his first words. The tape is wound back to the preceding graphic of the map for Sheridan to try again.

This report has been compiled so that visuals are switched to fit the rhythm of speech, and shots are changed at the start of a paragraph. When mistakes need correcting, it is a simple matter of winding back to the start of the paragraph and going again. Sheridan revoices that section a little faster. This time it fits perfectly and the slight change of pace is undetectable. Without pausing, he finishes reading his script. It is now twenty to one.

The report is run through for a final check and it meets with approval. It is two minutes and one second in duration, seventeen seconds longer than planned, but worth every second.

The writer is back. There is a further discussion about supers. She vanishes again. Sheridan looks satisfied. The VTR with the completed report is cued-up ready to go at the director's bidding. (Figure 70)

Figure 70 Sheridan's script is printed out from the computer. Graphics, pictures and interview are slotted into place (courtesy ITN)

msherida Wed Aug 20 11:46 page 1

SLUG MAIN NEWSROOM SYSTEM Status Time

READY 1:18

==

The image of the refugee has made such an impact on the western public's concience in the last two years that pictures like these may already have lost their power to shock.

But that doesn't diminish the problem, nor does it mean that the outpouring of public generosity has done a great deal to stop its growth.

The United Nations defines a refugee as a person who has left his or her country and is in fear of their life if they return.

By those standards the U.N. says there are about ten million refugees in the world -- that's bigger than the populations of many small countries.

These pictures are from Africa, the continent whose plight has got most attention, but the problem goes much further than that:

TAKE VT8D

It affects Central America, torn by civil war and killings of native indians.

In Southern Africa, thousands are on the move fleeing regional conflicts.

Best known, the plight of millions in the horn of Africa.

And tens of thousands have fled Afghanistan.

To the east, the legacy of the Indochina wars leaves millions displaced.

msherida Wed Aug 20 11:46 page 2

EENGULAY:

The responsibility for refugees lies with the United Nations, but its main agency simply hasn't got enough cash to handle the size of the problem.

Sof Stephen Sinclair UNHCR

If more money isn't committed, then the plight of people like these Afghan refugees will get worse, as their numbers inexorably increase.

'GOING LIVE . . .'

In the studio, cameramen are standing by, and the newscaster, fresh from make-up, takes his place behind the desk. Plugging in a piece of kit affectionately known as a deaf-aid, he can hear what is being said in the control room, where the director and his team are working to put the programme on air.

The atmosphere during the countdown is one of controlled chaos. Everyone appears to be talking at once. The array of monitors is bewildering. Timing is split-second. This is not the place for the faint-hearted or indecisive.

Every word uttered in the control room is injected directly into the newscaster's ear; every command to every cameraman and tape operator, every curt discussion between director and newsroom over late items, and of course, any instructions aimed at the newscaster himself. It is a little like standing in a crowded room and trying to listen to ten conversations at once.

'*We don't have story two and we don't have story three*,' a strained voice heightens the tension in the darkened room summoning an oath from the director, who has even more pressing problems to contend with. A pop star has appeared in court on a heroin charge and the picture chosen for the headlines doesn't look anything like him.

'***I want the slide with long hair, please!***' Exasperation. It's the second time of asking.

'*The headline for story two has just walked in.*'

'*One minute to transmission.*'

'***I haven't got the script!***'

'*Forty seconds to transmission.*'

'*Has Alastair got the script yet?*'

'*No, but I'll get it in a second.*'

Another oath, and the five second countdown begins.

'***On air.***'

'*Duration, Lesley.*'

Lesley hands him a note as the titles are rolling.

The newscaster finishes reading the lead and the first story begins.

'*Has anyone got the length? We don't know how long this is.*' Silence. They are flying blind.

'***That's it!***' says a writer as the untimed tape comes to an end. The script is allowed to fall to the floor, as dead as yesterday's news.

During each item writers watch the transmission monitor like hawks, calling out which captions should be put on air and when.

The barrage of instructions continues unabated in the ear of the newscaster as he unflinchingly conducts a live interview.

'*One minute to go.*'

'*Ten seconds. Try to come out on time.*' He does. To the second.

Now the story on refugees begins. A handwritten and much amended running order, issued just before the start of the programmme, shows an earlier item had to be ditched, upping Refugees to sixth position. (Figure 71)

As the worlds
refugee population
swells to ten
million: the
United Nations
issue an urgent
appeal for help.
We've a special
report.
And: near
disaster in the
skies over the
west country: but
then the marines
achieve the
biggest ever para-
stack.

Figure 71 Autocue script. The refugee report has made the headlines (Courtesy ITN)

The report goes out as planned without a hiccup, the only addition being the supers giving the names of the reporter and places shown.

Now it is time for the recaps, giving the main points of the news. The credits roll and another *News at One* is at an end, almost, it seems, before it began. The clamour of instructions ceases. Order is restored. Calm descends. Sighing and stretching as the tension unwinds.

The director turns to a bewildered and almost breathless onlooker. '***Easy, isn't it?***' The astonishing thing is, he means it!

FIELDWORK

1 Record a TV news programme and scrutinise one particular report. Watch it again to see how it was constructed. Note every shot, giving its type, duration and subject. Note also the supers and graphics and their duration. Look out for cutaways and noddies.

Now transcribe the commentary and reconstruct the script in its entirety giving commentary, camera shots and visuals.

2 Discuss ways to improve that report. Could the script be tightened? Could it say more or should it say less? What do you think of the camera shots? Were they dramatic and interesting enough? Can you think of any better shots they could have taken? Why do you think they didn't?

3 Get together in teams of four if possible and imagine you are preparing the day's news from scratch. Your brief is to provide a thirty minute programme of national and international news. Using only the national newspapers as prompts draw up plans for enough items to fill your half hour and to make a balanced programme. If you do follow the newspapers, make sure your ideas take the story a stage further than the press – don't resort to covering their old ground. Think about item length and the shape of the programme.

4 Now put together some proposals for graphics and visuals to provide extra illustrations for your reports.

5 Think up a scenario for an interview, based on one of your ideas for a news item. Find a willing volunteer to play the part of the interviewee and give him time to get briefed on the subject. There's a catch – he is to play the part of someone who has never before been interviewed and is very nervous. Conduct the interview, under lights in a TV studio if you have one, and record it if possible with a single camera. Do your best to reassure your interviewee and put him at ease. Discuss the interview afterwards and see if there are ways you could improve your 'bedside' manner.

25 The story of TV

This is a book for reporters rather than engineers, but most news organizations would be happier places if reporters had at least some idea how their equipment worked and a little sympathy for the struggles of their hard-pressed colleagues, who are often more at home in silent contemplation over a soldering iron than attempting to describe in lay person's terms the technical limitations of the satellite receiver.

The TV reporter has to spend many long hours on the road co-operating with and attempting to win the co-operation of colleagues in charge of lighting, sound and camera equipment. A little understanding of how that equipment works will even up the chances in an argument, and might save the reporter being blinded by science!

EARLY DAYS
(Figure 72)

The world's first true television pictures flickered into life in a Soho attic in the autumn of 1925. A reluctant office boy by the name of William Taynton grudgingly accepted a half-crown bribe to become the first person to appear on the small screen.

By January the following year, John Logie Baird, Scottish engineer, one time soap manufacturer and inventor of the absorbent sock, was ready to unveil his new discovery before the august and critical gaze of members of the Royal Institution of Great Britain. The first television programme featured a ventriloquist's dummy called Bill. *The Times* described the image as 'faint and often blurred' but recognizable. The experiment was a success. Telephony with vision – television – had arrived.

The breakthrough which made it possible had been made in 1888 with the invention of the photo-electric cell, a device which converted light into electric current. The stronger the light, the greater the current it produced. If light can be turned into electricity, then electricity can be turned back into light – one of the basic principles behind television.

The invention of the amplifier, to boost those weak electric signals to the point where they became usable, brought the dream of television closer to reality. What was needed now was a way of transmitting and receiving a picture.

Baird developed a way of scanning a picture, line by line, so each line could be sent by wire to a television receiver. The process was reversed at the other end and the picture reformed line by line into an image of the original.

Baird's original 'camera' divided the picture into thirty lines. Some cameras today break the picture into more than a thousand lines and scan it many times a second. The technology has moved on, but the principle remains the same.

Baird's first pictures by wire were the forerunner of cable television, but before long he had succeeded in transmitting his signals through the air by wireless.

By the time of the first monochrome transmission on the BBC in 1929, the first colour television pictures had already been seen, produced by scanning an image through red, green and blue filters and overlaying all three to produce a single colour picture. Modern colour cameras operate on a similar principle.

EMI developed the first electric camera and convinced the BBC of its merits in 1934. Baird, ahead of his time, but still obsessed with the idea of mechanical TV, plunged himself into relative obscurity trying to record television pictures on disc, a breakthrough which has been perfected comparatively recently using digital techniques and laser discs (Figure 73).

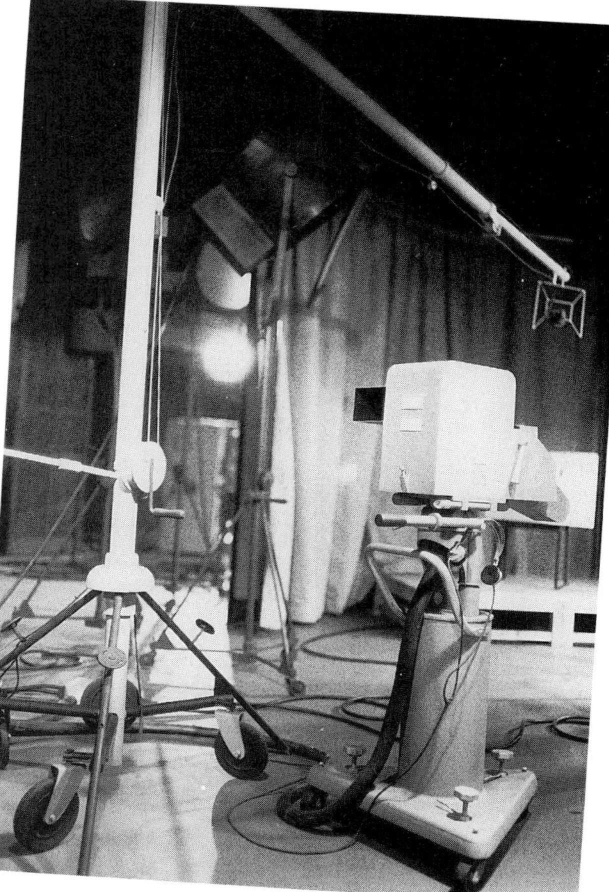

Figure 72 Model of John Logie Baird's first mechanical television camera. Light flashed through the holes in the rotating disc to scan the head of the ventriloquist's dummy. Critical observers pronounced the image produced by the crude machine 'faint and often blurred' – but recognizable (Andrew Boyd)

Figure 73 The first electronic television camera was produced by EMI and paved the way for the studio cameras of today. Here, a model of the original stands beside the boom microphone (Andrew Boyd)

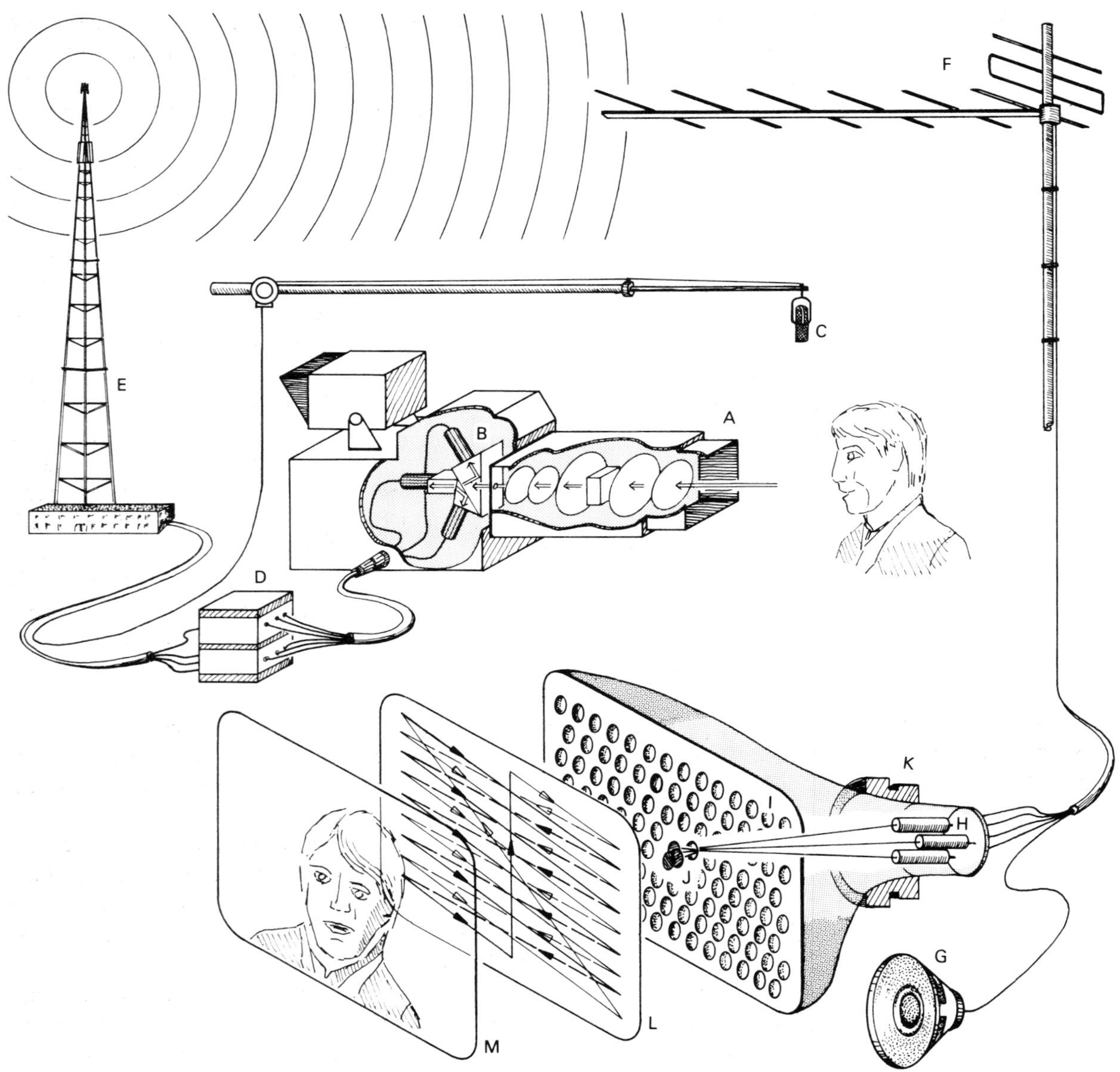

Figure 74 From TV camera to TV screen. The TV camera (A) picks up coloured light reflected from the presenter and breaks it down into its basic elements of red, green and blue, by filtering it through a series of mirrors within the camera (B). At the same time, the studio mike (C) picks up the presenter's voice. The picture signals then pass to an adder, (D) which forms black and white signals, and an encoder, which strengthens the colour signals. The sound and vision signals are sent to the transmitter (E) and beamed out, to be picked up by the TV aerial (F). The audio signal goes to the loudspeaker (G) while the picture signal is sent to the red, green and blue electron guns (H). These guns respond to the original colour signals produced by the camera and fire their stream of electrons at the TV screen. The electrons pass through a precision-engineered mesh covered with thousands of tiny holes, known as the shadow mask (I). These holes focus the electrons onto tiny coloured dots of phosphor on the inside of the screen, grouped in triplets of red, green, and blue (J). The system is designed so the beam from each gun will hit only the dot of the corresponding colour. When the dot is hit, it lights up, and combinations of dots produce different colours. An electromagnet (K) deflects the stream of electrons from side to side until the entire screen has been scanned (L) and the picture has been made up (M)

THE CAMERA

The colour camera works on the principle that every image is made up of a combination of red, green and blue light. When the camera focuses on a picture, light passes through the lens and is then separated inside the camera into its red, green and blue elements by passing through a series of coloured mirrors.

Each different coloured image is then focused on to a separate picture tube. Cameras usually have a tube for red, green and blue and may have a fourth for black and white.

The face of each tube is coated with thousands of light-sensitive dots, made out of a lead-based substance. An electron gun at the back of the tube scans this coating. When the electrons – negatively charged particles – hit a light patch on the picture tube a lot of current can flow through. When they hit a dark patch, less current can flow. So the voltage rises and falls according to the brightness of the image. This changing voltage is the signal coming out of the tube. The three signals, one for each tube, are combined and the signal is amplified and sent along a cable to the transmitter. The sound is sent at the same time, either separately or combined.

Another type in use today is the ENG (electronic news gathering) camera (also known as the PSC – portable single camera) where picture tubes have been replaced by solid state electronic sensors. These CCD cameras start instantly, require no warm-up time, are more robust and work in lower temperatures and in poorer light conditions than were previously possible.

HOW TELEVISION PICTURES ARE TRANSMITTED

Television pictures are transmitted by piggy-back. TV and radio programmes ride on the back of high frequency signals called carrier waves which are transmitted at up to millions of times a second. The number of waves each second is given as the *frequency*.

TV programmes are superimposed upon the carrier wave by altering that wave electronically until it precisely matches the TV signal. The modified carrier wave whisks its superimposed signal through the air to a receiver where the process is reversed and the signal is converted back into the original picture and sound.

Television transmitters are effective up to a distance of about 120 km, providing the landscape puts no obstacles in the signal's path. To carry them further signals are picked up by relay stations, which pass them by microwave or cable to local transmitters.

Alternatively, the signal can be bounced off a satellite and reflected down to a receiving dish the other side of the earth, which will then pass the signal to a transmitter.

From there it is picked up by individual TV aerials and passes along a cable to the television set.

Cable television works by sending TV signals directly to subscribers along underground cables.

THE TV SET
(Figure 74)

Most viewers have a better idea about what goes on under the bonnet of their cars than about the way their TV sets work. Hi-tech. reliability means TV sets start quicker than most cars and require a lot less servicing. But while the lag between pressing a button to getting the picture on the screen may seem negligible, a major operation is taking place inside the set.

When viewers select which channel to watch, a tuner inside their TV locks on to the signal and hands it over to a vision and sound amplifier. This separates the picture and sound signals from the carrier wave and hands each of them to another amplifier.

On the video side, information about the colour of the picture and its brightness is decoded, and the separate red, green and blue signals are passed to the picture tube. While this is happening the sound has been despatched to the loudspeaker.

The red, green and blue picture signals each make their way to an electron gun, one for each colour.

The inside of the TV screen is covered with thousands of tiny dots of coloured phosphor, grouped in triplets or bands of red, green and blue. But before the electrons can light these up, they have to pass through a mask covered with masses of tiny holes or slits, each drilled with incredible precision.

These holes focus the electrons, which zip through the mask in groups of three, one for each colour signal, to light up the corresponding triplet of phosphor dots on the screen. The electron beams touch more than 8 million points on the screen each second, scanning from left to right and then top to bottom.

To eliminate flickering, they scan every odd line of the picture (lines 1, 3 and 5 etc.) and then return to fill in the even lines. The strength of each electron beam determines how brightly the dot of phosphor it hits will light up, and the combination of red, green and blue dots in different strengths make up other colours, like mixing paints on an artist's palette. When all these coloured dots across the screen are lit up, which takes a fraction of a second, they form an accurate reproduction of the image seen by the TV camera.

The whole process from transmission to reception happens so quickly there is usually no appreciable time lag between the transmission of the live picture in the studio, and its reception at home on the set.

Although television operates on broadly the same principle across the world, systems differ slightly in operation, and are incompatible. The European system builds up the picture from 625 lines, and generates twenty-five different pictures per second (frames per second). The US system works on 525 lines with thirty frames per second.

The colour systems are different too, which means if a nation using a different system supplies another with a news report, those signals will first have to be converted to the different standard.

Meanwhile, Joe Public sinks into his armchair, blissfully unaware of the astonishing activity taking place behind the screen or of the years of sweated labour scientists have spent perfecting the process.

Nor does he realize his television set is deceiving him. Scanning takes place faster than his eye can follow, and tricks his brain into believing it is a moving picture which fills the screen, and not just a rapidly moving point of light.

SATELLITE TV

(Figure 75)

Satellite TV began as the dream of science fiction writer Arthur C. Clarke whose imagination was fired by the war-time rockets used by the Germans. He figured that a spacecraft in orbit 36,000 km (22,000 miles) above the equator would keep pace with the earth's rotation and appear to be hanging stationary above the planet's surface. These could be used as mirrors to bounce communications signals half way round the world. If this could be achieved, the technology would revolutionize broadcasting.

In August 1960 his dream started to come true when the first communications satellite was launched – a giant reflective balloon known as ECHO. Two years later, after a huge leap in technology, Telstar was put into orbit, relaying black and white TV pictures across the globe. Many satellites have since followed, ringing the world with a communications chain, sending back colour TV pictures, telephone calls, radio transmissions, navigation and weather information and a host of other data. The speed is phenomenal. A signal can cover the 50,000 miles between India and London (via space) in a quarter of a second.

Figure 75 Intelsat V – one of a growing number of satellites in stationary orbit 36,000 km above the earth, where they beam the news back across the globe (courtesy BBC External Services)

Satellites have brought television to remote areas where reception would otherwise have been impossible, especially regions outside the range of ground-based transmitters and away from TV cabling projects. India is installing more than 100,000 community viewing sets in villages across the country. Thousands of villagers are now able to receive educational TV for the first time. India's own satellite, INSAT IB, was put into orbit in 1983. The scheme is being widened by relaying satellite pictures across the surface using ground-based transmitters. Some 70 per cent of the country can now be reached by TV, and India's satellite programme is continuing.

Mrs Ghandi said when INSAT began: '*India is economically backward today... because we missed the industrial revolution. If we miss what is happening now in the new advances of science, then we haven't got the ghost of a chance of making up for lost time.*'*

FIELDWORK

1 Visit a TV station and ask the engineer to show you all the stages the picture goes through from studio camera to transmission.

2 Find out how fast the picture travels from transmission to the TV set, and how it is checked for quality at the TV station.

3 Find out which type of cameras are better – colour tube or CCD. What are the advantages and drawbacks of each?

4 Find out if any new satellites are due to be launched from your country and what difference these will make to the viewing available.

5 What are carrier waves? See if you can find a way of explaining them in not more than fifty words so *anyone* could understand.

* Suzanne Franks, 'Satellite to the Villages', *The Listener*, 16 October, 1986.

26 Gathering the news

FILM VERSUS VIDEOTAPE

In television, where the free flow of money makes radio seem a poor relation, technologists have had the incentive to come up with new ideas to satisfy the never ending demand for faster news.

Electronic news gathering (ENG – also called EJ (electronic journalism)), ECC (electronic camera coverage), PSC – (portable single camera), is the technocrat's solution to that problem.

ENG is fast replacing film in news gathering organizations around the world, though the cost of re-equipping can be prohibitive.

ENG uses smaller, lighter, more robust cameras, capable of being edged right up to the forefront of the action and sending back live reports. In the US, when they were first used, these were known as 'creepie peepies'. In Britain, both major news organizations, the BBC and ITN, have gone over to ENG in the wake of pioneering work carried out by American companies.

ENG cameras record directly on videotape, which unlike film, needs no developing and can be replayed instantly.

Immediate replay means the cameraperson can check difficult shots by running them back through the viewfinder and can retake them if need be. With film, he/she will have to wait until the prints come back.

A film camera with a 400 feet magazine can record for ten minutes (see Figure 76). A single professional videocassette will last for up to half an hour.

Digital ENG cameras store the images in a form that cannot be corrupted, even after generations of copying.

A further advantage is that video pictures can be repeated. Good shots from a report can be used as headlines at the start of a programme. Film shots can be used only once. The trade-off is that videotape editing is less flexible. It is difficult to correct mistakes once the report is finished – you cannot cut out a sequence or insert an extra shot in the middle of a report without having to re-lay all the shots that follow. With film, you just snip a section out or cut one in.

THE CAMERA CREW

Technology is developing too rapidly for there to be any single worldwide standard for television equipment. Some TV companies are sticking to film, while others with more money to lavish have re-equipped with ENG. A further complication is there are different types of ENG, all of which makes it impossible to speak in anything other than generalities. So, generally speaking, a typical news crew using film or ENG would comprise two or three staff: a cameraperson, a recordist, and for shooting indoors or in poor light, a lighting technician.

Where ENG crews are equipped with *cam-corders*, which record sound in the camera instead of on a separate recorder, the recordist may sometimes be dispensed with – union agreements permitting. Some news reports need only natural background sound which the camera can record automatically. Reports with interviews will need careful balancing of background and foreground sounds, which requires the expertise of a recordist.

Cameraperson and recordist may form a close working partnership, often permanently assigned together and usually travelling in a company car which has been kitted out to take their equipment. This may be a large estate car (shooting brake), fitted with extra security locks or a strong steel

Figure 76 Recording a location interview for Grampian's Gaelic current affairs programme *Crann Tara*. The tripod-mounted video camera is set up to shoot over the reporter's shoulder. To capture the sound a rifle mike (centre) is positioned between the reporter and interviewee, while a sound reflector (left) prevents their voices being snatched away by the wind. There is enough daylight to make the recording without complementary lighting (courtesy Grampian Television)

cage to keep out prying hands. It will also have a two-way radio to keep in contact with base.

The reporter may travel to the story with them, or meet the crew at the scene. Four in a car would be too many, especially with a bulky lighting rig, so the lighting technician will usually head for the news separately, meeting the rest of the crew on location.

Some organizations opt for the all-in-one approach and go for a higher profile, sending crews out in colourful mini-vans bedecked with the TV company's name and logo. The advantage of travelling separately is it offers the assignments editor greater flexibility. He/she can mix and match reporters and crews who may already be out on location.

Camera crews may sometimes work without a reporter to get rush shots back to base. Commentary can be added later after the pictures have been studied. Sometimes a crew will be sent to record material for library shots – general views of a scene which can be kept on file for later reports.

Cameraperson
(Figure 77)

The cameraperson's stock in trade is likely to be a 16 mm film camera or an ENG videotape camera. Both will be equipped with a zoom lens, operating on a ratio of around 10:1, which means the same camera can cover ultra-wide angles to close-ups without having to be moved. The zoom can be operated by hand or at the touch of a button by electric motor.

Some news outfits use Super 8 film gear, which was originally intended for amateur use. This is light and extremely portable, but is losing out to videotape cameras which have slimmed down over the years from a hefty fifty pounds to not much bigger than the Super 8 – but offering far better results.

Film cameras record sound directly on the film, or on reels of audio-tape on a separate recorder. With the separate system the pictures and soundtrack are synchronized later. ENG cameras record pictures and sound on the videotape.

The standard camera kit will include a tripod, a lens hood to cut out glare, rechargeable battery packs, spare videocassettes, or magazines and cans of film in 400 feet lengths.

If the camera does not have a built-in light meter, the cameraperson will carry his/her own. For filming in the dark, in circumstances like a battlefield where lights would be inappropriate and dangerous, the cameraperson may also pack an image intensifier to replace the normal camera lens and give the camera night vision.

One-person cameracrews – where union arrangements allow – will usually pack a portable light, though a single light produces shadows and the result can never be as good as with a full lighting rig.

Some cameracrews using film may also carry a silent (mute) camera. This comes into its own when the main sound camera has to be specially set up for an event like a news conference. While that remains in position, the silent camera, which is smaller, less conspicuous and much more portable, can be used for filming additional crowd shots and scene-setters.

Figure 77 On location with an ENG camera (courtesy Visnews)

Where film is used, the cameraperson will also need a light-proof changing bag to allow him/her to take exposed film from the camera and change it for fresh, and may use a clapperboard to synchronize sound and vision. (See pages 315, 316.)

Past form has been for camera operators to make a note of each different shot on a *dopesheet* which lists the subject and type of shot, stating whether it was a close-up or a long shot, etc. The dopesheet is used to help select the best shots for editing. Videotapes will still be labelled – it would cause chaos otherwise – but detailed shot-lists are rapidly becoming things of the past, or are confined to circumstances where the luxury of time permits. Even so, a detailed dopesheet can save hours in the editing suite.

At the scene, the cameraperson will place the camera in position, on its tripod or on his/her shoulder, check the colour balance by focusing on a piece of white paper or card, adjust the exposure, and set up the shots.

The cameraperson and reporter will usually work as a team. In current affairs or documentary work, the crew will include a director, but for news they will be on their own.

The reporter and cameraperson may both have ideas about which shots to use in the report. Some friendly rivalry usually exists, often accompanied by a degree of mutual leg-pulling. Get them on their own and most camerapeople would say *they* call the shots, while most reporters would argue that the credit goes to them.

Experienced camera operators will have a well-developed news-sense of their own, and will often take fledgeling reporters under their wing. But in the end it falls to the reporter to act as director; he/she will have to pull the item together and write the script so should have the last word about the story treatment. However, the shrewd reporter will quickly find that tact and diplomacy are better means of persuasion than dictatorship.

News camera operators are paid to be artisans rather than artists. Their filming is direct and to the point. Long, evocative zooms, sweeping pans, and shots filmed at artistic angles may go down well in the movies, but are guaranteed to give an editor apoplexy when it comes to assembling a news report. How do you cut into a pan or a zoom? How *do* you follow a shot looking up an interviewee's left nostril?

What the editor wants is a sensible selection of angles and sequences of long shot, medium shot and close-up. He/she also wants a minimum of film to sort through. For a news report of about two minutes, there can be no justification for using half an hour of tape. **Use the camera like a sniper's rifle – not a machine gun.** Every unnecessary shot is a waste of two people's time – the camera operator's and the editor's, so every shot is made to count, with the aim of filming on a ratio of better than 3:1; where one metre in every three metres of film will be used in the final report.

Recordist

US news practice is often to do away with the recordist, leaving the cameraperson to set up and monitor the levels, occasionally aided by the reporter.

This approach has been largely rejected in Britain, where a combination of union insistence and the quest for perfection have safeguarded the role of the recordist – for the time being. The recordist is generally regarded as a vital part of the team. As well as adjusting and monitoring levels, he/she is traditionally the team's fixer, who makes the arrangements and gets the right doors opened at the right times.

The recordist – and reporter – usually stick as close as possible to the cameraperson. There is more to this than mere chumminess. All three are often linked with cables, which can make the going difficult in a fast-moving situation such as a riot.

If the crew is recording film and sound separately, the recordist's kit will include a portable reel-to-reel tape recorder. To be certain the recorded sounds match the movement of the lips, the recorder will be synchronized with the camera. Where background noise only is recorded, the soundtrack is referred to as *wildtrack* or *NAT SOF* (natural sound on film).

The recordist will usually pack a wide selection of microphones. Most mikes are susceptible to wind noise, when even a slight gust across the top can be transformed into a roaring hurricane. Outdoor mikes will be protected by a windshield, which is usually made of acoustic foam.

A directional rifle mike is standard kit for location recordings. The recordist can stand or kneel out of vision and the mike will pick up sound from the direction it is pointed across a narrow angle. It can even isolate individuals within a group. The recordist's aim has to be good. A couple of degrees out and the gun mike will pick up the wrong person or background noise instead.

Another drawback with the gun mike is that with its cover off it can look a little too like its namesake, so it is best avoided in battle zones unless the recordist wants to become a target. The alternative for interviews out of doors is for the reporter to hold a stick mike with a windshield, similar to those used in radio.

Indoors, where wind noise will not be present, a pair of tie-clip or neck mikes (lavaliers) are usually favoured. Neck mikes are hung by a cord and both types can usually be concealed behind a tie or a jacket without losing too much sound quality. Disadvantages are that they can pick up clothing rustle, and because they work on the condenser principle, can draw in spurious background noise, such as the rumble of traffic or air-conditioning. An alternative is to use a couple of directional desk top mikes.

Another important part of the kit will be a radio mike which works like a walkie-talkie. This frees the reporter from his/her leash and is useful for situations where lengths of microphone cable would be a handicap, such as in crowds where the reporter might get separated from the recordist, or where it is necessary to film the reporter walking on his/her own, without the unnatural accompaniment of 15 m or so of trailing cable.

There can often be a personal price to pay for that freedom. Users of radio mikes have been described as walking radio stations. They will have to carry a transmitter, which is a small box with a length of dangling wire. This is most conveniently clipped to the back of the belt, away from the camera, or put in a pocket.

Problems arise when the reporter or interviewee has neither a belt nor a pocket. To keep the mike out of sight, it may mean secreting it down a trouser leg or inside a dress. Women will sometimes have to clip the mike to a bra strap, or if their dresses are tightly cut, tape the transmitter to the inside of a thigh.

Fortunately, radio mikes are usually small, being similar in appearance to tie-clip microphones, but are seldom very robust and are prone to interference. Users in America and the UK require a licence and an approved frequency before they can transmit.

For documentary and current affairs work, where sound quality may be a greater priority than saving time, a boom mike, like those used in the studio, may be included in the recordist's kit.

Lighting technician

Not all news reports require the services of a lighting technician or assistant. Modern cameras can cope perfectly well with outdoor shots in bright daylight, and as technology develops, they may even be able to dispense with artificial lighting indoors.

What they will never do away with is the lighting assistant's artistic touch, which can render unflattering subjects attractive and work wonders with a poor complexion or indifferent bone structure.

The lighting technician's basic kit will include three or four lights for indoor use, each producing between 750 and 1000 watts, enough to light an average room.

The lights model the subject, pick it out from the background and eliminate unwanted shadows. Three tasks, for which at least three lights are required.

The first of these is the *key*. This is the main light which is usually placed up to 5 m (15 ft) away from the subject at an angle of about 45 degrees to the camera. The light will be positioned to compensate for the brightness and colour of the room and the skin colour of the subject.

Harsh shadows created by the key are softened and filled by the second lamp, the *fill*. This will be of lower power or have a diffuser to widen the beam and cast a softer glow. The fill is set up behind or beside the camera to the other side of the key to eliminate its shadows. Small extra lights may be brought in to remove maverick shadows and an eye-light may be used to give a little extra sparkle to the eyes.

The third of the trio is the *backlight*, which is placed out of vision, behind and to one side of the subject. This adds depth to the picture, creating an image which is more solidly three dimensional, and helps separate the subject from the wall behind. It also fills in areas such as the top of the shoulders which the others may have missed (Figure 78).

If the subject is filmed against a window or natural daylight the back-

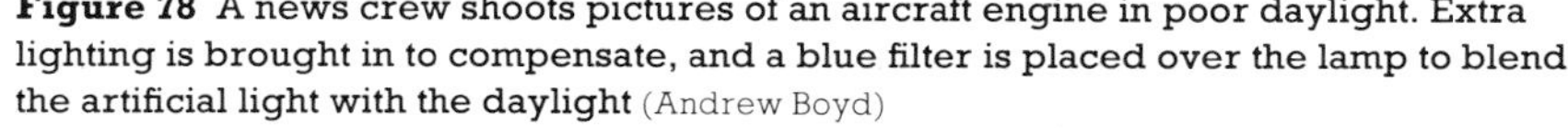
Figure 78 A news crew shoots pictures of an aircraft engine in poor daylight. Extra lighting is brought in to compensate, and a blue filter is placed over the lamp to blend the artificial light with the daylight (Andrew Boyd)

light may be omitted. Where the predominant light is daylight but extra lighting is required, a blue sheet of clear plastic will be placed over the lamp (possibly attached by clothes pegs) to act as a filter. This tones down the yellow artificial light to match the bluer balance of natural daylight. Cameras incorporate built-in colour filters which the camera operator will adjust for different lighting conditions.

The lamps are powered from the mains, and will usually be fitted with moveable flaps, known as barn doors, to direct the stream of light.

In the equipment, the lighting technician will also have one or two small hand-held battery-powered lamps, such as Sun Guns, for occasions where larger, tripod-mounted lights would be inappropriate, such as in a moving crowd (Figure 79).

For extra flexibility, an array of smaller lamps may be included, with spares, extension leads and sun reflectors for outdoor shooting.

Larger scale lighting, to flood an entire hall, would usually be supplied by a contract lighting company.

Some low-budget TV stations, in the US particularly, do away with the lighting assistant by using cameras with a built-in light. Others which really want to scrimp dispense with the cameraperson, recordist and lighting assistant entirely, by using a one-person crew, where the reporter is jack-of-all-trades (and usually master of none). This means either conducting the interview from behind the camera while shooting, or mounting the camera on a tripod, focusing it on the subject, rushing round in front of it and firing the questions, while hoping the shot stays in focus!

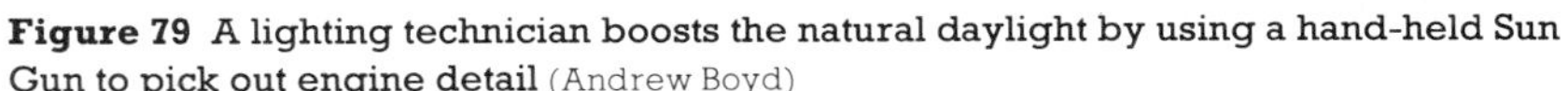

Figure 79 A lighting technician boosts the natural daylight by using a hand-held Sun Gun to pick out engine detail (Andrew Boyd)

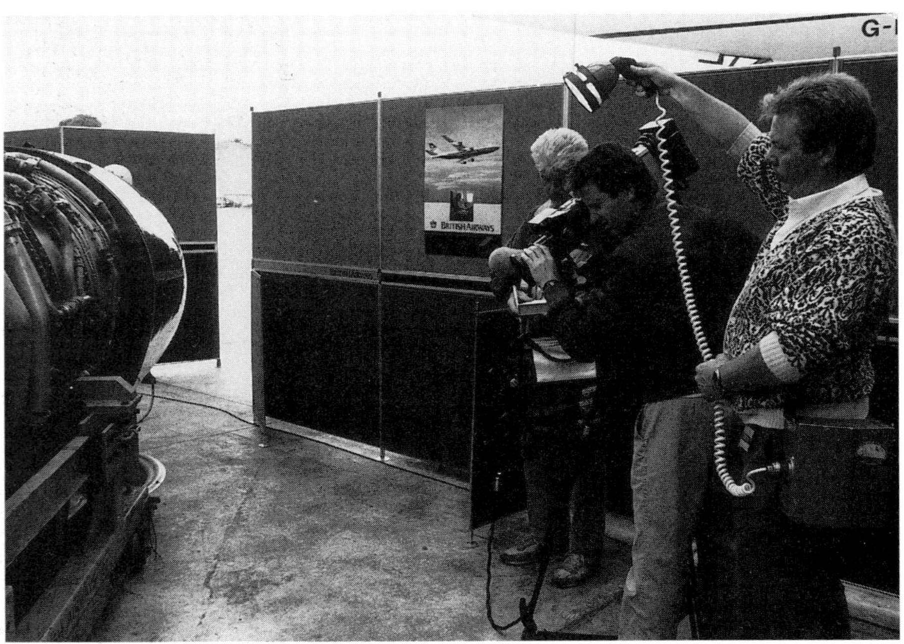

THE OUTSIDE BROADCAST
(Figure 80)

The outside broadcast (OB) no longer requires an operation on the scale of a military manoeuvre to get live pictures on the screen. In times past, even the most basic OB would tie up crowds of highly paid professionals and tons of expensive equipment. Thanks once again to ENG, that has begun to change. Live pictures can be sent anywhere across the world by a two-person crew.

But when it comes to televizing set-piece events with multiple cameras – particularly in the world of sport – then it is back to the full-blown OB unit.

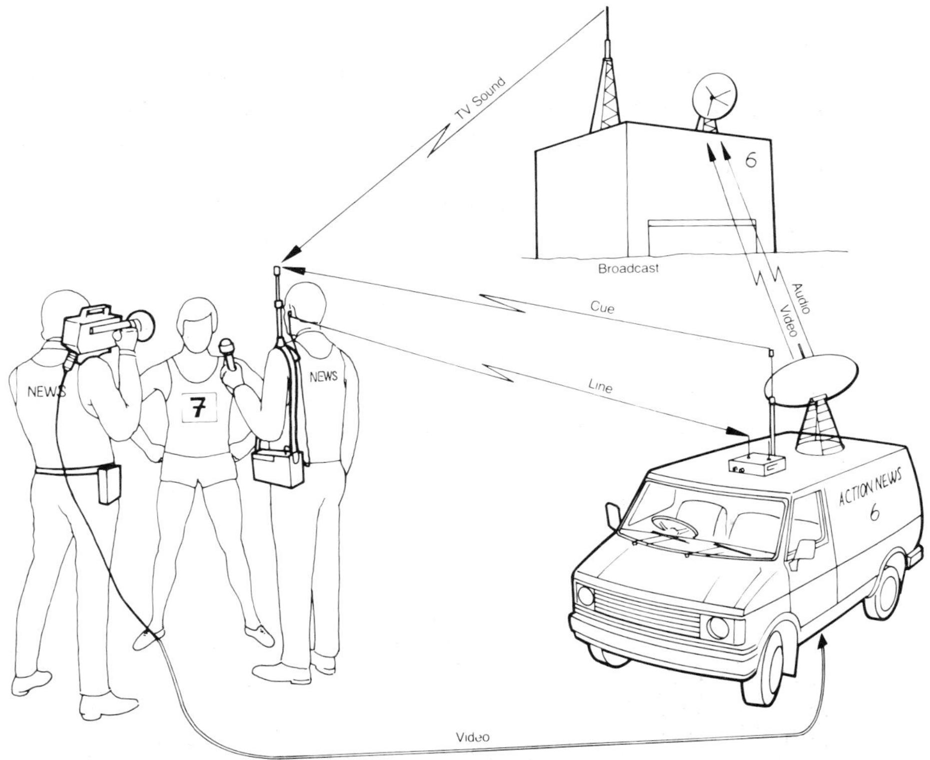

Figure 80 (*above*) Live broadcasting in action. The camera sends its signal by cable to the outside broadcast (OB) van. The reporter's sound signals are sent via a transmitter carried by the reporter and aerial strapped to his shoulder. Sound and vision signals are then beamed by microwave dish to a receiver at the TV station. The reporter can hear his report going out and receive his cues from the control room via another antenna on his shoulder (courtesy Sony Broadcast Ltd)
(*right*) Full-blown OB unit in action for ITN (courtesy ITN)

Figure 82 Portable ground-stations are used to beam news reports into space, where they are bounced off satellites and relayed to transmitters the other side of the world (courtesy ITN)

This is a complete mobile TV operation, minus only the studio set. Almost anything that can be done in a television studio indoors can be done on location.

The OB unit can comprise up to thirty people, several vehicles including a generator truck, and between three to five cameras, though news OBs – even the non-ENG variety – tend to be leaner, sleeker and built for speed.

At the heart of the unit is a large van, like a furniture removal van, called a *scanner*. This is a control room on wheels, with its own director/producer, engineers, vision mixers, bank of monitors for checking the action, and telephones for keeping in touch with the outside world and base (Figure 81).

The director has a talkback intercom providing spoken communications with all the cameraoperators. Their headphones have swing down microphones, so they can reply to his/her instructions.

Commentators will take their cues through hidden earpieces, if they are to appear in vision, or through headphones. Their microphones will also carry a talkback channel so they can reply to the director.

Outside broadcast commentators often work in crowded, noisy environments, so unless they are appearing on camera, they will use the same kind of lip microphones as their colleagues in radio to cut out unwanted background noise.

Incoming pictures, plus commentary and graphics, are relayed back to the TV station's master control room along a cable or microwave link.

For really big set-piece events, such as a royal wedding or state occasion, requiring multiple camera and commentary positions, several outside broadcast units will be combined.

GETTING THE STORY BACK

Rushing camera crews to an event and producing good pictures is only half the job. Newsgathering is not finished until those pictures are back at base being edited to go out on air. Every newsroom wants those pictures as soon as possible, and preferably half an hour ago.

On the rare occasions when there is time to spare and the story is breaking close to home, the crew will take their tape or film back with them for editing.

If a bulletin is approaching and the crew may have to stay at the scene, their videotape or film will be sent back by despatch rider. Some stations employ their own riders who form part of the camera crew's entourage, following them out and standing by until they are needed.

Film will have to be processed, which can take around forty minutes, but videotape recordings can be played back immediately. Raw tapes can be turned into polished reports in as little as a quarter of an hour by an editor back at base.

If time is very short, recordings will be sent back by microwave link. Microwaves transmit in a fine beam, like a pen-light torch. The narrow beam means transmitting and receiving aerials have to be lined-up very carefully.

A *links vehicle* is parked within line of sight of a receiving dish, which will be mounted as high as possible on a tall building or mast.

Links vehicles have masts stretching to 12 m or so to see over buildings. These can be adjusted by remote control from the vehicle.

An alternative to the microwave link is to send the signals along a cable but this is usually limited to short distances. Another option is to send the report by satellite. Satellite time has to be booked by the minute and is expensive but, increasingly, TV companies are buying portable ground-

Figure 81 Outside broadcast vehicles (scanners) are compact control rooms on wheels. Programmes are put together on location and beamed back to the TV station for transmission (courtesy ITN)

stations which can transmit pictures from the scene of the news up to a satellite which will then relay them back to base. This has opened the way for live pictures to be sent from previously inaccessible places (Figure 82).

Where access to a satellite is not possible from a particular country the report can be taken to another nation which does have a satellite link, or, failing that, it can be flown back. Where the crew have to stay in a country, and are not able to return with the film, this means finding a willing passenger to act as a 'pigeon'. He/she will escort the tapes or film back home, where they will be picked up at the airport by a TV company representative.

The era of instant communications does have its drawbacks. The shrinking world has opened the way for more news, tighter deadlines and faster travel to ever more remote regions, but one piece of bad news is that foreign reporting is not the plumb job it was. Spare time for reporters to relax and soak up the local ambience has been drastically reduced. With networks operating maybe four or five different news programmes a day, or providing 24 hour news – the pressure is constantly on for instant updates.

MASTER CONTROL ROOM

Master control can be likened to a glorified automatic telephone exchange, only instead of dealing with calls, it handles every signal coming into the television station, passing through it, and going out of it. MCR receives incoming reports from other television companies, both at home and abroad; it takes sound and vision from outside broadcast units, and receives feeds from remote cameras in key areas such as Parliament. It also maintains the quality of outgoing pictures.

FIELDWORK

1 If you can, practise using film and video cameras and compare the results. Which do you think offers the better quality picture?

2 Compare the advantages and disadvantages of film and video. Which do you think is more suitable for newsgathering/documentary making?

3 If you have access to lighting equipment, find a willing subject and practise using the three light set-up. Experiment by adjusting the position of the lights to get the best results.

4 Similarly, practise using a rifle mike on location. Do not forget to use headphones at the same time so you can monitor the results.

5 What kind of mikes would you use to record (a) an interview indoors with a single interviewee; (b) that same interview out of doors; (c) a discussion with a group of striking pickets; (d) an interview with someone on the big wheel at a fairground?

27 Camera shots

THE SHOTS

The camera is only a clumsy impersonator of the human eye, but with one important advantage – it can zoom in and out of a scene. But while we lack Superman's telescopic vision, each of us is acting like a movie director most of the time, for what the human eye lacks in mechanical facility is made up for by the mind, which zooms in and out of what the eye sees by concentrating on details or taking in the whole picture.

The TV camera imitates this with three shots which form the basis of all camerawork – *long shots*; *medium shots* and *close-ups*.

These expand into at least six different shots in everyday use. The following shows how they would be used for screening a person:

- The long shot (*LS*) takes in the whole person from head to feet.
- The medium long shot (*MLS*) cuts in closer, revealing the head to just below the knees.
- The medium shot (*MS*), reveals the head to the hips.
- The medium close-up (*MCU*) gives head and shoulders.
- The close-up (*CU*) shows head only.
- The big close-up (*BCU*) fills the screen with the features of the face.

Different news organizations may have their own names for these and will probably subdivide the categories further. Whatever you call them, the shots refer to the distance the subject is from the camera, and therefore how much of that subject fills the screen – long shots show the subject a long way off, while close-ups draw them nearer the viewer.

On location, where the camera is also taking in the surroundings, the long shot would give a view of the whole picture: the tanks rolling over the hillside, the burning building with the firemen in front, or the angry mob advancing.

Medium shots reveal more detail: the tank commander perched in his turret snapping instructions into his radio; a jet of water swallowed up by flames billowing from a top floor window; ringleaders urging on the mob.

The close-up focuses in on the action: the strain on the tank commander's face; the nozzle of the fire hose with spray bursting out; the wild eyes of the mob leader.

Another shot used commonly for scenes rather than people is the *general view (GV)* or *very long shot* (*VLS*) which gives a panorama of the entire scene.

Figure 83 This report of a ministerial visit to war-torn Ulster reveals most of the basic camera shots.

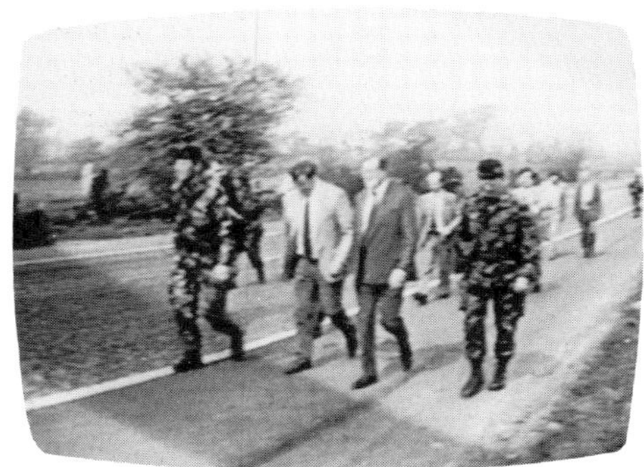

1 very long shot;

2 long shot;

3 medium long shot;

4 medium shot;

5 medium close-up with super (titles);

6 close-up;

7 graphic combining video still with electronic map and supers
(1–6 courtesy ITN; 7 courtesy BBC)

Local TV stations will have a stock of GVs showing important buildings such as hospitals which feature regularly in the news. You can choose your camera shots by running the sequence through in your mind's eye and deciding which shots would go best together.

CAMERA POSITIONS

Another set of shots describes the relative height of the camera to the scene:

- The *top shot* gives a bird's eye view.
- The *high shot* looks down on the scene from the front.
- The *level shot* is in line with the subject's eyes.
- The *low shot* has the camera looking up.
- The *low-level shot* takes a worm's-eye view of the world.

Single shots, two shots, three shots and *group shots* relate to the number of people in vision.

As well as zooming in and out the camera can crank up and down (*elevate* and *depress*), it can be moved backwards and forwards (*track*), sideways (*crab*), swivel (*pan*) and tilt (*cant*).

Zooming, tracking, panning and canting tend not to feature too largely in a single news report, which would prove impossible to edit and bear more than a passing resemblance to some obscure psychological 'B' movie from Eastern Europe.

SEQUENCE OF SHOTS

Edited camera shots should cut from one to the other smoothly and logically and follow a train of thought. If this rule is broken, the images that result are likely to be jerky, unrelated and confusing and will detract from the story.

Every change of scene or sequence has to be properly set up to register with the viewers. Long shots are often used as *openers* or *establishing shots* to set the scene.

We see the angry mob advancing and get an idea of the scale of the disorder. As we begin to wonder who the trouble makers are, a medium shot cuts in to reveal the ringleaders striding ahead and urging on the crowd. They look wild and unstoppable. As though to confirm our fears, the close-up picks out the crazed expression on the face of the leader.

Rearrange the sequence of these shots and you remove the context and offer the viewer more questions than answers.

Begin with the close-up and you have no idea of the scale of the disturbance; cut then to the long shot and the action appears to be moving backwards. Unless you cut progressively and smoothly – like the human eye – the logic of the sequence will be destroyed. **It is easier to follow the action if the close-ups and long shots are bridged by medium shots.**

SHOT LENGTH

Every shot should say something and stir up interest. The moment a shot has delivered its message and its appeal begins to wane, it should be cut. Action and movement generally hold interest longer than static shots. The pace is kept up if the cuts are made on movement.

How long you should hold a shot depends on a number of different factors:

- The instinctive decision by the editor about what the shot is 'worth.' Four seconds may capture the action. Five seconds may linger too long. Three seconds may 'feel' right, slipping into the overall rhythm of the item, or the shot may be cut to deliberately vary that rhythm with a change of pace.
- Shot length may be determined by the length of the sound bite. Here, a long quote need not dictate using the same visual of the speaker throughout. If visual interest wanes the editor can switch to another picture, while the soundtrack continues to run beneath. This may be a *reversal*, showing the reporter and the interviewee together, or a visual chosen to illustrate the subject under discussion.
- Where visuals are being matched to the script, the shot will be cut to fit the section of narrative.
- If the scene includes a pan or a zoom it could be difficult to cut. The shot will need to be taken in three parts. It should establish itself before panning or zooming, and then be permitted to settle down. Lingering on the establishing and closing shots effectively gives you three shots in one.
- Shots may be held to allow them to be dissolved into one another, as the extra length creates space for the overlap.
- Where the shot contains so much detail that it becomes impossible to take in at a glance, the editor may hold the picture for a while to let the scene register or give viewers time to read words on banners or placards.

The most obvious place for a change of shot is at the beginning of a new sentence or paragraph. This has a certain logic but can soon become stale and repetitious. You can provide welcome relief by illustrating a single sentence with a number of different shots.

Long sequences can be broken up with general views of related subjects. A longish commentary on the space programme could be relieved by adding shots of the space centre, technicians working, employees walking, over the soundtrack of the commentary.

The action can be brought closer to the viewer by using *insert shots*. These are the close-ups of the clenched fists, marching feet, spinning tyres, etc.

When it comes to editing, shots like these are called *overlays* because they are laid over the existing soundtrack. They should only be added once the soundtrack has been cut to its final length, otherwise they would have to be retrimmed to fit.

GRAB ACTION SHOTS FIRST

In a four-bedroomed house in a well-heeled suburb of town a cornered gunman is holding a wife and her five year old child hostage after they disturb him burgling their home. The TV crew gets there as a fresh wave of police reinforcements arrives at the scene.

This is no tidy, set-piece predictable story like a conference, where the crew will try to take pictures in the order they will appear in the final report. *Editing on camera*, as this is called, saves time and makes it easier to put together the item, but is often impossible with breaking news.

But at a shotgun siege or other fast moving story the cameraperson becomes the hunter; his task is to '*shoot it quick before it moves*', to capture the moment before it disappears.

After establishing with a glance that the gunman is out of sight and regrettably cannot be filmed, the cameraperson quickly grabs a long shot of armed police piling out of their vehicles and taking up positions behind parked cars.

Like the shots which come later of the gunman firing wildly from behind the curtain, and the police teargas driving him from the building, these pictures can never be repeated; they have to be grabbed while they are available.

The interview with the police chief, close-ups of his men and shots of the housefront can wait until a lull in the action. The temporary shots – shots that will go away – are filmed first.

SHOOT FOR IMPACT

Pictures which have the greatest impact are those which capture the action at its height. The sports photographer will try to snap the ball going through the posts or the batsman being caught; the news photographer will go for the champagne smashing against the side of the hull, or the ribbon parting the moment it is cut.

TV is the same, but the moving picture sequence takes the viewer up to the point of action and follows it through.

News is about action and change, so news cameras should be looking for things that are moving or are in the process of change – a new printing press whirling into action, the ship going down the slipway, the plane taking off or landing.

CONTEXT

There is more to most news stories than high drama and fast-moving action. Just as important are the reasons behind the drama; the consequences of it; its effect on people.

A major criticism of TV news is that by featuring the short scuffle with police or single ugly scene during a three-hour picket viewers are left with the distorted impression that the whole demonstration was violent or unruly.

This is where it becomes vital for the reporter to explain the context of what has been shown and to screen other shots offering a clearer, more normal representation of the event.

Reporters have to bear in mind how they plan to construct their report when they start calling the shots to the cameraperson.

With the siege there are five phases: the build up of police; attempts to negotiate; the gunman's violent response; police action to overpower him, and his arrest and the release of the hostages.

Shots should be picked to illustrate each phase of the story and the main points within each phase.

News is about events that affect people, and the most powerful way to bring home the impact of the story is to show its effect in human terms, and that means focusing on the people the item concerns.

PICTURES SHOULD COMPLEMENT THE NARRATIVE

As well as recounting the action at the shotgun siege the reporter will want to talk about the police presence and illustrate the long anxious wait before the gunman is flushed out.

This could be done with close-ups showing the tension on the faces of the police and the worried looks of neighbours peering from behind their curtains.

If the husband has turned up at the scene, pictures of his anguish as he stands powerless on the sidelines will illustrate his harrowing experience more eloquently than any scripted reference to '*tension in the air*'.

After shots like those, to say, '*The atmosphere was tense while police waited for the chance to move in*' becomes redundant and trite. *Show* the tension. *Show* the police waiting, and either say nothing or enhance the pictures with information that develops the story rather than simply repeats what we have already seen.

A two minute TV report will probably contain fewer than 200 words. To say word for word what is blindingly obvious from the pictures would be wasteful as well as pointless. There are times when pictures should be best left to speak for themselves. The reporter's script should never repeat what the viewer can clearly see, but should clarify, contextualize and explain what is shown on the screen.

If film of an accident on the highway shows a tailback of traffic receding into the distance, do not repeat the visuals by saying: '*The queue of trucks and cars stretched back as far as the eye can see*'. Add to the visual information. Tell us, '*the tailback stretched for almost 8 km*', or better still: '*The accident brought traffic to a standstill for almost two hours.*'

SOUND

The sound of the story adds to the viewer's sense of being there.

At the siege, sounds of gunshots, barked instructions, sirens approaching, warnings through the loud-hailer, are all essential to the story, and the narrator should pause to let them come through.

Effects that are off-mike and fail to come out can be dubbed on later from the sound effects library, though the aim of this is to clarify rather than exaggerate the sounds that were there.

The microphone has an infuriating habit of amplifying stray sounds that the human ear would filter out. The trouble is, when those sounds are played back, the ear becomes almost perversely aware of them. It can be frustrating for the viewer, who can spend more time trying to work out where that mysterious '*chugga, chugga, chugga*' is coming from than in concentrating on the report.

There are three ways around this: turn off whatever is making the sound, do your filming elsewhere or show us at the start where the noise is coming from. A little background noise, where relevant to the story (such as a shipyard), adds atmosphere.

Even more important are the *sound-bites* (*grabs* – Australia), or interviews in the report. With TV's emphasis on pictures, these are likely to be shorter than those used in radio. The sound bite should encapsulate the main point of the argument; the strongest opinion or reaction.

Again there is a danger of distortion by over-emphasizing the already emphatic and polarizing a point of view, and this can only be eliminated by carefully explaining the context in which the remarks were made.

To cover the siege story, the reporter will want to interview the police chief, the husband, and any witnesses.

The camera will usually be set up to feature the interviewee in three-quarters profile, looking to one side and slightly towards the camera, as he answers the reporter's questions. The prerogative of addressing the camera directly is usually left to the reporter.

CUTAWAYS

Back to the siege and the reporter has just got the police chief to explain that he will use force if he has to, when the chief is interrupted by a call on his radio. After a brief conversation, he tells the reporter that police marksmen will shoot to kill if necessary.

The reporter wants to run both statements together, but decides to cut out the interruption on the radio, because it was garbled and largely irrelevant.

The difficulty here is that the police chief was standing in a different position when he made his second statement. If the two answers were edited together there would be an unsightly jump on the tape.

The reporter resolves to ask the chief to do the interview again, when another urgent message comes on the radio and he is called away.

The reporter has no choice. She has to go with what she's got. What she needs now is a *cutaway*.

In a radio interview the first and last sentences may be edited together, while the rest is discarded. Providing the editing is professionally done, no one will notice the join. But in TV, the join would be all too obvious. The sound may flow smoothly across the two sentences, but the picture would leap about the screen as the subject jerked in an instant from one position to another.

To cover the join, the original pictures either side of the edit are replaced with a different sequence. This is known as *intercutting*. The pictures shown should be of a related scene, such as the reporter nodding or an illustration of the speaker's remarks, which could be a shot of a police marksman with his rifle or the house under siege. The original soundtrack of the answers is retained, but the jump in the film or tape is covered by the new pictures.

Cutaways are necessary where the shots of the subject are similar. It may be possible to do without them when the cut is made from a medium shot to a close-up. The switch to a different type of shot may cover the jump.

Telescoping the action

Cutaways also serve to telescope time and drive the action forward.

Switching from our siege report to another story; a motorcade carrying a foreign head of state is approaching in the distance. The camera follows the arrival of the car and its motorcycle entourage for twenty-five seconds until it reaches the steps of the Parliament building. The cameraperson continues filming for a further nine seconds as the VIPs are escorted inside. This is more than is required for the report, and to telescope the action the editor decides to join the shot of the motorcade approaching in the distance, to the last twelve seconds of the cars pulling up and the VIPS bundling into the building.

The editor links the two shots with a cutaway taken earlier of a clutch of armed guards scanning the crowds for the first sign of trouble. Another which would have worked was an earlier picture of the fenced-off crowds straining to catch sight of the approaching motorcade. These are related to the original scenes and tell us something new about them.

Reverses

Cutaways of the reporter are known as **reverses**. These are used when the report is being made with only one camera, which is trained on the interviewee. Where two cameras are used they shoot across one another to film each person in three-quarters profile.

A common reverse is the *noddy* where the reporter is filmed after the interview appearing to be listening hard to the interviewee and nodding. Care has to be taken otherwise it can look as though the reporter is supporting the interviewee's point of view. On controversial issues, instead of nodding, the cutaway may be of the reporter listening intently – a difficult piece of acting to portray convincingly.

Another common reverse is the *two shot*, where the camera pulls out to show the reporter and her subject. This is often shot from behind the interviewer and over her shoulder where the camera cannot see the mouth moving, so the picture can be cut over the soundtrack of the interviewer's question without appearing to be out of sync.

Reporters may also re-voice their questions to camera after the interview, and use one of those as a cutaway. To help remember the exact wording they may have taped the original interview on a small cassette recorder tucked out of sight of the camera.

Some news organizations believe there are ethical problems with cutaways. By using them deviously, the reporter could reassemble the interview in any order she liked to produce whatever effect she desired. Re-voiced questions may also differ in tone or content from the original to give a distorted impression.

> *'[The aim of editing is to] produce a clear and succinct statement which reflects fairly, honestly and without distortion what was seen and heard by our reporters, cameras and microphones.'* – CBS NEWS, USA

CBS lays down in its news standards that reverse shots are to be made in the presence of the interviewee if he/she requires, and the producer should compare questions asked in reverse with the originals to make sure there has been no distortion.

Some stations have a policy of not using cutaways at all, preferring to leave in the less slick, but more veracious jump cuts. Some take this further, insisting that edited answers are kept strictly in the order in which they were given in the interview. (See also a story is born, page 256.)

THE LINE

For cutaways the cameraperson will position the reporter so she seems to be looking at the interviewee. If they both appeared on screen looking in the same direction it would seem as though they were talking to a third person and not one another. TV people would say the camera had *crossed the line*.

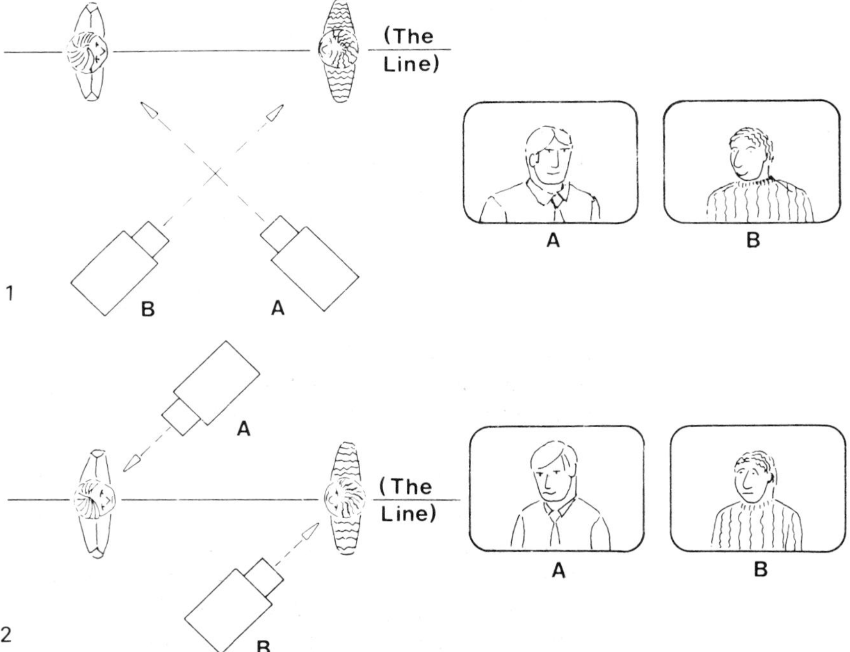

Figure 84 The line

1 Cameras are positioned to shoot across one another, showing each speaker in three-quarters profile. Providing neither camera crosses the line, when the speakers appear alternately on the TV screen they will be seen facing one another in conversation

2 If a camera does cross the line the speakers will be shown facing the same way, as though talking to someone else off-camera. The impression of conversation will be broken

The *line* is an imaginary border separating the two people. Providing the camera doesn't cross it, it can move anywhere and the two will appear to be facing each other in conversation. As soon as the line is crossed, the two will face the same way and the illusion will be broken (Figure 84).

The line has to be observed with action shots as well. Returning to our earlier example of the advancing tanks, if the cameraperson films them from one side, then crosses the column to film the other, the intercut shots will show the tanks advancing first in one direction and then turning tail and retreating. Crossing the line seems bizarre to the viewer because it is as though the observer of the scene has shifted rapidly from one viewpoint to another.

Where you have to cross the line, the switch in direction can be disguised with a *buffer shot*. The camera can stand in front of the moving object and show it coming towards it, or pan to show the object approaching and then passing.

CONTINUITY

Edited reports have a way of telescoping time which can play tricks on the unwary reporter. Someone may be filmed in a long shot wearing a hat, and again three minutes later in close-up without it. During that brief interlude he may also have loosened his tie, removed his jacket, put on his reading glasses, taken the nearby phone off the hook and closed the curtains behind him.

Cut those two shots together and the effect would be interesting, if not weird. At the very least it would distract from what he was saying. Always keep a weather eye open for good continuity.

PIECES TO CAMERA

Most reporters like to enhance their reports – and their reputations – by appearing on camera from time to time.

Figure 85 A reporter does a piece to camera in the fillings fields of Kampuchea. The dramatic dropback tells the story every bit as eloquently as the reporters' own words. Always make the most of the background in stand-up shots (courtesy ITN)

Figure 86 Prompting on location, with a lightweight, hand-operated, battery powered roller prompter (courtesy EDS Portaprompt)

(Figure 85) These shots, known as *pieces to camera* (or *stand-ups* or *stand-uppers*) usually feature the reporter standing in front of the scene in question. If this is a carnival with lots of colour and movement, there is no excuse for the kind of stand-upper which has a blank wall in the background. This has been described as 'execution photography', where the reporter is put up against a wall and shot! The action should be used as the backdrop. It adds variety and shows audiences that the TV station goes where the news is – to the war zone, fire or factory opening – that its reporters are out and about.

The piece to camera may be used at the beginning of an item to set the scene, in the middle to act as bridge linking two threads of the story and at the end as the reporter's way of signing-off; TV's equivalent of radio's standard out-cue.

Stand-uppers are usually short – their static nature can slow down the action and the reporter's memory may not be very good! Memory aids include a clip-board judiciously held out of camera, key words chalked on the ground, even a portable prompter which can be set up beside the camera (Figure 86).

Another useful trick is to write the commentary and record it on a portable cassette recorder. You can listen back to it through a concealed ear piece and take your prompt from that.

If none of these solutions is available and there is too much to remember in one take, the commentary may be split over two takes and joined by cutting from a long shot to a close up.

At times the reporter may have to voice the entire script on location. This can happen when the deadline is close and film or tapes have to be rushed back to the studio by despatch rider.

Where *voice-overs* (*VO*) are to go over natural sound on film or tape, the VO should be made in a quiet location such as a hotel room or inside a car. If they are to go over a portion of silent film, then the background sound in the VO should closely match the sounds behind the stand-upper or other items, to prevent a stop-start effect in the background. This may mean recording the VO in the same location.

PLANNING – THE FULL TREATMENT

Full scale planning is a luxury increasingly reserved for the world of TV current affairs. This differs from news in four respects: subjects are usually covered in more depth, larger crews are required to put the longer items together, there is more time at their disposal, and more detailed planning of coverage is necessary if television's expensive resources are to be allocated as efficiently as possible.

A documentary crew will include a field producer or director whose job it will be to plan and supervise filming. Camera crews will be given a scheme to work from and will rely less on shots taken 'on the hoof'.

A researcher will be despatched in advance to investigate the subject, explore locations, arrange interviews and gather background material. From the researcher's findings a draft script will be prepared listing the main shots that will make up the programme. This is the *treatment*. Plans might change later, but the treatment offers a route map to show where the team is starting from, where it is heading, and how it plans to get there.

Producing a treatment gets your ideas out in the open where they can be examined instead of waiting until you start filming to find they do not work. Once they are on paper they can be knocked into shape. Anything that has been left out can be added, sidetracks can be sidestepped and blind alleys avoided. You can also see if you've got enough good ideas to sustain a programme.

In *On Camera*, Harris Watts* draws up a simple formula for preparing a treatment. His advice is to decide what you want to say and what pictures you want to go with it. Jot down the headings the programme will follow, with visuals on the left and commentary on the right. Allow fifteen seconds for each point and a little longer for points made by interviewees. Add something for opening shots, scene setters and pictures with no narration. Cutaways shown over existing narration will take no extra time. Work out the duration for each sequence of the programme and aim to run up to 25 per cent over length as the assembled programme will probably be tighter and more polished after it is trimmed down.

After the treatment, a shooting schedule will be drawn up to minimize time wasted dashing to and fro.

* BBC, 1984.

Every shot taken is listed on a *dopesheet*. News crews sometimes dispense with these under pressure of deadlines; instead the reporter will return with the tape and talk the editor through the footage. Even then the cameraperson will usually have made some record of his/her work, be it only a hastily scrawled note on the videotape box. For longer items, like a documentary, this information is vital if the team is to keep track of all the material.

Once the shooting is finished an *editing script* can be produced listing the takes that are to be included in the final programme.

FIELDWORK

1 Record a TV news programme and look at an interesting location report. Study the camerawork and note the different shots that are used (LS, MS, CU, etc.). Do they follow a logical order? Are there any examples of jerky editing? How could the sequence of shots be improved?

Now identify the camera positions (from top shot to low-level shot) and note how the camera was used. Do you think the cameraman could have been more adventurous? How? Note the length of each shot and discuss why each would have been cut to that length. How do the shot changes relate to the structure and rhythm of the commentary?

Which shots would you say had impact? Why?

2 How do the pictures and narrative compliment one another? Is there any point where the words simply repeat what the pictures were saying?

3 If there is a camera you can use, load it with film or tape and get out and about practising the different types of camera shot. Experiment with the camera positions as well.

4 Write up a forty-five second court story and practise doing a piece to camera in the open air without reading from your notes. (If you have not got a camera you can still try this – though I suggest using a microphone and recorder as props if you do not want the men in white coats to take you away!) Try memorizing the text first of all and recording it in two takes. Then try other improvised ways of prompting, including the cassette and earpiece method.

How difficult was it to remember your script? Which prompt technique did you find the most effective? Did you feel embarrassed about 'performing' in the open-air? How can you overcome that embarrassment?

5 If you are in a class and have access to equipment, find a news story to cover and then form a crew and produce a report. Do your planning in advance. Film in sequence and aim for a shot ratio of around 3:1. Do not forget your openers and cutaways. When you come to edit your report, work hard at getting shot lengths that suit the rhythm of the piece and keep interest. Write the commentary to compliment the pictures.

Compare your work with that of other crews in the class. What can you learn from one another?

28 Writing the script

'I was doing a story for the News at 5.45. I was so late back I had to do it live. You sit in a little booth behind the studios and as they broadcast the piece, when the pictures come up you read into a microphone off your printed script.

'Because it was such a last minute thing I had to scribble my script in pencil on the back of a couple of envelopes. I had one minute before the bulletin and mine was the lead story. With 30 seconds to go, somebody came in to check my headphones were on and everything was OK, and they slammed the door and my two envelopes were blown out beneath it.

'Then the newsreader went straight into my story, and I was sitting there thinking, "Oh, my God, I've got nothing, but I can't go out because they're starting the piece". So I started talking and my mind went into automatic. I was talking off the top of my head, trying to remember what I'd said, and it got to a stage where I almost repeated myself, but just managed to change the words around. When it was all over I signed off "Kim Sabido, ITN" and sat there gasping, with sweat pouring off me when this guy came in and said, "Why did you repeat yourself?" and I said, "because you blew my script under the door. Look, there it is . . . you're standing on it!" I just went to the bar and had a lot to drink.'

— ITN REPORTER KIM SABIDO

The first stage in compiling any report is to decide whether to write the script to suit the pictures, or to match the pictures to the script. Reporters differ in their opinions. Some argue that as TV is a visual medium, the pictures must come first.

Others will maintain the first job of a TV news report is to tell a story – the pictures merely serve to illustrate that story. Perhaps the truth lies somewhere in between. In practice, shot selection and script writing often take place together.

But where the script is to be written to the pictures, split-second timing is required to precisely match the spoken words with the images on screen. A shot list is produced giving details of the camera shots (GV, LS, CU, etc.) the subject and the duration of the shots. This gives reporters a clearer idea of what they are writing to. Once again, in the hectic world of the newsroom, the shot list may often be sacrificed for speed.

The shot list adds together the duration of all the pictures to give the cumulative time:

Shot	*Time*	*Cumulative time*
GV Crowds at demonstration	4 seconds	4 seconds
MS Police cordon	3 seconds	7 seconds
MS Crowd faces and banners	4 seconds	11 seconds
CU Leaders chanting	5 seconds	16 seconds
MS Policeman in riot gear	4 seconds	20 seconds
MS Crowd tries to break police lines, panning to	6 seconds	26 seconds
CU Demonstrator falling	5 seconds	31 seconds
LS Police vans appear with re-inforcements	4 seconds	35 seconds
MS Police charge	3 seconds	38 seconds
LS Crowd retreats, police pursuing	4 seconds	42 seconds

In forty-two seconds the reporter could cram in around 130 words – and that would have him/her speaking solidly throughout – but for dramatic shots like these the reporter's script should be deliberately sparse, pausing to let the pictures tell the story. Less than half the sequence will be taken up with narration.

THE CUE (LEAD, or LINK)

The cue is the writer's way of preparing the viewer for what is to come. It grabs the attention and shouts, '*Hey you! Listen to this. This is important, this is interesting. Let me tell you what happened . . .*' The lead is the bait, but once the viewer is hooked, the writer still has to play him in.

The bait may be made more appealing by dressing it up with a visual which illustrates the story. Newsreaders will not be expected to refer to that visual any more than they would be likely to say: '*in the piece of film coming up*', or, '*as you can see from these pictures*'.

Newsreaders may finish the cue before the report begins, or talk over the first few seconds of the establishing shot, providing they stop before anyone speaks on the report.

WRITING TO SOUND

Adjectives which describe what can be heard or seen on the screen are best avoided. Phrases like, '*screeched to a halt*', '*deafening blast*' or '*dramatic siege*' are unnecessary. If the screech of tyres and roar of the blast can be heard on air, then viewers will already know about it. If the sounds are not there, they will feel cheated or suspect the reporter of sensationalism. Likewise, viewers watching the siege will draw their own conclusions about the drama or otherwise of the incident.

Where the commentary has to pause for a sound-bite or effect, the reader will need a clear indication of when to break the narrative and when to take it up again. The pause will be indicated by a break in the script or the word *cue*. The reader will know when to resume the story either from the duration and the last words of the sound bite given in the script, or from a signal given by a *cue light* operated by the writer. The cue light should go on half a second before the commentary is due to begin to give the reader a moment to draw breath.

Effects which are to be played in live should be clearly noted in the script alongside the commentary with the precise times they should start and end, and copies of the script should be given to each member of the production team.

The line of script which leads into a sound bite is known as the *throw line*. A throw line which requires an immediate response may well be regretted when the script is narrated live. Even a moment's delay in the soundtrack will make it appear as though both the reporter and the speaker were lost for words:

> *'turning to the Prime Minister, the opposition leader shouted...* (silence)*'*
>
> **Better to say:** *'the opposition leader turned to the Prime Minister, and launched an angry attack.'*

That sentence ends on a downturn in the voice and does not leave us poised in mid-air waiting for what ought to follow immediately.

The throw line should never repeat what is about to be said:

> **not:**
> Reporter: *'The Home Secretary said the situation was dire...'.*
> Home Secretary: *'The situation is dire. It can't be permitted to continue...'.*
>
> **but:**
> Reporter: *'The Home Secretary said he had no choice but to intervene...'.*

Where names are given, the last mentioned name should belong to the face which is about to appear on screen. If we are cutting from the cue to an interview with Peter Smith the cue should *not* be:

> *'Peter Smith believes a rise in bus fares is now inevitable, as he explained to Alison Bell.'*

The sentence can be turned around or both names can be left out of the cue, unless one is newsworthy in its own right, or it is house style to give the reporter a name check. Names and titles can clutter and confuse, and are often better left to the caption generator. So our throw-line becomes the more streamlined and pointed:

> *'A rise in bus fares may now be inevitable...'.*

When Peter Smith has been on screen for about a second, his name will appear in the lower third of the picture, where it will linger for about four seconds and disappear. When the reporter appears on camera he/she will get the same treatment.

Where live commentary is to be added, care must be taken to avoid writing so many words that the film ends ahead of the commentary. Far better to have fewer words and be certain of pictures at the end of the report than to leave the newsreader mouthing a marvellous narration over a blank screen.

KEEP DETAIL TO A MINIMUM

Newspaper reporters tend to pack stories with as much detail as possible. Try that with the spoken word and you would lose your listeners before the end of the second paragraph. If the information is to sink in, the focus of the story has to be as tight as possible. Any unnecessary detail which would overload the listener has to be cut. Titles, places and geographical relationships should be dealt with by captions and graphics.

This rule applies equally to pictures. Too many snippets of film or different shots in a report will forcefeed the mind. Images may run through so quickly it can be impossible to take the information in. The viewer is left with the same sense of breathlessness that might come from listening to a presenter trying to read at 200 words per minute.

Visuals are to illustrate and clarify a report – not to add to the general clutter. A visual has to contain just enough information to get its message across in a few seconds. The fewer words, distractions and details, the better.

Television, like radio, is a medium of impression, not precision. Just enough should be said and shown to leave the viewer with a strong general impression of the story. Too much detail swamps the images and saturates the senses. Simplicity is the watchword if the audience is to retain what it sees.

SCRIPT LAYOUT

TV scripts are laid out differently from those in radio because they have to carry a lot more information. As well as the story, the TV script has to give details of camera shots, graphics and their durations.

TV stations lay out their scripts according to house style, but, for the sake of clarity, visual and narrative information is usually separated into two columns – visual on the left and script on the right.

The information in the left-hand column tells the director the visuals that will accompany the story. These are placed opposite the point in the narrative where the visuals begin.

For a *tell story* where only the newsreader appears in vision, his/her name will be given in the column at the start of the script:

ALASTAIR I/V:	Cricket now – and tomorrow England face a crucial test at the Oval, in their third and final encounter in the Cornhill Series against New Zealand. England can't win the series but if they can beat New Zealand in the Oval test, they can at least salvage a draw.

From ITN *News at One*

I/V is short for *in vision* and tells the director that the presenter should appear on camera at that point. Where the presenter is out of vision, *OOV* is written. Visuals used to illustrate a story are marked alongside the script showing clearly where each begins and ends:

PAULA I/V	Three top Indian officials have been suspended for failing to prevent this morning's assassination attempt on Indian Prime Minister Mr Rajiv Ghandi.
SLIDE (Ghandi)	/Mr Ghandi wasn't hurt in the attempt, which police say was carried out by a lone gunman with no political motive.
PAULA I/V	The Indian leader was attending a religious festival when the first shot was fired. Security guards assured him it was just a fire-cracker, but as Mr Ghandi left,/
STILL (caption) (B & W gunman – pistol ringed) (zoom in to pistol)	the gunman, hiding in bushes, fired again, using a home-made and wildly inaccurate pistol.
MIX TO STILL (B & W assassin arrested)	/Security men – the Black Cats – told Mr Ghandi it was a car backfiring. Mr Ghandi had to tell THEM he was being shot at. They acted quickly – the would-be assassin surrendered.
PAULA I/V	Officials in charge of Mr Ghandi's security have been suspended, pending a full inquiry into the attempt on his life.

The term *caption* is BBC jargon for a still photograph. *B & W* means the photograph is black and white.

Where the cue goes into a pre-recorded report, basic details of that report will be given in the video column at the foot of the script:

JACK I/V	A Hercules transport plane laden with food and medical supplies is now on its way to bring some much needed aid to Southern Sudan.
CAPTION (Map)	/The plane, which has been chartered by relief organizations, is heading for the famine-stricken city of Malakal.

MIX TO ENG: 2

IN WORDS: 'Despite warnings that . . .'

SUPERS: TUNNY 35″
MALAKAL 1'02″

OUT WORDS: Sign off

TIME: 1'22″

Mix to ENG: 2 tells the director the report will appear on ENG (video-cassette) machine no.2. *Mix* is an instruction to dissolve from the graphic of the map to the report, so one picture gives way to the other.

The *in words* are the first words on the report, which can be referred to to make sure the correct report is being played.

Supers are the captions and titles which are inserted live. The times given show the time from the start of the report when those supers should be displayed. They will usually be left on screen for a few seconds and faded out.

Out words are the last words in the report so the director knows when to cut back to the newsreader; in this case it is a sign off, or standard out-cue, such as '*This is John Tunny, for the 6 o'clock News in Malakal.*'

The *time* gives the length of the report. Some stations prefer to give the *running time* (R/T) which indicates how long the programme should still have to run after the present report is completed. This gives the director an instant point of reference to see whether he/she is running ahead or behind and needs to pad or drop an item.

When a reporter is writing a script to fit visuals that have already been edited, which can happen when a live studio voice-over is required, the details of each shot may also be marked alongside the script. Cues show the time from the start of the report when the reader should commence reading that part of the script:

POLAND/FILEY	***6 O'CLOCK NEWS***	***Mon. Sept. 21***
CUE 02″		
N/READER OOV	*SUPER*	*/More than 50,000 people gathered from*
(LS crowds)	*Czesto-chowa 2″*	*throughout Poland in the biggest display this year of public support for the banned trade union, Solidarity.*
CUE 10″		*/This outdoor mass at the Czestochowa*
(GV crowds at monastery)		*monastery follows the release /last week*
(MS crowd with banners)		*of nearly all the country's political prisoners in an amnesty.*
CUE 18″		*/Solidarity leader Lech Walesa talked*
(MS Walesa with leaders)		*privately with newly released underground leader, Zbigniew Bujak, but made no public speeches.*
MS Walesa/SOT 25″ *IN: 'We will have . . .'* *OUT: 32″ '. . . to the church.'* *CUE 34″*		
N/READER OOV		*/But today the church nailed its colours to the mast yet again, describing the 225 released*
(MS priest)		*under the amnesty/ as 'prisoners of*
LS Crowd SOT 44″ *(Actuality applause)*		*conscience.'*
CUE 48″		*/It's understood the Solidarity leadership has*
(MS Walesa and Bujak)		*been discussing whether the banned union should continue to operate underground/ or*
(CU Walensa)		*risk a new wave of imprisonments by conducting its affairs in the open.*
MS PIECE TO CAMERA SOT 59″ *IN: 'Top of the . . .'* *OUT: sign off.* *R/T: 1'21″.*	*SUPER: Filey 1'00*	

Cues are given after a pause to let the pictures or soundtrack speak for themselves.

The contents of the sound-bite or piece to camera would not be included in the script, as these would have been recorded beforehand, but are given below to make sense of the story:

Walesa: *'We will have a statement, but not here and now because we don't want to cause any harm to the church.'*

Reporter: *'Top of the agenda for Solidarity's leaders will be whether the union should continue to work underground or conduct its affairs like today's mass – out in the open. And tied up with that will be a renewed campaign to get Solidarity legalized and recognized – and to pave the way for other trades unions to be established in Poland.*

'This is Alison Filey for the 6 o'clock News in Czestochowa.'

As Filey is reporting on location, her piece to camera would show the crowds assembled for the mass with the monastery buildings in the background.

BALANCING WORDS WITH PICTURES

> *'Too much broadcast journalism tells me what I can already see, it doesn't tell me what it's about. The writing has to explain what you are seeing.'* – HARRY RADLIFFE, LONDON BUREAU CHIEF, CBS NEWS

Some reporters like to run the first and last scenes of their reports a little longer to give the opening pictures time to establish and to let the closing shots leave an impression.

Another good reason for leaving a couple of seconds at the start of the film before beginning the commentary is in case the report is put on air slightly late. If you look back to the Poland story above, the opening shots last two seconds longer than the narrative.

When it comes to switching scenes, note that some fresh shots appear at the beginning of a sentence, while others change in the middle. Where that happens, if you read that sentence out loud, you will see the new shots follow the rhythm of speech by coming in during a natural break.

The length of the shot may determine the number of facts that can be selected to accompany it. If all you have is a five second shot of troops scrambling up a hill towards a fortress, then it would not be possible to write:

Defying heavy machine gun and rifle fire from the troops inside the fortress, Afghan rebels laid down a curtain of smoke and clambered towards the summit.

9 seconds

Too long. One way to retain all that information would be to add a three second covering shot of the fortress at the beginning – if one were available. Failing that, the script would have to be rewritten to length:

	Under heavy fire, Afghan rebels laid down a curtain of smoke and clambered towards the fortress. 5 seconds

Occasionally, a shot will be so good that it begs to run a little longer than the script might require. Such a shot should speak for itself, or be complemented with useful additional information:

LS seamen running up Jolly Roger on ferry 9 seconds	The men made it crystal clear they had no intention of handing back the ferry. 4 seconds
Better:	The crew's response to the company's demands came almost immediately – [pause] No mistaking the message of the skull and crossbones. 9 seconds

The rewritten version fills the time while letting the visual speak for itself by pausing to let the message of the Jolly Roger sink in.

Stations which use prompting machines will type the story in large capitals on a narrow strip of paper for feeding into the machine, or will key the story into a computer which will automatically display it in a narrow column on a monitor screen.

Some reporters prefer narrow scripts which keep the copy to about three words per line. Each line then represents about one second of speech and the process of timing becomes simpler.

Different coloured copies of completed script are handed out to all the staff involved in the programme.

USING THE LIBRARY

Most TV stations have their own libraries to provide a back-up service for reporters. The library will keep an archive of valuable footage and stills to illustrate and enhance reports, as well as reference material to help with research.

Cuttings are kept of newspaper stories dating back several years. To save space, these are often photographed, reduced in size, and stored on microfiche – transparent folios which can be read with the aid of a special magnifier.

Cuttings may also be cross-indexed by subject, so a reporter wanting to find out about, say, accidents in the nuclear industry, can get speedy access to all the material that has appeared in the papers on that subject dating back as many years as he/she wants.

The library may also offer access to large computerized databases such as World Reporter, which store millions of words from many international newspapers and magazines. A powerful research tool – but costly to use.

Background information not found in cuttings or on database may be available in the library's reference section, where books will be on hand listing such information as the names and personal details of members of Parliament or Congress, background on companies and corporations, or census material showing changes in the population and social trends. Regional TV libraries will also file and index the local newspapers.

Research aside, the library plays an important, though seldom appreciated, part in the final report which will appear on air. Archive footage, slides, useful graphics and black and white agency photos are usually stored to provide extra illustrations for reports. (For more details, see also film library, page 323.)

> *'On one occasion we were looking for some lively material on the SALT talks [Strategic Arms Limitation Talks], and we went through our library and couldn't find it anywhere, and then someone uncovered it under the heading of Food and Drink.'* – UK NEWSREADER MARTYN LEWIS*

FIELDWORK

1 Rewrite the following TV throw-lines to tidy them up and give your reasons for any changes that you make:

'Our reporter George Frederick caught up with Peter Brown at the Opera House and first of all he asked him how much money the Opera House needed to keep going . . .'

'. . . the decision to expel them from the party was regrettable, but there was no alternative, as Mr Chadha explained to our reporter Gurinda Bhattacharaya . . .'

'In an angry outburst, Mrs Stellar said the voting had been rigged, the results were loaded, and her contempt for the judges was absolute. She called them all a . . .'

2 Working on the principle of keeping detail to a minimum, find a hard news story in a newspaper – the more complex the better (financial story, perhaps?) – and attempt to boil it down to its bare bones. Jot down headings of the crucial points. Then write up the story in just ninety words.

If you are in a class, call for two volunteers who are not familiar with the story. Get one to leave the room, while you read your version of the story out loud to the other. Without seeing your script he/she is to write up the main points of that story in thirty words or less.

Call the other in and give him/her the newspaper version of the story. Without conferring, he/she is then to boil that down to thirty words.

When they have both finished, compare versions. Do they sound like the same story? Do they differ in substance or detail? If so, why? Do both versions retain the important points of the story? If not, why have some been left out? Were some important points left out of the original ninety word rewrite? Discuss the differences.

* *It'll Be Alright on the Night*, London Weekend Television

3 Record and watch a TV news programme. Do not make notes, do not confer, and do not read the next paragraph until you have finished watching the programme and half an hour has passed.

Now, without discussing it with anyone, list all the stories in the order in which they appeared, and describe the main points of each story in thirty words or less. (Thirty words per story.)

Then try to recall the pictures and graphics that accompanied those stories.

Now watch the programme again and see how good your memory was. Did you get the order of the items right? Were your summaries of the items accurate? What did you find easier to remember, the pictures or the commentary? Could you remember the graphics? Compare how you got on with other members of the class and discuss what made some items more memorable than others.

4 Now find another newspaper report of a strong news story and turn it into a TV script. Break it down into its component parts and decide what treatment to give the story – which pictures you would want to take and which of the interviews in the write up you would want to include. Think also about graphics and illustrations and any pieces to camera. Aim for a duration of one minute and twenty seconds and produce a full two-column script for your report. Take care not to repeat in your narrative what you plan to show in your pictures.

5 Now do some research so you can find out what tools are available to you. Working on your own and using a library as your main source, find out the following (*use the telephone only as a last resort*):

(a) The population of your electoral boundary (both local and national government).
(b) The numbers of abortions that took place in your region during the past year.
(c) The phone numbers of any prisons in your area and the names of the governors.
(d) The name of the Bishop of your area (or other religious leader, if applicable) and how you would address him.
(e) The title of the company that employs the most people in your area, the number it employs and the name and phone number of the managing director.
(f) The name of the *previous* Mayor or Council Leader in your area and details of his/her history in active politics.
(g) The date and brief details of the last major aircraft hijacking to happen anywhere in the world, with the name of the organization responsible.

When you have finished compare your answers with others in your class and swap notes about how you got that information.

29 Editing videotape and film

Writing the script is only half the story. Once the crew is back from location their raw tapes or films have to be edited, library pictures sought and graphics or captions added. This section deals with the mechanics of editing videotape and film and compiling the report.

Figure 87 News reports are put together in the editing suite. The videotape editor (left) shares a lighter moment with newsreader Martyn Lewis. Note the Ampex VTR on the left and the edit controller in the centre (courtesy ITN)

EDITING VIDEOTAPE

The tape

Videotape bears a family resemblance to its audio cousin, but has to work considerably harder. It carries a good deal of information besides the picture: it also stores the soundtrack, cue information for editing, and control information for the *videotape recorder* (VTR). All this is stored on four different tracks.

The video signal is scanned by up to four heads mounted on a revolving drum, which flies rapidly past the tape, reading it at an angle. Editing machines can search for a picture at up to thirty times normal speed and can freeze a frame indefinitely.

Alongside the picture heads are audio heads which erase, record and play back the soundtrack. Another set of heads deals with the cue and control information. Some machines offer hi-fi stereo sound and others record digitally for even higher quality.

The tape editor

The job of assembling different video shots to make a report usually falls to a specialist tape editor, though in some small operations the camera-person or reporter may be required to do his/her own editing.

Unlike film editing, there is no actual cutting involved. Tape editing takes place by re-recording (*dubbing*) pictures from one tape to another until the final report is complete.

The original tape is viewed by the reporter and editor. The shots they decide to use are dubbed in sequence on to a master tape. Shots such as the reporter nodding can be inserted later by dubbing over the top of existing shots. This is called an *insert edit*.

The editing suite

(Figure 87)

The action takes place in an *editing suite* (or *videotape booth*) which contains a lot of expensive hardware. Along with the VTRs and possibly VCRs (*videocassette recorders*) will be an *edit controller* to make the edits, a *vision mixer* to blend scenes together, an *audio mixer* for handling the soundtrack, a *talkback system* for speaking to personnel around the building, and a bank of monitors, including one for each video machine and others for looking at graphics and watching station output.

The timer

Superimposed on the pictures is a *time code*, which is a special clock for timing the edits. This counts the number of hours, minutes, seconds, and frames which have elapsed since the start of the report. British TV works on twenty-five frames per second; US and Canadian TV operates on thirty (see Figure 90).

The editing process is quick and clean and usually carried out with the aid of the ubiquitous microprocessor.

The *rushes* – unedited tapes – are run through back and forward in fast and slow motion, freezing frames for closer scrutiny, until the editor decides the exact scene he/she wants to use in the report.

The chosen sequence might begin at 00.16.25.21 (zero hours, 16 minutes 25 seconds and 21 frames), and end just under 11 seconds later at 00.16.36.09.

The edit controller

These timings are logged in the edit controller, which puts pulses on the cue track of the videotape at the beginning and end of the sequence.

It then automatically dubs that sequence on to the master, starting the recording at the first pulse and ending it at the second. (See also page 261.)

Editors can then check that sequence through on the monitor. If they do not like it, they can take it again. The rushes are not recorded over, so the original scene is always there for a re-take.

Video mixing

The above process describes a straight cut from one sequence to another. Dissolving one scene into another, by fading one out as the other fades in, or wiping one picture off the screen to reveal another, involves overlapping two separate images. This requires one VTR for each sequence and a third to dub them on to.

The tapes will be lined up, so the end of one scene overlaps the start of the other, and the vision mixer will be used to fade the first image down and fade the other up. A more sophisticated version of this, capable of a wide range of effects is used in the control room for mixing live TV programmes.

Next comes the sound mixing. Editors can handle the sound separately or with the video. They have three choices: using the audio and video together; the audio without the video; or the video without the audio.

Recording the commentary

By now the reporter is probably ready to record the commentary, which is made in an adjoining *commentary booth*. There the reporter has eye contact with the editor through glass and verbal contact on the talkback. As the reporter watches the report going out on a monitor, he/she reads the commentary into a microphone, and this is dubbed by the editor on to the soundtrack.

If the timing is out, they go back to the start of the last shot and take it again. The editor takes care to balance the reporter's voice over the natural sound on the tape (NAT SOF) so the commentary is never drowned out.

Audio mixing

As much care should be taken over the mixing of sounds as in the editing of the pictures. A cut from a busy street scene with roaring traffic to the near silence of a waving cornfield, or the acoustically dead atmosphere of a studio would be abrupt to the ear, so the soundtrack of the traffic will probably be allowed to continue for a second into the next shot, with the editor fading out the traffic gradually, as the natural sounds of the countryside are faded in.

Using the audio mixer, editors can keep the natural soundtrack if they wish, fade it down under the reporter's narration, fade two soundtracks together so they overlap like a vision mix, or supplement the natural sound with special effects. These come in handy if the sounds of, say, a police van pulling up outside a court building are off-mike or too quiet on the original tape.

The soundtrack should be faded up slightly in advance of the pictures and never permitted to lag behind them. When sound emerges before pictures it makes for a smooth transition from one scene to another, but a moment of silence after the pictures have begun seems very odd indeed.

The TV station will probably keep a bank of hundreds of audio cartridges of different effects which can be added to a report, ranging from oars splashing to explosions. These are being increasingly kept on compact disc or computer which offer a substantial improvement in quality. If time is short, effects will be played live from the sound control while the report is going out on air.

Graphics and other illustrations, such as captions, can be put in at the editing stage, or inserted live. (For more details, see graphics, page 323.)

PLAYING THE TAPE ON AIR

The video cartridge

The completed report, now wholly transferred to the master tape, can be played into the news programme live by the editor from the editing suite, or, time permitting, can be re-dubbed on to a video cartridge. The advantage of the cartridge is that it can be played back instantly at full speed, while VTRs need a pick-up time of several seconds.

Like so much of the equipment, the *automatic cartridge recorder* (ACR) is computer controlled. Cartridges are loaded into a carousel and can be fired at the touch of a button in a pre-programmed sequence, which can be altered at the last moment. The control room director will tell the operator over the talkback which report is required next, and the operator will key the name of that report into the computer. To put the report on air, all he/she has to do is press the play button at the director's command.

VTR playback

(Figure 88)

Reports which are too long to fit on a cartridge will be played in from a VTR or VCR. The tape will be wound back to display a countdown clock which has been recorded immediately prior to the report.

Usually five seconds before the report is due on air, the director will call the editor on the talkback and give the instructions, *'roll VTR'*.

The tape will be gathering speed while the cue to the story is still being read, and the operation will be timed to the second so the report begins the moment the newsreader finishes the last word of the cue.

Figure 88 The countdown clock is displayed on screen before the start of the report. The white block moves from left to right to show the tape is running. The figure in the centre counts down the seconds and the time code at the bottom counts up the hours, minutes, seconds and frames. When the time code reaches zero (24) the report will go on air (courtesy BBC)

EDITING FILM

The film

Compared with videotape, film is old technology. Editing is mechanical rather than electrical. But old does not necessarily mean bad. Years of development and roots that go beyond Hollywood have made film editing a highly refined art capable of producing what some would argue are still unrivalled results.

But before editing can take place, the film has to be developed and a print produced called the *rushes* (*workprint* or *cutting copy*).

As soon as the rushes return from the lab the film editor and reporter can get down to compiling the news item. Shots are run through a viewer and the ones intended for use are marked out. The remainder are known as *out-takes*. Never throw a shot away until you have finished editing – it just might come in handy.

The chosen shots are then joined together in the right order to form a *rough cut*. This is checked for content and length, then each shot is listed, giving its roll number (which batch of film it belongs to) shot number, take number, and possibly the subject, duration and soundtrack details. Armed with this *shot list*, the reporter or writer will go off and hammer out the script.

The rough cut is trimmed and tightened. 10 per cent or more can be shed in this way. Cuts are checked to see they flow smoothly from one to the other, that there are no jumps or jars, and that the eye is not snatched from the foot of the screen to the top.

The *final cut* is then returned to the lab where the original negative is cut to match it exactly.

Then the colours are improved (*graded*), and a new print is produced from the negative called the *answer print*.

This may be screened on air, or the lab may be asked to improve it again to produce a *showprint*. The process can take several days.

Reversal film is more commonly used for news, because it is faster to process. Original stock can be back from the lab within half an hour ready for transmission. The drawback is that the colour cannot be improved and any damage done to the master is permanent.

A way round this which takes more time is to edit a copy of the master and then cut the master to match. A showprint could be made to improve the quality further, but that would cancel out the time advantage of using reversal stock.

Different types of film

Of all the types of film in use, *silent* (*mute*) film is the easiest to edit. The editor runs the film through a viewer and marks out the parts he/she wants with a grease pencil. These are cut out and joined in the right sequence. The process is similar in principle to editing audio tape.

Silent film is often used with a separate soundtrack, recorded in synchronization with the camera. This is known as the *double system*, or *sepmag* (*separate magnetic*) because it uses a separate magnetic soundtrack. The sound recording is edited alongside the film, and cuts are made to match the cuts in the pictures.

For news coverage, sound and pictures are more commonly combined on the same film. This *single* system *(stripe)* or *commag (combined magnetic)* records the soundtrack on a magnetic strip alongside the pictures. This is favoured for news coverage because it offers faster results, although they may not be as good as with the separate system.

Editing sound on film

The problem with editing sound is that it is not possible to record sound and pictures side by side. The soundtrack is on a magnetic stripe running alongside the pictures, but because the sound recording head cannot occupy the same position as the camera's picture gate, the sound is recorded on the film *before* the pictures. Optical soundtracks in early single systems were recorded twenty-six frames in advance, and the more common magnetic soundtrack is recorded twenty-eight frames ahead.

Modern projectors and editing machines compensate for this by placing the sound head in front of the picture gate, so the sound and pictures are in synchronization.

Where that equipment is not available an out of sync soundtrack becomes very noticeable with speech. People may appear to speak without moving their lips, or move their lips without speaking. This is known as *lip-flap*. Lip-flap is less visible on long or medium shots, but more obvious with close-ups.

It can be hidden by switching to a second picture on another projector, such as a cutaway of a reporter or a long shot of the scene, before returning to the first projector. This process, where the soundtrack runs into a different scene is known as an *overlap cut*.

The double system

With the double, or sepmag system, sound is recorded on a separate recorder and transferred across the full width of magnetically coated film.

A *clapperboard* (*clapstick, clapboard US*) is used to synchronize pictures with soundtrack. The clapperboard is filmed with the arm coming down, and the soundtrack captures the crack that it makes. To synchronize pictures and sound, the editor simply lines up the clap of the board with the picture of the arm shutting.

Written on the clapperboard are details such as the title of the film, the names of the cameraperson and director, and the number of the shot and the *take*. A single shot may be filmed a number of times to get the best result. Each attempt is known as a take (Figure 89).

If it is not possible to record the clapperboard at the start of a shot, it can be filmed at the end. To make it clear it belongs to that shot and not the one that follows, the board is turned upside down.

To make doubly sure the film is matched to the correct soundtrack, the number of the shot and the take may be spoken into the mike before the arm of the clapperboard is brought down.

Where silence is required such as during the filming of an important ceremony or speech, the clap can be replaced by filming the recordist tapping the mike.

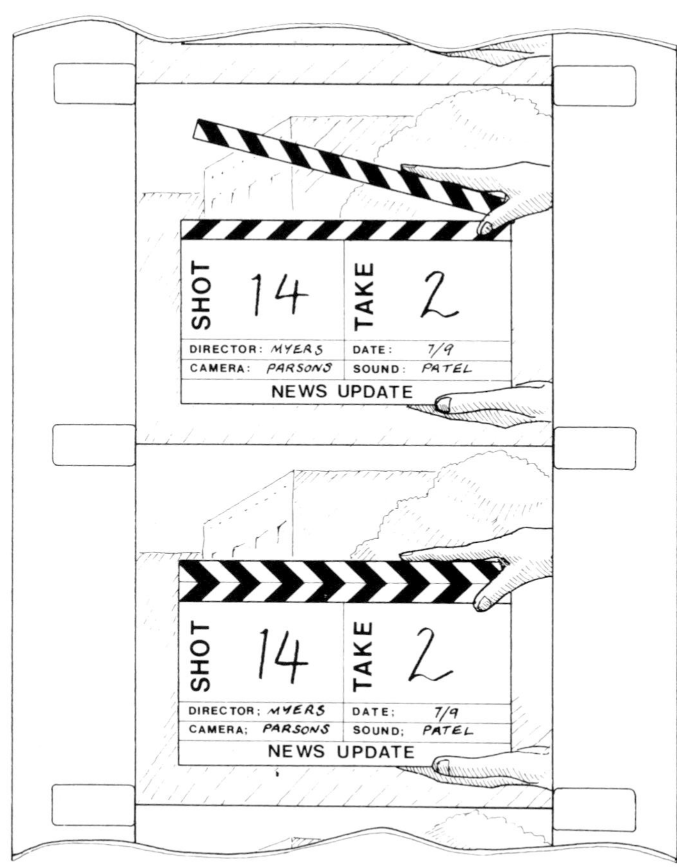

Figure 89 The clapperboard (clapstick). Details of each shot are chalked on for easy identification in the cutting room. The clap of the arm coming down is used to synchronize the soundtrack where film and soundtrack are recorded separately

An alternative to the clapperboard is a mechanism in the camera which generates a flash of light on the film and a synchronized bleep in the sound recorder.

THE FILM EDITOR'S EQUIPMENT

The enemy within

Next to time, the news film editor's worst enemy is dust. If you have ever had a set of photographs back from the developer's with scratch marks or blemishes on them, you will see why. Those same minute particles which caused the damage on large prints will wreak far greater havoc in a tiny 16 mm image. Great care is taken to keep dust and sharp edges away from film.

Editors will usually wear white cotton gloves to protect the film from them, and them from the film. Fingerprints can leave permanent marks and film edges can cut fingers.

Grease pencils are used to mark the film for editing, and these marks are wiped off with the cotton gloves before the film is spliced.

Sequences of film which have been cut out ready to be joined will be hung inside a *trim bin* which has been lined with cloth to prevent scratching. The film clips may be stuck to the rim with tape or hung over the bin on a wooden frame.

Edited film is wiped with film cleaner to remove stray particles.

The editing bench
(Figure 90)

An *editing bench* holds the film editor's equipment. The film is held vertically on reels for editing, or placed horizontally on a flat-bed editing machine such as a Steenbeck, Moviola or Kem. The editor watches the film as it passes through a viewer which magnifies it, or a projector which displays the pictures on a screen.

Editing machines allow pictures and soundtrack to be edited simultaneously. These are motorized and have a variable speed control.

The sound reader (pic sync.)
(Figure 91)

The soundtrack is dubbed from quarter inch audio tape on to magnetically coated film for editing. It is transported through a *sound reader* which plays it back through a loudspeaker. Modern sound readers are motorized to run the track through at projection speed, and can synchro-

Figure 90 The Steenbeck flatbed editing machine permits the editor to review the film on screen while listening to the soundtrack (Andrew Boyd)

Figure 91 The film synchronizer allows the film and up to three separate soundtracks to be cut to match one another. The tracks are cranked through the synchronizer by hand or drawn through by an electric motor. The editor views the film through the screen on the right, while the amount of film passing through the synchronizer is measured by counters in the foreground (Andrew Boyd) nize several different soundtracks at a time, which can then be put through a *dubbing mixer* to form a single track.

The sound reader will usually have a counter for timing the soundtrack in feet, or minutes and seconds.

Sound can be recorded magnetically, or optically using patterns of light on the film, which are read by a photo-electric cell. Some readers have optical and magnetic heads to play both types of sound.

Marking the edits
(Figure 92)

Trial edits are marked on the film using a grease pencil. Editors can see how the shot looks through the viewer before making the final cut. If they have second thoughts they can rub out the grease mark and try again.

The type of mark used will indicate the edits they intend to make.

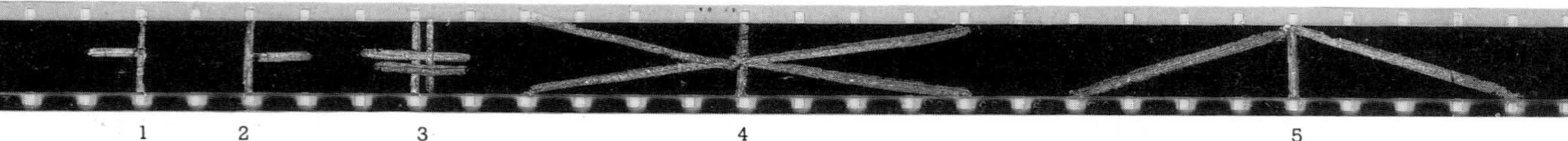

Figure 92 Film editing marks: 1 Cut film to left; 2 Cut film to right; 3 Ignore cutting mark; 4 Fade down and fade up; 5 Dissolve
Marks are made up with a chinagraph (grease) pencil and can be wiped clean

When the sections of film have been cut out for use they are hung by pegs, clips or tape in the trim bin. Each will be marked with a different number to show its place in the final sequence and a full record of each shot will be kept on a *continuity sheet*, giving details of shot type, subject, and duration.

Splicing
(Figure 93)

Sequences are joined together on a machine known as a *splicer* using film cement or transparent tape. Where cement is used, joins are made by overlapping the ends of the film.

Before cementing, the emulsion on the facing side of the film is scraped away where the overlap joint is to be made. Cement is applied with a brush, and the join is held by a clamp in a *cement joiner* until the cement hardens, which takes about fifteen seconds. A hot splicer can be used to speed up the process.

Leadering and cues

The film is leadered at the beginning with a leader incorporating a count-down sequence so the director knows exactly when the film is about to begin.

To offer some leeway in the timing, the film can be extended slightly at the start, so if the director goes on air too soon, the audience will see pictures instead of numbered leader tape. These extra pictures, inserted after the leader, are known as *buffer frames*.

Instructions to the director indicating when a sequence is about to end can be made by giving precise timings and verbal cues from the soundtrack, or marking the film with a *cue marker*, which removes a spot of emulsion from the corner of a number of frames. When the director sees the spot on the monitor, he/she knows the film is about to end.

Assembling the print For documentary work, where there may be time enough for a counsel of perfection, trial and error cuts will be made on a print of the film, and only when editing is completed will a blade be taken to the original, which will be cut to match.

When effects like dissolves or fades are wanted, the film negatives will be assembled on two rolls which are laid over one another in the lab to produce a single composite print. Dissolves are created by overlapping two film sequences over a required length.

The rolls are assembled by cutting out and numbering each scene and alternating it with black leader tape the same length as the scene that will follow. Scenes 1, 3, 5, 7 with leader in between are compiled on roll A, and scenes 2, 4, 6, 8, also leadered, go on roll B. This is called the *chequerboard* (*checkerboard* US) system, because if the two rolls were laid side by side they would create a chequerboard pattern. The edited soundtrack can then be added with illustrations, captions and effects.

The advantage of this system is that it hides splices. The disadvantages for news is that it gobbles up time.

Figure 93 Using a film joiner. Editors normally wear white gloves to protect their film from their fingers and their fingers from the film (Andrew Boyd)

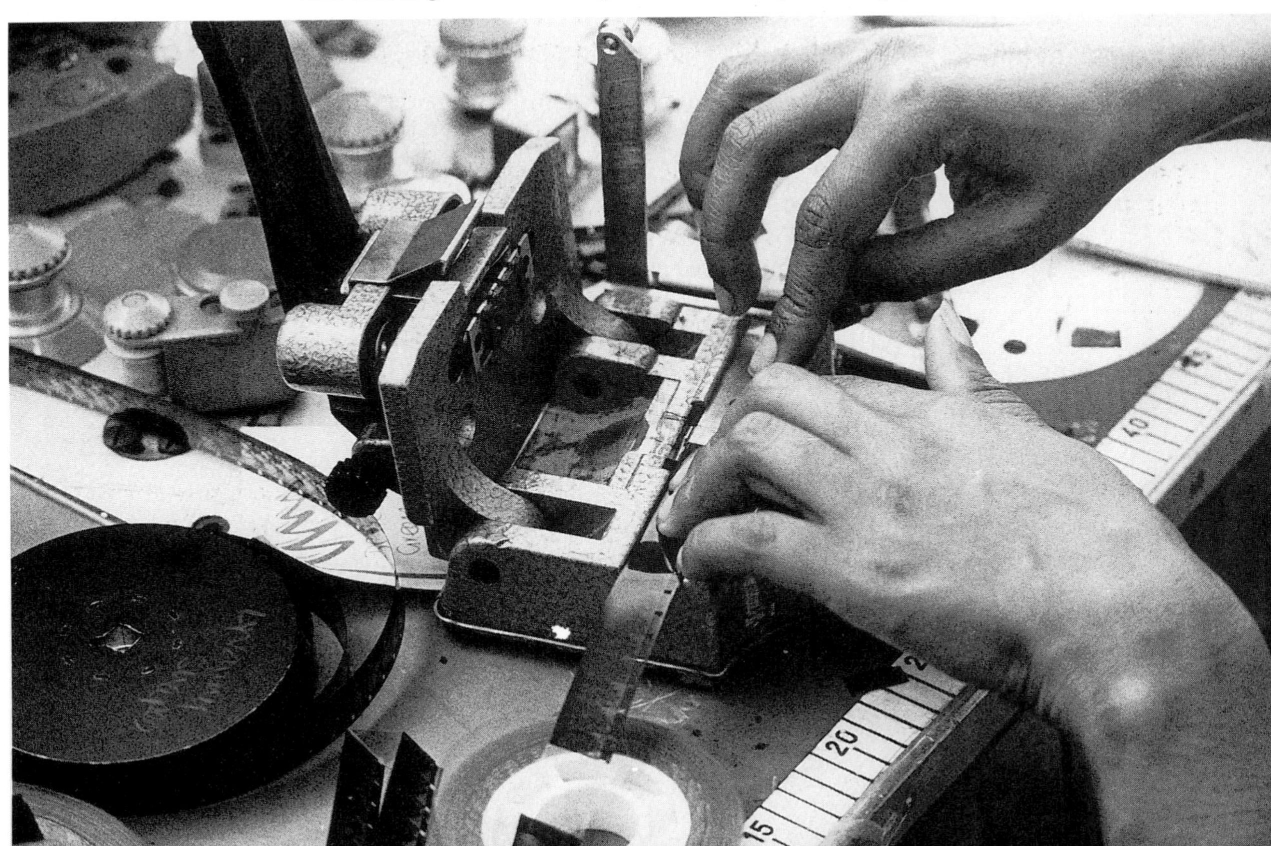

PLAYING THE FILM ON AIR

Telecine

A machine known as a *telecine* (*TK, film chain* US) is used to transfer the film image to television. In its simplest form the telecine is basically a television camera looking at a projected film.

More sophisticated machines use the *flying spot* method, which uses light reflected from a rotating prism to scan the picture line by line.

Two machines are used to screen cutaways to hide edits and make dissolves. This is known as *double chaining*. Detailed instructions about when the director should switch from one machine to the other will be given on the script.

Where the sound has been recorded separately, a second machine will play back the soundtrack.

Telecine machines are also used for screening slides. For complex production work including film clips and slides, several telecines may be linked together or *multiplexed*.

The roll-through (roll-thru US)

Live TV reports may be linked by newsreaders. While the camera is on the reader the film continues to roll but not on air. The gap between the sound bites is timed to match the link, so as soon as the newsreader finishes, the director cuts back to the film and the sound bite appears on air – right on cue.

The portion of film linking the two sound bites is called the *roll-through*. Where this does not appear on air it will be either surplus film or leader tape. But where the pictures are shown and the newsreader gives the link off-camera, the roll-through may be silent film or pictures with the soundtrack dipped down.

FIELDWORK

1 Open a file on editing for TV. Get permission to visit videotape and film editors at work and watch them edit an item all the way through. Ask them to describe the process and to say whether they prefer working with tape or film – and why.

2 Watch a TV news programme and note the fades and dissolves. Look for when they are used and how long they last. Listen for sound mixes as well. Describe the techniques used.

3 If you have access to the equipment, practise editing pictures on both videotape and film.

Which process do you think offers the most scope to be creative? Which is easier? Which is faster?

4 If you are able to use film equipment, try shooting some sepmag and commag shots of people speaking.

With the commag shots, does the equipment you use give you a problem with lip-flap? Can you get away with it?

5 Practise synchronizing sound and vision conventionally and then by dubbing on to videotape. Which gives the best results?

30 Visuals

Thanks to advances in electronics, TV news is no longer the poor relation to newspapers and magazines in putting over information which cannot easily be explained in words. Facts can now be displayed on the screen as three-dimensional and animated graphics, offering a depth and clarity of explanation previously achieved only on the printed page. Stylish visuals make the images on the screen more attractive too. The term 'visuals' covers a multitude of tricks, from stills, slides and captions, to charts, graphs, and full-screen images which fill the wall behind the newsreader.

STILLS

TV camera crews may attempt to be first at a breaking story, but they will not always succeed. News agencies with more troops on the ground will sometimes beat them to it.

Agencies send out hundreds of photographs daily which are reproduced on photowire machines in newsrooms. These pictures are often mounted on cards and archived – a technique which consumes much time and space.

The modern alternative is to receive agency pictures directly into an electronic *picture store* which holds them digitally as information in a computer.

The picture can be reduced, enlarged or cropped electronically or zoomed in and out. Contrast and tone may be enhanced, and the final picture may be reproduced on a laser printer or put to air electronically, doing away with the need to mount it on a board in front of a TV camera. An electronic picture store represents a considerable investment, but large savings can be made on the cost of processing agency photographs.

Most TV stations will have a stock of coloured slides of leading politicians and personalities. For people much in the news, a variety of stills are usually kept showing different moods and expressions. If the Prime Minister has just sacked a cabinet colleague, it would hardly do to show a picture of either minister grinning, so a stern and determined looking shot of the Prime Minister would probably be chosen, accompanied by a suitably grim-looking picture of the hapless cabinet minister. A big TV library may have up to half a million transparencies in store, indexed alphabetically.

But the electronic revolution is changing that too. Advances in video freeze-frame techniques mean stills from videotape can be used instead, so a recent taped report of the Prime Minister addressing a conference may throw up four or five new shots which can be used in the same way as stills. These can be updated the next time a report is made of the Prime Minister.

Screening stills

Where picture stores and video stills are not available, photographs can be screened in a variety of ways. The simplest method is to mount them on 30 by 23 cm cards, put them on a caption stand and point a camera at them (Figure 94).

Another method is to take a photographic slide of the still, and screen it on a telecine machine. The slides are loaded in a magazine and projected one by one by remote control.

Slides are usually 35 mm, although formats of 2 in by 2 and $3\frac{1}{4}$ in by 4 are also used. The TV station's library will probably have thousands of slides, usually offering different shots of politicians and personalities as well as views of the neighbourhood. Pictures from 16 mm news film can also be screened by holding the film on a telecine machine and viewing a single frame.

Stills can be displayed together by mounting them side by side to form a *composite* (Figure 95). Care must be taken to balance the size and shape of the shots. Where the stills are of faces, they should be looking slightly towards each other to lead the viewer's eye into the picture. Another type

Figure 94 A studio camera focuses on a picture stand used for screening still (courtesy ITN)

Figure 95 Composite shot. The faces of two key newsmakers are combined in a single frame. The balance between the two shots is critical. Here the composition of each is almost identical and both pairs of eyes appear to be focused on the same object, but the face shown on the left is dominant because it is larger

of composite is a split screen with the face on one side and a quote on the other.

FILM LIBRARY

As well as stills, most TV stations will try to keep as many moving pictures as possible. Copies of news programmes and reports will be stored in the film library.

Reports may also be itemized shot by shot and indexed. So if a riot breaks out in a city centre and the reporter wants to run footage of a previous riot to compare the scale, the film library should be able to come up with those shots in a matter of moments. The files may even list whether the shot is close, medium, or long.

Material which cannot be unearthed from the TV station's own vaults can often be obtained from one of the many commercial film libraries. (See also library, pages 307, 323.)

ELECTRONIC GRAPHICS

Since television news was put on a diet of microchips it has developed a growing appetite for complex illustrations and special effects – graphics – and larger stations will have their own specialized graphics departments.

Visual Production Effects (VPEs) machines have made it possible for the graphic artist to dispense with mechanical contraptions of glue, cardboard and string, and have opened the floodgates to a faster, more polished method of graphics design, where the only limits to creativity are the electronic memory of the machine and the designer's imagination.

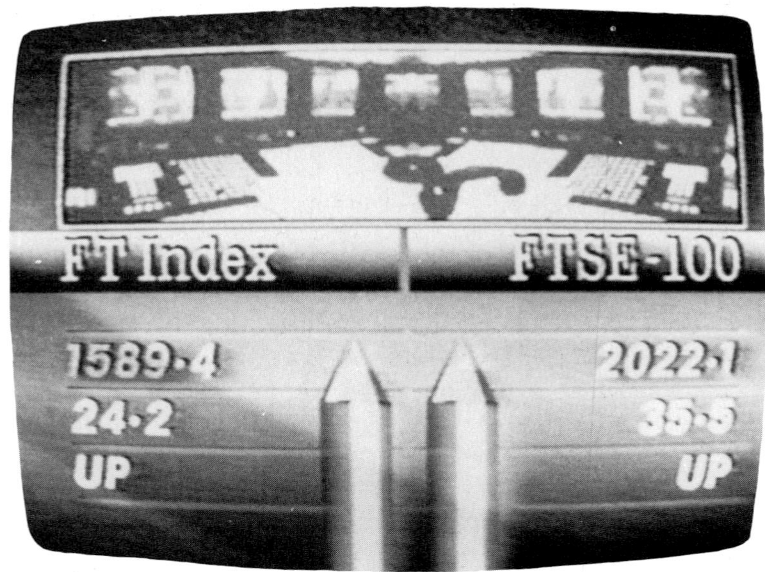

Figure 96 Graphics focus attention and help audiences remember key points. They are especially useful for visualizing figures and numerical relationships. Here, the graphic is combined electronically with a picture to add visual interest (courtesy ITN)

Graphic stills and animations
(Figure 96)

Graphics fall into one of two categories: still and animated. Still graphics include such items as the intertwined flags of two nations, maps with illustrated place names or a bristling clutch of nuclear missiles. Animated graphics include moving bar charts representing complex relationships such as the rise and fall of the economy, or three dimensional images of solid objects such as rockets launching, which can be reproduced with almost photographic realism by computer graphics machines.

Stills taken from videotape can also be called up on screen and the image edited to change its colour, stretch it, rework it, combine it with a graphic or isolate a section of it and reproduce just part of the original.

Painting with light

Using an electronic graphics machine, such as Paintbox, comes close to working with a brush and paints, but with no risk of getting your clothes dirty and with a greater variety of colours and brushes. Instead of oils, you are painting with light (Figure 97).

A light pen is moved across the screen, or a stylus is drawn across a touch tablet. Wherever it passes, corresponding lines appear. Their thickness can be varied by selecting different 'brush' sizes from a fine point to an airbrush.

Dots can be drawn and joined up to form a shape. That shape can be stretched or bent and moved round the screen at will, and filled in at the touch of a button with the artist's choice of colour, which is mixed on an electronic palette.

Pictures can be duplicated many times, and altered or moved a little each time to produce a very swift form of animation.

These machines work by dividing the screen into thousands of tiny dots known as pixels. Each has a precise location such as 840 pixels across by 635 down, and each can be painted whatever colour the artist desires, while the precise colour of each pixel is stored in computer's memory, so any graphic can be instantly recalled at any time.

What would have taken weeks in the old days of cardboard and dry transfer lettering can now be done in a matter of hours.

TITLES AND CAPTIONS

Titles or captions are valuable additions to TV reports. They can give the names of people and places, dates, sports scores and other statistics that can be shown on screen leaving the newscaster free to press on with the story.

Charts, maps and diagrams can clarify an item and may show in a moment what it might take minutes to explain – which makes for tighter

Figure 97 A graphics machine allows picture stills and electronic images to be combined to produce a wide variety of effects. Every move the artist makes with the special stylus is converted into colourful brush strokes or lines on the screen (courtesy ITN)

scripting. Holding statistics on screen can also make it easier for the viewer to digest the information.

Through extensive use of subtitling, TV news has been opened up to a whole new audience – the deaf. Titles also do away with the problem which besets radio reporters of having to include a line of script to introduce each speaker.

For example, Professor Julius Hallenbach is invited to talk about his book on espionage that accuses the Government of setting up hit-squads in foreign countries. Hallenbach appears twice in the report, at the beginning, and later in reply to an official denial.

The first time he may be introduced by the reporter, but for his later reply the report will cut straight into his quote. After a second or two, when Hallenbach's picture has had time to register, his name will be superimposed in the lower third of the screen. *Supers* are also referred to as *lower thirds*. They are usually kept in vision for up to five seconds and faded out.

If the TV station's budget allows, captions and titles will be created electronically by a *character generator*. These come with a wide range of typefaces and can be programmed to store captions or supers which can be recalled on screen at the touch of a button.

For election coverage for example, the generator could be pre-programmed with the name of every candidate in every constituency with all the results from the previous election, so as the results begin to come in, all the relevant information can be flashed up on screen in an instant (see Figure 96.)

Electronic character generators replace paraphernalia such as title cards, slides, and mechanical caption machines which operate like miniature printing presses. The older method is to make up sets of titles and superimpose them on the screen. Titles can be scrolled using a *roller caption machine*, or mounted on rotating boxes, drums or flip-cards. Where cards are used these should be roughly the shape of the television screen – around three units in height by four units in length.

Lettering can be printed, cut out, stuck on, rubbed off, hand-drawn or carved out of wood. For card-mounted titles, white lettering is normally used against a black background. When the title is superimposed on the picture, the black background vanishes.

All these approaches require a camera to be kept permanently trained on a caption machine. Another advantage of the electronic character generator is that it does away with the need for this camera. Character generators can also be combined with graphics machines to produce sophisticated illustrations.

The middle ground between the hand-cranked roller caption and the electronic graphics generator is occupied by machines which permit titles and credits to be crawled up and down the screen or across the bottom. These are driven by electric motors.

Care must be taken to make sure captions and titles can be clearly read. Letter height should be kept above one twenty-fifth of the screen height, and the letters will need to be placed so they do not obliterate important parts of the picture beneath. To make allowances for badly adjusted sets, titles should be positioned within a part of the screen known as the *safe area* where there will be no danger of slipping off the bottom of the picture or falling off the side. Viewfinders of TV cameras are usually marked so the cameraperson can see when the picture is straying outside the safe area.

Caption information should be kept as brief as possible to avoid overloading the viewer or the screen, and should be displayed for long enough to allow even slow readers to take it in.

Complete rehearsals of news programmes are seldom possible, but where complex opening sequences are used, featuring a mix of titles, graphics and animation, these will usually be compiled in advance of transmission and recorded on videotape. This covers the embarrassment of the production team by giving them the chance to rehearse and correct mistakes off-air.

OVERLAYS

Chromakey

(Figure 98)

Chromakey is an electronic means of displaying still or moving pictures behind newsreaders. Pictures can fill the entire screen behind them or occupy a rectangular box to one side of the presenter. These are known as full-frame graphics or window graphics respectively. An onlooker in the studio will see only newsreaders at their desk sitting in front of the brightly coloured back wall of the set. Only the production team and viewers at home will see the newsreader and pictures combined.

Chromakey, or *colour separation overlay (CSO)* as it is sometimes called, works by eliminating one colour from the screen and replacing it with a picture or graphic.

Unseen by the viewer, the back of the set is a coloured backdrop of lurid blue, yellow or green. This colour is switched out automatically by

Figure 98 Chromakey (CSO) can be used to create a window beside the newsreader (*left*) where still or moving pictures can be displayed, or to create an electronic backdrop (*right*) to fill the screen behind the presenter (courtesy BBC and ITN)

the vision mixer and replaced with a picture or visual from a second camera, VTR or graphics machine. Blue is commonly used for the backdrop because there are few shades of blue in white human skin.

By using chromakey the studio set with its bright blue drape can be transformed, for example, into an attractive backdrop of graduated wedgewood blue created by a graphics machine.

This image can then be replaced with a full frame still or moving shot of a news story, or supplemented by a window in the top right or left-hand corner showing a picture.

The only problem is when newsreaders decide to wear the same colour as the one switched out by the chromakey. If the newsreader's tie is a matching shade, that too will disappear, leaving what appears to be a hole punched right through him to the photograph or scene behind. No self-respecting newsreader wants to be seen on air with troops marching across his chest or politicians draped across his midriff, so care is taken to avoid clothing which matches the chromakey colour.

Bright blue eyes may also accidentally trigger the effect, but in practice the shade chosen is so unnaturally vivid that the problem of accidental switching seldom occurs.

A more common shortcoming is that the chromakey background can appear to sparkle at the edges where it gives way to the subject, particularly through the hair.

Back projection (rear projection, US)

An older alternative which has been largely superseded by electronic picture insertion is *back projection*, where a slide or moving image is projected from behind the set on to a translucent screen. One scene can be replaced by another using a second projector.

This is less expensive but less flexible than the electronic system and requires extra studio space for the projector. *Front projection* saves that space, but the image is being projected into a well-lit studio and may appear to be less bright. The lighting also has to be carefully set up to avoid the newsreader's shadow falling across the screen.

Other alternatives are to project television pictures on to a large screen behind the newsreader, or, more simply, to display pictures on a monitor which is in vision, though this can cause problems with colour balance.

Inlay

Where chromakey and electronic effects are not available, it is possible to create visual effects mechanically using the inlay method.

To produce a *wipe*, where one picture is wiped off the screen to reveal another, three cameras are required. Camera one views the scene going out on air. Camera two looks at the second scene, while camera three is focused on an illuminated ground glass screen. A sheet of cardboard is placed across the screen blocking out the light. To create the wipe, the cardboard is simply pulled across the glass screen, revealing the light beneath. As the light is revealed, the image in front of camera three changes from black to white.

The light going into the camera operates an electronic switch which activates camera two. As the cardboard begins to move, the output of camera two is displayed on the TV alongside that of camera one. Camera two's image occupies the bright area seen by camera three. As the cardboard is pulled across, the image on camera two takes up more of the screen, and the effect is of one scene wiping the other off the screen. Cardboard can be made up into many different shapes to provide different wipe and overlay effects.

Digital video effects (DVEs) machines, which are a form of electronic mixer, permit all this to be carried out automatically and add a variety of special effects, such as shrinking the picture, rotating it or turning it over like the leaves of a book.

FIELDWORK

1 Open a file on *visuals*. Watch, and record if possible, a number of news programmes. Note the types of visuals used. Is chromakey or back projection used? Are several types of visual on screen at the same time? For how long are supers displayed on the screen? Do they appear and disappear instantly or are they faded in and out?

2 Try to visit a studio which uses VPEs and another which produces visuals mechanically and compare the processes. Which is the most creative, and why?

3 Listen to a recording of an extended news programme on the radio. Imagine that same programme on TV. Story by story, what visuals and graphics would you commission to illustrate those items? If you are in a class, split into groups of four and draw up your proposals.

4 Make design sketches of one of the graphics you would use. Decide whether it should be still or animated, accompanied by words or figures, how long it should be kept on screen, and most importantly, whether it adds to the story and makes it clearer.

5 What are the advantages and disadvantages of chromakey over front or rear projection?

31 'Standby for transmission . . .'

'. . . thick padded doors and walls, anything from two to five cameras looking hungrily for something to shoot, a flock of technicians waiting behind double-thickness glass (bullet-proof perhaps?) for the producer's every word (and mistake?) – all this could just as well be a torture chamber as a television studio.

'Once you know how to do it, directing a studio can become addictive, an exhilarating drug which can stimulate you to a "high" it takes hours to come down from.' – ON CAMERA*

The clean uncluttered lines of the TV newscaster's desk and the pleasing decor of the studio set are as much an illusion as the tasteful graduated blue chromakey backdrops favoured for many newscasts.

Walking into a news studio is like stepping into a barn or factory. It will either be many times smaller than it appears on screen, or cavernously large. The first impression is one of disarray and overwhelming untidiness.

To the first-time visitor, the news studio is a bewildering array of lights and a snakes-nest of cables. Ceilings are high and incredibly cluttered with lamps of all shapes and sizes. The floor is a man-trap of wires and the cameras bristle with flex and look as brutal and uncompromising as ships' engines.

Even the set which appears so swish and urbane on the screen, looks uninviting in daylight. The illusion is all in the lights and the tricks of the camera.

THE SET

The news programme may have its own studio, or it may share a set with the rest of the TV station.

Sets vary in sophistication. They may have elaborate desks with panelling behind giving the impression of an affluent sitting room, or be incorporated into the newsroom itself, presenting a backdrop of bustle. Alternatively, the background may be a picture window which appears to

* Harris Watts, BBC, 1984.

be looking out on a local scene, but is in reality a picture projected from a slide.

Increasingly, set sophistication is giving way to electronic illusions created in the control room, offering full-screen graphics, windowing and chromakey backgrounds. Behind the desk, the backdrop may often be nothing more than a set of painted wooden panels or highly coloured cloth.

Where several programmes use the same studio, sets may be constructed to fit inside each other, so instead of dismantling one to make way for the next programme, another may simply be placed over it or around it, while the boards behind, known as *flats*, are turned round to reveal a surface of a different texture or colour.

On the desk in front of the newscaster but out of view of the cameras, will be a pair of lights: one red, the other green. The red tells the newscaster he/she is on air, and the green is for rehearsals.

Built into the desk will often be a microphone, clock, and a monitor to show what is going out on air. A second monitor off-camera may show a preview shot of the next item. Plenty of space is left on the desk for scripts.

Beside the newscaster may be a hotline for the sub-editor to give instructions live into the programme. This is used only in emergencies. Another phone sits on the desk for conducting live telephone interviews. Instead of a bell which could interrupt broadcasts, it has a light which flashes when a caller is on the line.

A third telephone may be kept behind the desk in case the newscaster needs to contact the producer. This equipment is duplicated for each newscaster and the assorted clutter on the desktop is concealed from the cameras by a raised lip at the front.

Lighting

Each news programme will require its own particular array of lights to provide the illumination which best suits the camerawork used on the programme.

When different programmes regularly use the same studio, permanent lighting rigs for each will be kept in place. This results in duplication, but saves having to re-set all the lights for each change of programme.

Some lights are floor-mounted, but most are suspended by cables and poles from a framework of girders across the ceiling called a *lighting grid*. They range in power from a meagre 750 watts to a searing 10 kilowatts. The lighting director fades them up and down from a control panel.

In some studios the lights can be programmed to function automatically. Floodlights bring up the overall level of lighting to within the operating range of the cameras; large, square, matt fillers provide diffuse light to brighten up the studio, while spotlights act as the keys, lighting and modelling the subject. These have 'barn-door' style flaps which can be adjusted to alter the spread of light.

Backlights pick the newscaster out from the background and add sparkle to his/her hair and areas that other lights might have missed, such as the tops of shoulders. Additional lamps may be used to illuminate the set and add sparkle to the newscaster's eyes.

Cameras

A typical TV studio will have between two and four cameras mounted on mobile pedestals. Each will have a zoom lens which can shift the picture from long shot to big close up without having to move the camera closer to the scene. Another knob or lever adjusts the focus.

The operator sees the picture through a viewfinder on top of the camera. This displays a black and white picture, even on colour cameras, as a monochrome image is clearer and easier to focus.

The camera is mounted on a pedestal and the head can be raised, lowered, tilted or swivelled (*panned*). A *panning handle* is used to adjust its position. Fitted to this is the zoom control which is similar to a motorcycle twistgrip.

The camera may be mounted on a lightweight tripod or heavyweight dolly which can be remote-controlled. Between these two extremes is the pedestal, the camera mounting most commonly used in TV studios. It can be operated by one person and is adjustable for height. The studio floors are carefully levelled to allow the cameras to move smoothly across them without jumping or bumping on the screen.

Some cameras have pre-set controls which allow the operator to select the appropriate shots with the zoom lens and programme them into the camera's *shot-box*. Instead of adjusting the lens by hand, he/she can then go straight to the shot at the touch of a button.

When the director puts a camera on air, an indicator will glow in the viewfinder, and a red *cue-light* on top of the camera will light up to let the presenter know the camera is live.

The cameraperson can line up the picture with another by superimposing the picture from the second camera into the viewfinder.

Each camera has its own intercom, so the operator can hear and reply to the director's instructions.

Pictures from the different cameras are selected and mixed in the control room. The vision mixer, or technical director, can cut directly from one camera to another, or can use a variety of *wipes*, *fades* and *dissolves* to gradually change between pictures.

TV news programmes are usually presented from a fixed set, with the newscasters in the same position each night. This means the camerawork is fairly predictable. To streamline the chain of command from director to cameraman, some stations use one or more remote-controlled cameras which are operated from the control room.

Sound

The walls of the studio are acoustically treated to eliminate echo and provide a natural sound. Three different types of microphone are commonly used. Newsreaders will usually be fitted with a personal mike which can be clipped to the tie or hung round the neck on a cord. This means that if newsreaders turn to one side to conduct a live interview the microphone will move with them and there will be no danger of going off-mike. A desk top mike will usually be in position as a back-up.

Where the presenter is likely to move around, *a boom microphone* will be operated by a sound engineer (See Figure 73) or the presenter will be fitted with a radio mike. Both these solutions do away with the problem of trailing cables. The boom mike will either be a microphone on the end of a pole, known as a *fishpole*, or a more sophisticated sound boom which can stretch up to 6 m and be adjusted for length, height and tilt.

The floor manager

At first glance, the *floor manager* looks a cross between mime artist and racecourse tic-tac man (bookie). With a combination of hand signals and gestures he/she acts as the director's link person and makes sure that everything runs smoothly on the studio floor. In the run-up to the programme the floor manager sees that all the props and equipment are in place, and during the programme guides the presenters and instructs the studio crew. He/she hears the director's instructions through an ear-piece or headphones and passes them on by means of hand-signals (Figure 99).

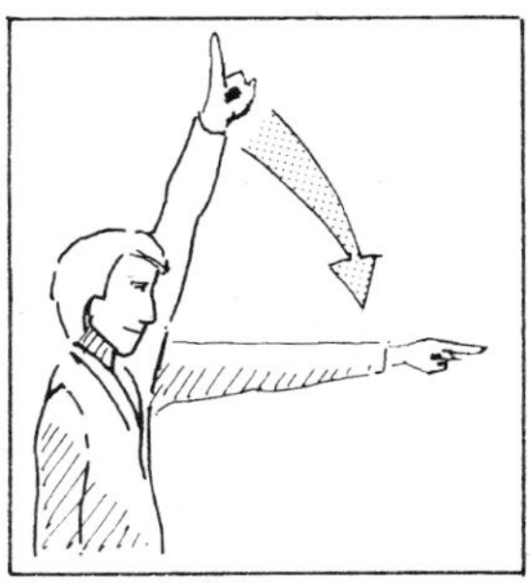

Figure 99 The floor manager passes on the director's instructions by gesture.
A CUE . . . now! (stand by . . . begin your item now!)
B WIND-UP (come to an end)
C CUT! (stop now!)

Prompting

Newsreaders never work without a script on the table, though they may seldom refer to it. Few things look worse than the top of newsreaders' heads as they glance down to read the script, and the more professional TV stations get round this problem by using prompting devices. The most effective of these are machines like the *autocue* or *teleprompt* which display the script on a screen in front of the camera, so the reader is always looking straight at the lens.

The script is typed out in large print on a long narrow strip. This is run over a roller in front of a small camera. The picture of the moving script is displayed on a television screen, which is reflected on a glass sheet in front of the studio camera. This is invisible to the camera lens which looks right through the glass sheet at the reader (Figure 100).

Corrections and last minute changes to the script are made by sticking gummed white strips of paper over the words and hand writing the changes on top (Figure 101).

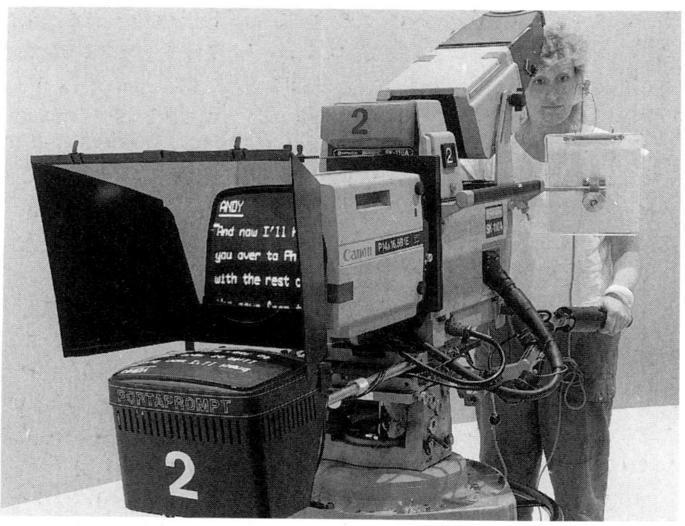

Figure 100 The camera operator takes her cue from the camera script (crib cards). The automatic prompter reflects the presenter's script on to a sheet of glass in front of the camera lens (courtesy EDS Portaprompt)

HEADLINES

Hello. Good
afternoon.
Police have
said
yesterday's
explosion in
Kensington was a
bomb: The Terrorist
squad have taken
over the investigation.
The Iranian
Consulate say it
was
intended for them.
Suspended police-
chief John Stalker
should face an
independent
inquiry according

Figure 101 Last minute corrections to the programme script are handwritten on gummed strips which are stuck in place over the autocue roll (courtesy ITN)

The speed at which the script is run through the machine is regulated by the operator who matches it as closely as possible to the reading speed of the presenter. (See also page 151).

The hi-tech alternative is to produce the script on computer and display the computer screen in front of the camera. Cheaper options include flip cards beneath the camera, scripts boards held to one side, and roller prompters on top or to one side of the camera.

CONTROL ROOM

'45 seconds to transmission.'
'Stand by ACR6, VT1, EJ1, VT2, VT3, and EJ2 and cameras 1 and 3.'
'20 to transmission.'
'On air in fifteen, fourteen, thirteen... three, two..'
'ACR6 roll.'
'... zero. On air.'

You have seen those submarine movies. The dim red lights, the atmosphere taut with expectancy. Each man at his post, every eye straining at a flickering dial or gauge. Reflexes that are nerve-end sharp, breathing that is shallow and rhythmic. The captain's instructions are terse and clipped, his utterances in a technical tongue. Not a word is wasted. Each cryptic command triggers a response from the crew as swiftly as tripping a relay. And when the crisis finally passes the atmosphere discharges like the night air after a thunderclap. To the uninitiated it is a little like that in the TV control room.

The director

The control room captain is the TV *director*, who sits at the centre of the control desk, cueing the cameras and calling the shots from the studio. The red light for action stations is the red transmission warning. A bank of monitors dominates the wall in front of the director, displaying a more bewildering variety of pictures than most television showrooms. Each image and sound that makes up a programme; all the camera pictures, pre-recorded news reports, slides, graphics and titles, are fed into the control room gallery where the director reigns supreme, deciding when each picture, report or caption should go to air (Figure 102).

The *transmission* monitor shows what is currently on air. Another displays the picture the control room is working on. Beside that the next shot is lined up ready to go. A fourth monitor displays a caption to be added to a report. Another has a graphic. Three more show what each camera is looking at in the studio. Several more display countdown sequences for each tape and telecine machine that has a report standing by ready for transmission. On another is the picture called up from the electronic still store. A black and white monitor repeats the transmitted scene to offer a clearer image for checking the focus. Another shows what the network is seeing so the director can tell exactly when to opt in and out of network with the programme. And to make sure the station is keeping up with the

Figure 102 Into rehearsal for the *News at 5.45* at ITN. Banks of monitors in the control room preview different shots and graphics (courtesy ITN)

opposition another monitor reveals what is currently going out on the rival station.

The director tells the telecine and videotape operators to stand by. They reply with a buzzer. One buzz for 'yes', two means 'not ready'.

Located in a prominent position is a large and accurate clock. In the background the programme sound is being played over the speaker. On the long desk in front of the monitors are the rows and clusters of illuminated buttons and switches that make up the control panel.

Each picture on show can be switched to air. The director has to keep an eye on these and remain in constant verbal contact over the talkback with cameras and crew as well as acting on split-second decisions by the producer about the running order of the programme.

Presented with the need to have more heads than the Hydra, if only to keep watch on all those monitors, the director on larger TV stations farms out a number of responsibilities to other personnel.

Other personnel

The *production assistant* (PA) or *production secretary* keeps one step ahead of the programme. Some scripts are numbered shot by shot. He/she calls these shots and cues in items on telecine (TK) and videotape (VT, EJ), allowing five seconds (usually) for these machines to pick up speed. The PA knows exactly when to cue them, because before the programme began he/she worked back in the script and marked every word which fell five seconds before the picture was due on air. As soon as that word is uttered by the newscaster, the PA cues the machines to roll. Five seconds later the newscaster completes the cue and the pictures are up to full speed and running.

The PA is responsible for copying and distributing scripts and for the timekeeping of the programme. He/she has timings for everything from stories to stills, knows exactly how long the programme should run and can tell from the stopwatch at any given time whether it is running over or under. If the times mismatch, items will have to be cut, dropped or added in. (On some stations the PA's task falls to the *assistant director*. On others, the production assistant directs, and the timekeeping is carried out by the production secretary.

Where a script has to be altered, the *chief sub-editor* will whittle it down or pad it out with extra sentences or lines, carrying out a constant process of fine tuning to make it fit. Prime targets for tinkering are the recaps at the end of the bulletin. The chief sub has a telephone link with the newscaster to pass on any emergency instructions.

At the director's command, *the vision mixer* (*switcher, technical director*, US) fades or cuts from one shot to another, punches up outside broadcast cameras, or plays tricks on the screen with special effects. Where effects are used extensively a second vision mixer may be on hand simply to operate those.

While all this is happening, a constant check is being made on the circuitry to make sure there are no technical hitches. This is carried out by the *technical manager* (*operations supervisor, senior engineer*). At the first hint of trouble, he/she will be on the hotline to the engineers in master control. Meanwhile the *vision controller* is checking and adjusting the quality of all the pictures.

At the end of the control desk, or in an adjoining room with visual contact through a plate glass window, is the *sound controller*, who regulates the sound levels of all the microphones in the studio. With him/her may be a *grams operator* who plays the jingles (sounders) and signature tune and adds any sound effects. These used to be kept on sound effects records, hence the title grams operator, but increasingly effects are being stored either on tape, compact disc, or computer.

From a panel in the control room or an adjoining room a *lighting director* and his/her *console operator* work the studio lights. The lighting 'plot' may be keyed into a computer, which will operate the lights throughout the programme according to the pre-set plan.

If the programme is introduced by an announcer, he/she will sit in an adjoining *announcement booth* (*presentation area*).

Personnel and their roles will almost certainly differ from station to station.

Running order

With so much material to be co-ordinated from so many sources, the director and his/her team could not be expected to rely on their memories to guide them through the programme.

As much as possible is scripted, though news programmes are fast moving and likely to change as stories come in. Every item will be on a separate page so pieces can be dropped or added as needs be. Each page of script will include details of camera shots and visuals such as stills and graphics, as well as a duration for the item.

Each item and lead is timed. Ad-libs are discouraged. The programme may opt out of the network to offer regional news or may supply national news to the entire network. Either way, split-second timing is essential. On television an unscheduled two-second delay can feel like infinity.

Each programme will have a running order, but with ENG making instant updates a possibility, complete running orders are becoming something of a rarity. More often it will be unfinished and smothered in handwritten corrections and additions. A new lead may arrive five minutes before the programme is due on air. Stories may be cut to make way for others, and extra items may have to be included to make up time. This is where a short copy story illustrated by a still can come in handy. Where a story has yet to arrive, a blank sheet known as a *skeleton* (or *blank*) is inserted into the script, to be replaced with the story as soon as it is finished.

The producer makes decisions about the content of the news programme, the director makes those decisions work on air. With news the problem is seldom one of having to fill: scripts may have to be edited and shortened even while the programme is going out.

The nearest the director may come to rehearsing the show is the pre-recording of the title sequences shortly before the programme begins.

That a news programme ever gets on air without a mistake seems little short of miraculous to an onlooker.

> ***'I have never known a programme that doesn't change. Sometimes we can go on air and not have the lead story, nor the second lead nor the third lead and start half way down the running order. We get into the VTR (taped report) and try and sort ourselves out to find out what we can go on to next. It can be an absolute mess!'***
>
> – MALCOLM JOHNSON, DIRECTOR, ITN *NEWS AT ONE*

When mistakes do occur, there is always an inquest to find out how and why and to prevent them happening again but, with the shrinking world's news coming in thicker and faster, that uncomfortable sense of teetering even closer to the brink can only continue to grow. It is a tribute to the team's professionalism that, somehow, it never seems to show.

FIELDWORK

1 If you have access to a TV studio construct a set that is suitable for a news programme and arrange the lighting for single-headed and then double-headed presentation.

2 Find a willing subject to act as a newsreader and practise using a TV camera. Concentrate on framing your subject well and keeping him/her in focus. Zoom in and out for best effect. Shoot some tape or film and see how well you have done.

How should the zoom be used during a news programme? Watch a bulletin and see if you can notice the cameras zooming or panning.

3 Make a recording of yourself reading the news from a teleprompter and criticize your performance. Is your expression natural or are you staring or peering at the camera? Are your eyebrows glued in position? Try again, taking care to relax and iron out any ticks or peculiar expressions.

4 Watch a number of news programmes and see which wipes, fades and dissolves they use. Do you think the producers could have been more creative? How?

Try your hand at vision mixing. Experiment with different types of wipes, fades and dissolves. Which work best for news?

5 Arrange to visit a TV control room to watch a live news programme going out. Find out exactly who is doing what and see if you can follow the action as the programme is broadcast.

PUSHING BACK THE FRONTIERS

32 Tomorrow

THE COMPUTERIZED NEWSROOM
(Figure 103)

News is about getting information and getting it fast. Small wonder newsrooms are abandoning typewriters and tubs of correction fluid in favour of the fastest of all information systems – the computer.

Computers cut down on paper, make information available to more users and allow almost instant recall of items that might otherwise be buried in a boxfile or impaled under forty other stories on a spike.

One computer network to be adopted by an increasing number of newsrooms is the Basys system, owned by ITN in London, who liked it so much they bought the company. It has been installed by Ted Turner's

Figure 103 The computerized newsroom – faster, more efficient and more flexible than typewriters but proof there is no such thing as the paperless newsroom (courtesy ITN)

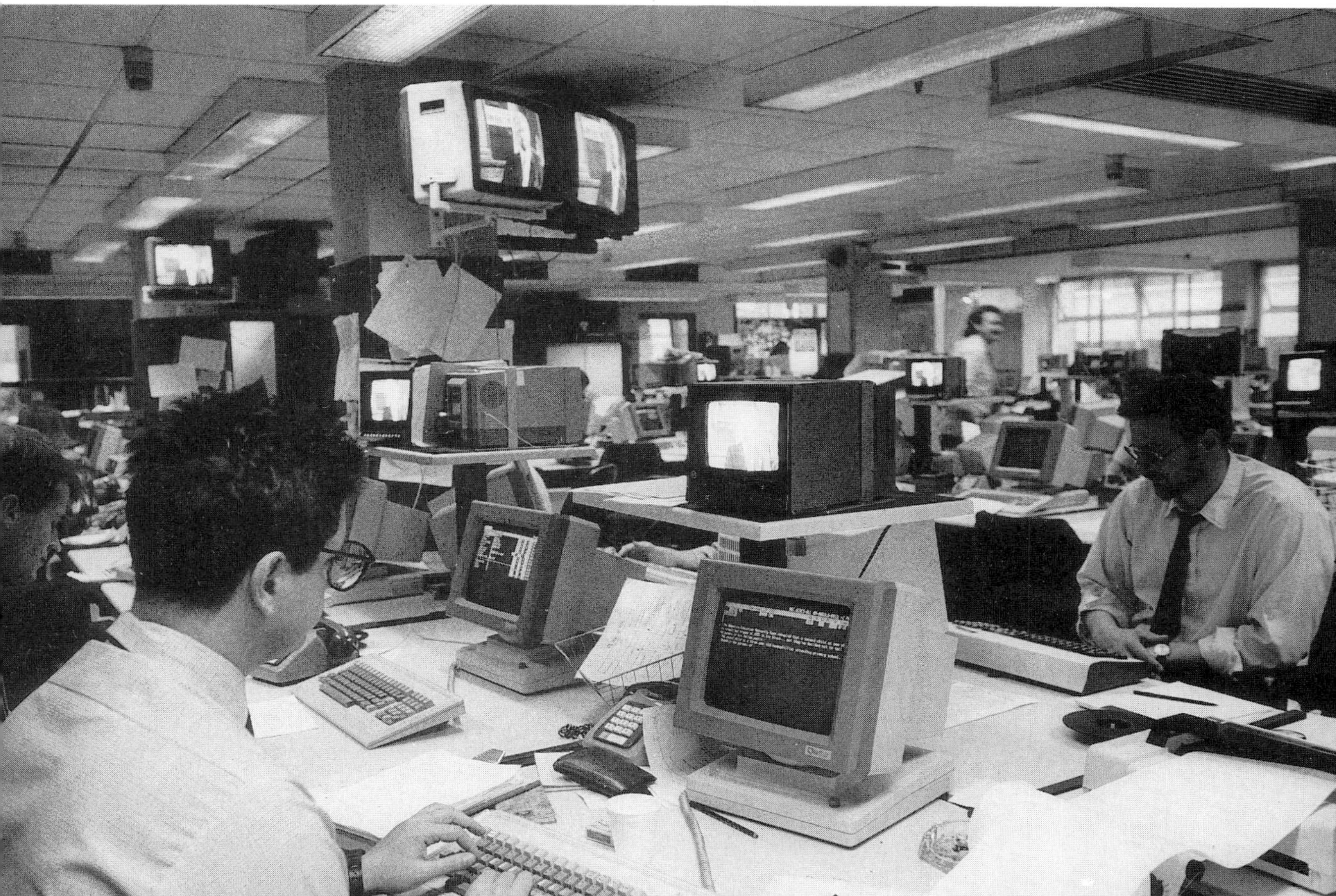

24 hour Cable News Network in Atlanta, Georgia, by NBC and ABC in New York, BTQ-7 TV in Brisbane and the Broadcasting Corporation of New Zealand. Even ITN's arch-rivals the BBC have adopted the system, claiming the investment will pay for itself with a big increase in news output and a faster turnaround of stories. Similar systems are also finding their way into a growing number of radio stations including BBC Radio London and the Macquarie Radio Network in Australia.

Basys keeps as much information as possible in the computer and off the newsroom floor, receiving all the news wires and incoming telex messages. Journalists key their stories directly into the computer and sub-editors call them up for rewriting.

Basys and systems like it are more than just wordprocessors. Reporters can program in their reading speed and the computer will automatically time their copy. Items can be assembled into a programme and the computer will calculate the total running time. If there are any changes, the duration can be recalculated at the press of a button and a new running order drawn up on screen.

The system does not allow stories to go through unchecked. The writer initials the finished copy. Then the chief sub approves it and adds his/her initials, which are joined by the newsreader's initials once the story has been checked through. Split-screen editing allows the original story to appear alongside the rewritten version. The computer can also produce scripts, TV style, with text on the right and video and graphics instructions on the left.

Where paper copies are required, pages can be printed automatically and labelled with the time, date, page number and name of the person summoning up the printed copy. But no paper is needed for the archives. Every word of every bulletin can be kept electronically for as long as the station requires.

It can also access other computer archives for rapid recall of paperless cuttings, and large commercial databases such as World Reporter or Nexis, which keep the contents of newspapers and magazines on file.

The same computer system can also be used to streamline routine administrative chores, such as rosters and reporters' expenses.

Journalists are renowned for being ham-fisted with equipment. If there is any way of fouling-up a machine, give it to a reporter for half an hour and he/she will discover how. So for the computerized newsroom to work, it had to be journalist-proof. Basys and others like it can run without the help of resident experts or nursemaids, and reporters do not even have to be in the building to use them.

Portable computers, increasingly used by newspaper journalists, allow reporters to type their stories on location and feed them into the newsroom computer down the phone. Or, to save precious moments hunting for a call-box, the portable computer can be hooked up to a personal cellular phone. With international direct dialling, the computer is accessible even to reporters working abroad. And when the editor goes off-duty, journalists need not think they can relax. Senior editors may even

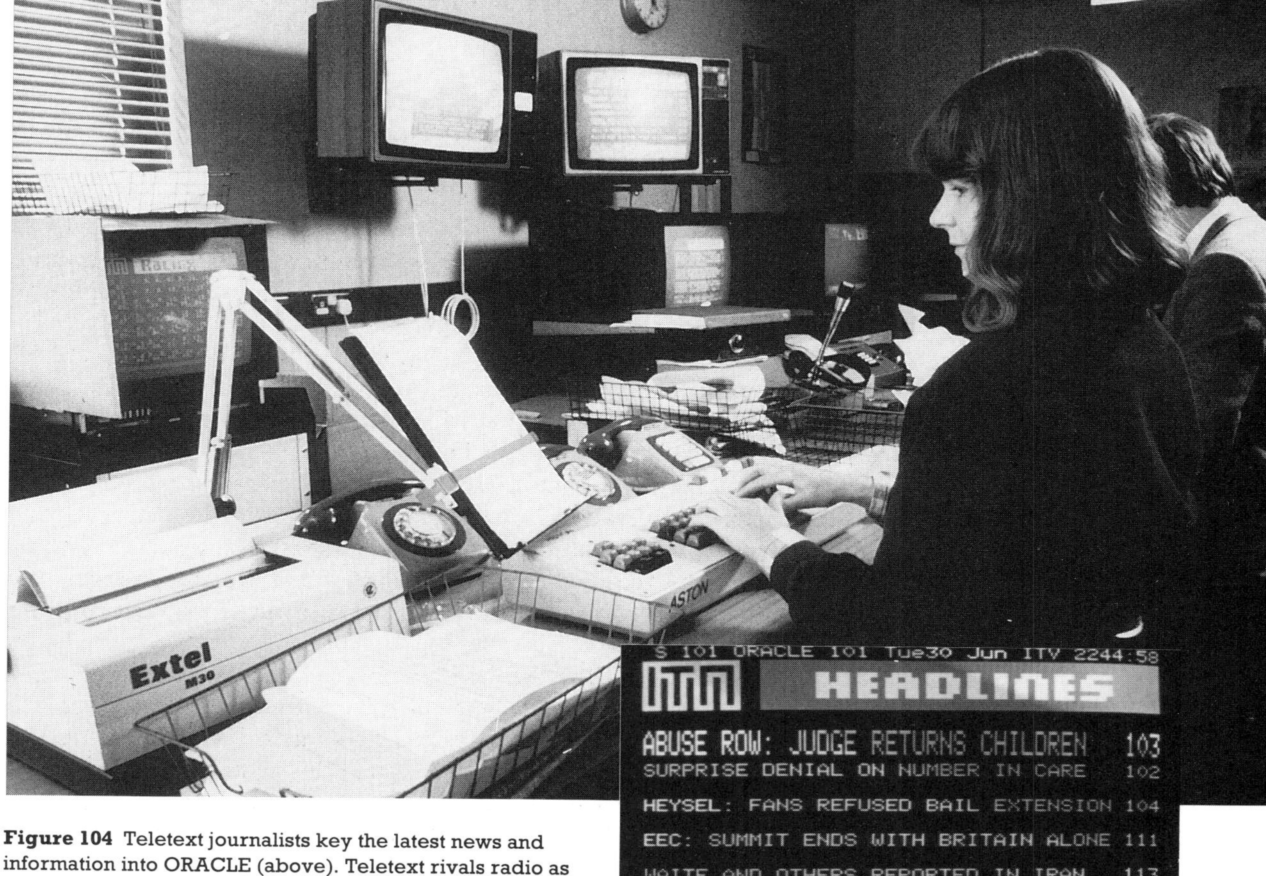

Figure 104 Teletext journalists key the latest news and information into ORACLE (above). Teletext rivals radio as the fastest source of news. Stories can appear on screen the instant they have been written (*right*). The index at the foot of the screen shows the extensive variety of information available on Teletext (courtesy ITN)

have terminals in their homes so they can keep tabs on what is happening back in the newsroom.

ITN Head of Operations, Derek Taylor, says: '*It can inform everyone what ITN are doing about all the breaking stories. As a manager, at the flick of a button I can find out what every writer is watching.*'

To make sure outsiders cannot tap in on what is often highly sensitive information, security includes the use of personal passwords to get into the system.

It may sound complicated, but a four-day course has been regarded as training enough to use it successfully.

TELETEXT
(Figure 104)

There is another dimension to television news which is fast gaining a sizeable audience and is able to offer considerably more information than could be packed into any conventional news programme.

Teletext is a relatively new offensive in the television onslaught. A sort of newspaper of the airwaves, offering a similar service – only faster and free of charge – to anyone with the right kind of TV set.

In the decade that teletext was launched, the audience exploded from a couple of hundred to around six million. In Europe that audience has topped 25 million, and teletext is gaining in popularity in Australia, New Zealand, Singapore, Malaysia, Japan and South Africa. That the US has been slow on the uptake has been put down to the '*not invented here*' syndrome*. In its country of origin, Britain, the theoretical readership of teletext already exceeds that of any national newspaper and is increasing by a million a year.

Two teletext services exist in Britain: CEEFAX, operating on BBC channels, and ORACLE on the ITV network. ORACLE's editorial director, David Klein, has described the service as: '*The world's biggest and most widely distributed free newspaper*.'† CEEFAX is funded from the BBC licence fee, while ORACLE is paid for wholly by advertising.

Teletext employs a growing number of journalists and has the capacity to get news on air even faster than radio. While the radio reporter is still typing the script, that same story can be displayed directly on the viewer's TV screen.

'*It's not only quick, it's continuous,*' says ORACLE's manager, Peter Hall. '*When we get a story we can have it on air within a minute of hearing about it. And the viewer can get information at any time, without having to wait for a specific bulletin.*'

The most popular services are the TV guide, weather and travel information provided by organizations like the Automobile Association and British Rail. Next come news and sport. Agencies feeding the news service include PA, Reuters, AP, Extel and IRN.

More than a thousand editorial changes are made each day to the news, sport and business sections alone. The copy style – concise and to the point – is closer to that of broadcast news than newspapers. A testimony to the speed of teletext is the way it is assiduously pirated by many radio stations – especially for its sports news. There must be few stations in Britain without a teletext set permanently on the newsroom or studio.

Other features include regional information, music, theatre reviews and business news. ORACLE's computer is linked to the dealing room computer of a major bank, which updates details of price fluctuations every two minutes – a service tantamount to bringing an international dealing room into your home free of charge. It is paid for by featuring the name of the bank on the screen. By the same arrangement, a British Airways computer gives the times of plane arrivals.

Teletext subtitles have been a boon to the hard of hearing, who no longer have to lip read or turn up the volume to catch the latest news. Subtitles in different languages are also a possibility.

The system looks set for steady expansion, believes David Klein: '*The potential in teletext is tremendous and as more open up there will be more jobs for journalists.*'‡

* 'Dealing with the "not invented here" syndrome', *Broadcast*, 31 October, 1986.
† 'World's Biggest Free . . .', *UK Press Gazette*, 8 September, 1986.
‡ Ibid.

ORACLE stands for Operational Reception of Announcements by Coded Line Electronics. It works by using some of the extra lines on a television screen that are not used for carrying pictures. These carry codes instead, which are translated into letters, numbers, graphics, and colour by the special teletext receiver.

Individual characters are transmitted one after another, which is why viewers will have to wait several seconds for their chosen page to appear. They select the page with a remote control keypad which draws the information into the TV set's computer.

Every page is given a number, so if the viewer keys-in page 118 carrying the headlines, the teletext receiver will count through all the incoming pages until 118 is reached. The computer will store that page in its memory and then display that information on the screen (Figure 104).

NEXT STEPS

The next steps are to increase the number of pages; reduce the time it takes to select a page; enhance the ability to provide printouts of information from the screen; develop the regional teletext service and improve the quality of the text and graphics – '*It's still quite embarrassing that we are unable to produce a decent curved line!*' says Peter Hall. The technology exists to do all this.

Consumer choice – and job opportunities for journalists – will widen as teletext is transmitted internationally by satellite, and, ultimately, teletext may be linked to home computers to offer an information service that is universally available and two-way, so viewers may be able to do their shopping and banking from home and send their mail along the phone lines to appear on their friend's television screen. If teletext does not rise to that challenge, the contender waiting in the wings is cable TV which is planning a range of interactive services.

AND THEN . . .

The technical history of television reads like a quest for not one but two Holy Grails – quality and quantity – better pictures and more of them. From the first days, the aim was to produce the most lifelike pictures possible and get them on to our sets in the quickest possible time. That aim has not changed. Big advances in picture quality that will make 625 lines look like a fuzzy photograph are just around the corner with high definition TV (HDTV) and digital TV. Pocket sized television sets have been around for years, and manufacturers have long been hinting tantalizingly of the large, but ultra-thin flat-screen TVs that will one day hang on our walls like pictures.

Digital TV

Where tape has largely superseded film, tape itself could be replaced before long – by the computer. The same revolution that looks set to change radio is likely to have an even greater impact on television.

Film or tape simply stores information – information which could be held directly in the memory of a computer. Computer storage would do away with tape and make the process of storing and editing pictures faster, more reliable, and infinitely more creative.

The breakthrough will come when computer memories can store enough to take a report or an entire TV programme. For the present, systems are available which store pictures on optical discs which can be read by lasers. Again, storage space is limited.

Computers store pictures and sound as a set of numbers. Each piece of information, such as the precise hue or brilliance of a single dot along with its exact position on the screen, is given a code number. When that number is read, the computer reproduces the right coloured dot in exactly the right place on the screen.

In the same way as a groove in a gramophone record represents a sound which can be reproduced by running a stylus along it, each number represents a tiny portion of the video. But where the grooves on a gramophone record wear out, and the signals on a tape deteriorate, as long as the recorded numbers can be accurately read back, the digital signal can be reproduced perfectly, time and again, which means there will never be the loss in quality which has blighted every other form of recording.

The other attraction is that unlike videotapes which have to be wound back and forth digital pictures can be summoned almost instantly and edited together in any desired sequence.

With the random access of pictures, editing becomes faster and new creative possibilities open up. Storage problems are overcome and the library packed from ceiling to floor with archive material could become a thing of the past. By keeping every report on computer, retrieval of archive footage becomes even faster.

The full advantages of digital techniques will only be realized when information can be stored in abundance on computer. Once computer memories can be made large enough to store the masses of digits which would make up a report or full-length programme, the digital revolution will have truly arrived.

Developments in space
(Figure 105)

In the quest for speed, electronic news gathering has brought instant pictures into the home, and the explosion in satellite communications has meant those live pictures can now come into our living rooms from around the globe.

Home video recorders and satellite and cable television offer the viewer wider choice and greater autonomy than ever before. Viewers with the right equipment can now choose what they want to see and when they want to see it. Satellite and cable have made possible many more TV channels each offering a degree of specialization. As radio stations offer different types of music to cater for a particular audience, so satellite and cable TV stations are tending to specialize in their programme output, opting for music, children's programmes or films, even news. Instead of a few TV stations trying to please all the people all of the time, people are choosing the channels that suit their tastes and dipping in and out of them as they please.

Ted Turner's Cable News Network in Atlanta may have been the first with 24-hour news, but it will certainly not be the last. The diet of never

Figure 105 Satellite earth station at Santa Paula. How long before there are reporters, as well as satellites, in space? (courtesy Visnews)

ending news is here to stay, and with it, for its reporters, the pressures of never-ending deadlines.

As mass production leads to falling equipment costs, and competition leads to falling prices, satellite TV will become more universally available. Even the days of that most conspicuous status symbol, the dish aerial, appear to be numbered. Higher powered satellites will send signals that can be picked up by smaller aerials. At the same time aerials will become more powerful. It is possible to sandwich thousands of tiny antenna into a single flat surface to create a satellite aerial not much bigger than a dinner plate. A single small receiver like this will be able to lock on automatically to whichever satellite the viewer chooses.

Even nations which cannot afford the hardware are joining the satellite scramble. In Poland, people are picking up satellite TV with dishes made of dustbin lids, and in India signals are being pulled in with constructions made of chicken wire.*

TV companies will make increasing use of their own portable satellite transmitters, and at the same time, satellite exchanges between news companies will grow.

* Elizabeth Ray, *The BBC Goes Worldwide*, February, 1987

Pictures from low orbiting 'spy in the sky' satellites will be made increasingly available to TV companies to show in remarkable detail events happening on the surface of the earth hundreds of kilometres below.

While military satellites are able to photograph objects as small as your hand from space, pictures from commercial satellites such as The Spot, launched in 1986, can reveal your house quite clearly. Pictures of missile sites in Libya, flooding in Utah, war damage to oil installations in Iraq are typical of the shots being made available to television. Tomorrow's hardware will make even that level of performance seem as obsolete as the service offered by the first ECHO satellite.

Where innocent nation-watching for news turns into spying will be a problem for the legislators to figure out.

While shots from unmanned satellites, once a science-fiction dream, have become today's reality, the stuff of today's fantasies may be just around the corner.

> *'Some time during the working lives of many of you, there will be news bureaux on the Moon and on Mars. Some of you may even be competing to become their bureau chiefs, and others may be using the tag line... "reporting from outer space"'*
>
> – DR JAMES FLETCHER, DIRECTOR OF THE US SPACE ASSOCIATION NASA*

FIELDWORK

1 Try to visit a TV station which uses a newsroom computer and find out what it can do and what the staff think of it. Has it speeded up their work? What extra facilities does it offer? How many of the journalists would want to go back to a typewriter? Are there any drawbacks?

2 Teach yourself to use a wordprocessor or enrol on a course. Soon every newsroom will have them!

3 If there is a teletext set you can look at, compare the news headlines with news bulletins on radio and TV. Describe the similarities and the differences. How up to date is the teletext news compared with the others? Is the sports service more or less comprehensive?

Find out about the job opportunities for journalists in teletext in your country.

4 '*Too little hard cash and too many hard unions mean the technical revolution in TV will be slow in coming and may never happen.*' Discuss.

5 Where do you think that spy in the sky pictures available to TV cease to become legitimate news and start to become a matter for national security? Where would you draw the line? Give some examples and discuss.

* Jim Wilson, 'Reporting from Outer Space', *Broadcast*, 26 September, 1986

APPENDIX 1

A career in TV and radio

> *'Practically everyone works at high speed. Telephones ring, people shout, crises pop up all the time, and deadlines keep thundering down. It's not an environment for the weak of heart.'*
>
> – PHILIP O. KIERSTEAD, ALL-NEWS RADIO*
>
> *'No one thinking of working in radio or television should have any illusions about the disruptive effect it can have on family and social life and the toll it can take on health.'*
>
> – JULIA ALLEN, *CAREERS IN TELEVISION AND RADIO*†

Ask journalists what they think about their chosen profession, and the chances are they will bemoan the anti-social hours, unreasonable stress, flogging to meet constant deadlines, time wasted waiting on the telephone, destruction of family life and home existence, but when the griping is over and you ask them what else they would do, the chances are they would shrug and smile and tell you, 'nothing'. Few professions can match broadcast journalism for its rewards in terms of job satisfaction, interest, variety, sheer challenge – and for the select few, fame and wealth.

Radio and television stations belong in one of three leagues: *local*, *major market* (big city or regional), and *national* (network). TV usually pays better than radio, and as one might expect, the higher the profile of the position and the bigger the audience, the greater the salary. Network television journalists tend to be the highest paid of all, with salaries in the UK at around double the average industrial wage.

Broadcasting is on the move. Developments in cable and satellite TV mean more jobs. Radio is increasingly mirroring the changes in TV and branching out into smaller, leaner, more specialized units. These open up new opportunities for broadcasters, who also benefit from the pull-through effect of new jobs in television, which create vacancies throughout the industry.

Jobs in broadcasting range from behind-the-scenes writers and producers, to on-air reporters, newsreaders and presenters. Network and bigger stations offer more scope for specialization, while smaller stations,

* *All-News Radio*, TAB, 1980.
† Kogan Page, 1986.

like those in remote parts of America and Australia, often employ a jack-of-all-trades who can turn his/her hand to everything from reading the news to selling advertising and handling the payroll.

JOBS IN RADIO

For the radio journalist the career path is likely to run from reporter to producer and into management as news editor, though some organizations rank reporters above producers. Higher level management includes programme organizer or station manager, or equivalent. For those who prefer to remain in the field as a reporter, finding a specialism such as industrial, political or foreign correspondent is often the answer.

The larger the station, the more opportunity there is to specialize and the greater the variety of positions available. Some employ specialist announcers and newsreaders, who do nothing else, and writers who only rewrite other people's copy. Networks and some larger stations also employ current affairs reporters to make documentaries.

Rob McKenzie gave up a career as an engineer to train as a broadcaster on the radio journalism course at the London College of Printing before joining one of Britain's biggest independent stations, Capital Radio, to produce the award-winning *The Way It Is* programme:

'It's an exciting life I'm sure thousands would envy because of the opportunities I get to do things. Getting in is a matter of luck – being in the right place at the right time and being good at your job. There also has to be a spark inside you which says, "I'm determined to do this". I think you've got to be able to grasp a subject quickly and be able to put it across in a simple, direct, manner.'

TELEVISION

> *'In American television there is more opportunity for training than in British TV. Any major market station will have at least an hour's news broadcast preceding or following the network newscast. People get out of university and go to work on small stations where they can afford to make mistakes covering things that are not earth shattering, then they go on to bigger markets and some of them end up in the networks.'*
>
> – PAUL CLEVELAND, ASSIGNMENT MANAGER, ABC NEWS

Television is often a natural progression from radio. TV journalists may start as sub editors, writing and re-writing copy, and may move up to become reporters, and from there follow a similar career path to that of radio, into speciality reporting, production or management.

Kim Sabido began his career in local radio, progressing to become a network reporter with Independent Radio News. He covered the Falklands War for IRN, sending back vivid accounts of the fighting, before moving into television to be a reporter with ITN:

'There's a lot more independence and personal freedom with radio and in a way it's more rewarding. In independent radio as it was then, I was given total freedom as a respected reporter. On television you have a lot of masters and your material can be seen, reprocessed, packaged and edited by other people beyond your control.'

Some reporters and presenters start out as researchers, the unsung heroes of television, whose job it is to come up with programme ideas, set up interviews, collect background information, hunt for archive material and possibly write scripts.

FREELANCING

> *'Freelancing, especially foreign freelancing, is for the birds. It is a profession without security, grossly, almost laughingly, underpaid. It is the province of maladjusted freaks, outsiders who cannot work in the system back home, characters who inhabit a twilight, pension-less world . . .'* – KIERAN COOKE, BBC STRINGER IN ATHENS*

Freelances travel the country or work a region, filling in for newsroom staff who are sick or on leave, or filing reports and stories on a commissioned or casual basis. They are paid a daily rate or by the item.

Freelancing offers a greater variety and range of experience to newly trained reporters, and is the most effective foot-in-the-door method of getting employment. When a job comes up, the good freelance becomes the benchmark against which all other applicants are judged. He/she has been tried and tested, is familiar with the radio or TV station and its patch and already knows many of its news contacts. Vacancies are not always advertised. Many stations prefer to invite known contacts to apply. News editors will often cultivate freelances to provide a steady supply of replacement staff.

A good freelance will often earn more than a staff reporter, but the drawbacks are insecurity, no sick pay, paid holidays or perks, living out of a suitcase, constantly having to work flat out to prove yourself to a prospective employer and putting up with stations which can take weeks to settle their accounts. If you decide to follow the freelance path, make sure you keep meticulous accounts, send regular invoices (be prepared to send reminders) and can call on the services of a good accountant.

UNION MEMBERSHIP

Freelances would be well advised to join a recognized union which should be prepared to fight on their behalf if a station is reluctant to pay the going rate, or if it tries to take in too many 'volunteers' who might affect their chances of getting shifts.

Some stations will refuse to employ non-union members, and may be reluctant to buy stories and tip-offs from someone who is not registered with the union.

GETTING STARTED

> *'What we want are people steeped in news. As long as they've got good writing ability and a nose for news we can quickly teach them the video part. Radio is fantastic training ground, perhaps the best place to begin.'*
> – DAVID NICHOLAS, EDITOR ITN

* From 'Twilight, underpaid world of freelancing abroad', *UK Press Gazette*, 30 March, 1987.

The industry's training commitment in Britain ranges from weak to variable. On-the-job training is usual for the fortunate few taken direct from school or university. Bigger organizations such as the BBC and ITN operate highly selective graduate trainee schemes, for which they pick only a handful of candidates from the thousands who apply.

Coming from newspapers is another way into radio or television at a writer or sub-editor level. Broadcast newsrooms look favourably on trained reporters from local papers who know the station's area.

Network TV and radio recruit heavily from local and regional stations. During holiday times promising scriptwriters step into the front line and amass some airtime, putting themselves in prime position for a reporting job when one comes up.

Many newsroom secretaries or technical assistants go on to make excellent journalists with the benefit of this head start.

Once established as a journalist, it is often easy to hop from one branch of the media to another.

Starting out in Australia

'Most people will start one of two ways. Either they'll get a cadetship with one of the broadcasters – usually the ABC, but they're as scarce as hen's teeth and only the privileged few get those. Others start as virtually indentured labour with some of the commercial radio stations, starting with secretarial work and working their way through. The other well-recognised course is to begin with the newspapers right on the ground floor.' – IAN HENDERSON, TV NEWS CORRESPONDENT FOR EUROPE, AUSTRALIAN BROADCASTING CORPORATION

Approaching news editors

I usually give the following stark advice to prospective candidates for my broadcasting course – the industry has never heard of you, and right now, it neither needs you or wants you. Being brilliant is not enough. You have to *prove* how good you are: market yourself, persuade them they would miss out if they did not agree to see you. To succeed you need wit, charm, subtlety, persistence – and heaps of talent.

The saying it is not *what* you know but *who* you know that counts is probably truer of broadcasting than many other professions. Broadcasting is a village industry. By the time a job is advertised the news editor may already have a candidate lined up, so you should make your play before the job ads appear.

The best way to put yourself in the running is to visit news editors and talk to them for twenty minutes to find out what they are looking for, tell them what you can do and see what opportunities are coming up.

Plan your campaign. Begin by sending a demonstration tape of your work and a curriculum vitae, and follow these up within a week with a phone call asking for a meeting.

The demo tape should be short, succinct and superb. For a job in radio news it should be on one side of a cassette and comprise a three minute bulletin with actuality clips (interviews with household names preferably, and all your own work) followed by a gripping interview of not longer than two and a half minutes and a sparkling package of the same length. The tape should be professionally presented and labelled. For TV send a short demo of your work on videocassette (VHS).

Your CV should be typed and well laid out. It should give your name, address, phone number(s), date of birth, relevant broadcast experience (including freelance work), broadcast training, educational qualifications (briefly), language skills, brief *relevant* details of previous employment, whether you hold a driving licence, a note of *interesting* personal hobbies and achievements, and the names and addresses of two referees. If you can, put your CV on a word processor and tailor it to suit each application.

> *'When I get your application form, the first thing I look at is your previous experience,'* says former BBC External Services Editor, Terry Heron, *'what you have done, where you have been. That is the priority.* ***Then*** *I look at the panel which shows your educational achievements.'*

The interview

Preparation is everything. Know your station, be familiar with its output, its style. Know about the area – its industry, politics, and stories. Be familiar with the news the station is running that day and have constructive comments to make about its output and ideas on how to develop those stories. Be well briefed in current affairs. Be prepared to face newsreading, news writing or screen tests. Be early. Be smart.

The best way to be briefed is to talk to staff members who are doing the job you have applied for. Be prepared for standard interview questions:

- Why do you want the job?
- What can you offer us?
- What do you think of the station's output?
- What do you see yourself doing in five years time?
- Do you work well in a team?

Come over as confident, positive, lively, interesting and above all, enthusiastic.

TRAINING COURSES

> *'I took a journalism course once. They told me if I put everything in a certain order I would be a journalist.'* – WELLS TWOMBLY, US SPORTS JOURNALIST
>
> *'I think you've got to go on a course these days. If you want to be good, a course gives you a far greater breadth of ideas and gets rid of bad habits before you start.'*
> – ROB MCKENZIE, PRODUCER/PRESENTER CAPITAL RADIO

Increasingly, news editors are recruiting only people who have had substantial experience or professional training. Courses are variable, but there are some clear indicators that will tell you whether a course is worth applying for.

Figure 106 There are many routes into broadcasting, but one of the best training grounds is the one year vocational course. Here, a radio journalism student presents a programme in the training studio at the London College of Printing (Andrew Boyd)

First, it should offer a thoroughly practical training, with as much hands-on experience of broadcast equipment and practical reporting as possible. The course should possess at least one studio, ample editing equipment and enough portable tape recorders to issue one per student.

Second, the course should see itself as vocational first and academic second. Academic areas which have to be covered are law, ethics and public administration, but these should be closely integrated into the practical side of the course. Chief among these is law for journalists, as no news editor would chance his reputation with a reporter who might land him with a libel suit or have him prosecuted for contempt of court.

The third indicator of a good course is its record. What jobs have past students got, and how long did they have to wait to get them?

But perhaps the most telling test is to ask prospective employers for their recommendations and look for courses that have been recognized by the industry. It is useful to have the backing of the major journalists' union, which should produce a current list of approved courses.

Ideally, begin by looking for a course that is run by a radio or TV station, and preferably one which pays the trainee a wage while he/she is learning the ropes. An alternative is to seek sponsorship from a broadcast company to pay for your training at college.

Courses range in length from a weekend to several years, from part-time to full-time. A word of warning – the cost of a course will not always be an accurate indication of its value to the student. Conversion courses also exist for newspaper reporters who want to move into broadcasting.

DEGREE, OR NOT DEGREE...?

Many courses and employers will require a degree and some evidence of commitment to your chosen career in the form of broadcasting experience. Sufficient experience will sometimes override the need for a degree.

It is usually better for school leavers to take a degree before beginning their careers. It may not be essential at first, but can be useful for promotion. The degree subject is of little importance, although a related course, such as media or communication studies, can provide an interesting overview of broadcasting. A course with a practical element which offers an attachment to the industry, can give a head start later when applying for vocational courses or jobs, but academic courses of the media-watching variety can frustrate and disappoint students who want to work within the media rather than stand on the sidelines and criticize. A good general-purpose degree would be in English – preferably at a university or college with campus radio and TV facilities.

PERSONAL QUALITIES

'The only qualities for real success in journalism are ratlike cunning, a plausible manner and a little literary ability. The capacity to steal other peoples' ideas and phrases... is also invaluable.'
– NICHOLAS TOMALIN, BRITISH JOURNALIST

'The qualities I look for in a radio reporter are: a good nose for a story, a determination to ferret out the details despite the obstacles, an interest in, and a genuine awareness of, current news and issues, a lively imaginative mind, and a sense of humour.'
– SIMON ELLIS, NEWS EDITOR, BBC ESSEX

'A good reporter is someone who is up-front with self confidence, bright, and who knows what a story is... the reporter you send out on one story who comes back with two others as well, and who can find the offbeat in the run of the mill event. Those people will always get to the top very fast.' – PENNY YOUNG, NEWS EDITOR, BBC RADIO NORTHAMPTON

Employers and training courses alike are looking for special personal qualities from people who think they have what it takes to make a broadcast journalist.

Top of the list is commitment. Reporters must have the stamina to cope with shift work whose varying patterns could take them from three in the morning one day for a twelve hour shift, to from ten at night a couple of days later.

The reporter must be able to deliver peak performance even in the face of deep-set fatigue, and still remain a cheerful team member. Prima donnas and fragile personas who need nannying and constant encouragement will last only a short while in the brusque atmosphere of the newsroom with its relentless deadlines. He/she should also be self-reliant and capable of working with a minimum of guidance and supervision.

Intelligence, curiosity, creativity and writing ability are basic qualities. Added to this, our paragon will need that essential spark. Vitality, vivacity, energy, drive, enthusiasm – call it what you will – news editors are looking for that extra something that will set one applicant above all others.

> ***'If you have a man who is a good journalist, you generally find he has a positive personality. A correspondent has to be not only competent, he has to show others that he is competent. And be a little assertive and probing and questioning – I'm hovering on the word aggression, but I don't mean to go that far. He has to make his presence felt. He has to be personable, otherwise people won't talk to him or rate him highly. Most correspondents are people who are confident.'***
>
> – TERRY HERON, FORMER EDITOR, BBC EXTERNAL SERVICES NEWS

Malcolm Dowsning, the Australian Broadcasting Corporation's chief correspondent in London looks for a quality that is rarer still, especially when coupled with these other virtues. '*Humility – the opposite of the assumption that you know it all.*'

Increasing numbers of women are setting out on careers in broadcasting. Women now outnumber men in a growing number of BBC local radio newsrooms but the influx has yet to filter up through the hierarchy.

'*I think there* **is** *discrimination,*' says BBC Radio Northampton news editor Penny Young, '*and another problem is that women tend to get diverted because they get married and have kids, but if they really want to succeed, the opportunities are there.*'

The BBC has been criticized for recruiting too few black journalists, but has altered its recruitment policies to help redress the imbalance.

Trevor McDonald was Britain's first black newscaster. He began his career in Trinidad in 1962 where he was an interviewer for local current affairs programmes. Five years later he joined the BBC in London.

His advice for those – black, white, male or female – who are starting out, is: '*Come equipped with the best qualifications you can get, such as a good degree in English, and then read voraciously – the information will stick and you will be more confident about going out into this curious world of journalism.*'

APPENDIX 2

Addresses of vocational and pre-vocational courses in broadcasting

The US alone boasts more than 10,000 radio stations and 1600 TV stations, all reliant upon an unfailing stream of trained personnel. To that end, more than 40,000 students are studying broadcasting at degree or vocational level at more than 500 different schools. A comprehensive list of course opportunities in America alone would probably fill a book, so this index of courses worldwide cannot claim to be exhaustive, but is compiled from returns made to the author's inquiries. It includes courses thought to be of direct interest to would-be broadcasters and contact numbers for organizations which can provide fuller lists of courses available. Telephone numbers are in brackets.

AUSTRALIA

Australian Film, Television and Radio School, PO Box 126, North Ryde, NSW 2113 (02-887-1666). Full-time courses for announcers, and short, specialized courses.

Canberra College of Advanced Education, Centre for Communications Studies, School of Liberal Studies, PO Box 1, Belconned, ACT 2616 (062-52-2111). BAs in professional writing; communication.

Capricornia Institute of Advanced Education, Rockhampton, QLD 4700. (079-36-1177). BA majoring in journalism.

Curtin University of Technology, School of Communications and Cultural Studies, Western Australian Institute of Technology, Bentley, WA 6102. MA (English) in journalism.

Darling Downs Institute of Advanced Education, School of Arts, Darling Heights Post Office, Toowoomba, QLD 4350 (076-31-2100). BA majoring in journalism.

Deakin University, Media Studies, Humanities School, VIC 3217. (052-47-1111). BA majoring in journalism.

Mitchell College of Advanced Education, School of Communications and Liberal Studies, Bathurst, NSW 2795 (063-332-530). BA arts and communications.

Queensland Institute of Technology, School of Business Studies, GPO Box 2434, Brisbane, QLD 4001. (07-223-2371). Bachelor of Business Communication with journalism major.

Royal Melbourne Institute of Technology, Department of Humanities, 124 La Trobe St, Melbourne, VIC 3000 (03-662-0611). BAs in: media studies and journalism; associate diploma in journalism.

South Australian College of Advanced Education, Faculty of Business, Communication and Cultural Studies, Lorne Avenue, Magill, SA 5072 (08-333-9411). BA in journalism.

University of Queensland, Journalism Studies, St Lucia, Brisbane, QLD 4067 (07-377-2501). BA majoring in journalism.

For more detailed information, contact:
Federation of Australian Broadcasters, 8 Glen Street, Milsons Point, Sydney, 2061 (02-929-4866).

CANADA

The Canadian Bureau for International Education lists the following colleges as offering programmes in or similar to broadcast journalism.

Algonquin College of Applied Arts and Technology, 1358 Woodroffe Ave, Nepean, ONT K2G 1V8. National diploma in technology, BEAC member.

Canadore College of Applied Arts and Technology, PO Box 5001, North Bay, ONT P1B 8K9. National diploma in technology. BEAC member.

Centennial College of Applied Arts and Technology, Kitchener PO Box 631, Station (A), Scarborough, ONT M1K 5E9. National diploma in technology. BEAC member.

Concordia University, 1455 De Maisonneuve Boulevard West, Montreal, Quebec, H3G 1M8. BA in journalism.

Fanshawe College of Applied Arts and Technology, PO Box 4005, London, ONT N5W 5H1. National diploma in technology, 2 years. RTNDA, CAB, BEA recognized.

Humber College of Applied Arts and Technology, 205 Humber College Boulevard, PO Box 1900, Rexdale, ONT M9W 5L7. National diploma in technology. BEAC member.

Loyalist College of Applied Arts and Technology, Wallbridge Loyalist Road, PO Box 4200, Belleville, ONT K8N 5B9. National diploma in technology. BEAC member.

Mohawk College of Applied Arts and Technology, PO Box 2034, Hamilton, ONT L8N 3T2. National diploma in technology. BEAC member.

Mount Royal College, 4825 Richard Road South West, Calgary, Alberta, T3E 6K6. National diploma in technology. BEAC member.

Northern Alberta Institute of Technology, 11762–106 Street, Edmonton, Alberta, T5G 2R1. National diploma in technology. BEAC member.

Seneca College of Applied Arts and Technology, 1750 Finch Avenue East, Willowdale, ONT M2J 2X5. National diploma in technology. BEAC member.

The Conestoga College of Applied Arts and Technology, Kitchner Campus, 229 Don Valley Drive, Kitchener, ONT N2G 4M4. National diploma in technology. BEAC member.

The Confederation College of Applied Arts and Technology, PO Box 398, Thunder Bay, ONT P7C 4W1. National diploma in Technology. BEAC member.

In addition:

The University of Western Ontario, Graduate School of Journalism, Middlesex College, London, ONT N6A 5B7 (519-661-3383). MA in journalism and short courses in law and economics for journalists.

University of Windsor, 401 Sunset Avenue, Windsor, ONT N9B 3P4 (519-253-4232). BA and MA in communications studies.

The following institutions are members of the Broadcast Education Association of Canada:

British Columbia Institute of Technology, Broadcast Centre, 3700 Willingdon Avenue, Burnaby, British Columbia, V5G 3H2 (604-434-5734). National diploma of technology.

College de Jonquiere, 65 St Hubert Street, Jonquiere, PQ G7X 7W2 National diploma in technology.

Lambton college, PO Box 969, Sarnia, ONT N7T 7K4. National diploma in technology.

Niagara College, PO Box 1005, Woodlawn Road, Welland, ONT L3B 5S2. National diploma in technology.

Ryerson Polytechnical Institute, 50 Gould Street, Toronto, ONT M5B 1E8

Other addresses:

Association of Universities and Colleges of Canada, 151 Slater, Ottowa, ONT K1P 5N1 (This lists eighty-six member colleges.)

Canadian Bureau for International Education (CBIE), 85 Albert Suite, 1400 Ottowa, ONT K1P 6A4 (613-237-4820)

INDIA

Punjab Agricultural University, Department of Journalism, Languages and Culture, Ludhiana, India. Short journalism course.

Punjabi University, Department of Journalism and Mass Communication, Patalia 147002. Degree and postgraduate degree courses.

University of Poona, Department of Communication and Journalism, Ranade Institute Building, FC Road, Pune 411 004 (54069) Bachelor of communication and journalism (post-degree degree course)

Xavier Institute of Communications, St Xavier's College, Bombay 400 001 (415-1366) One year, part-time course in journalism, short workshops on video production, announcing and broadcasting for radio and TV.

NEW ZEALAND

University of Canterbury, Christchurch 1, New Zealand. 1 year Postgraduate diploma in journalism.

TANZANIA

Tanzania School of Journalism, PO Box 4067, Dar Es Salaam (64208). Mass Communication, majoring in radio.

UK

BBC Engineering Training Department, Wood Norton, Evesham, Worcestershire, WR11 4TF. Introduction to audio operations – 10 weeks; introduction to television operations – 10 weeks; introduction to radio operations – 9 weeks; qualified audio operators – 4 weeks; qualified technical operators – 4 weeks.

BBC International Relations, Broadcasting House, London W1A 1AA Short courses in newswriting, TV production and direction.

BBC Radio Training Department Room 403, Grafton House, Broadcasting House, London W1A 1AA. Radio production – 4–8 weeks; Radio trainers – 4 weeks; Radio management – 8 weeks.

BBC Television Training, Room N313, BBC Elstree Centre, Clarendon Road, Borehamwood, Hertfordshire, WD6 1JF. Overseas production Course – 8 weeks.

Brighton Polytechnic, Moulsecoomb, Brighton BN2 4AT (0273–693665). News training course in radio and TV – 3 months.

Broadcast Training Centre (Viewplan Ltd), Springfield House, Hyde Terrace, Leeds University, Leeds. Television Production – 13 weeks.

Central Office of Information, Hercules Road, London SE1 7DU. News and feature writing – 12 weeks.

Christian Broadcast Training, PO Box 38, Newmarket, Suffolk, CB8 7EG. Cambridge radio course – 4 weeks.

City of Birmingham Polytechnic, School of English and Communications Studies, Perry Barr, Birmingham B42 2SY. BA in communications studies.

City University, Graduate Centre for Journalism Studies, Northampton Square, London EC1V OHB. Diploma in radio journalism – 1 year, JACTRJ recognized; diploma in periodical journalism – 1 year; MA international journalism – 1 year.

Cornwall College of Further and Higher Education, Killigrew Street, Falmouth, Cornwall, TR11 3QS (0326–313326) CNAA post-graduate diploma in radio journalism. 1 year, JACTRJ recognized.

Coventry Cable Television, London Road, Coventry, CV3 4HL. Station assistant and technical operators training – 12 weeks.

Coventry Lanchester Polytechnic, Faculty of Art and Design, Gosford Street, Coventry CV1 5RZ. BA in communications studies.

Darlington College of Technology, Cleveland Avenue, Darlington, Co. Durham, DL3 7BB (0325–467651). Diploma in journalism. 7 months.

Dorset Institute of Higher Education, Cranford Avenue, Weymouth, Dorset DT4 7LQ. BA (Hons) communication and media production.

Goldsmith's College, New Cross, London, SE14 6NW (01–692–7171). Diploma in communications, BA in communications and sociology.

Gwent College of Higher Education, Faculty of Art and Design, School of Film and Photography, Clarence Place, Newport, Gwent NPT 5XA. BTEC HND in film and television practice – 2 years.

Highbury College of Technology, Department of Communication and Media Studies, Cosham, Portsmouth, Hants PO6 2SA (0705–383131). Postgraduate diploma in broadcast journalism. 1 year, JACTRJ recognized.

Lancashire Polytechnic, Preston, Lancashire, PR1 2TQ (0772–22141) Post-graduate diploma in radio and television journalism. 1 year, JACTRJ recognized.

Leeds Polytechnic, Media Services, Calverley Street, Leeds LS1 3HE. Video production course (Level 1 and Level 2). 1 week each.

Napier College, Department of Print, Media, Publishing and Communication, Colinton Road, Edinburgh EH10 5DT. HND journalism studies. 2 years.

National Catholic Radio and Television Centre, Oakleigh Road, Hatch End, Middlesex, HA5 4HB. Full production course – 10 weeks; introduction to broadcasting and electronic media – 4 weeks; radio course – 1 week; full production course, 10 weeks.

National Council for the Training of Journalists, Short Courses Department, Carlton House, Hemnall Street, Epping, Essex. CM16 4NL. Electronic journalism – 2 days.

North Cheshire College, Padgate Campus, Fearnhead, Warrington WA2 0DB. BA in media and communications.

Polytechnic of Central London, Faculty of Communication, 18 Riding House Street, London W1. Short courses in radio presentation/production; basic radio skills; basic radio journalism; basic video skills; BA media studies.

Radio Worldwide Training Unit, Hurchington Manor, Little Common Road. Bexhill-on-Sea, East Sussex. Radio programme production. 12 weeks.

Sandwell College of Further and Higher Education, Woden Road, South, Wednesbury, West Midlands WS10 0PE. Television and audio production – 9 months; video production – 15 days; technical operation for broadcast studio – 2 weeks.

Sunderland Polytechnic, Department of Languages and Cultures. Forster Building, Chester Road, Sunderland SR1 3SD (76191). BA/BA (Hons) in communications studies.

The London College of Printing (a constituent of the London Institute), Journalism and Business Studies Department, Elephant and Castle, London SE1 6SB (01-735-9100 ex 359) CNAA postgraduate diploma in radio journalism – 1 year, JACTRJ recognized; BA (Hons) film and video.

The Polytechnic of Wales, Department of Behavioural and Communication Studies, Pontypridd, Mid Glamorgan CF37 1DL. BA in communication studies.

University College Cardiff, Centre for Journalism Studies, PO Box 78, Cardiff, CF1 1XL. (0222-44211). Post-graduate diploma in journalism studies – 1 year; MA course for mid-career journalists; PhD journalism studies – 2 years (7 years part time).

University of Bristol, Arts Faculty House, Senate House, Bristol 8, Postgraduate certificate course in radio, film and television 1 year.

University of Leicester, Centre for Mass Communication Research, 104 Regent Street, Leicester LE1 7LT. MA in mass communication. 1 year.

University of Stirling, Stirling, Scotland, FK9 4LA. BA film and media studies – 3 years; BA (Hons) film and media studies – 4 years.

University of Ulster at Coleraine, Cromore Road, Coleraine, County Londonderry, BT52 1SA (0265–4141). BA media studies.

Visnews International, Cumberland Avenue, London, NW10 7EH. TV studio production course 10–12 weeks; advanced documentary production course in video and film – 10–12 weeks; television news 10–12 weeks; basic video/film production – 10–12 weeks; cable operations – 4 weeks.

Other addresses:

Association of Independent Radio Contractors Ltd, Regina House, 259–269 Old Marylebone Road, London NW1 5Ra.

BBC, Broadcasting House, London W1A 1AA (for radio).

BBC Television Centre, Wood Lane, London W12 7RJ (for television).

BBC External Services, Bush House, Strand, London WC2B 4PH.

Independent Broadcasting Authority, 70 Brompton Road, London SW3 1EY.

Independent Television Companies Association Ltd, Knighton House, 56 Mortimer Street, London W1P 0AU.

Joint Advisory Committee for Radio Journalism Training, C/O NUJ, Acorn House, 314–320 Gray's Inn Road, London WC1X 8DP.

National Union of Journalists, 314–320 Gray's Inn Road, London WC1X 8DP.

Royal Television Society, Tavistock House East, Tavistock Square, London WC1H 9HR.

The British Council, Media Group, 10 Spring Gardens, London SW1A 2BN.

The City and Guilds of the London Institute foundation course in media techniques is offered by a number of further education colleges. For more details contact:
CGLI, 76 Portland Place, London W1N 4AA (01–580–3050).

USA

Arkansas State University, Arkansas 72467. BSc and MSc majoring in radio-television.

California State University, Department of Journalism, Northridge, Cal. 91330. BA in broadcast journalism.

Memphis State University, Department of Journalism, Memphis, Tennessee 38152. BAs in journalism and theatre and communication arts; MA journalism.

Medhill School of Journalism, Northwestern University, 1845 N. Sheridan Road, Evanston, Ill. 60201. MA in journalism.

The American University, School of Communication, 4400 Massachusetts Avenue, NW Washington DC 20016 (202–885–2060). BA in broadcast journalism, MA in journalism and public affairs.

The University of Alabama, Department of Broadcast and Film Communication, PO Box D, Alabama 35486 (205–348–6350).

The University of Kansas, The William Allen White School of Journalism and Mass Communications, Stauffer-Flint Hall, Lawrence, KS 66045 (913–864–3991). BA majoring in broadcast news.

There are many more courses available. The Broadcast Education Association (address given below) lists forty-one schools specializing in radio and TV, 320 colleges and universities offering degrees in broadcasting; thirty-seven colleges and universities offering broadcasting courses and 152 two-year colleges offering courses in broadcasting. For comprehensive lists contact:

American Film Institute, 501 Doheny Road, Beverley Hills, CA 90210.

Associated Press Broadcasters Association, KOBE, Drawer X, Las Cruces, NM 88001.

Broadcast Education Association, 1771 North Street, NW, Washington DC 20036.

National Association of Broadcasters, 1771 North Street, NW, Washington DC 20036

WEST INDIES

University of the West Indies, Caribbean Institute of Mass Communication, Mona, Kingston 7, Jamaica (927–6661). TV and radio courses.

ZIMBABWE

Harare Polytechnic, Division of Mass Communication, PO Box 8074, Causeway, Rhodes Avenue West, Harare, Zimbabwe. 2 year. National diploma.

For further details of courses available within the Commonwealth: Commonwealth Broadcasting Association, CBA Secretariat, Broadcasting House, London W1A 1AA.

GLOSSARY

Actuality Interviews or sounds recorded on location.

Agency tape (wire copy) Information received on news agency teleprinters.

Analogue recording Where sound and/or pictures are recorded directly on to a recording medium (without being digitally encoded).

And finally *See* Tailpiece.

Angle An item of information in a news story that a journalist chooses to emphasize. It may be a *new angle*, giving the latest development in a story, or a *local angle*, emphasizing the point of relevance of that story to a local audience.

Archive File in which previously broadcast material is stored, possibly with clippings and background material.

Aston Brand name for a type of electronic caption generator.

Audio mixer (control panel) Control desk for mixing sound sources such as grams and mike.

Autocue, Teleprompter, Portaprompt Mechanical or electrical prompting devices which allow presenters to read a script while looking at or towards the camera.

Automatic cartridge recorder (ACR) Machine for recording video news reports on to cartridge for instant replay on air. Carts are stored on a carousel.

Automatic level control (ALC) Electronic device to reduce or boost the incoming signal to a tape recorder.

BA Fire service jargon for breathing apparatus.

Back announcement (B/A, back anno) A final sentence giving extra information to be read by the anchor or presenter at the end of a recorded item or report.

Backlight Lamp shone behind interviewee to pick him/her out from background, eliminate shadows and highlight hair. *See also* Key, Fill.

Back projection Where pictures are projected on to a screen behind the newsreader. *See also* Front projection.

Barn door Adjustable flaps around a studio light used to direct the beam.

Bias High frequency current combined with audio signal to reduce recording distortion.

Bi-directional mike A microphone which will pick up sound in front and behind it.

Blank *See* Skeleton.

Boom mike Microphone held on a long telescopic boom manoeuvred by a sound technician.

Breaking news (spot story US) A story that is happening right now.

Brief Instructions given to a reporter about how to cover a story.

Buffer frames Extra frames at the start or end of a report to allow for minor delays in screening.

Bulk eraser Powerful electromagnet used for erasing entire reels of tape.

Camcorder Hand-held camera and videocassette recorder combined.

Capacitor mike Battery-operated mike, often of the tie-clip variety.

Carrier wave Frequency wave which is modulated to carry a video or audio signal.

Cartridge (cart) Loop of tape in a plastic case used for recording and playing inserts into bulletins or items into programmes. May be audio or video. Self-cueing.

Catchline A one or two word name used to identify a story, for example: world record. Also known as a *slug*.

Cathode ray tube (CRT) Vacuum tube containing electron gun emitting a controlled and continuous beam of electrons against a phosphorescent screen.

Character generator Electronic caption machine.

Charge-coupled device (CCD) Solid state sensor comprising light sensitive diodes. Used in place of conventional tubes in some modern cameras.

Check calls Regular newsroom calls to the emergency services and hospitals to find out whether news is breaking.

Chromakey (colour separation overlay, CSO) Method of electronically replacing a single colour with a second picture or image.

Clapperboard (clapstick, clapboard US) Board with movable arm used to synchronize film with soundtrack. The board is marked with the details of the shot and take. Picture and sound are synchronized by matching the clap of the arm being brought down with the picture.

Clip *See* Newsclip.

Clipping When all or part of the first word of a report is cut because the cart or tape is incorrectly cued.

Contact Source of news information.

Contribution circuit Network of landlines linking member stations of a network, along which news material is sent and received.

Contributions studio Small studio for sending reports 'up the line' to the network station.

Control panel *See* Audio mixer.

Copy story News story with no accompanying audio or visuals.

Copytaster Senior journalist who sifts incoming mail and agency copy to select items that are considered to be worth running.

Crocodile clips Metal clips used for connecting a lead from a tape recorder to a telephone for sending recordings along a phone line.

Cue 1 Introduction to a record item.
2 Instruction to a presenter to start and stop speaking. This may be given verbally, or by gestures or in writing. *See also* In-cue, Out-cue.

Cue dot (cue marker US) Small mark on corner of film to warn projectionist when the reel it is about to begin or end.

Cue-light Light on top of camera to tell presenter the camera is live. Also used in a commentary box to cue live narration.

Cue pulse Inaudible pulse recorded on tape just before the start of audio or pictures. When the tape recorder finds the pulse it will stop and the tape will be cued-up ready to play.

Cut *See* Newsclip.

Cutaway The insertion of a shot in a picture sequence which is used to mask an edit.

Deaf-aid Earpiece used by presenter to listen to instructions from the studio control room.

Decibel (db) Unit of loudness.

Delay A recorded delay of several seconds in playing back a 'live' phone-in programme to trap obscene calls. *See also* Obscenity button.

Digital recording The storage of sound and/or pictures which have been encoded as a series of numbers. Playback translates those numbers back without the noise or distortion of conventional (analogue) recording.

Directivity pattern (pickup) Area over which a microphone will pick up sound.

Dissolve Where one picture is faded out and another is faded in simultaneously.

DOA Dead on arrival. Emergency services jargon for a victim who has died either before help could arrive or before the ambulance could reach the hospital.

Dolby System for reducing audio noise and improving high frequency response.

Dope sheet (camera report) Camera operator's written record of each camera take.

Double chaining Where two telecine (film chain) machines are used alternately to screen a report.

Double system (sepmag) Where film and sound are recorded separately to be synchronized later. *See also* Single system.

Drive-time The period during radio listening when a substantial part of the audience is travelling in cars – early morning, lunchtime, early evening.

Dubbing Duplication of a recording from one recorder to another. System of electronic editing.

Edit controller The heart of a computerized tape editing system which is programmed to control the precise location of each edit.

Embargo 'Not to be released until' date on a news release. Device intended to control the publication date of an item of information.

ENG (EJ, ECC, PSC) Electronic news gathering (electronic journalism; electronic camera coverage; portable single camera) with portable video cameras. *See* Camcorder.

Equalization Improving audio quality by altering the frequency characteristics.

Erase head Magnet in tape path which erases the recording by realigning the magnetic pattern on the tape.

Fade out 1 Where a picture fades out, usually to black or to white. 2 Gradually bringing down the volume of an audio signal until it disappears.

Feature opener Informally written introduction to a soft news story designed more to arouse curiosity and to entertain than to inform.

Federal Communications Commission (FCC) The US governing body for broadcasting.

Fill Lamp casting a soft light to fill in shadows. *See also* Backlight, Key).

Fillers (or pad) Second string items used as makeweights to bring a bulletin or programme up to length.

Fishpole Hand-held sound boom. *See Boom mike.*

Flats Boards used as a backdrop to the set.

Frequency Rate at which a sound or light wave or an electronic impulse passes a given point over a specific time. *See* Hertz.

Front projection Where pictures are projected from in front of the newsreader on to a screen alongside.

Full-track Recording made across the full width of the tape. Other common types are *half track, quarter track* and *multi track*. Tapes recorded on one type of machine will not give satisfactory reproduction if played back on another.

Futures file File in which stories and news events which are known to be happening on a certain date are placed, so that coverage may be planned in advance.

FX Shorthand for sound effects.

General view (GV) Camera shot showing an entire scene to establish location.

Gobbledygook Jargon-laden and often garbled officialese intended to confuse rather than communicate.

Half-track Recording over half the width of the tape. *See also* Full-track, Quarter-track.

Handling noise Unwanted clicks and sounds picked up by a microphone as a result of handling and moving it.

Hard news Information of importance about events of significance.

Hard news formula A hard news story will cover most of the basic facts by asking the questions, who? what? where? when? why? and how?

Headline Short summary of a news story given at the start or end of a bulletin or grouped with other headlines in lieu of a longer bulletin. Also known as *highlights* or *summaries*. *See also* Teaser.

Headline sentence *See* Intro.

Hertz (Hz) Frequency of sound measured in cycles per second, for example 800 hertz is 800 cycles per second. 1000 hertz is a kilohertz (kHz).

High definition television (HDTV) TV system of more than a thousand lines resulting in improved quality.

Highlight *See* Headline.

Holding copy The first version of a story left by a reporter to be run in his/her absence while he/she is out of the newsroom getting further information on that story.

Ident Piece of recorded music played to introduce or identify a particular programme, feature or presenter. Also known as *stab, jingle, sounder*.

In-cue and out-cue These are written instructions to say when a report begins and ends. The in-cue is the first few words of that report, and the out-cue the last few words. The in-cue is a useful check that the right report is being played, and the out-cue tells presenters, directors and technical operators when the report is finishing.

Independent Broadcasting Authority (IBA) British governing body for independent television and radio.

Independent Radio News (IRN) Company which supplies hourly bulletins of national and international news to independent radio stations in the UK.

Input The newsgathering operation of a newsroom. *See* Output.

Insert *See* Newsclip.

Intro (Introduction) 1 The first, audience winning, and most important paragraph of a news story, giving the main angle of the story and the central facts. 2 The introduction (cue or lead) to a report or recorded item. Also known as the *headline sentence*.

Independent Television News (ITN) Company which supplies programmes of national and international news to the UK's other independent TV companies.

In vision (IV) Instruction on script to indicate presenter should be on camera at that point.

Jingle *See* Ident.

Jump cut An edit in a sequence of shots which has the subject jerking from one position to another.

Key Main lamp providing a hard light for modelling a subject. *See also* Backlight, Fill.

Key words One or two words which sum up the most important point of a news story.

Kicker *See* Tailpiece.

Kilohertz *See* Hertz.

Land line Cable transmission for audio and/or video.

Lavalier Cord used to hang a throat mike around performer (lavalier mike).

Lead First item in a news programme or the written cue to a news item or report.

Leader Tape or film which leads up to the start of an item. On audio tape the leader is transparent or coloured, on film it is usually numbered with a countdown sequence.

LED Light emitting diode. Low powered light used for electronic displays (on/off indicators, level meters, etc.).

Lighting grid Construction suspended from the ceiling of a studio to support the lights.

Links Narrative linking or bridging interviews in a report, summarizing or giving additional information. *See also* Package.

Links vehicle Mobile vehicle used as a platform for a microwave transmitter. *See also* Microwave.

Lip-flap Where filmed mouth movements are out of synchronization with the soundtrack.

Local angle *See* Angle.

Lower third Caption or super in the lower third of the picture.

Mandrel Small pronged grip used to retain a spool of tape on a tape recorder.

Marking-up Marking a story with important details, such as who wrote it and when and the catchline.

Menu Collection of tasters at the start of a programme giving forthcoming attractions.

Microwave System for relaying audio and video signals on very short wavelengths.

Mini-wrap Brief package, often used in the news.

MPX filter Electronic filter used to cut out interference when recording from FM radio.

Multi-angled story One which carries a number of different angles on the same story. *See also* Umbrella story.

Multi-track Tape normally used in a music studio to record separately a combination of different sounds. *See also* Full-track.

Natural Sound On Film (NAT SOF) Location sound recorded on the film or tape as the footage is taken.

Newsbooth Small studio where bulletins are presented on air.

Newsclip (cut, insert) Short extract of an interview to illustrate a story.

Newsflash (bulletin US) Interruption of normal programming to give brief details of an urgent breaking story.

Newsmix A news summary comprising a mixture of local and national news.

News release Publicity handout from an organization or public relations company informing the newsroom about a possible news item. *See also* WPB.

Newsroom conference Discussion between producers and the news editor about what stories to run in the news and how they should be covered.

Newsroom diary (prospects) A diary or sheet in which is listed all the known stories and news events that are taking place that day and require coverage.

Nipkow disc After inventor Paul Nipkow. A circular disc with a spiral of holes used in the earliest TV apparatus for scanning scenes and converting them into television pictures.

Noddies Shots of the reporter nodding or listening intently recorded after an interview to be cut in later to mask edits.

Noise reduction The electronic reduction of interference induced by the transmission system.

OB Outside broadcast.

Obscenity button (profanity button) Switch used for taking a programme instantly out of delay to prevent an obscene caller from being heard on the air. *See also* Delay.

Omni-directional mike Microphone with circular pickup pattern.

Opt-in and opt-out 1 The process of switching between local and network transmissions. Opting-in occurs when a local station goes over to a live network programme and opting-out takes place when it returns to its own programmes. 2 Opt-out is an early point at which a report may be brought to an end.

ORACLE Optical Reception of Announcements by Coded Line Electronics. A teletext system which displays words and graphics on a television screen by transmitting them along spare television lines.

Outcue Prearranged verbal cue to show that a tape or a bulletin has come to an end. A standard outcue is the regular ending to a voice report, such as 'John Smith, Independent Radio News, Nottingham.'

Out of vision (OOV) Instruction on TV script to show the narrator is not to appear in vision while reading the script.

Output The programme-making operation of a newsroom. *See* Input.

Out-takes Discarded pictures edited from a report.

Package Report comprising edited interviews separated by narrative links.

Padding *See* Fillers.

Paintbox Electronic graphics machine.

Panning handle Handle used to turn the head of a camera.

Peak programme meter (PPM) Meter for measuring peak signal level. Its specially damped action prevents flickering and produces a steady reading. *See also* VU meter.

Phono Report or interview made by telephone. Also a type of lead used to connect one piece of equipment to another.

Photo-electric cell Device to convert variations in light to electrical impulses.

Picture store Device for electronically storing wire pictures.

Piece to camera (stand-upper; stand-up) Information given by a reporter on location facing the camera.

Pixel Single dot of information on a video screen. Pixels are combined to form the pictures.

Planning board Large board used in some newsrooms to show the stories that are being covered and which reporters have been assigned to them.

Playback head Tape head which plays back previously recorded material by translating the magnetic pattern on the tape into electrical current.

Portaprompt *See* Autocue.

Pre-fade Listening to an item without playing it on air. Used to check levels, cue records and check the network signal before opting-in to the network news.

Profanity button *See* Obscenity button.

Promo *See* Trail.

Prospects *See* Newsroom diary.

Quarter-track Where the recording is made over two pairs of stereo tracks. *See also* Half-track and Full-track.

Question and answer (Q&A) When a reporter is interviewed on air about a story he/she has been covering.

Reading-in This is when a reporter, coming on shift, reads all the copy and items produced by the previous shift to familiarize himself with the stories the newsroom has been following.

Recording head The head of a tape recorder or VTR which makes the recording. It has one or more magnetic gaps which realign the magnetic particles on the tape as it passes.

Recordist Member of camera crew who operates sound and/or video recording equipment.

Remote studio Small, often unmanned, studio some distance from the radio or TV station where guests who cannot make it in to the station can be interviewed. It may be linked to the main station by satellite or cable, permitting studio quality sound and pictures for TV.

Ribbon mike Sensitive directional microphone, frequently used in recording studios.

Rifle mike (gun mike) Directional mike for picking up sound at a distance.

Rip and read Stories sent by wire service and received on teleprinter where they can (in theory) be ripped off the printer roll and read out on air.

Roller caption Mechanical caption machine.

Roll-through (roll-thru) A portion of film linking two sound bites.

Recording of (off) transmission (ROT) Tape of the output.

Rough cut First rough edit of film.

Running story One that is developing and constantly changing, throwing up new information that requires frequent revision and updates.

Rushes Raw shots that are ready for editing.

Safe area Central area of the screen where pictures and captions are unlikely to be cut off by poorly adjusted TV sets.

Scanner 1 Radio which automatically tunes in to broadcasts by the police and emergency services. 2 Outside broadcast vehicle. 3 Telecine machine. 4 Caption scanner.

Scrambler Device for scrambling satellite TV signals so only authorized viewers equipped with an unscrambler can receive them.

Self-opping When a presenter operates his/her own control desk without technical assistance.

Sepmag *See* Double system.

Sexy story A story that has instant audience appeal. Usually light and amusing. Very occasionally sexy in the usual sense.

Shot box Switches used to preset the zoom of a studio camera.

Signposting In a news programme, this means comprehensively headlining and forward trailing the programme to keep up audience interest. During a story, it means highlighting the central theme of the story at the start, amplifying that theme in a logical manner, repeating key points where necessary, and pointing the story forward at the end.

Silly season The time of year over the summer holiday period when nothing seems to happen and the news media resorts to covering trivia.

Single system (commag) Where the soundtrack is recorded optically or magnetically on to the film itself.

Skeleton (blank) Programme script which has gaps between the pages for insertion of new and late items.

Slug *See* Catchline.

Sound bite (Grab – Australia) Portion of an interview or snatch of actuality selected for screening.

Sounder (jingle, stab) *See* Ident.

Sound on film (SOF) *See* NAT SOF.

Sound reader Editing device used to play back optical and magnetic soundtracks.

Spike Newsroom anachronism. A metal prong on to which incoming copy and background material which is not required immediately is impaled.

Splicer Device for joining manually edited film or tape.

Splicing tape Sticky tape used to join physical edits made by cutting the recording tape or film.

Spot story (US) An item of breaking news, such as a fire or an air crash.

Stab Short, emphatic jingle. *See* Ident.

Standard outcue (payoff) *See* Outcue.

Stand-upper (stand up) *See* Piece to camera.

Stereo A recording made using left and right channels to separate and spread the sound.

Stringer Freelance correspondent.

Summary 1 *See* Headline. 2 News programme or bulletin rounding up the most important news events.

Super (caption) Title or caption mechanically superimposed or electronically generated on the picture.

Switching pause Short pause in transmission before and after the network bulletin to permit local stations to opt-in and out cleanly.

Syndicated tapes Tapes sent out to radio stations by PR and advertising agencies to promote a company or product.

Tailpiece (kicker, and finally) Light hearted story at end of bulletin or newscast.

Talkback Intercom device for talking to station staff on location or in other parts of the building.

Talking head Disparaging term used for a story which features dry expert opinion rather than the views of 'real' or ordinary people.

Teaser, taster Snappy, one-line headline, usually at start of programme (*see* Menu), designed to tease the audience into wanting to find out more. May include a snatch of actuality.

Telecine (TK, film chain) Device for converting film pictures into TV pictures and for screening stills.

Telephone balance unit (TBU) Device used in the making of recorded telephone interviews. Permits interviewer to use a studio microphone and balances the levels of the two voices.

Teleprompt *See* Autocue.

Teletext Process for transmitting written and graphic information on to TV using the spare lines of a TV signal. *See also* ORACLE.

Ten code Spoken communication code used by the emergency services, where the word 'ten' indicates that the code is being used, and the number spoken after it carries the message, i.e. '10–31' means crime in progress. The code numbers used will vary.

Time base Device used to synchronize the picture sweep of a TV set with the transmitted image.

Tip-off Call from a stringer, tipster or member of the audience to let the station know that a story is breaking.

Tipster *See* Tip-off.

Touchscreen studio Where all the studio equipment is controlled electronically by touching part of the screen of a computer.

Trail (or promo) Telling the audience about items which are to follow.

Trim bin Bin with protective lining in which edited strips of film are hung.

TX Shorthand for transmission.

Umbrella story A single story incorporating a number of similar items under one banner. *See also* Multi-angled story.

Uni-directional mike Microphone which responds mainly to sounds directly in front of it.

VCR Videocassette recorder.

Vérite Actuality programme or feature made without accompanying narrative or commentary.

Vision mixer (switcher, technical director) 1 Operator who controls, fades, wipes and dissolves in the studio control room. 2 Device used to fade, wipe, dissolve. *See also* Wipe.

Visuals The visual element of a TV report: photographs, film or tape footage or graphics.

Voice over Commentary recorded over pictures by an unseen reader. *See also* OOV.

Voice report (voicer) Details and explanation of a story by a reporter or correspondent. More expansive than a copy story. Permits a change of voice from the newsreader.

Vox pop Latin 'vox populi' or 'voice of the people'. Refers to street interviews conducted to poll public opinion. (US – man in the street interviews.)

Visual production effects machine (VPE) Computer graphics system used in TV.

VT80 Visual production effects machine invented by ITN. *See also* VPE.

VTR Videotape recorder.

VU meter Volume unit meter. Imprecise meter for monitoring recording and playback levels. *See also* PPM.

Wildtrack Recording of ambient sound for dubbing later as background to a report.

Wipe Crossing from one picture to another, giving the impression that one is wiping the other off the screen.

Wire service News agency which sends copy out to newsrooms along landlines (wires) where it is received by teleprinters or directly into computers.

WPB The ultimate destination of 90 per cent of a newsroom's incoming mail – the waste paper bin.

Further reading

ABC of Plain Words, Sir Ernest Gowers, HMSO, 1951.

All-News Radio, Phillip O. Kierstead, TAB Books, 1980.

Broadcast News, Radio Journalism and an Introduction to Television, Mitchell Stephens, Holt, Rinehart and Winston, 1980.

Broadcast News, The Inside Out, Julius K. Hunter and Lynne S. Gross, C.V. Mosby, 1980.

Careerscope – Careers in Radio, John Keats, Hamilton House Publishing.

Careers in Television and Radio, Julia Allen, Kogan Page, 1986.

Editing and Design, Book One: Newsman's English, Harold Evans, Heinemann, 1972.

Effective TV Production, Gerald Millerson, Focal Press, 1983.

Fundamentals of Radio Broadcasting, John Hasling, McGraw Hill.

How it Works... Television, RPA Edwards, Ladybird Books, 1984.

Local Radio, Barrie Redfern, Focal Press, 1978.

McNae's Essential Law for Journalists, Walter Greenwood and Tom Welsh, Butterworths, 1985.

News, Newspapers and Television, Alastair Hetherington, Macmillan, 1985.

On Camera, Harris Watts, BBC, 1984.

Radio, A Guide to Broadcasting Techniques, Elwyn Evans, Barrie and Jenkins, 1977.

Radio Programme Production, A Manual For Training, Richard Aspinall, UNESCO, 1977.

Reporting for Television, Carolyn Diana Lewis, Columbia University Press, 1984.

See Inside a Television Studio, George Beal, Hutchinson, 1977.

See It Happen: The Making of ITN, Geoffrey Cox, Bodley Head, 1983.

Television – Behind the Screen, Peter Fairley, Independent Television Productions, 1976.

Television: Here is the News, Anthony Davis, Independent Television Productions, 1976.

Television News, Irving E. Fang, Hastings House, 1972.

The Broadcast Communications Dictionary, Lincoln Diamant, Hastings House, 1978.

The Spoken Word, A BBC Guide, Robert Burchfield, BBC, 1981.

The Technique of Radio Production, Robert McLeish, Focal Press, 1988.

The Technique of Television News, Ivor Yorke, Focal Press, 1987.

The Technique of Television Production, Gerald Millerson, Focal Press, 1985.

The Techniques of Radio Journalism, John Herbert, A & C Black, 1976.

The Work of the Television Journalist, Robert Tyrell, Focal Press, 1981.

Work in Local Radio!, Geoffrey Roberts, Bradford College Print Centre.

World Communications, UNESCO, Gower Press/Unipub/The Unesco Press, 1975.

INDEX

AAP (Australian Associated Press), 23
Abbreviations, 72
ABC (American Broadcasting Company), 23–4, 42, 132, 167, 249, 340, 348
ABC (Australian Broadcasting Corporation, 56, 350
Abstractions, 45–6, 96
  ladder of abstraction, 46
Accidents, 6
Accuracy, 22, 58–60, 88, 98, 171, 177, 182, 230
  accurate English, 44–5, *see also* Hyperbole
ACR (Automatic Cartridge Recorder), 313, 360
Acronyms, 72
Action, 165
  action shots, 290–1, 296
Actuality, 31, 100, 103, 112, 119–20, 123, 166, 170, 182, 190, 193–4, 196, 203, 238, 360
Actuality, Radio 4, 104
Adjectives, 40, 65–6
Ad-libs, 27, 129, 141–2, 337
Adrenalin, 90–2, 139–40, 191
Advertising code, 20
  advertising pressure, 170–1
AFP (Agence France Presse), 176
Africa, 23–4, 27
Air India air disaster, 50–1
ALC (Automatic Level Control), *see* Levels and Limiter
All India Radio, 24
Allaun, Frank, 165
Allen, Julia, 347
Alliteration, 48
All-news radio, 105
Ambiguity, 73
Amin, Mohammed, 260
Ampex, 206
Analysis, 81, 169, 251
Anchors, 106, 131–5, 139, 143
  anchors versus newsreaders, 132–3
And finally . . . , 112, 128, 366, *see also* Tailpiece and Kicker
Angle, news, 4, 19, 26, 30, 32–3, 35, 50–2, 60, 89, 92, 112, 122, 167, 224, 250, 258, 360
  human angle, 82
  local angle, 6–8, 10, 33, 50, 54
  multi-angled (umbrella) stories, 51, 363, 366
Announcement booth (presentation area), 337
Announcer, 133, 337, 348
AP (Associated Press), 23, 176, 342
Archive, 15, 107, 259, 261, 308, 321, 340, 344, 349, 360
Assignments, 248, 277
  assignments editor, 106
Assistant director, 336
Assistant editor, 176–7, 182, 185
Aston, 253, 360
Attention span, 42
Attribution, 66–7
Audience (listener, viewer), 6–8, 19–20, 30, 33, 36, 40–1, 43, 46–7, 50, 53–4, 58, 67, 71, 75–6, 80, 82–3, 89, 96, 105–6, 108, 112–13, 118–23, 125, 130, 138, 140–1, 144–5, 147–8, 152–3, 166, 168, 188, 192, 196–7, 202, 232, 243, 262, 297, 301, 303, 326–7, 342, 344
  audience loyalty, 8, 103, 117–18
  audience ratings, 5, 30, 102, 131, 169–70
  audience reaction, 3–4, 10, 33, 111, 154, 167
  target audience, 5, 118, 242
Australia, 23–4, 56, 105, 134, 158, 172, 185, 249, 293, 340, 342, 348, 350, 354–5
  Australian Broadcasting Commission, 158, 354
  Australian Broadcasting Tribunal, 158
Authority, 37, 75, 132–5, 170, 194
Autocue, *see* Prompter
Automatic level control, *see* Levels

Back announcement (back anno, BA), 58, 197, 203, 360
Back projection (rear projection), 328, 360
Background information, 31–2, 79, 88, 97–8, 257, 308
Background noise, 277, 280, 284, 292–3, 298
Backtiming, 130
Baird, John Logie, 268–9
Balance of news, 30, 121
  balancing words with pictures, 306–7
  programme balance, 30, 103, 121–2
Balmforth, Katrina, 52
BBC, 12, 23–7, 40, 60, 76, 78, 92, 105, 109–10, 119–21, 133, 135–6, 140–1, 143, 147–8, 151, 157–62, 165–6, 168, 174–89, 205, 216, 231, 235–6, 247, 249, 269, 275, 340, 342, 350, 353–4, 357–8
  BBC Essex, 37, 120
  BBC External Services, 12, 14, 32, 39, 43, 52, 103, 108, 120, 141, 147, 151, 161–2, 174–90, 205, 351, 354
  BBC General News Service

(GNS), 25, 60, 176
BBC Mark 1 desk, 236
BBC Mark 3 and 4 desks, 138, 231, 235
BBC Monitoring Unit, 12, 176
BBC Radio Bedfordshire, 235
BBC Radio Bristol, 27
BBC Radio 4, 81, 94, 113, 133, 95
BBC Radio London, 340
BBC Radio Northampton, 65, 148, 353
BBC Radio Solent, 14, 102
BBC 6 O'Clock News, 109
BBC Television South and West, 27
BBC TV News, 109, 113, 120
BBC Ulster, 130
BBC World Service, 175–89, *see also* BBC External Services
Broadcasting House, 143
Bush House, 175
BCC (Broadcasting Complaints Commission), 158
BCNZ (Broadcasting Corporation of New Zealand), 24, 340
Berry, Colin, 123
Bestic, Richard, 4, 75
Bias, 17, 80, 96, 135–6, 160–2, 164, *see also* Prejudice
camera bias, 164–5
Bias (recording), 211–12, 219, 360
Black, Jim, 133
Body language, 91, 221
Bosworth, Annette, 7, 106
Bradlee, Ben, 3
Breaking news (spot story), 15–16, 26, 30–2, 59–60, 99, 103, 191, 193–4, 197, 206, 321, 360, *see also* Running story
Bremer, Hans, 183
Brevity, 88
Bridge, 58, 129, 297
Brief, the, 31–3, 89, 360
Broadcast News of Canada, 38, 42
Broadcasting unions, 27, *see also* NUJ
CBU (Caribbean Broadcasting Union), 27
EBU (European Broadcasting Union), 27
Inter-American Association of Broadcasters (AIR), 27
URTNA (Union of National Radio and Television Organizations of Africa, 27
Brooks, Peter, 182
BTQ-7, 340
Buerk, Michael, 162
Buffer frames, 318–19, 360
buffer material, 127
buffer shots, 296
Bulk eraser, 207–8, 360
Bulletin, 15, 17, 25–6, 32, 55, 78, 83, 87–8, 103, 108, 111–13, 119, 125, 128, 153, 169, 177–9, 184, 192–3, 195, 199, 202, 210, 261, 336, 340
Burnet, Alastair, 160, 247, 254

Cable TV, 102, 105, 269, 271, 274, 343, 347
Camera, 139, 153, 258–9, 269–71, 275, 277, 280, 282, 287–99, 327–9, 332–6,
Camera bias, 164–5
Camera crew, 104, 106, 163–4, 168, 248, 250, 258, 275–82, 285, 298–9, 321, 336
Camera kit, 277
Camera mountings, 332
Camera positions, 289
Camera script (crib cards), 334
Camera shots, 254, 278–9, 287–300, 303, 335, 337
action shots, 290–1, 296
buffer shots, 296
camcorder, 276, 360
CCD, 271, 361
closing shot, 290
establishing shot, 259, 289–90
insert shots, 290
overlays, 290
pan, 279, 289–90, 332
portable single camera, (PSC), *see* ENG
shoot for impact, 291
shooting schedule, 298
shot box, 332, 365
shot changes, 290
shot length, 290
shot list, 278, 300–1, 314
shot ratio, 279
shot rhythm, 290
shot sequence, 279, 289
silent (mute) camera, 277
16 mm film camera, 277
two shot, 294
zoom, 279, 287, 289, 321, 332
Cameraperson, 165, 248, 258–9, 266, 275–9, 282, 284, 291–2, 295, 299, 315, 332, 327
Campaigning journalism, 162
Canada, 24, 38, 42, 50–1, 57, 69, 105, 135, 244, 356
Capital Radio, 9–10, 90–1, 126, 348
Caption, 115, 263, 266, 303–5, 310, 319, 321, 325–7, 335
caption generator, 302, *see also* Character generator
caption machine, 326 *see also* Supers
Careers in TV and radio, 347–54
Carrier wave, 271, 272, 360
Carroll, Lewis, 154
Cartridge (cart), 208–10, 236–7, 243, 360
Cassette, 206, 211, 214, 218–20
cassette recorder, 214, 218–20, 228–9
Catchline (slug), 181, 360
CBC (Canadian Broadcasting Corporation), 24, 69
CBS (Columbia Broadcasting System), 17, 24, 105–6, 134, 167, 188, 295
CBU (Caribbean Broadcasting Union), 27
CEEFAX, *see* Teletext
Censorship, *see* Freedom of the media
Channel 4 News, 109–10, 134, 249, 251, 255
Channel 9 (Australia), 23, 249
Character generator, 326, 361
Charisma, 132, 139
Check calls, 12, 15–16, 361
Chequerboard (checkerboard), 319

Chiltern Radio, 52, 125, 207, 235
Chinagraph (grease) pencil, 226–7, 314, 316, 318
Chromakey (CSO – colour separation overlay), 327–8, 330–1, 361
Citizens' band radio, 10
CKCU-FM, 244
Clapperboard (clapstick, clapboard US), 278, 315–16, 361
Clarity, 72, 147
Clarke, Arthur C., 273
Clauses, 41–2
Cleveland, Paul, 42, 132, 167, 348
Clichés, 43, 62–5
Clifford, Brian, 123
Clip (cut, insert), 32, 83, 87–9, 199, 202, 210, 237, 363
Clipping, 209
CNN (Cable News Network), 105–6, 344
Coast to Coast, 26
Cockburn, Alexander, 161
Code of conduct (NUJ), 171
Colloquialisms, 46
Colour balance, 258, 278, 328
Commag (combined magnetic), 315
Comment, 161–2, 169, 171, 199
Commentary, 238, 251, 277, 290, 297–8, 300–7, 312
  commentary booth, 263–4, 312
  commentator, 213, 284
Commercial break, 119, 122, *see also* pre-commercials
Communication, 40–1, 48, 222
Compact disc, 236, 337
Compiling the report (TV), 259–67, 300–1, 310–29
Composite, 322–3
  composite print, 319
Computer, 15, 23, 39, 64, 180–2, 211, 241–4, 249, 251, 259, 261, 307, 321, 325, 334, 339–41, 343
  Basys computer, 260, 339–41
  computer graphics, 118
  computer sound storage, 211, 337
  computerized editing, 225, 229, 243, 261–2
  computerized newsroom, 15, 243, 339–41
  database, 15, 308, 340
    Nexis, 340
    World Reporter, 340
  portable computer, 238, 340
Concise Oxford Dictionary, 3, 65
Concrete English, 45–6, 69, 96
Confidentiality, 171
Confirmation, 58, 67
Conflict, 7–8, 165
Conrad, Joseph, 157
Contacts, 13, 22, 33–5, 59, 89–90, 349, 361
  chasing contacts, 33–4
  contacts book, 13–14, 17
  contacts file, 33
Contentious statements, 67–8
Context, 230, 253, 291–3
Continuity, 296
  continuity sheet, 318
Contractions, 47
Contribution circuit, 26, 193–4, 196, 202, 361
Contributions studio, 236–7, 361, *see also* Newsbooth
Control room, 142–3, 153, 252, 254, 266, 283–4, 313, 332, 334–8
  control desk (panel), 138, 231, 236–7, 241, 335–7
  control room personnel, 335–7
  gallery, 335
Controversy, 7, 10, 35, 67, 76
Cooke, Keiran, 349
Copy story, 193–4, 361
Copyright, 26
Copytasting, 19, 30, 106, 178, 248, 361
Corbin, Jane, 93
Corpsing, 145
Correspondents, 20–1, 23, 106, 177–8, 180, 182, 187, 354, *see also* Stringers
  agency correspondents, 23
  foreign correspondents, 177, 184–7, 239, 348
Countdown clock, 313, 335
County Sound, 40, 54
Cox, Geoffrey, 122
Crann Tara, 276
Credibility, 5, 37, 58, 133–5, 145, 182
'Creepie peepie', 275
Crime reporting, 6–7, 15, 163
Crisis, 9
  Cuban missile crisis, 68
Crocodile clips, 238–9, 361
Cronkite, Walter, 131–2
Cue, 79, 194–5, 197, 202, 237, 254, 259, 301–2, 304–6, 313, 336, 361, *see also* Lead
  cue light, 302, 332, 361
  cue marker, 319, 361
  cue pulses, 208–9, 261–2, 311–12, 361
  cue sheet 54
  film cues, 264, 318–19
Current affairs, 255, 278, 280, 298, 348, 351
Curriculum vitae, 350
Cut, news, *see* Clip
Cutaways, 259, 293–5, 298, 315, 320, 361
Cutting the programme, 127–30

Dana, Charles, 3
Database, *see* Computer
Day, Robin, 78
DBX noise reduction, 219
Dead air, 143
Deadline, 22, 30, 32–7, 43, 64, 90, 237, 249, 255, 286, 298, 345, 347, 353
Decibels, 210, 361
Degree, university, 353
Delay system, 240–2, 361
Demonstration tape, 350–1
Deregulation, 243
Desert Island Discs, 95–6
Detail, 303
Developing stories, *see* Running stories
Developing the story, 56
Development of TV, 268–74
Diary, *see* Newsroom diary
Digital delay, 242
  digital recording, *see* Recording
  digital tape, 206
  digital TV, 343–4
  digital video effects machine (DVE), 329

Dimbleby, Richard, 119–20
Director, 27, 116, 252, 254–5, 264, 266–7, 278–9, 284, 298, 304–5, 313, 315, 318–20, 330, 332–3, 335–8
  assistant director, 336
Disorder, reporting, 163–4
Dissolve, 290, 312, 319–20, 332, 361
Distortion, 165, 168, 171, 230, 291, 293–5, *see also* Hyperbole and Sensationalism
Distortion to recording, 211–12, 231, 293
Documentary, 103, 278, 280, 298–9, 348
Dolby noise reduction, 212, 219, 361
Doorstepping, 248
Dopesheet (camera report), 278, 299, 361
Double system, 314–16, 361
Downing, John, 164
Downing, Malcolm, 56, 354,
Drama, 5–6, 291
  drama documentary, 103
Drive time, 9–10, 361
Dubbing (audio), 292, 312, 361
  dub editing, 214, 219, 226, 228–9
  dubbing mixer, 318
  video dubbing, 209, 261–3, 311–12
Dunhill, David, 135–6, 140, 142–3, 150
Dunn, Tony, 162
Durant, Will, 108

Earpiece (deaf aid), 27, 153, 251, 254, 266, 333, 361
Easy Listening Formula, 44, 48
EBU (European Broadcasting Union), 27
ECC (electronic camera coverage), *see* ENG
Editing:
  assembly editing, 261, 275
  computerized editing, 225, 229, 243
  digital editing, 242
  dub editing, *see* Dubbing
  edit controller, 262, 310–12, 361
  edit timer, 311
  editing bench, 317
  editing block, 226–8
  editing booth, 259
  editing on camera, 291
  editing room, 36
  editing script, 299
  editing sound on film, 315
  editing suite (videotape booth), 225, 259, 310–11, 313
  editing videotape, 249, 261–2, 275, 295, 310–20
  film editing, 275, 279, 289, 290, 294, 299, 314–19
  rough editing, 100
  tape editing, 202–3, 214, 224–34, 238, 289, 293, 295
  unethical editing, 165, 230
  videotape editor, 259–60, 262, 264, 279, 290, 294, 299, 310–13
Editorial conference, *see* Newsroom conference
Editorial freedom, *see* Freedom of the media
Editors, 19, 21, 106, 177, 180, 250–1, 253, 256
  assignments editor, 106
  assistant editor, 176–7, 182, 185
  chief assistant editor, 162, 168
  chief sub-editor, 336
  deputy news editor, 29, 177
  desk editor, 106
  duty editor, 107, 180, 184, 250
  editor-in-chief, 251–2
  foreign editor, 106, 251, 256
  home editor, 106, 251
  input (intake) editor, 106–7, 177, 182, 202, 204
  managing editor, 177
  news editor, 13–14, 26, 29–33, 36, 54, 69, 107, 113, 165, 169, 179–80, 191–2, 199, 203, 238, 250–1, 256, 348–51, 354
  output editor, 251
  programme editor (producer), 106
  senior duty editor, 177
  senior editor, 340
  sports editor, 106, 194
  sub-editor, 106, 177, 180, 331, 340, 348, 350
EDS Portaprompt, 152
Edwards, James, 161, 176–7, 182, 185
EJ (electronic journalism), *see* ENG
Electrons, 270–2
  electron gun, 270–2
Ellis, Simon, 37, 120, 353
Embargo, 19–20, 361
Emergency services radio, 16
EMI, 269
Emphasis, 71, 149–50
ENG (electronic news gathering), 249, 253, 258–9, 271, 275–8, 283, 337, 362
Entertainment, 5, 8, 30, 46, 50, 55–6, 102, 106, 112, 123, 138, 158
Equalization (tape), 212, 219, 240, 362
Essex Radio, 22, 353
Establishing programme identity, 117–18
Ethics, 156–72, 230, 240, 294
  code of conduct (NUJ), 171
  responsible reporting, 157, 163–72
  unethical editing, 165, 230
Eurovision, 249, 251
Evans, Harold, 43, 62
Extel, 342
Eye contact, 75, 90–2, 148, 153, 222

Faction, 103
Fades, 230–3, 319, 332, 362
  fader (slider), 231
  pre-fade, 130, 232, 364
Falklands Conflict, 162
Familiar words, 44
Fang, Irving E., 44, 48
Feature, 30, 55–6, 129, 169
  feature openers, 55–6, 362
Federal Communications Commission (FCC), 158, 242, 362
Federation of Australian Broadcasters, 172
Figures, 72
Files, 14–15, 30

Fillers (padding), 20, 30, 123, 362
  filling, 128–30
Film, 249, 275, 314–20, 343
  answer print, 314
  assembling the print, 319
  chequerboard (checkerboard), 319
  composite print, 319
  film cues, 318–19
  film editing, 314–19
    cement joiner, 318
    cue marker, 319
    editing machine, 317
    film editor, 290, 314, 316–19
    film joiner, 319
    film leader, 318–19
    hot splicer, 318
    sound reader (pic sync.), 317
  film library, 259, 323
  film playback, 320
    roll-through, 320
    telecine, 320
  film processing, 285
  film traffic, 259
  film types, 314–15
  film versus videotape, 275
  final cut, 314
  grading, 314
  reversal, 314
  rough cut, 314
  showprint, 314
  silent (mute) film, 298, 314, 320
  splices, 316, 319, 365
Fishpole, 333, 362
Flats, 331, 362
Fletcher, Dr James, 346
Flewin, John, 249–50
Floor manager, 246, 333
Fluff, 143
Fly-on-the-wall, 104
Follow-up, 7, 26, 30, 51, 88
Ford, Anna, 71, 151
Foreign correspondents, *see* Correspondents
  foreign coverage, 113, 175–89, 286
  foreign desk, 248–9
  foreign editor, 251
Foreign Office (British), 177, 179
Forward planning, 127, 129, 250–1
Forward trail, 119
Fowler's Modern English Usage, 70
Freedom of the media, 157–60, 171
  censorship, 157–60, 171
  editorial freedom, 13
  government interference, 158–60, 172
  independence, 13, 158–9, 170, 175, 179
  media control, 160
  self-regulation, 172
Freelance, 20–1, 30, 106, 182, 185, 187, 248–9, 349, *see also* Correspondents and Stringers
Frequency, 210, 271
Front projection, 328, 362
Futures file, 14, 362

Gall, Sandy, 247
Gallery, 335
Galsworthy, John, 65
Gardner, Andrew, 71, 151
Gate, 142
Gau, John, 122
Getting the story, 29–37
Ghandi, Mrs Indira, 93, 274
Gilbert, Richard, 105
Gobbledygook, 43, 49, 362
Godoy, Julio, 160
Good taste, 123, 166–7
Gopher, 193, 197
Government reporting, 7
Grabs (Australia), 290, 293, 301, *see also* Sound bites
Grampian Television, 276
Grams operator, 337
Graphics, 31, 45, 53, 103, 107, 115, 121, 129, 249, 252–4, 259–60, 265, 288, 303–4, 308, 310, 323–5, 327, 335, 337, 343
  animated graphics, 321, 324, 327
  electronic graphics, 249, 260, 323–5
  full-frame graphics, 327, 331
  graphic artist, 106, 252, 323, 325
  graphic stills, 288, 322, 324
  graphics machine, 253, 259–60, 325–6, 328
  Paintbox, 253–4, 324, 364
  Visual Production Effects machine (VPE), 323, 366
  graphics operator, 259, 262
  window graphics, 327, 331
Grease pencil, *see* Chinagraph pencil
Greensmith, Jim, 112
Groupings, 122–4
Guiding formula, 179
Gunter, Barrie, 123

Hall, Peter, 343
Hammond, John, 167
Handling noise, 213, 362
Hanson, Lord, 92
Happy talk, 132, 169–70
Hard news, 30, 50, 52–3, 55–6, 106, 110, 121, 251, 257, 362
  hard news formula, 52, 55, 61, 362
Harris, Joel Chandler, 50
Harris, Sim, 125
Hayakawa, S.I., 46
HDTV (high definition television), 343, 362
Headline, 192–4, 254, 261, 362
  headline sentence (intro, lead), 51–3, 55–6, 58, 66, 68
    double intro, 51
  headline shot, 263
  headlines (highlights), 32, 118–19, 124, 192, 236, 266, 275
Health, 8
Hemingway, Ernest, 38
Henderson, Ian, 350
Heron, Terry, 179, 187, 188, 351, 354
Hertz, 210, 362
  kilohertz, 210
Hetherington, Alastair, 7
Hitler, Adolf, 157
Hoaxes, 21–2
Holding copy, 31–2, 194, 362
Home editor, 251
Home Office, 158
Home Secretary, 158
Homonyms, 70–1
Housham, David, 105
HTV, 75

Human angle, 82
Human interest, 8, 50, 55, 108, 111, 121, 257
Humphrys, John, 113, 133, 139, 153
Hyperbole (hype), 63, 65, 166, *see also* Distortion and Sensationalism

IBA (Independent Broadcasting Authority), 123, 158, 362
Image intensifier, 277
Immediacy, 3–4, 9–10, 53, 68–9, 98, 108, 111–12, *see also* Time references
Impact, 3–4, 50, 113, 260, 291–2
material impact, 111
shooting for impact, 291
Impartiality, 67, 158, 160–2, 170, 179
Imperial Echoes, 175, 182, 188
Importance, 3, 6, 10, 30, 33, 46, 56, 108, 118, 121, 179
Impression, 45, 57
In the Psychiatrist's Chair, 81
Independence, 13, 158–9, 170, 175, 179
Independent Broadcasting Authority, *see* IBA
Independent radio network (UK), 20, 24–5, 27
India, 23–4, 50–1, 93, 274, 345, 356
Industry, 8
Inflection, 40
Inlay, 328–9
Input, 106–7, 248, 362
input (intake) editor, 106
Insert, 199, 202, 237
Insert edit, 311
Insert shot, 290
Inspiration, 64–5
Intake, 106, 248
intake editor, 106, 202, 204
Integrity, 5, 13, 161, 170
Inter-American Association of Broadcasters (AIR), 27
Intercutting, 293
Interest, 4–5, 19, 46–7, 53, 124–5, 179, 290
Internal pressures on reporting, 169–70
Interview, 18, 27, 31–6, 75–101, 190, 194, 197–9, 202, 213, 218, 221–2, 224–5, 230, 237–8, 240, 243, 258–9, 263, 265, 276
approach, 89–92
arrangements, 89
before the interview, 220–3
pre-chat, 90–1, 257–8
distractions, during, 221
interviewer, 76, 78, 80–2, 85–6, 90, 92–6
length, 199
questions, 88, 92–8
bridging questions, 95–6
double questions, 96
leading questions, 96–7
question scope, 94
short questions, 95
single idea questions, 95
yes/no questions, 94
setting up the interview, 87–101
setting up the interview room, 221
types of interview:
actuality, 82–3
adversarial, 80
emotional, 82
entertainment, 82
grabbed, 84–5
hard news, 78–9
informational, 79
interpretative, 81
investigative, 79–80
live, 127, 135, 184, 199
person-in-the-street interview (vox pop), 83
personal, 81–2
Q & A (question and answer), 99–100, 197, 364
telephone or remote, 83, 193, 237–9, 243, 331
TV interview, 257–9
vox pop and multiple, 83–4
winding up the interview, 98–9
Intro (lead, headline sentence), 51–6, 58, 66, 254, 266, 363
double intro, 51
Investigative journalism, 13, 122, 170
IRA, 18
Ireland, 50–1
IRN (Independent Radio News), 24–5, 75–6, 86, 342, 348, 362
Item length, 125
Item order, 110
Item selection and order, 108–16, 165, 171, 179
ITN (Independent Television News), 5, 23, 81, 93, 109–10, 115, 119, 121, 133, 157, 162–4, 168, 246–7, 275, 283–5, 296, 303, 335, 338, 340, 348–50, 362, *see also* *News at 5.45* etc.

Japan, 342
Jargon, 43, 96
Jenkins, Clare, 168
Jingle (sounder), 40, 191, 194, 209, 241, 337
Job interview, 351
Jobs in radio, 348
Jobs in television, 348–9
Johnson, Lyndon B., 158
Johnson, Malcolm, 338
Journalese, 64–5
Jump cuts, 259, 293–5, 362

Kampala, 23
Kenya, 4
Key words, 53, 55, 149, 297, 363
Kicker, *see* Tailpiece
Kierstead, Philip O., 347
Kingsley, Ben, 95
Kington, Miles, 124
Klein, David, 342
Kudelski, 219
Kurait, Charles, 188

Landline, 23, 363
Laser disc, 206, 211, 269
Last line, 57–8
Last words, 57–8
Law, 59, 170–1, 352
contempt of court, 352
copyright, 26
libel, 21, 80, 85, 170–1, 240, 352
monitoring police radio, 16
Police and Criminal Evidence Act, 164

Lawley, Sue, 118, 123, 138
LBC (London Broadcasting Company), 24, 106
Lead, 52, 194, 253–4, 259, 266, 301, 337–8, 363
Leader (film), 318–19, 363
  leader code, 228
  leader tape, 228, 363
    banding, 228
Leo, John, 64
Levels:
  ALC (Automatic Level Control), 215, 217–19, 231, 360, *see also* Limiter
  level check, 221–2, 237, 258
  recording levels, 215, 217–18, 221–3, 231–3, 240, 279
Lewis, Carolyn Diana, 118, 122
Lewis, Martyn, 308
Libel, *see* Law
Library, 14, 32, 253, 257, 259, 277, 308, 344, *see also* Film and TV library
Light pen, 324
Lighting, 331–2, 258–9, 277, 280–2
  backlight, 258, 281–2
  fill light, 258, 281
  key light, 258, 281
  lighting director, 337
  lighting grid, 331, 363
  lighting plot, 337
  lighting rig, 331
  lighting technician/engineer/elecrician, 248, 275–7, 280–2
Limiter, 219
Line, the, 295–6
Link, 202, 301, 320, 363
  linking, 124
  linking items, 112
Links vehicle, 285, 363
Lip-flap, 363
Lipman, Walter, 158
Listener, The, 105
Live reports, 36, 195–202, 238
Local angle, 6–8, 10, 33, 50, 54
  local considerations, 112–13
  local government, 7
  local news, 6, 10, 107, 122
  local newsroom, 6, 17, 24, 33, 90, 107, 354
  local stations, 13, 347
Logging the tape, 35–6, 215, 222
London College of Printing, 348, 352

MacGregor, Sue, 140
Macquarie Network, 340
Magazine programme, 106
Mailbag, 18–19, 251
Major market, 347–8
Malaysia, 342
Mallet, Sheila, 125
Marantz cassette recorder, 218–19
Marking up, 54, 181–2, 194, 363
Master control room (MCR), 286
Master tape, 226, 261–2, 311–13
Mayer, Martin, 4
MBS (Mutual Broadcasting System), 24
McCarthy era, 161
McDonald, Trevor, 134, 143, 254, 354
McEwen, Arthur, 3
McKenzie, Rob, 90–1, 124, 348, 351
McLeish, Robert, 140
McQuail, Denis, 165
Meacham, Steven, 169
Media control, *see* Freedom of the media
Media Touch Systems Inc., 241
Media Week, 162
Melby, Judith, 9, 135
Meltdown factor, 123
Menu, 118, 194, 199–200, 363
Mercia Sound, 27
Metaphors, 46, 64
Mexico, 105
Microphone, 214, 218–19, 221–2, 236, 279, 284, 292
  diaphragm, microphone, 212–13
  directivity (pick up) pattern, 212–13, 361
  microphone handling, 220–1
  microphone technique, 150–1, 222
  microphone types, 212–13
    bi-directional, 213
    boom, 269, 280, 333, 360
    capacitor (condensor), 212–13, 360
    cardiod, 212–13
      hyper cardiod, 212
    desktop, 280, 332
    dynamic, 213
    induction, 240
    lavalier, 213, 280, 363
    lip, 213, 284
    omni-directional, 213, 364
    moving coil, 212
    radio, 280, 333
    ribbon, 212–13, 365
    rifle (gun), 276, 279–80, 365
    tie-clip (neck), 213, 258, 280, 332
    uni-directional, 213, 366
  microphone voice, 136
  off-mike, 292
Microwave link, 83, 249, 271, 283–5, 363
Milne, Alasdair, 159
Mini-wrap, 202–4, 363
Mixing (sound), 230–3, 241, 312–13
  mixer, 184, 224, 232, 237, 311–12, 360
  video mixing, 260, 304, 312
    digital video effects machine (DVE), 329
  vision mixer (switcher, technical director), 284, 311–12, 328, 332, 336, 366
    dissolves, 290, 312, 319–20, 332
    wipes, 312
Modifiers, 70
Modulation, 150
Moger, Phil, 119, 121, 157, 252–4
Monitor Radio, 20
Monitoring other news media, 26–7, 30, 88, 109, 192, 203, 252, 335–6
Morris, Freda, 3, 20
MPX filter, 219, 363
Multi-angled (umbrella) stories, *see* Angle, news

Murrow, Edward R., 147, 161
Music, 129–30
Mute (silent) camera, 277
M & Y news agency, 59

NAB (National Association of Broadcasters), 158
NAB (News About Britain), 177
Nagra tape recorder, 219
Names, 71–2
Narration, *see* Commentary
narrative, 292, 303
NAT SOF (natural sound on film), *see* Sound
NBC (National Broadcasting Company), 3, 20, 24, 340
Neil, Ron, 109, 113, 120
Network, 6, 24–6, 60, 191, 193–4, 201–4, 232, 235, 237, 243
- Independent radio network (UK), 20, 24–5, 27
- *Network*, 168
- network TV news, 106–7
- networking, 24–6

New Zealand, 24, 185, 340, 342, 357
News:
- types of news, 5–10
  - hard news, 30, 50, 52–3, 55–6, 106, 110, 121, 251, 257, 362
    - hard news formula, 52, 55, 61, 362
  - soft news, 8, 50, 55, 110, 128
- what is news?, 3–11
  - change as news, 7, 69, 291

News agencies, 21, 23–4, 59, 69, 106, 176, 182, 248–9, 308, 321, 342, *see also* Wire services
News angle, 4, 19, 26, 30, 32–3, 35, 50–2, 60, 112
News at 5.45, 251, 300, 335
News at One, 167, 246, 257, 259, 267, 303, 338
News at Ten, 119, 121–2, 157, 160, 247, 251–5
News at 12.30, 251, 257
News clip, *see* Clip
News conference, 18, 32, 35–6
News consultants, 169–70
News coverage:
- radio, 190–204
- TV, 275–99

News cycle, 105–6, 123
News editor, 13–14, 26, 29–33, 36, 54, 69, 107, 113, 165, 169–70, 179–80, 191–2, 199, 203, 238, 250–1, 256–7, 348–52
News information, 14
News judgement, 18, 109–10, 113
News manipulation, 18
News peg, 103
News priorities, 30
News programme, 15, 102–30, 169, 192, 251, 330–2, 337–8
- establishing programme identity, 117–18
- making the programme fit, 127–30
- programme briefing, 253–4
- putting the show together, 117–26

News releases, 14, 18–20, 363
News selection, 108–9, 179, *see also* Item selection
News-sense, 4, 108, 134, 139, 278
News sources, 12–28
News studio (TV), 246, 249, 330–8
News values, 4, 113
Newsbeat, 126
Newsbooth, 194, 237, 363, *see also* Contributions studio
Newscaster, 113, 131–4, 246, 253–4, 259, 266, 330–2, 336, *see also* Newsreader
- women newscasters, 133

Newsdesk, 30, 248
Newsdesk, 177, 185
Newsflash, 60, 103, 191–2, 363
Newsgathering, 3–37, 120
- TV newsgathering, 248–51, 275–86

Newsmix, 26, 193–4, 363
Newsreader, 39–41, 53, 66, 68, 71–3, 106, 113, 118, 128, 131–7, 139–43, 145, 147–54, 180, 184, 187, 194, 209, 213, 236–7, 244, 300–3, 320–1, 327–8, 333, 347–8.
Newsreading, 40, 112, 138, 146–55, 351
- breathing, 147–8, 151
  - breath control, 147–8
- bringing the story to life, 154
- newsreading mechanics, 147–55
- newsreading speed, 125, 147, 180, 187, 334, 340
- sightreading, 137

Newsroom, 5, 13–14, 17, 19–20, 22, 24, 29–30, 68, 87, 107, 129, 142, 166, 169, 174–5, 177, 179–80, 182, 191, 194, 199, 202–3, 243, 251, 253, 256, 266, 285, 321, 330, 342, 350
- Channel 4 newsroom, 109
- computerized newsroom, 15, 339–41
- joint newsrooms, 27
- local newsroom, 6, 24, 33, 90
- newsroom assistant, 251
- newsroom conference (editorial conference), 29–30, 180, 251, 256–7, 363
- newsroom diary, 13–14, 30, 180, 363
- newsroom secretary, 107, 191, 350

Newswriter, 5, 41, 52–3, 253, 301–2, 314, 340, 347
Newswriting, 5, 40–1, 50–61, 69–71, 351
- active writing, 69
- colourful writing, 66
- conversational writing, 38–49, 53
- convolution, 41
- passive writing, 69
- positive writing, 69–70
- sentence construction, 41–4, 46–9, 71, 141
- inverted sentences, 43
- singular or plural, 71
- WHAT formula, 56
- writing for broadcast, 38–74
- writing for a mass audience, 40–1
- writing to sound, 301–3

Nicholas, David, 167, 251, 349
9 O'Clock News (BBC), 133, 139
Noddies, 259, 263, 294, 364,

see also Cutaways
Noise reduction, 212, 219, 364, *see also* Dolby/DBX
Northern Life, 29
Novelty, 108
NPR (National Public Radio), 24
NUJ (National Union of Journalists), 171
Union membership, 349

Objectivity, 81, 108, 136, 160–2
Obscenity button, 240–1, 364
Official Secrets Act (UK), 159
On-air light, 236, 331
On-air studio (radio), 235–6
On Camera, 298
On-the-spot report, 195–202, 237
Openers, 118, 327
Opening shots, 289, 298
Operations organizer, 106
Opinion, 67, 136, 161, 170, 194, 293
Optical disc, 344
Opting in and out, 25, 337, 364
ORACLE, 341–3, 364, *see also* Teletext
Orwell, George, 62
Outcue, 26, 201–2, 251, 305, 364, *see also* Sign off
Outpoint, 129
Output, 106–7, 248
output editor, 251
Outs, 129
Outside broadcast (OB), 283–4, 364
(OB) vehicle, 238, 283–4, *see also* Scanner and Radio car
Out-takes, 226, 314, 364
Overlap cut, 315, 318
Overlays, 290, 327–9

PA (Press Association), 23, 176, 342
Pace, 122, 125–6, 147, 187, 290
Package (wrap), 33, 84, 199–202, 224, 259, 364
Padding, 30, 50, 129
Pan, 279, 290
Panorama, 162
Paper-rustle, 150–1
Parkin, Leonard, 246
Parkinson, Michael, 95–6
Partridge, Eric, 62
Pauses, 66, 71, 301
Payoff (standard outcue, SOC), 197
Pennine Radio, 238
Performance, 5, 30, 90, 98, 138–9, 142, 353
Personality, 132–3, 135, 161
personalities, 8, 165
personality profile, 81
Philips, 206
Phillips, Harry Irving, 256
Phone-in, 240
phone levels, 240
phone reports (phonos), 36, 124, 238–40, 364
Phonetics, 72, 187
Photocalls, 18
Photo-electric cell, 268, 364
Pic sync., 317
Picture tube, 171–2
Pictures, 120–1, 300–1, 303, 313, 320–1, 325, 327, 335–6
picture scanning, 268–73
picture store, 321–2, 364
Pieces to camera (stand-ups, stand uppers), 296–8, 364
Pigeon, 286
Pitch, 150
Pixel, 325, 364
Plagiarism, 26
Plain English, 43
Planning, 7, 298–9
planning meeting, 256
Poland, 345
Police:
Police and Criminal Evidence Act, 164
police radio, 16–17
police stories, 15–17
Politicians, 17
Pooled news, 24, 26–7
Popping, 150
Portable tape recorders, 34, 89, 182, 214–23, 226, 238, 240, 279
Pot-point; pot-cut, 128, 232
Poulsen, Valdemar, 205
Power, 157
power, freedom and responsibility, 157–72
Powers, Ron, 170
PPM (peak programme meter), 231–2, 237, 364
PR (public relations), 18–20, 26, 192, *see also* Press office
Pre-fade, 130, 232, 364, *see also* Fades
Prejudice, 76, 135–6, 161
Presence, 139, 140
Presentation, 135
double-headed presentation, 105, 124–5, 134
presentation styles, 132–3
presenters, 26–7, 55, 106–7, 117, 124, 129–30, 132, 134–5, 138–9, 143–4, 149, 170, 184, 191, 197, 209, 240–2, 255, 304, 327, 332–3, 347, 349
presenting the news, 131–55
Press conference, *see* News conference
Press office; officers, 15, 34
Press release, 17, *see also* PR
Press Trust of India, 23
Pressure groups, 7–8, 17
Privacy, 82, 85, 167–8, 171
ordeal by camera, 167–8
Privilege, 33, 171
Producer, 20, 27, 29–31, 36, 54, 106–8, 114–17, 119, 121, 127, 129–31, 184, 197, 226, 236, 248, 251–6, 284, 295, 330–1, 336–7, 347–8
bulletin producer, 29
field producer, 298
programme editor (producer), 106
senior producer, 29
TV producer, 121
Production assistant (PA) (production secretary), 184, 336
Production team, 109, 302, 327
Production unit, 257
Profanity button, 240–1
Professionalism, 80, 133, 135–6, 145, 161, 258, 338
Programme assistant, 107
Programme balance, 30, 103, 121–2
Programme briefing, 253
Programme editor (producer), 106
Programme feel, 122, 124–5
Programme identity, 117–18, 124

Programme organizer, 348
Programme schedule, 127, *see also* News programme
Projection, 148
Promotion, 118–19, 197
Prompter, 151–3, 297, 361
  Autocue, 151
    Autocue script, 266, 334
  EDS Portaprompt, 152, 297
  prompting, 297, 333–4
  roller prompter, 334
Pronouns, 71
Pronunciation, 59, 72
Proofreading, 72–3
Propaganda, 15, 20, 68, 76, 163, 182
Prospects, 14, 250–2, 256
Protests, 17–18
Proximity, 3, 4, 108, 113
Public interest, 85, 168, 171
Public relations, *see* PR
Pumping, 218
Punctuation, 42, 71, 141, 229
Purvis, Stewart, 109

Quotations, 66

Radcliffe, Gerry, 238
Radio:
  radio car, 36, 193, 195, 237–8
  Radio Clyde, 10
  radio equipment, 205–44
  Radio 4, 81, 95, 104, 113, 124, 133, 136
  Radio Hallam, 112, 114
  Radio Mercury, 209
  radio news coverage, 190–204
  Radio Newsreel, 175, 177, 182–5
  Radio 1, 126
  radio scanner, 9, 16
  radio studio, 183, 191, 235–44
  radio tomorrow, 242–4
Radliffe, Harry, 17, 167
Rantzen, Esther, 214
Rapport, 90–2, 140–1
Reaction story, 7, 17, 81, 293
Reading-in, 32, 364
Rear projection, 328
Recall, 57
Recaps, 336
Received pronunciation (RP), 187
Record deck (gram), 236
Recording, 216–18
  analogue recording, 211
  digital recording, 206, 211, 226, 242, 269, 275, 311, 361
  principles of recording, 205–13
  recording head, 210, 364
  recording levels, 215, 217–18, 221–3, 231–3, 240
Recordist, 248, 258, 276, 279–80, 282, 315, 365
Recovery, 142–5
Redundant words, 69–70, 292
Reel-to-reel tape, 206–8, 216–17, 225
Rees, Norman, 162, 168
Reeve-Jones, Lawrence, 187
Referring-up, 110
Regional TV, 26–7, 122, 250, 337, 350
Regulation, 158
  deregulation, 243
  self-regulation, 172
Rehearsal, 91, 118, 254, 327, 337
Reinforcement, 119
Reiteration, 57
Relaxation, 145–6
Relevance, 3–6, 10, 19–20, 33, 46, 89, 96, 108, 113
  relevant questions, 96
Remote interview, 83
Remote studio, 83, 237, 365
Repetition, 57, 70
Report (TV), 254, 259–67, 300
Reporter, 6–7, 10, 13–18, 21, 27, 30–3, 35–6, 43, 58, 75–6, 80, 82, 84, 88–94, 96, 99–100, 103–4, 106–7, 127, 129, 131, 134–6, 162–3, 166–7, 191, 195, 197, 202, 222, 224, 229, 232, 237–40, 243, 248, 250–1, 253, 255, 257–9, 262, 268, 278–80, 282, 286, 290–4, 296–8, 300–3, 305, 311, 314, 323, 340, 342, 348–9, 353
Research, 14, 32, 190, 193–4, 249, 308
Researcher, 32, 259–60, 298, 349
Resources, 169
Reuters, 23, 176, 342
Reversal, 290
  reverses, 294–5
Reynolds, Michael, 205
Rhettie, John, 185, 187
Rhythm, 47–8, 122, 125–6, 150, 180, 264
  shot rhythm, 290
Rider, Chris, 239
Right of reply, 171
Rip and read, 24–5, 135, 365
Rodman, John, 117
Roll, 319
  roll-through (roll-thru), 320
ROT (recording of transmission), 199, 365
Rough cut, 314, 365
  rough editing, 100
Royal Charter, 158
Royal Television Society, 122
Running order, 30, 113–16, 127, 179, 252, 261, 263, 266, 336–8
Running story (developing stories), 50–1, 191, 256, 365
Running time (R/T), 305, 340
Rushes, 311–12, 314, 365
Ryan, Rocky, 22

Sabido, Kim, 248, 300, 348
Safe area, 327, 365
Satellite, 8, 23–4, 83, 102, 243, 249, 255, 271, 273–4, 284–6, 343–6
  ECHO, 273, 346
  INSAT 1B, 274
  Intelsat V, 273
  satellite TV, 105, 273–4, 344–5, 347
  Telstar satellite, 273
  The Spot, 346
Scanner (OB) vehicle, 284–5, 365
  scanner (radio), 9, 16, 243, 365
  scanning, 268–73
Scargill, Arthur, 76–8, 85–6
Scene setting, 57, 297–8
Scotland, 25
Screen test, 351
Screening a programme, 254–5
  screening stills, 322–3
Script, 154, 260–2, 264, 290,

292, 320, 326
script layout, 129, 303–7, *see also* TV script
scriptwriter, 350
Seasonal news, 8
Secondary items, 123
Secret Society, 159
Segmenting, 30, 122–3, 125
Selection, 108–16, 165, 169, 179
Self-operation, 184, 209, 237, 365
Sensationalism, 166, 301
Sepmag (separate magnetic), 314
Set, the, 330–4
Set-piece news events, 17–18
'Sexy' story, 47, 253, 365
Shadow mask, 270, 272
Shared material, 27
Shaw, Malcolm, 4
Sheridan, Michael, 257–65
Shewall, Christina, 131
Signal-to-noise ratio, 217
Significance, 6, 33, 50, 108, 111–12, 122, 166, 179
Sign-off, 251, 304–5, *see also* Outcue and Standard outcue
Signposting, 51–2, 57, 66–7, 123, 150, 192, 197, 202, 365
Silly season, 12, 256, 365
Simmonds, Posy, 156
Simmons, Edith, 162
Simplification, 44
Singapore, 342
Single system, 315, 365
Sissons, Peter, 110
Skeleton (blank), 337, 365
Slice of life, 104
Slug, *see* Catchline
Snap, 59
Snow, Jon, 142
Snowdesk, 9
Soft news, 8, 50, 55, 110, 128
Somerville, Julia, 133
Sony Broadcast Ltd, 226, 283
Sound, 210, 292–3, 332–3
sound bite (grabs), 290, 293, 301–2, 320, 365
sound check, 222, 258, 263–4, *see also* Levels
sound control, 313
sound controller, 337
sound effects (SFX), 31, 232, 292, 301–2, 313, 319, 337
sound engineer, 333
sound on film, 315
NAT SOF (Natural Sound on Film), 279, 298, 312, 363
sound reader, 317–18, 365
sound reflector, 276
soundtrack, 27, 263, 276, 279, 290, 294, 302, 311–16, 319–20
optical soundtrack, 315
wildtrack, 84, 279, 366
writing to sound, 301–3
Sounder (jingle), 191, 209
South Africa, 342
South African Press Association, 23
South Today, 26
Special local interest, 8
Specialisms, 21, 24, 112, 347–8
specialists, 13, 106, 194
Spelling, 71–2
SPL (sound pressure level), 210
Splicing film, 316, 318–19
splicing tape, 208, 226–7
Sponsored stringers, 187
Sponsorship, 20
Spools, 225
Sport, 8, 30, 106, 112, 128, 238, 342
sports editor, 107, 194
Spot story, *see* Breaking news
Staged events, 17–18
staged news conferences, 35–6
Stand uppers, *see* Pieces to camera
Standard outcue (SOC, payoff), 197, 297, 305, *see also* Sign-off
Standby item, 36
Station identity, 117
Station manager, 348
Stereo, 206, 210, 219, 365
Stereotyping, 165
Sterne, Lawrence, 38
Stewart, Stephen, 34
Stills, 115, 129, 153, 288, 304, 308, 321–3, 325, 327, 336–7
graphic stills, 322, 324
screening stills, 322–3
still store, 335
video still, 322
Story closing, 58
Story construction, 56
Story length, 192, 194
Story treatment, 190–204
Stringers, 20–1, 177, 181, 187, 365, *see also* Freelance and Sponsored stringers
Studio:
radio studio, 183, 191, 235–44
studio clock, 236
studio manager, 183–4
studio set, 327–38
flats, 331
studio tape decks (radio), 225–6, 342
talks studio, 99, 236
touchscreen studio, 241–2, 366
TV studio, 249, 254, 266–7, 330–8
Style, 21, 24, 42, 55, 69, 105, 108, 125, 342
broadcast style book, 62–74
house style, 5, 23, 65, 72, 302–3
presentation styles, 107, 132–3
Subjectivity, 4
Subtitles, 326, 342, 345
Sun Gun, 282
Superchannel News, 251
Super 8 film camera, 277
Supers, 253–4, 263–4, 267, 288, 305, 326, 335, 365
lower third, 326, 363
Surge (pumping), 218
Syndicated programmes, 20
syndicated tapes, 20, 366

Tailpiece (kicker), 5, 366
Take, 315
Talent, 131–2
Talkback, 195, 197, 201, 236–7, 262, 264, 284, 311–13, 331, 336, 366
Talking heads, 33, 123, 366
Tanzania, 357
Tape, 206–8, 343
master tape, 226
tape care, 208
tape editing, 214, 224–34

tape editor, 259, 311
tape heads, 206, 210, 311
erase head, 210, 362
playback head, 210, 364
recording head, 210, 364
tape logging, 222
tape loop, 241
tape noise, 209, 211–12, 214
tape path, 226
tape reclamation, 207
tape recorders (portable), 214–23
tape recorders (studio), 225–6
tape recording, 216–23
tape speed, 206
tape tracks, 210–11, 311, 362, 364
Taste, *see* Good taste
Tasters (teaser), 118, 194, 263, 366
Taylor, Derek, 350
Taylor, Shaw, 151
Taynton, William, 268
Technical assistant, 113, 135, 184, 250
Technical manager (operations supervisor, service engineer), 336
Technical operator (TO), 144, 209, 236
Telecine (TK, film chain), 320, 322, 335–6, 366
double chaining, 320, 361
flying spot, 320
multiplexing, 320
Telephone:
cellular phone, 196, 238, 340
telephone balance unit (TBU), 240, 366
telephone reports, 32, 238–40, *see also* Phone
Telescoping the action, 294
Teletext, 341–3, 366
CEEFAX, 342
ORACLE, 341–3, 364
Television, *see* TV
Tell story, 303
Telling the story, 38–40
Ten code, 16–17, 366
Terrorism, 18
The Way It Is, 126, 348
Throw line, 302
Time references, 68–9, 98
Timecheck, 26, 124, 142
Timecode, 261–4, 311, 313
Timing, 118
Tip-offs, 20–2, 349, 366
tipster, 21
Titles, 305, 325–7
safe area, 327
title sequence, 118, 337
Today Programme, 113, 133
Tomalin, Nicholas, 353
Topicality, 111
Touch tablet, 324
Touhey, John, 141, 151, 183
Traffic reports, 9–10, 106
Trail, 119, 366
forward trail, 119
Training, 348, 350–2
Transitions, 123–4
Transmission (TX), 270–1, 335, 342, 366
transmission warning light, 331–2, 335
Treatment, 298
Trigger words, 36, *see also* Key words
Trim-bin, 316, 318, 366
Tully, Mark, 90
Turner, Ted, 105, 339, 344
Tusa, John, 176, 179
TV, 245–346
how TV works, 268–74
TV library, 249, 257, 259, 307–8, 321–2, *see also* Film library
TV lighting, 258, 259, 280–3
TV lines, 269
TV news, 118
TV news coverage, 275–99
TV report, 259–67, 300, 323, 325, 335, 337
TV reporter, 134, 248, 259, 268, 276–80, 299
TV script, 129, 259–62, 264–5, 290, 292, 301–9, 320, 336–7, 340
TV scriptwriting, 300–9
TV set, 272–3
TV sound recording, 279–80
TV sound mixer, 263
TV studio, 139, 330–8
TV tomorrow, 339–46
TV transmission, 268–74, 284, 286
TV tuner, 272
Twain, Mark, 41
24 hour news, 105–6
Twombly, Wells, 351
Two-source rule, 182
Tyne Tees Television, 29

Uher tape recorder, 215–19, 221, 225
UK, 357
UK Press Gazette, 18, 22, 120
Umbrella, *see* Angle
UNICEF, 162
Union membership, 349
United Nations Resolution 59, 159
UPI (United Press International), 23, 176
URTNA (Union of National Radio and Television Organizations of Africa), 27
USA, 15–16, 20–1, 24–5, 103, 105–6, 117, 123, 132–5, 158, 161, 169–70, 185, 240, 242, 249, 275, 279–80, 282, 295, 340, 342, 348, 355, 359

Variety, 105, 111, 122–4
Verification, 59–60, *see also* Accuracy
Vérite, 103–5, 366
Vested interests, 17, 34
VHF, 243
Victimization, 80
Video:
video cartridge, 313
video mixing, 312
video playback, 313
video still, 289, 322
videocassette, 275
videocassette recorder (VCR), 206, 236, 311, 313, 344
videotape, 206, 211, 249 258–9, 263, 275, 277–8, 311–12, 321, 324, 327, 336, 344
videotape editing, 249, 261
videotape editor, 225, 259, 260–2, 264, 290, 310–13
videotape recorder (VTR), 206, 211, 261, 264, 313, 328
VTR playback, 313

videotape recordings, 211, 285
Viewer, *see* Audience
Viewfinder, 275, 327, 332
Viewpoint, 33
Vision controller, 337
Vision mixer (switcher, technical operator), 284, 311–12, 318, 332, 336, 366
Visnews, 23, 249, 260
Visual Production Effects machine (VPE), 323, 366, *see also* Graphics
Visuals, 31, 36, 103, 115–16, 190, 264, 290, 292, 301, 303–5, 321–9, 337, 366
Voice, 39–40, 131, 133–6, 141, 150
accent, 136
intonation, 141
microphone voice, 136
stress, 54, 150, *see also* Newsreading
Voice over (VO), 298, 366
Voicer (voice report), 193–4
Voltaire, 58
Voyeurism, 168
Vox pop, 83–4, 366
VU (Volume Unit) meter, 219, 232, 366

Wales at Six, 75
Walker, Stanley, 3
War reporting, 162–3
Watts, Harris, 39, 298
Weather, 8–9, 30, 106, 128, 236
snowdesk, 9
Webster, Mark, 253
WEEI, 7, 106, 117, 242
Wenham, Brian, 157
West Indies, 359
Westinghouse All-News Radio, 102, 105
WGST, 21
Wheaton, Bob, 109
Wind roar, 279–80
Wipe, 312, 328, 329, 332, 366
Wire services, 23–4, 30, 60, 248, 340, 366
World Service, *see* BBC External Services
WPB (waste paper basket), 15, 18–19, 366
Wrap, *see* Package
Writing, *see* Newswriting
WTN (Worldwide Television News), 23, 249

XTRA, 105

Young, Penny, 65, 148, 353–4

Zeebrugge ferry disaster, 167–8
Zoom, 279, 287, 289–90, 321, 332
zoom lens, 277
Zimbabwe, 359